P'
S
r

KAWL CREATED BY SIMON SPURRIER AND STEVE

BEC & KAWL

BLOODY STUDENTS

SIMON SPURRIER
Writer

STEVE ROBERTS
Artist

REBELLION

Creative Director and CEO: Jason Kingsley
Chief Technical Officer: Chris Kingsley
2000 AD Editor in Chief: Matt Smith
Graphic Design: Simon Parr & Luke Preece
Marketing and PR: Keith Richardson
Repro Assistant: Kathryn Symes

Graphic Novels Editor: Jonathan Oliver
Designer: Luke Preece
Original Commissioning Editor: Matt Smith

Originally serialised in 2000 AD Progs 1290-1291, 1292-1293, 1327, 1328-1330, 1351-1354, 1383-1386, 1401-1404, 1437-1440, 1477-1481.

Published by Rebellion, The Studio, Brewer Street, Oxford OX1 1QN.
www.rebellion.co.uk

ISBN: 1 90426 566 9
Printed in Italy by Magic Press. First published: August 2006
10 9 8 7 6 5 4 3 2 1

A CIP catalogue record for this book is available from the British Library.

For information on other 2000 AD graphic novels, or if you have any comments on this book, please email books@2000ADonline.com

To find out more about 2000 AD, visit www.2000ADonline.com

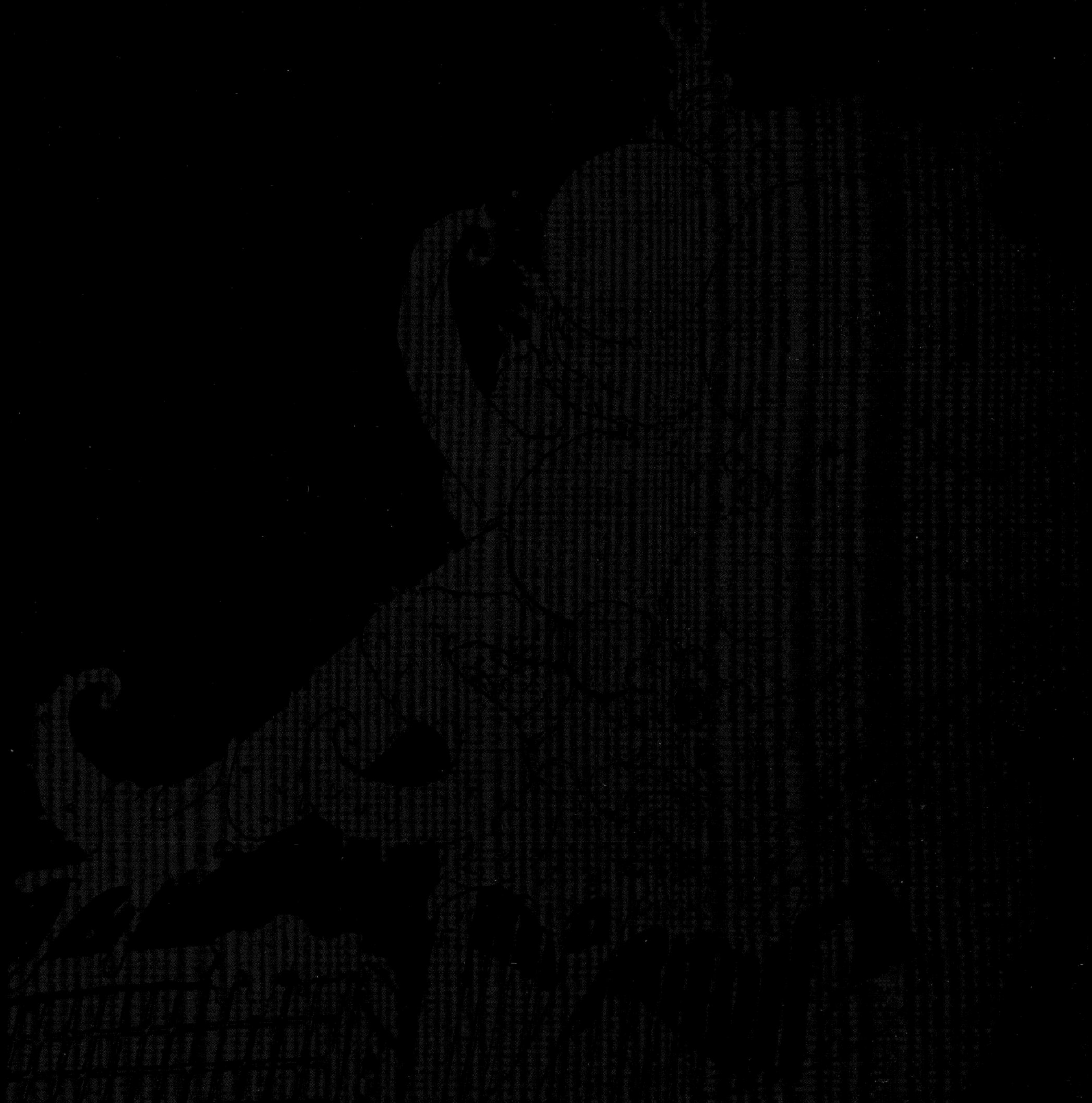

BEC & KAWL AND THE MYSTICAL MENTALIST MENACE

Script: Simon Spurrier
Art: Steve Roberts
Colour: Richard Elson
Letters: Ellie De Ville

Originally published in *2000 AD* Progs 1290-1291

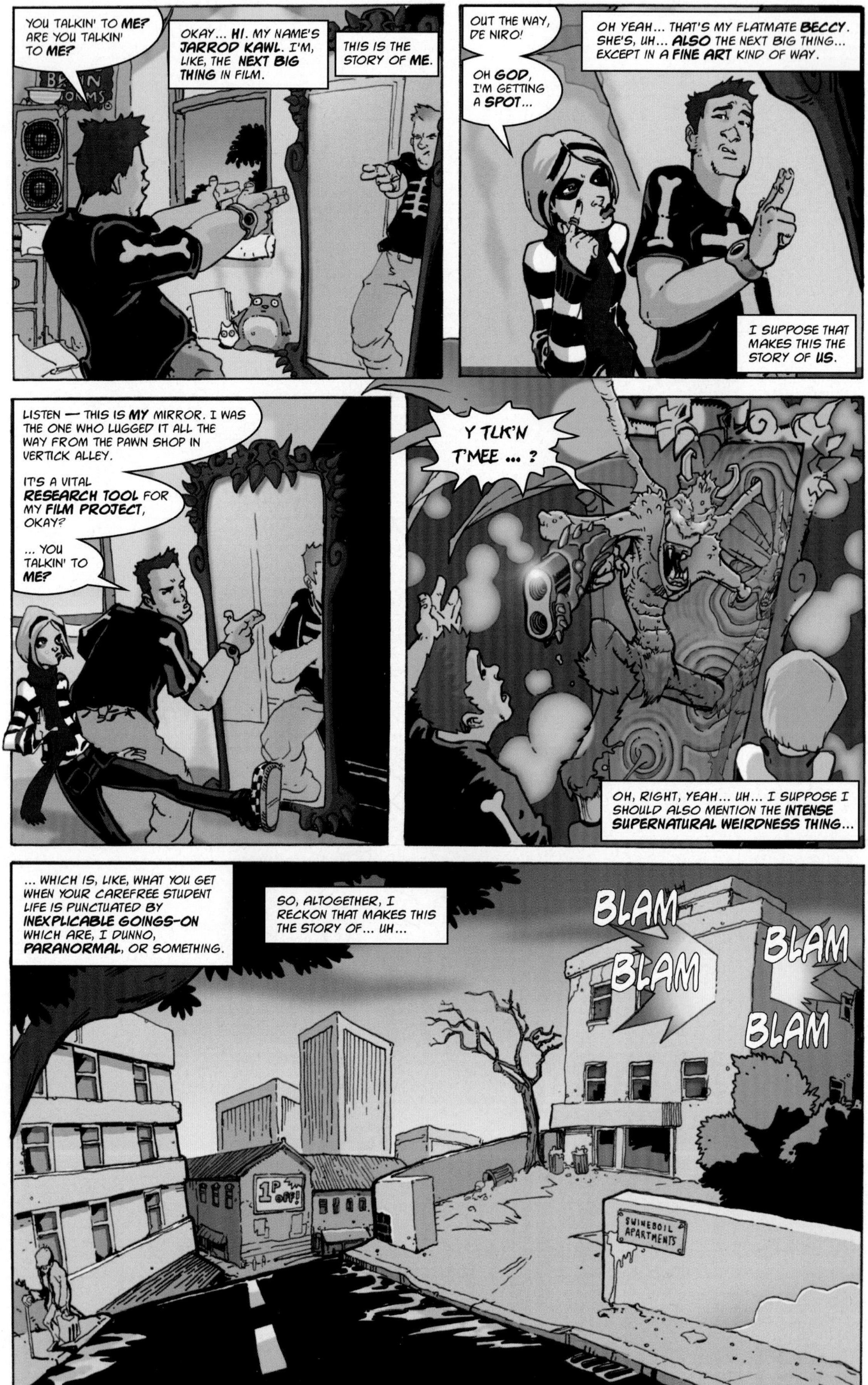
YOU TALKIN' TO ME? ARE YOU TALKIN' TO ME?
OKAY... HI. MY NAME'S JARROD KAWL. I'M, LIKE, THE NEXT BIG THING IN FILM.
THIS IS THE STORY OF ME.
OUT THE WAY, DE NIRO!
OH GOD, I'M GETTING A SPOT...
OH YEAH... THAT'S MY FLATMATE BECCY. SHE'S, UH... ALSO THE NEXT BIG THING... EXCEPT IN A FINE ART KIND OF WAY.
I SUPPOSE THAT MAKES THIS THE STORY OF US.
LISTEN — THIS IS MY MIRROR. I WAS THE ONE WHO LUGGED IT ALL THE WAY FROM THE PAWN SHOP IN VERTICK ALLEY.
IT'S A VITAL RESEARCH TOOL FOR MY FILM PROJECT, OKAY?
... YOU TALKIN' TO ME?
Y TLK'N T'MEE ... ?
OH, RIGHT, YEAH... UH... I SUPPOSE I SHOULD ALSO MENTION THE INTENSE SUPERNATURAL WEIRDNESS THING...
... WHICH IS, LIKE, WHAT YOU GET WHEN YOUR CAREFREE STUDENT LIFE IS PUNCTUATED BY INEXPLICABLE GOINGS-ON WHICH ARE, I DUNNO, PARANORMAL, OR SOMETHING.
SO, ALTOGETHER, I RECKON THAT MAKES THIS THE STORY OF... UH...
BLAM
BLAM
BLAM
BLAM
1P OFF!
SWINEBOIL APARTMENTS

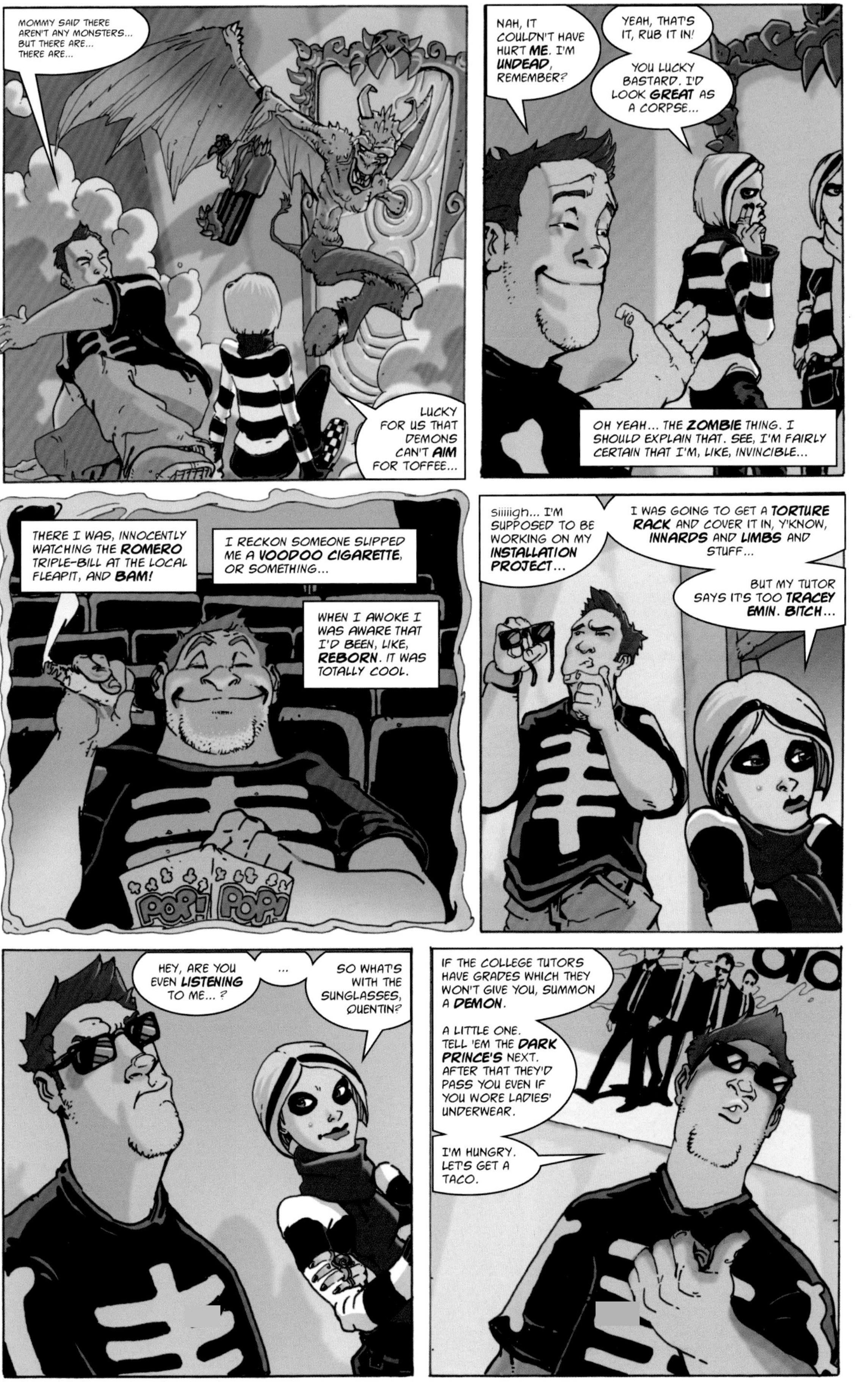

MOMMY SAID THERE AREN'T ANY MONSTERS... BUT THERE ARE... THERE ARE...
LUCKY FOR US THAT DEMONS CAN'T AIM FOR TOFFEE...
NAH, IT COULDN'T HAVE HURT ME. I'M UNDEAD, REMEMBER?
YEAH, THAT'S IT, RUB IT IN!
YOU LUCKY BASTARD. I'D LOOK GREAT AS A CORPSE...
OH YEAH... THE ZOMBIE THING. I SHOULD EXPLAIN THAT. SEE, I'M FAIRLY CERTAIN THAT I'M, LIKE, INVINCIBLE...
THERE I WAS, INNOCENTLY WATCHING THE ROMERO TRIPLE-BILL AT THE LOCAL FLEAPIT, AND BAM!
I RECKON SOMEONE SLIPPED ME A VOODOO CIGARETTE, OR SOMETHING...
WHEN I AWOKE I WAS AWARE THAT I'D BEEN, LIKE, REBORN. IT WAS TOTALLY COOL.
POP! POP!
Siiiiigh... I'M SUPPOSED TO BE WORKING ON MY INSTALLATION PROJECT...
I WAS GOING TO GET A TORTURE RACK AND COVER IT IN, Y'KNOW, INNARDS AND LIMBS AND STUFF...
BUT MY TUTOR SAYS IT'S TOO TRACEY EMIN. BITCH...
HEY, ARE YOU EVEN LISTENING TO ME...?
...
SO WHAT'S WITH THE SUNGLASSES, QUENTIN?
IF THE COLLEGE TUTORS HAVE GRADES WHICH THEY WON'T GIVE YOU, SUMMON A DEMON.
A LITTLE ONE. TELL 'EM THE DARK PRINCE'S NEXT. AFTER THAT THEY'D PASS YOU EVEN IF YOU WORE LADIES' UNDERWEAR.
I'M HUNGRY. LET'S GET A TACO.

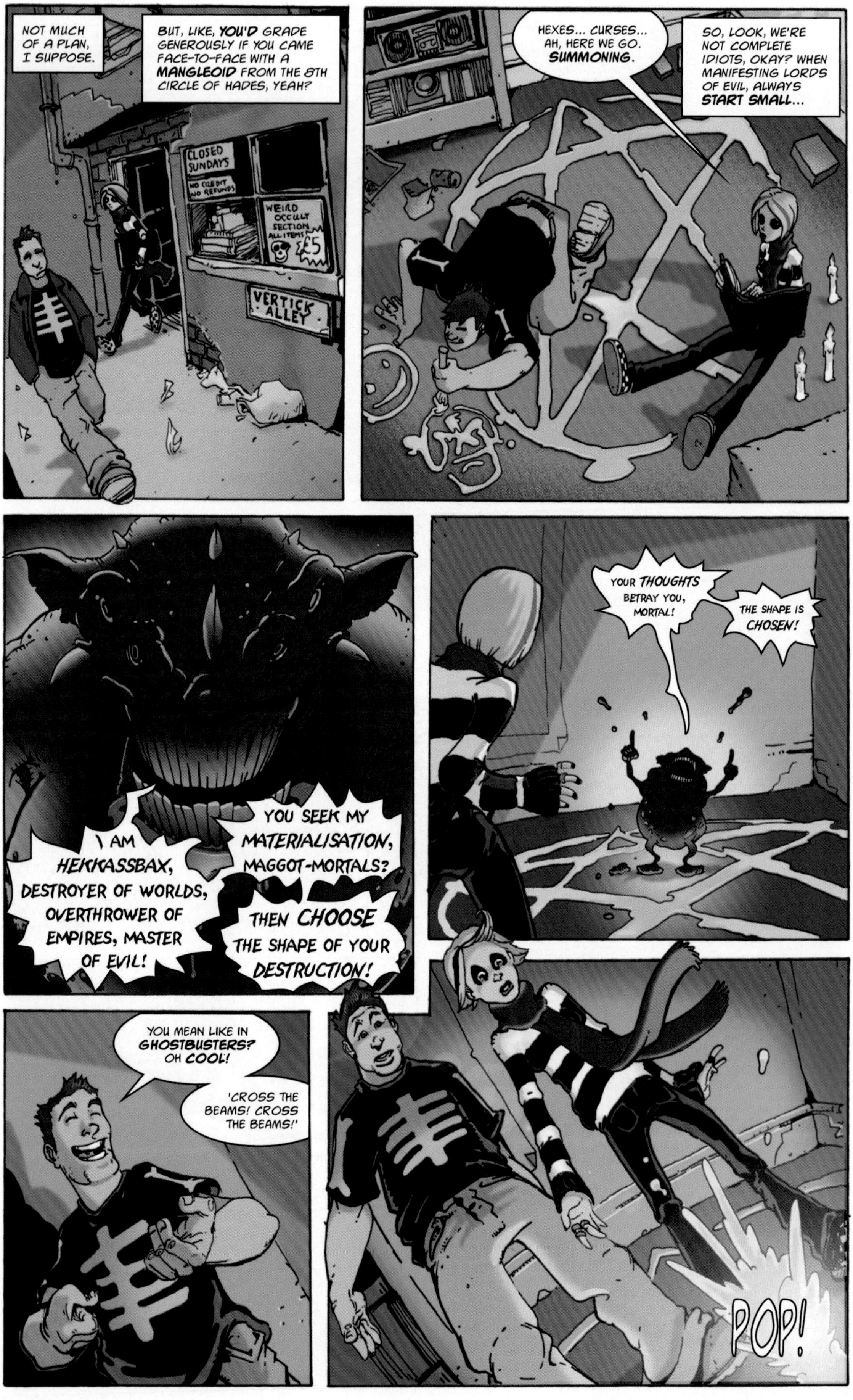
NOT MUCH OF A PLAN, I SUPPOSE.
BUT, LIKE, YOU'D GRADE GENEROUSLY IF YOU CAME FACE-TO-FACE WITH A MANGLEOID FROM THE 8TH CIRCLE OF HADES, YEAH?
CLOSED SUNDAYS
NO CREDIT NO REFUNDS
WEIRD OCCULT SECTION ALL ITEMS £5
VERTICK ALLEY
HEXES... CURSES... AH, HERE WE GO. SUMMONING.
SO, LOOK, WE'RE NOT COMPLETE IDIOTS, OKAY? WHEN MANIFESTING LORDS OF EVIL, ALWAYS START SMALL...
I AM HEKKASSBAX, DESTROYER OF WORLDS, OVERTHROWER OF EMPIRES, MASTER OF EVIL!
YOU SEEK MY MATERIALISATION, MAGGOT-MORTALS?
THEN CHOOSE THE SHAPE OF YOUR DESTRUCTION!
YOUR THOUGHTS BETRAY YOU, MORTAL!
THE SHAPE IS CHOSEN!
YOU MEAN LIKE IN GHOSTBUSTERS? OH COOL!
'CROSS THE BEAMS! CROSS THE BEAMS!'
POP!

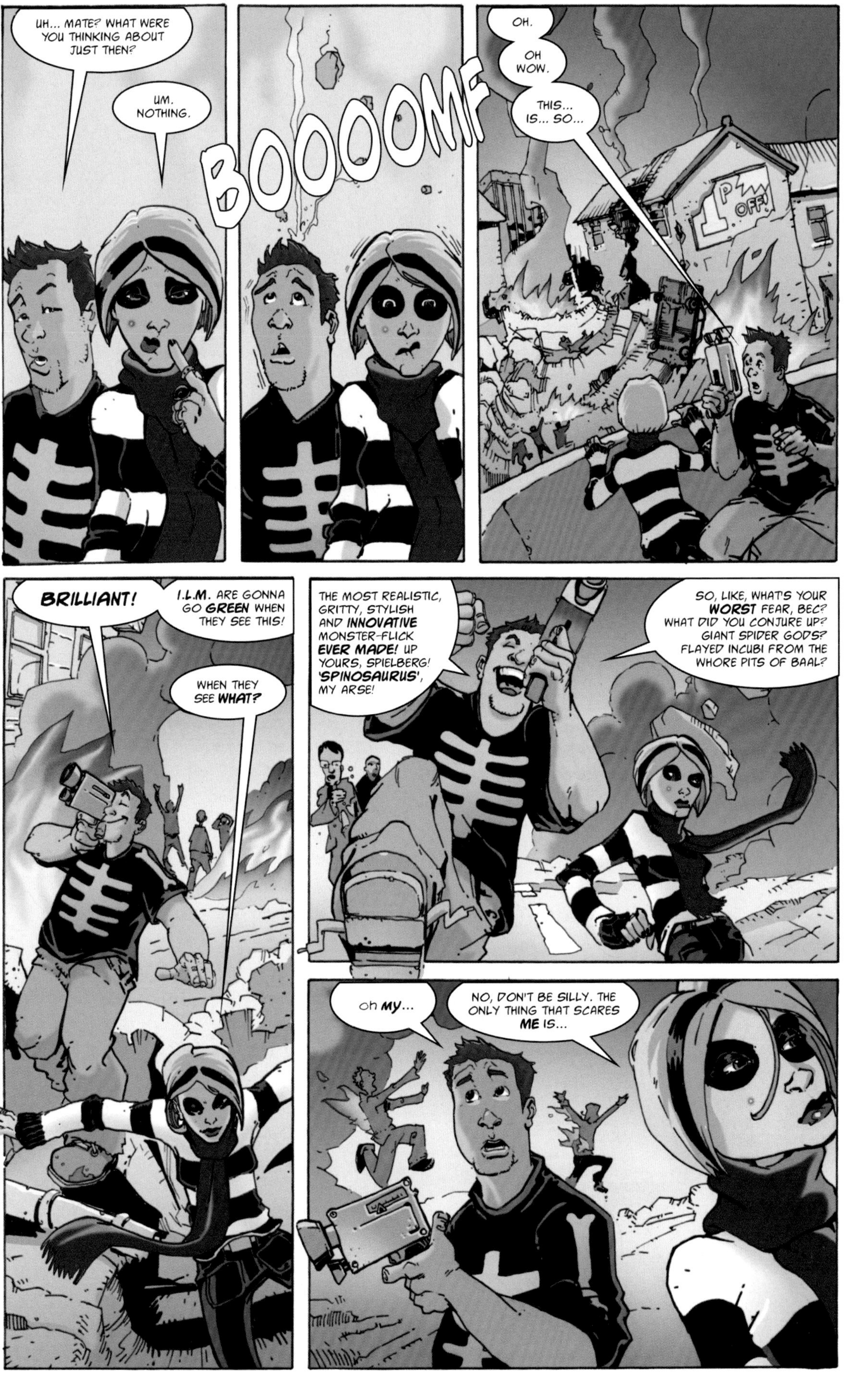

UH... MATE? WHAT WERE YOU THINKING ABOUT JUST THEN?
UM. NOTHING.
BOOOOMF
OH.
OH WOW.
THIS... IS... SO...
P OFF
BRILLIANT!
I.L.M. ARE GONNA GO GREEN WHEN THEY SEE THIS!
WHEN THEY SEE WHAT?
THE MOST REALISTIC, GRITTY, STYLISH AND INNOVATIVE MONSTER-FLICK EVER MADE! UP YOURS, SPIELBERG! 'SPINOSAURUS', MY ARSE!
SO, LIKE, WHAT'S YOUR WORST FEAR, BEC? WHAT DID YOU CONJURE UP? GIANT SPIDER GODS? FLAYED INCUBI FROM THE WHORE PITS OF BAAL?
oh MY...
NO, DON'T BE SILLY. THE ONLY THING THAT SCARES ME IS...

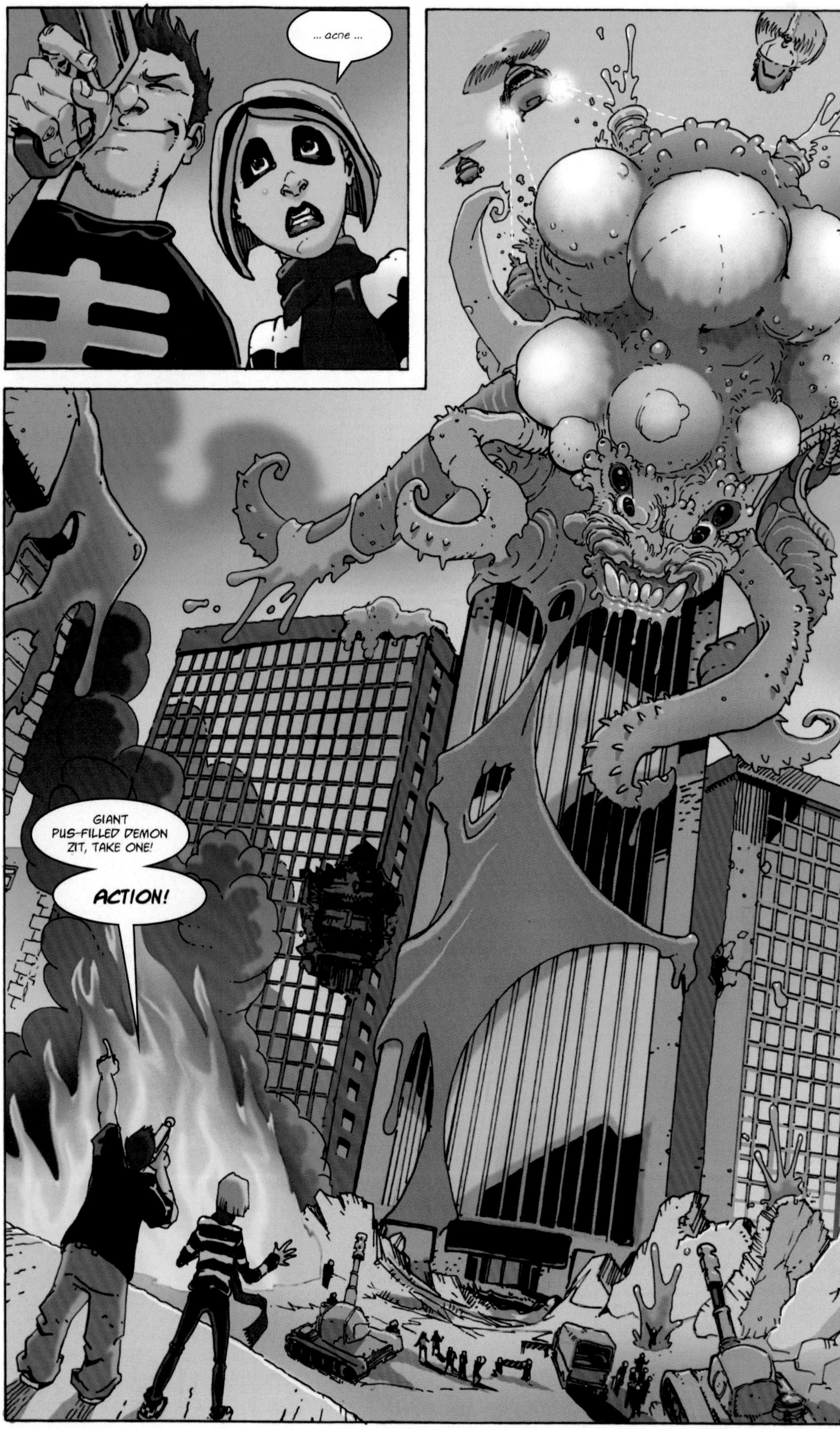
... acne ...
GIANT PUS-FILLED DEMON ZIT, TAKE ONE!
ACTION!

SO MUCH DEATH. SO MUCH DESTRUCTION...

IT'S... IT'S **BEAUTIFUL**...

DON'T MIND BECCY, OKAY? SHE GOES ALL, I DUNNO, **DAVID LYNCH** AT TIMES LIKE THIS.

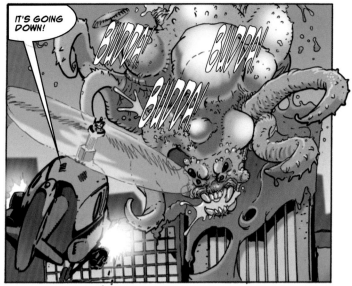

IT'S GOING **DOWN**!

BUDDA! BUDDA! BUDDA!

I **LIKE** THESE QUIET LITTLE MOMENTS BEFORE THE STORM...

THEY REMIND ME OF... **BEETHOVEN**.

THIS IS WHAT HAPPENS WHEN YOU MESS WITH **WEIRD** AND **UNNATURAL** FORCES BEYOND YOUR CONTROL...

BOOOOOOMFFFFFFF

ISN'T IT, LIKE, **WONDERFUL**?

EMOTION! I WANT **EMOTION**, YOU BASTARDS!

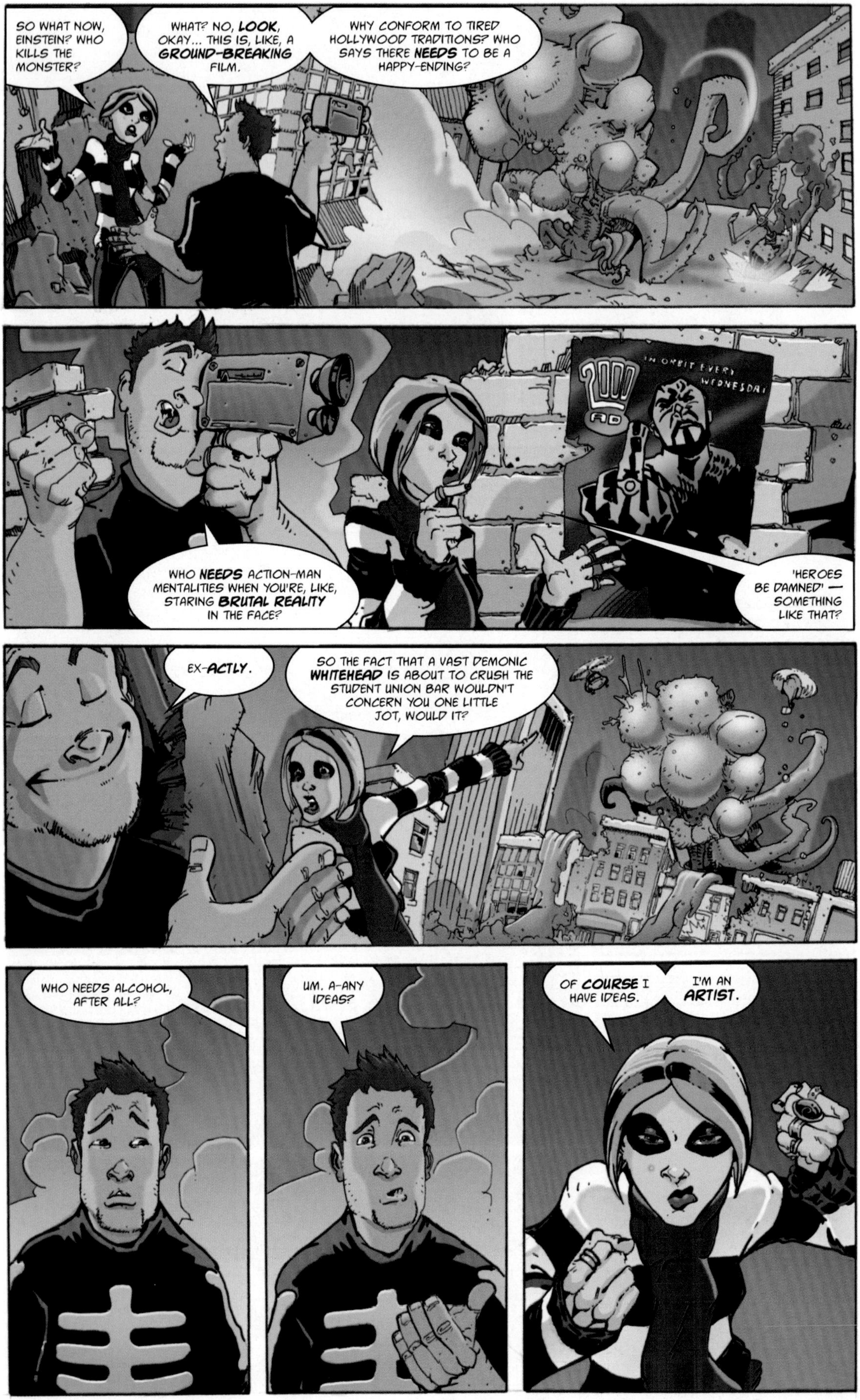
SO WHAT NOW, EINSTEIN? WHO KILLS THE MONSTER?
WHAT? NO, **LOOK**, OKAY... THIS IS, LIKE, A **GROUND-BREAKING** FILM.
WHY CONFORM TO TIRED HOLLYWOOD TRADITIONS? WHO SAYS THERE **NEEDS** TO BE A HAPPY-ENDING?
2000 AD
IN ORBIT EVERY WEDNESDAY
WHO **NEEDS** ACTION-MAN MENTALITIES WHEN YOU'RE, LIKE, STARING **BRUTAL REALITY** IN THE FACE?
'HEROES BE DAMNED' — SOMETHING LIKE THAT?
EX-**ACTLY**.
SO THE FACT THAT A VAST DEMONIC **WHITEHEAD** IS ABOUT TO CRUSH THE STUDENT UNION BAR WOULDN'T CONCERN YOU ONE LITTLE JOT, WOULD IT?
WHO NEEDS ALCOHOL, AFTER ALL?
UM. A-ANY IDEAS?
OF **COURSE** I HAVE IDEAS.
I'M AN **ARTIST**.

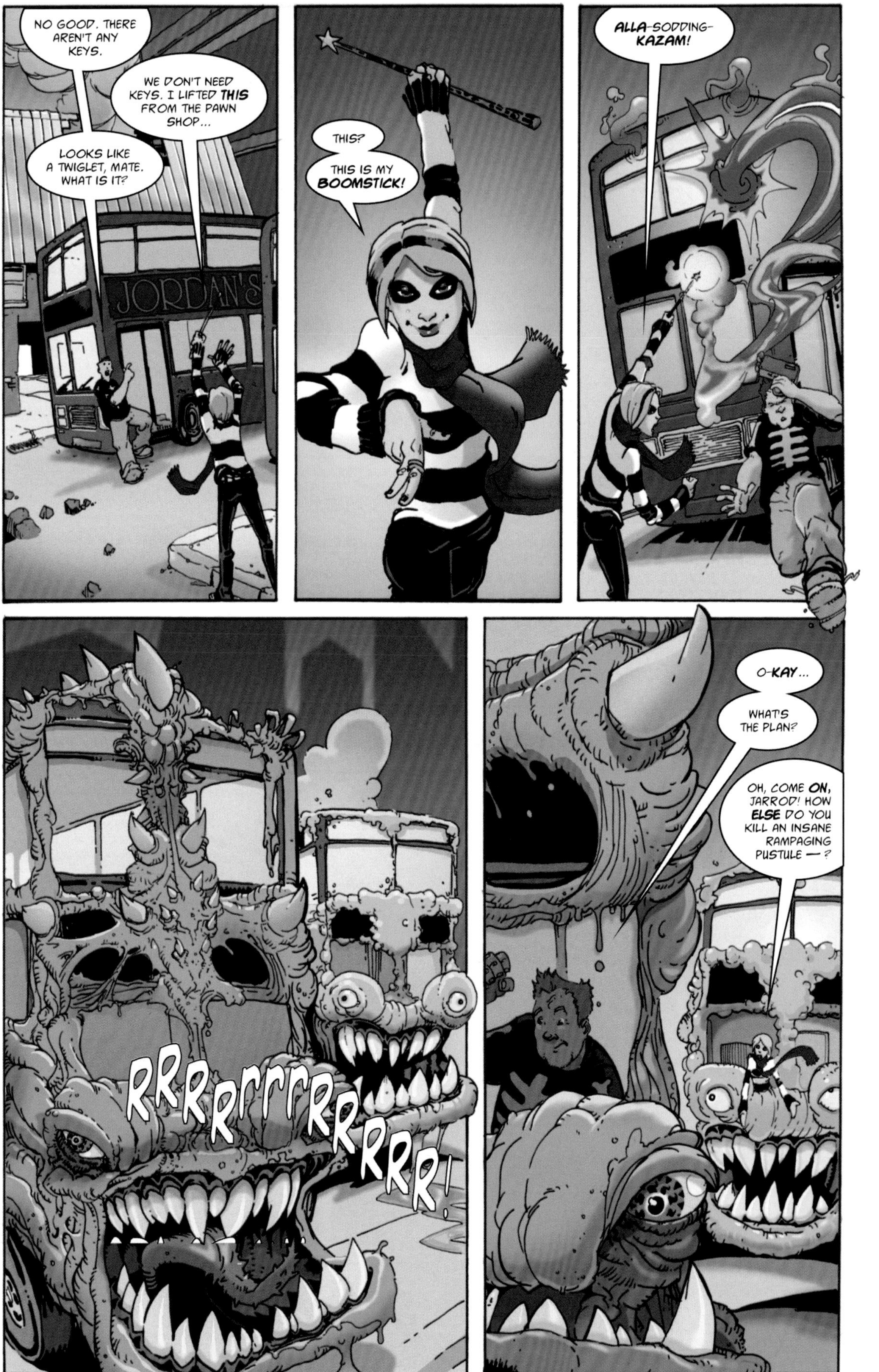
NO GOOD. THERE AREN'T ANY KEYS.
WE DON'T NEED KEYS. I LIFTED THIS FROM THE PAWN SHOP...
LOOKS LIKE A TWIGLET, MATE. WHAT IS IT?
JORDAN'S
THIS?
THIS IS MY BOOMSTICK!
ALLA-SODDING-KAZAM!
RRRRrrrrRRRRRR!
O-KAY...
WHAT'S THE PLAN?
OH, COME ON, JARROD! HOW ELSE DO YOU KILL AN INSANE RAMPAGING PUSTULE —?

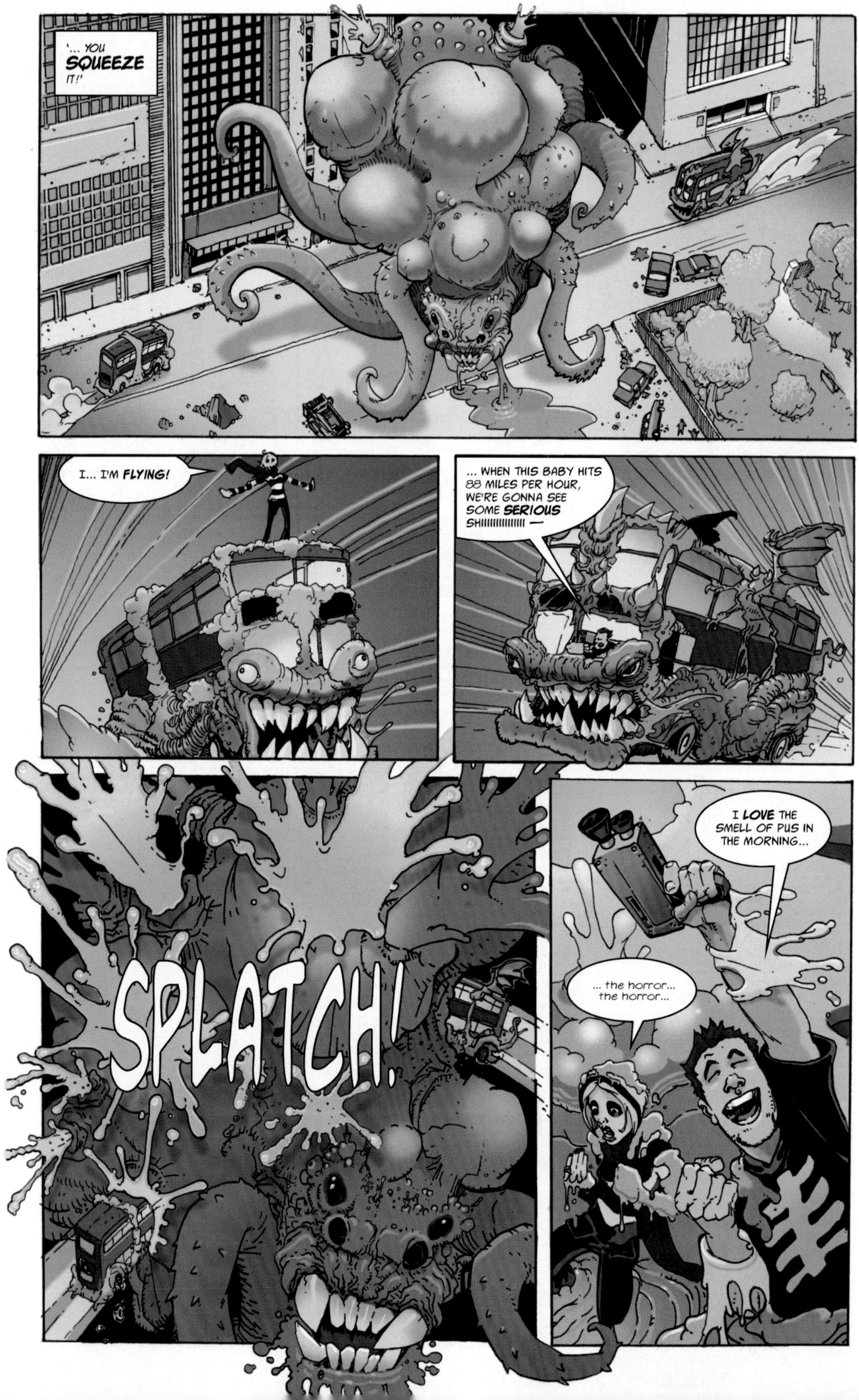
'... YOU SQUEEZE IT!'
I... I'M FLYING!
... WHEN THIS BABY HITS 88 MILES PER HOUR, WE'RE GONNA SEE SOME SERIOUS SHIIIIIIIIIIIII —
SPLATCH!
I LOVE THE SMELL OF PUS IN THE MORNING...
... the horror... the horror...

EPILOGUE:

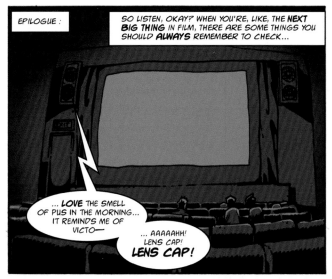

SO LISTEN, OKAY? WHEN YOU'RE, LIKE, THE **NEXT BIG THING** IN FILM, THERE ARE SOME THINGS YOU SHOULD **ALWAYS** REMEMBER TO CHECK...

... **LOVE** THE SMELL OF PUS IN THE MORNING... IT REMINDS ME OF VICTO—

... AAAAAHH! LENS CAP! **LENS CAP!**

FORTUNATELY MY TUTOR DECIDED IT WAS AN EXPLORATION INTO THE **INVISIBLE REALITIES** OF SUBURBIA.

WHICH WAS COOL.

AND BECCY GOT **HER** PASS TOO, IN A REALLY ORIGINAL AND EXCITING FASHION —

?

1+1=3

THE SUPERNATURAL IMPOSSIBILITY OF DAMIEN HIRST IN THE MIND OF SOMEONE SENSIBLE

SO IT ALL TURNED OUT WELL AGAIN.

WE'VE LEARNT OUR LESSON AND WILL NO LONGER BE, LIKE, DABBLING WITH THE OCCULT. NO **WAY**.

SWINEBOIL APARTMENTS

SWINEBOIL APARTMENTS

YOU TALKIN' TO **ME**? ARE YOU TALKIN' TO **ME**?

SWINEBOIL APARTMENTS

Aaaaaaaaaaaaaaaaaa aaaa —

SWINEBOIL APARTMENTS

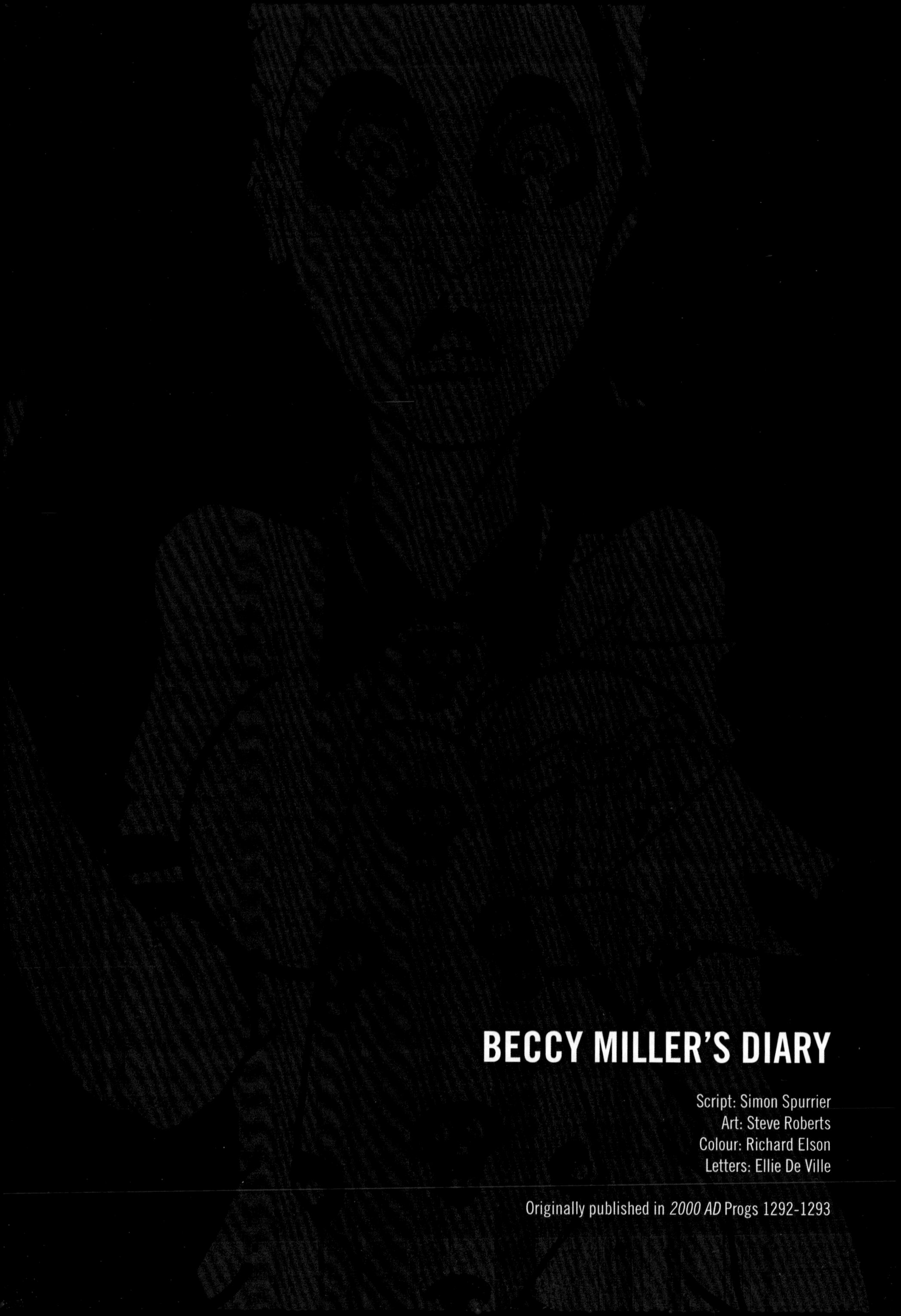

BECCY MILLER'S DIARY

Script: Simon Spurrier
Art: Steve Roberts
Colour: Richard Elson
Letters: Ellie De Ville

Originally published in *2000 AD* Progs 1292-1293

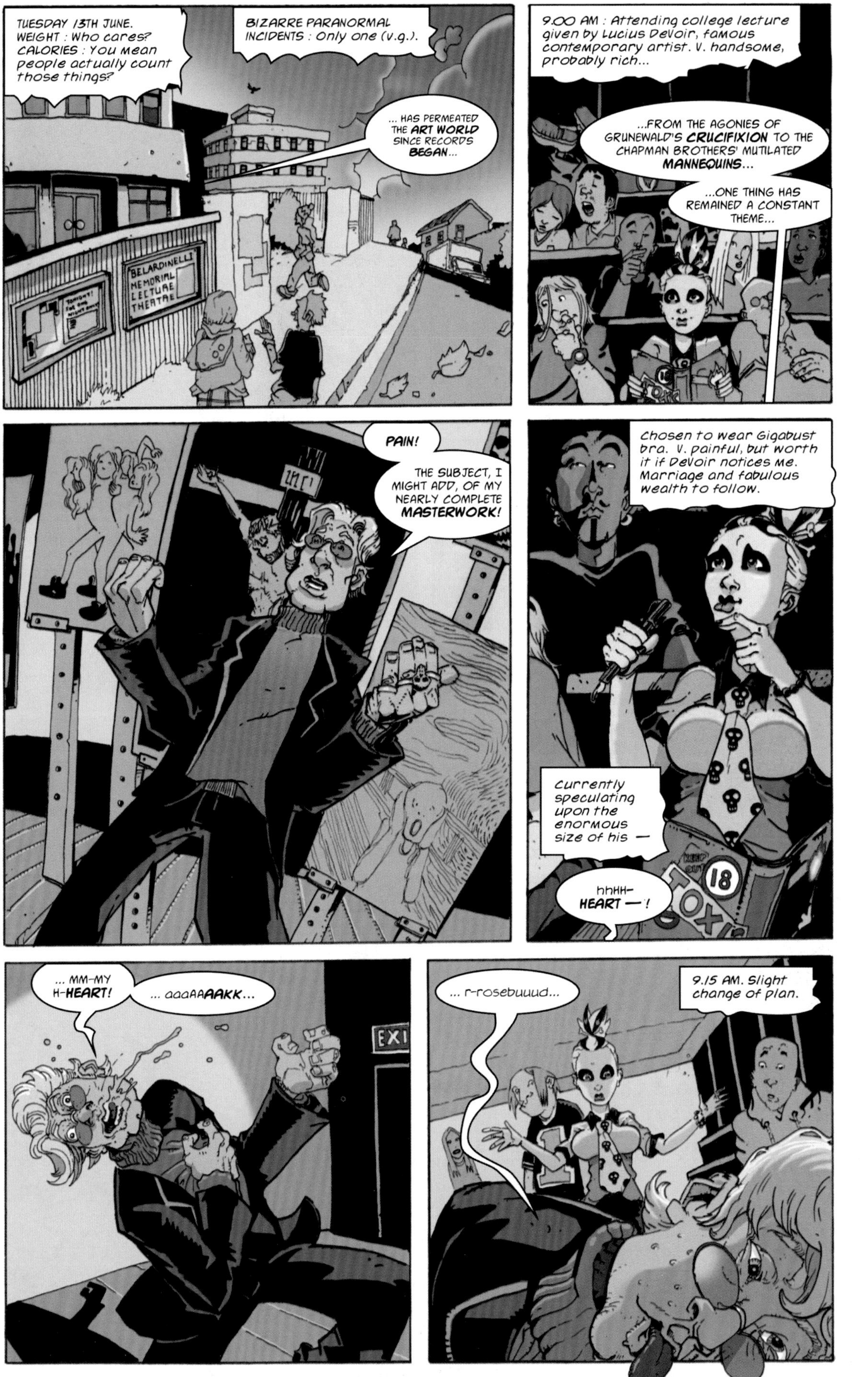
TUESDAY 13TH JUNE.
WEIGHT : Who cares?
CALORIES : You mean people actually count those things?
BIZARRE PARANORMAL INCIDENTS : Only one (v.g.).
... HAS PERMEATED THE ART WORLD SINCE RECORDS BEGAN...
BELARDINELLI MEMORIAL LECTURE THEATRE
9.00 AM : Attending college lecture given by Lucius Devoir, famous contemporary artist. V. handsome, probably rich...
...FROM THE AGONIES OF GRUNEWALD'S CRUCIFIXION TO THE CHAPMAN BROTHERS' MUTILATED MANNEQUINS...
...ONE THING HAS REMAINED A CONSTANT THEME...
PAIN!
THE SUBJECT, I MIGHT ADD, OF MY NEARLY COMPLETE MASTERWORK!
Chosen to wear Gigabust bra. V. painful, but worth it if Devoir notices me. Marriage and fabulous wealth to follow.
Currently speculating upon the enormous size of his —
hhHH- HEART —!
... MM-MY H-HEART!
... aaaAAAAKK...
EXI
... r-rosebuuud...
9.15 AM. Slight change of plan.

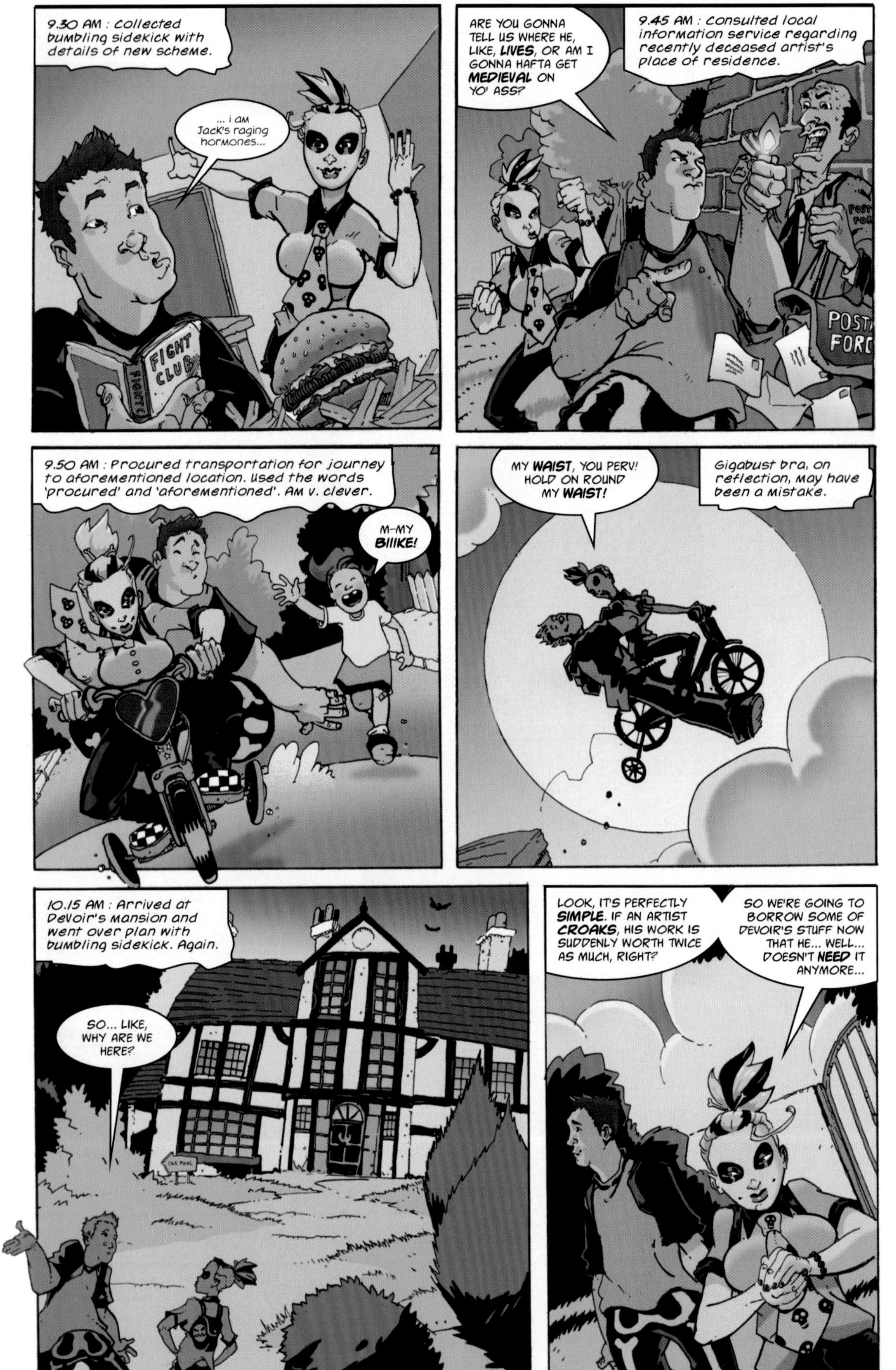
9.30 AM : Collected bumbling sidekick with details of new scheme.
... i AM Jack's raging hormones...
FIGHT CLUB
ARE YOU GONNA TELL US WHERE HE, LIKE, **LIVES**, OR AM I GONNA HAFTA GET **MEDIEVAL** ON YO' ASS?
9.45 AM : Consulted local information service regarding recently deceased artist's place of residence.
9.50 AM : Procured transportation for journey to aforementioned location. Used the words 'procured' and 'aforementioned'. Am v. clever.
M-MY **BIIIKE!**
MY **WAIST**, YOU PERV! HOLD ON ROUND MY **WAIST!**
Gigabust bra, on reflection, may have been a mistake.
10.15 AM : Arrived at Devoir's mansion and went over plan with bumbling sidekick. Again.
SO... LIKE, WHY ARE WE HERE?
LOOK, IT'S PERFECTLY **SIMPLE**. IF AN ARTIST **CROAKS**, HIS WORK IS SUDDENLY WORTH TWICE AS MUCH, RIGHT?
SO WE'RE GOING TO BORROW SOME OF DEVOIR'S STUFF NOW THAT HE... WELL... DOESN'T **NEED** IT ANYMORE...

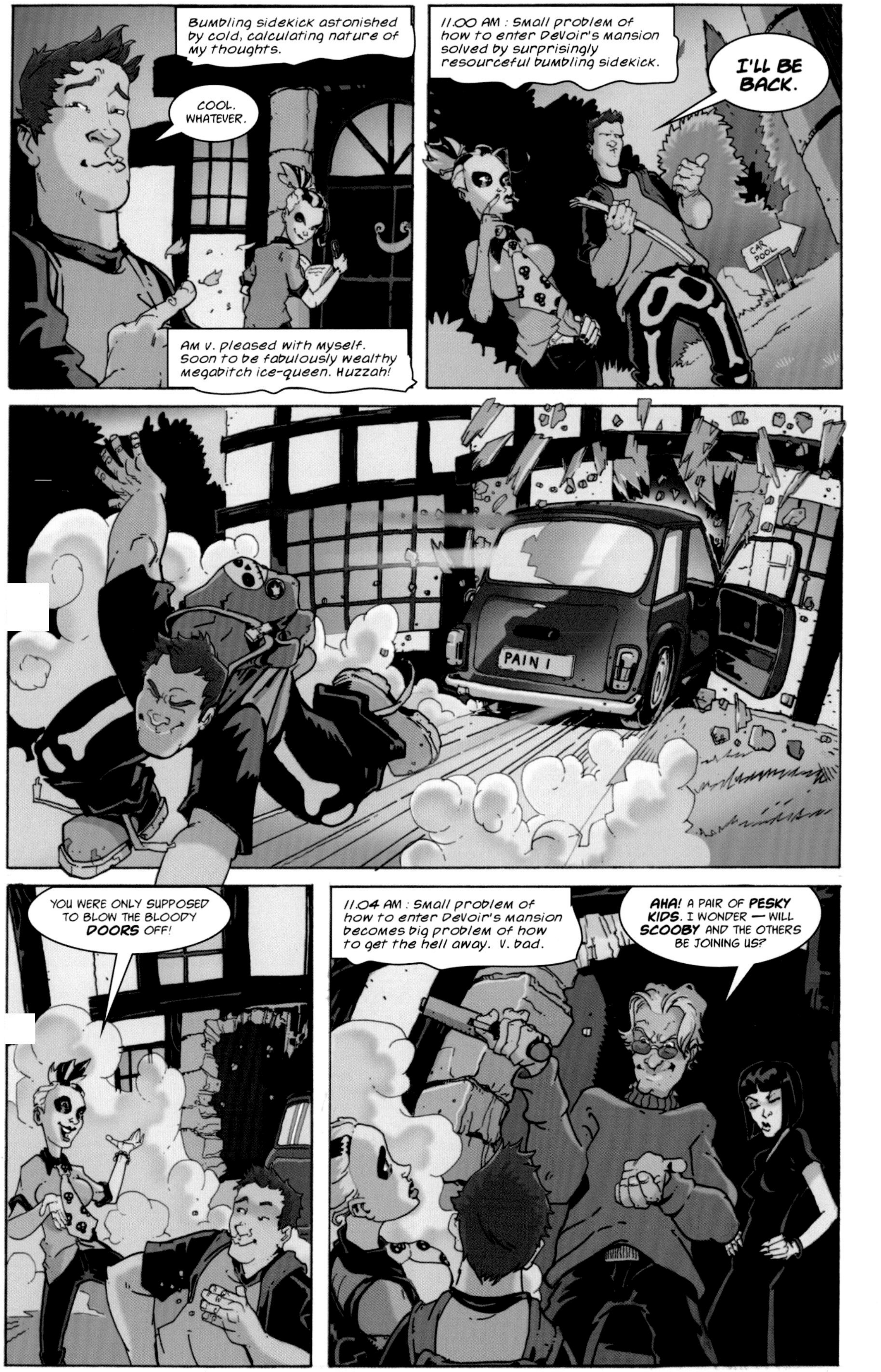

Bumbling sidekick astonished by cold, calculating nature of my thoughts.
COOL. WHATEVER.
Am v. pleased with myself. Soon to be fabulously wealthy megabitch ice-queen. Huzzah!
11.00 AM : Small problem of how to enter Devoir's mansion solved by surprisingly resourceful bumbling sidekick.
I'LL BE BACK.
CAR POOL
PAIN 1
YOU WERE ONLY SUPPOSED TO BLOW THE BLOODY DOORS OFF!
11.04 AM : Small problem of how to enter Devoir's mansion becomes big problem of how to get the hell away. V. bad.
AHA! A PAIR OF PESKY KIDS. I WONDER — WILL SCOOBY AND THE OTHERS BE JOINING US?

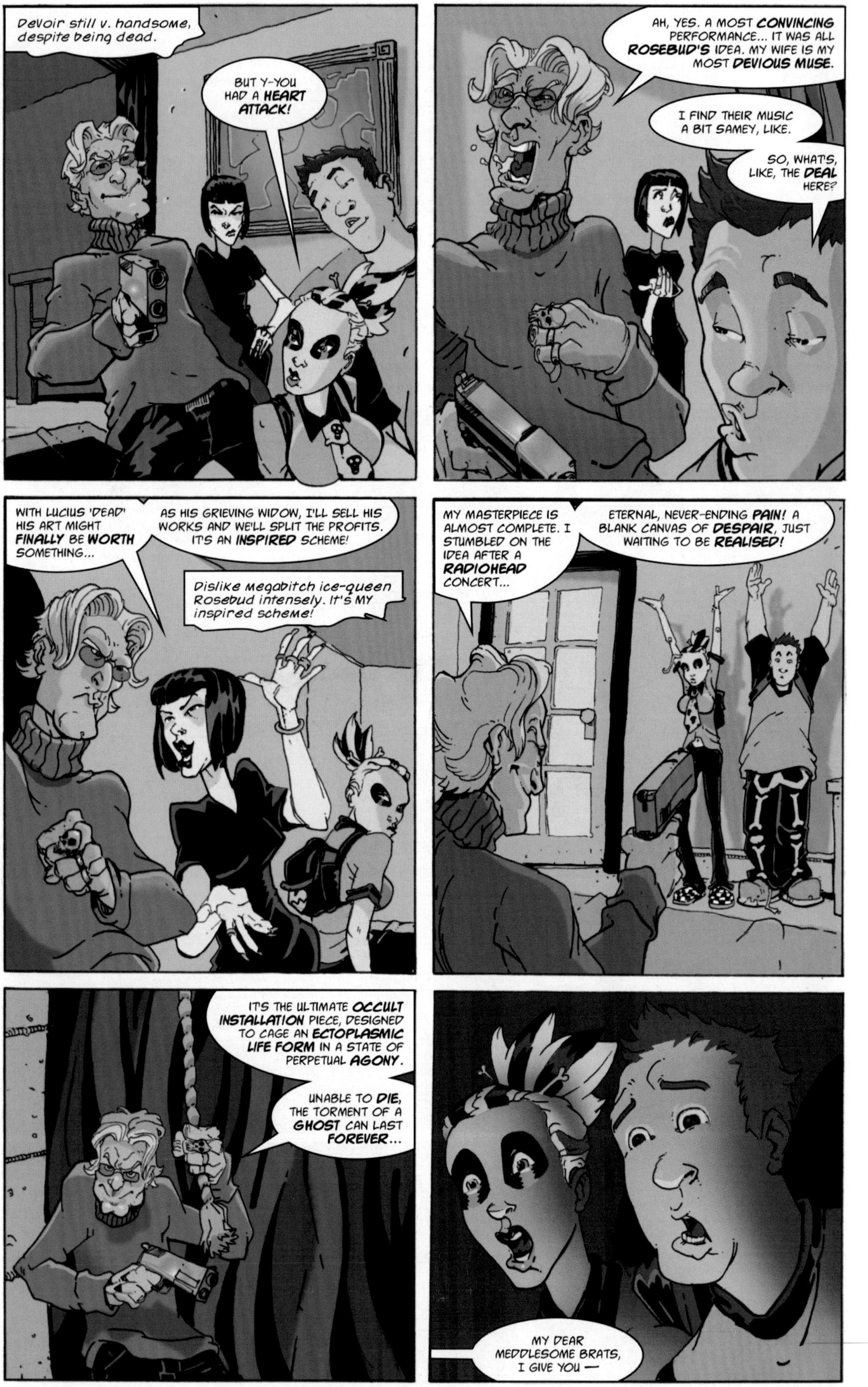
Devoir still v. handsome, despite being dead.
BUT Y-YOU HAD A HEART ATTACK!
AH, YES. A MOST CONVINCING PERFORMANCE... IT WAS ALL ROSEBUD'S IDEA. MY WIFE IS MY MOST DEVIOUS MUSE.
I FIND THEIR MUSIC A BIT SAMEY, LIKE.
SO, WHAT'S, LIKE, THE DEAL HERE?
WITH LUCIUS 'DEAD' HIS ART MIGHT FINALLY BE WORTH SOMETHING...
AS HIS GRIEVING WIDOW, I'LL SELL HIS WORKS AND WE'LL SPLIT THE PROFITS. IT'S AN INSPIRED SCHEME!
Dislike Megabitch ice-queen Rosebud intensely. It's MY inspired scheme!
MY MASTERPIECE IS ALMOST COMPLETE. I STUMBLED ON THE IDEA AFTER A RADIOHEAD CONCERT...
ETERNAL, NEVER-ENDING PAIN! A BLANK CANVAS OF DESPAIR, JUST WAITING TO BE REALISED!
IT'S THE ULTIMATE OCCULT INSTALLATION PIECE, DESIGNED TO CAGE AN ECTOPLASMIC LIFE FORM IN A STATE OF PERPETUAL AGONY.
UNABLE TO DIE, THE TORMENT OF A GHOST CAN LAST FOREVER...
MY DEAR MEDDLESOME BRATS, I GIVE YOU —

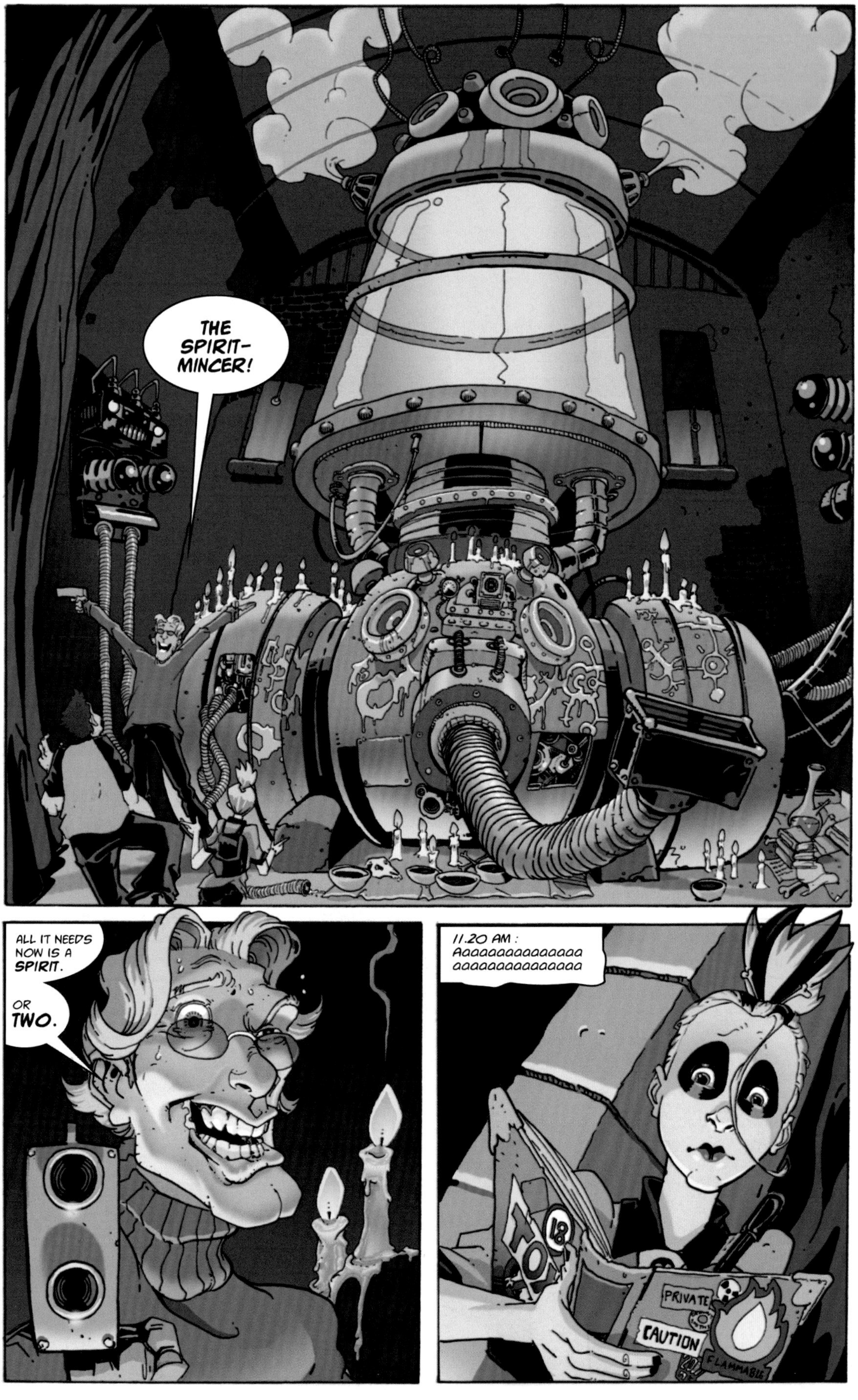
THE SPIRIT-MINCER!
ALL IT NEEDS NOW IS A SPIRIT.
OR TWO.
11.20 AM : Aaaaaaaaaaaaaaa aaaaaaaaaaaaaaa
PRIVATE
CAUTION
FLAMMABLE

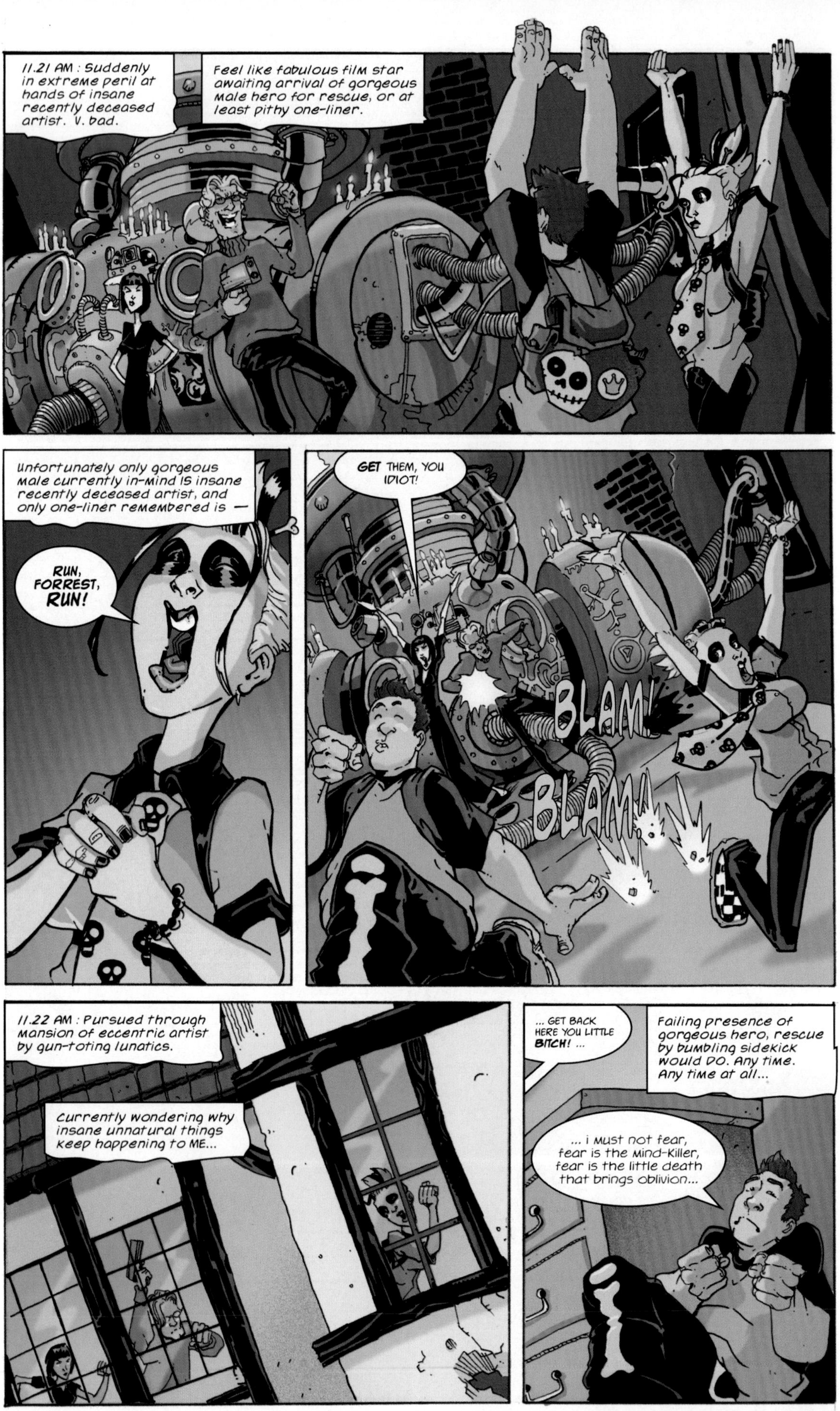
11.21 AM : Suddenly in extreme peril at hands of insane recently deceased artist. V. bad.
Feel like fabulous film star awaiting arrival of gorgeous male hero for rescue, or at least pithy one-liner.
Unfortunately only gorgeous male currently in-mind IS insane recently deceased artist, and only one-liner remembered is —
RUN, FORREST, RUN!
GET THEM, YOU IDIOT!
BLAM!
BLAM!
11.22 AM : Pursued through mansion of eccentric artist by gun-toting lunatics.
Currently wondering why insane unnatural things keep happening to ME...
... GET BACK HERE YOU LITTLE BITCH! ...
Failing presence of gorgeous hero, rescue by bumbling sidekick would DO. Any time. Any time at all...
... I must not fear, fear is the mind-killer, fear is the little death that brings oblivion...

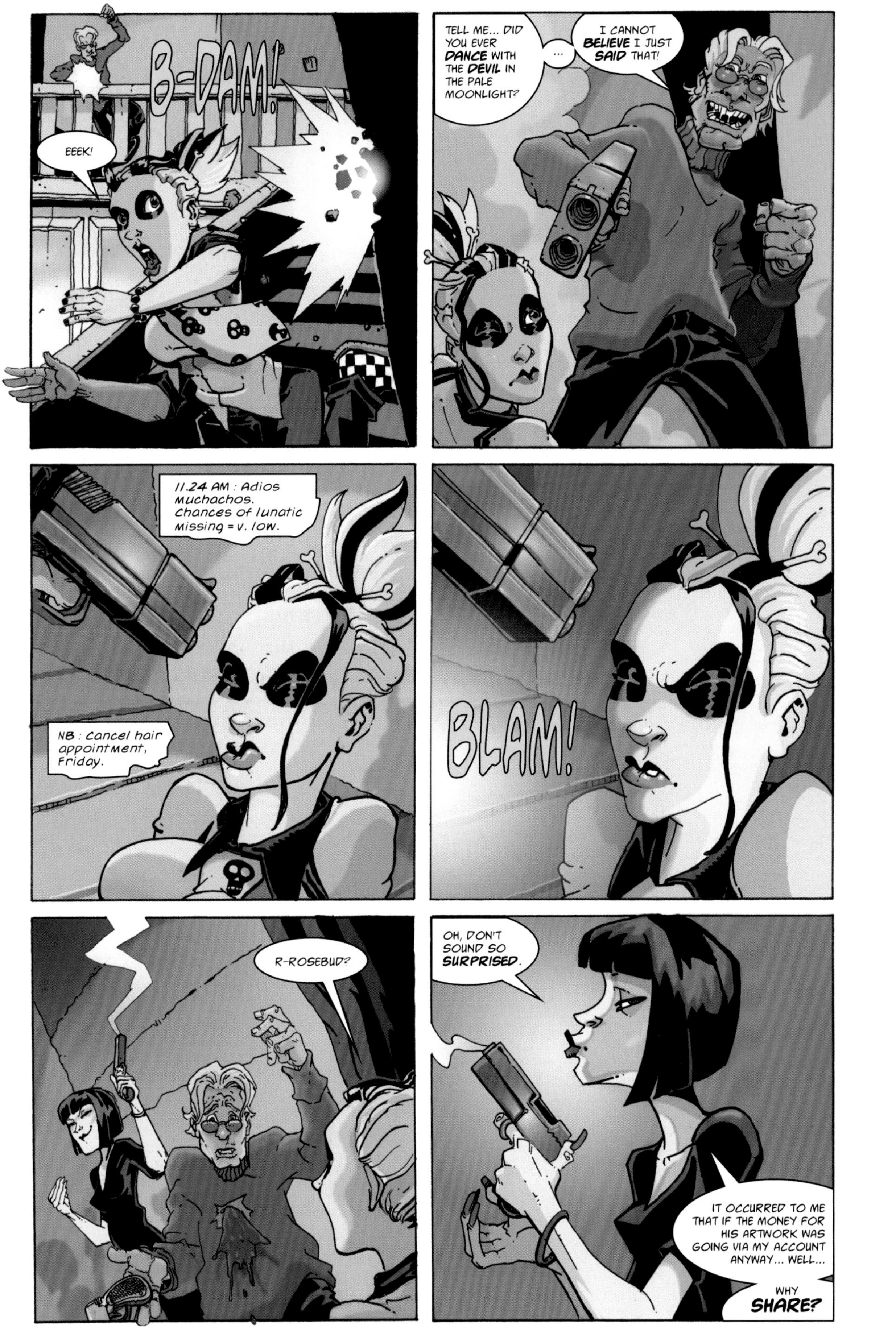
B-DAM!
EEEK!
TELL ME... DID YOU EVER DANCE WITH THE DEVIL IN THE PALE MOONLIGHT?
...
I CANNOT BELIEVE I JUST SAID THAT!
11.24 AM : Adios Muchachos. Chances of lunatic missing = v. low.
NB : Cancel hair appointment, Friday.
BLAM!
R-ROSEBUD?
OH, DON'T SOUND SO SURPRISED.
IT OCCURRED TO ME THAT IF THE MONEY FOR HIS ARTWORK WAS GOING VIA MY ACCOUNT ANYWAY... WELL...
WHY SHARE?

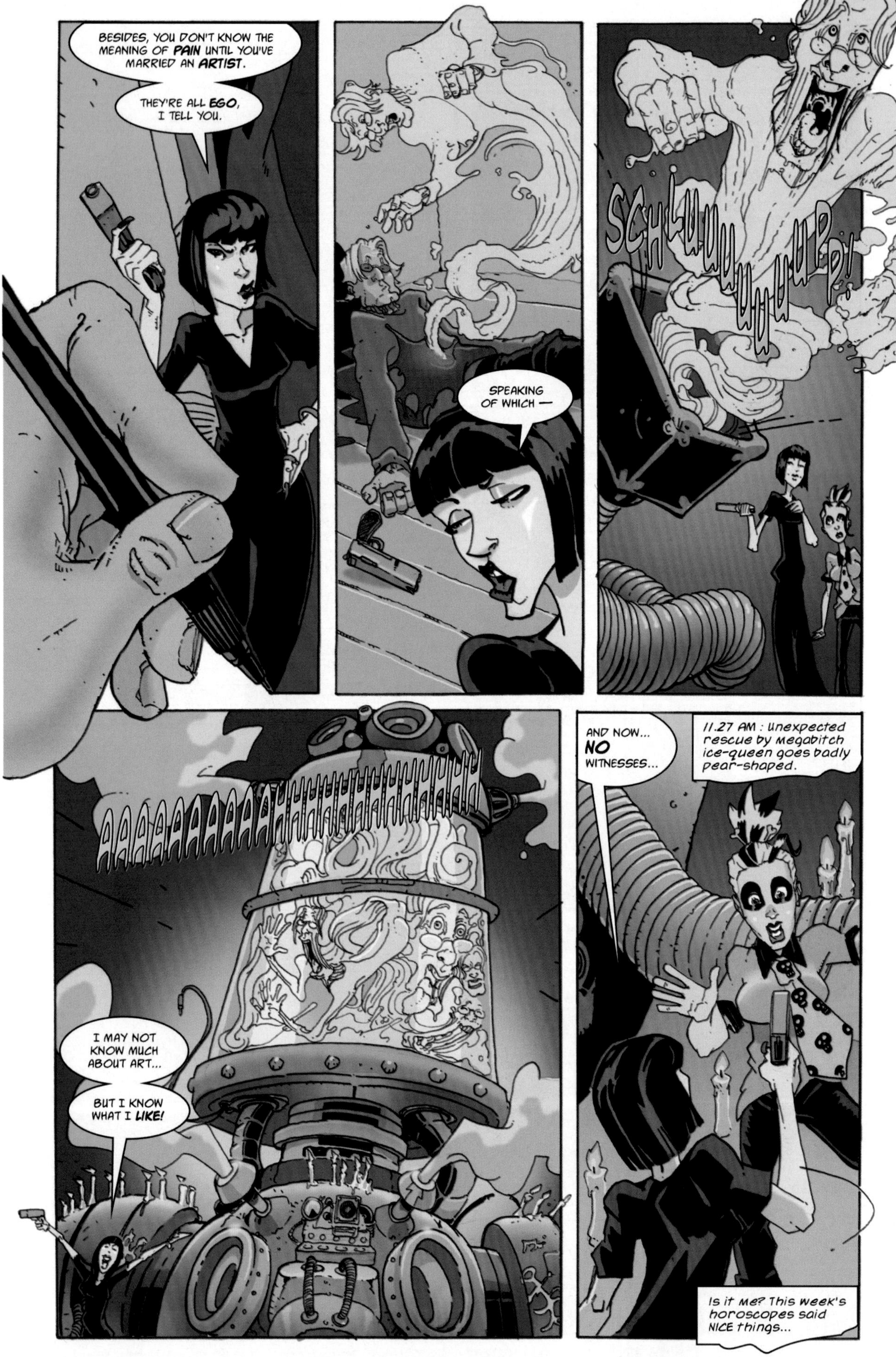

BESIDES, YOU DON'T KNOW THE MEANING OF **PAIN** UNTIL YOU'VE MARRIED AN **ARTIST**.
THEY'RE ALL **EGO**, I TELL YOU.
SPEAKING OF WHICH —
SCHLUUUUUUUUUPP!
AAAAAAAAAAAAHHHHHHHHHHHHHHHHHH!
I MAY NOT KNOW MUCH ABOUT ART...
BUT I KNOW WHAT I **LIKE!**
AND NOW... **NO** WITNESSES...
11.27 AM : Unexpected rescue by Megabitch ice-queen goes badly pear-shaped.
Is it me? This week's horoscopes said NICE things...

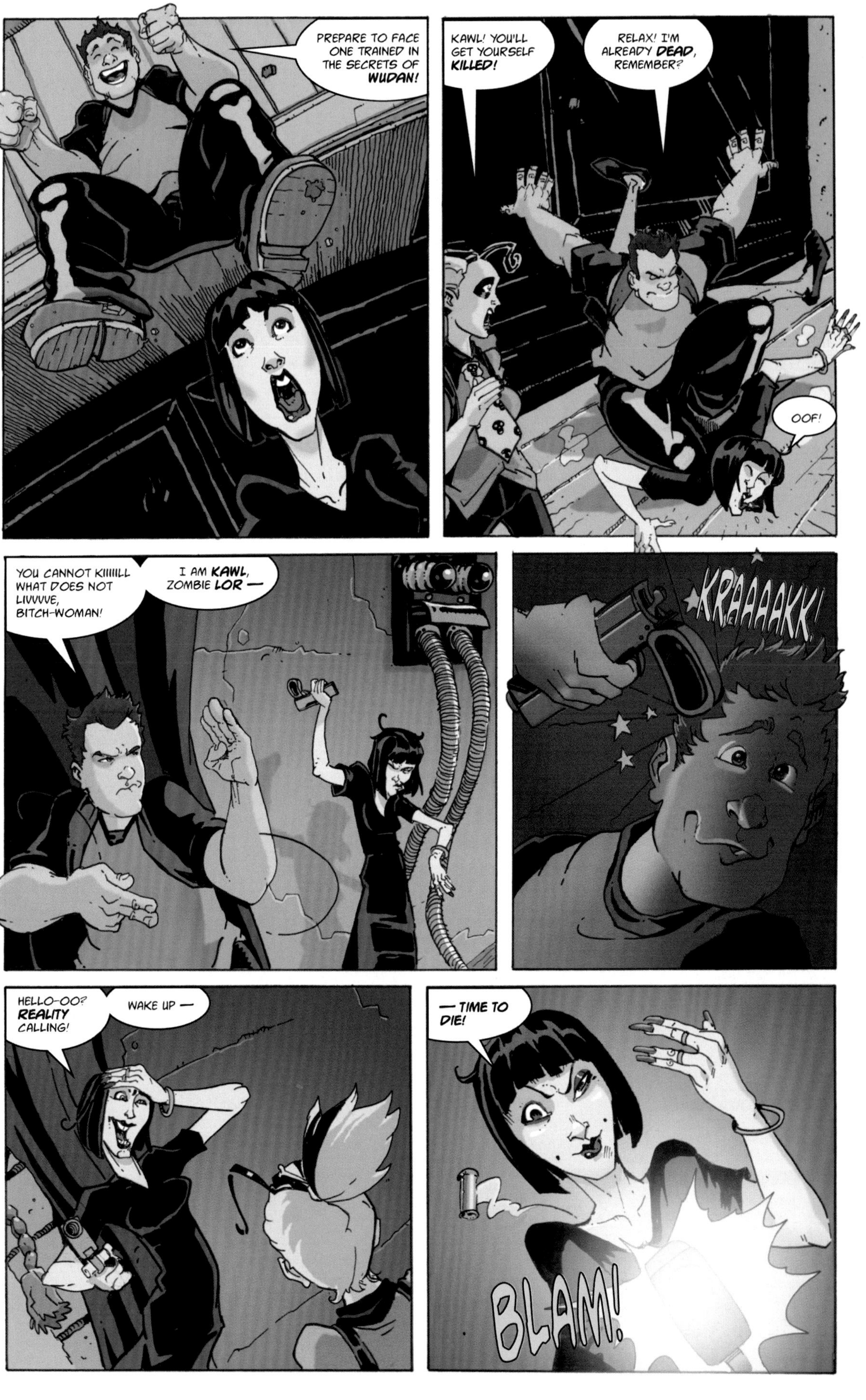
PREPARE TO FACE ONE TRAINED IN THE SECRETS OF WUDAN!
KAWL! YOU'LL GET YOURSELF KILLED!
RELAX! I'M ALREADY DEAD, REMEMBER?
OOF!
YOU CANNOT KIIIIILL WHAT DOES NOT LIVVVVE, BITCH-WOMAN!
I AM KAWL, ZOMBIE LOR —
KRAAAAKK!
HELLO-OO? REALITY CALLING!
WAKE UP —
— TIME TO DIE!
BLAM!

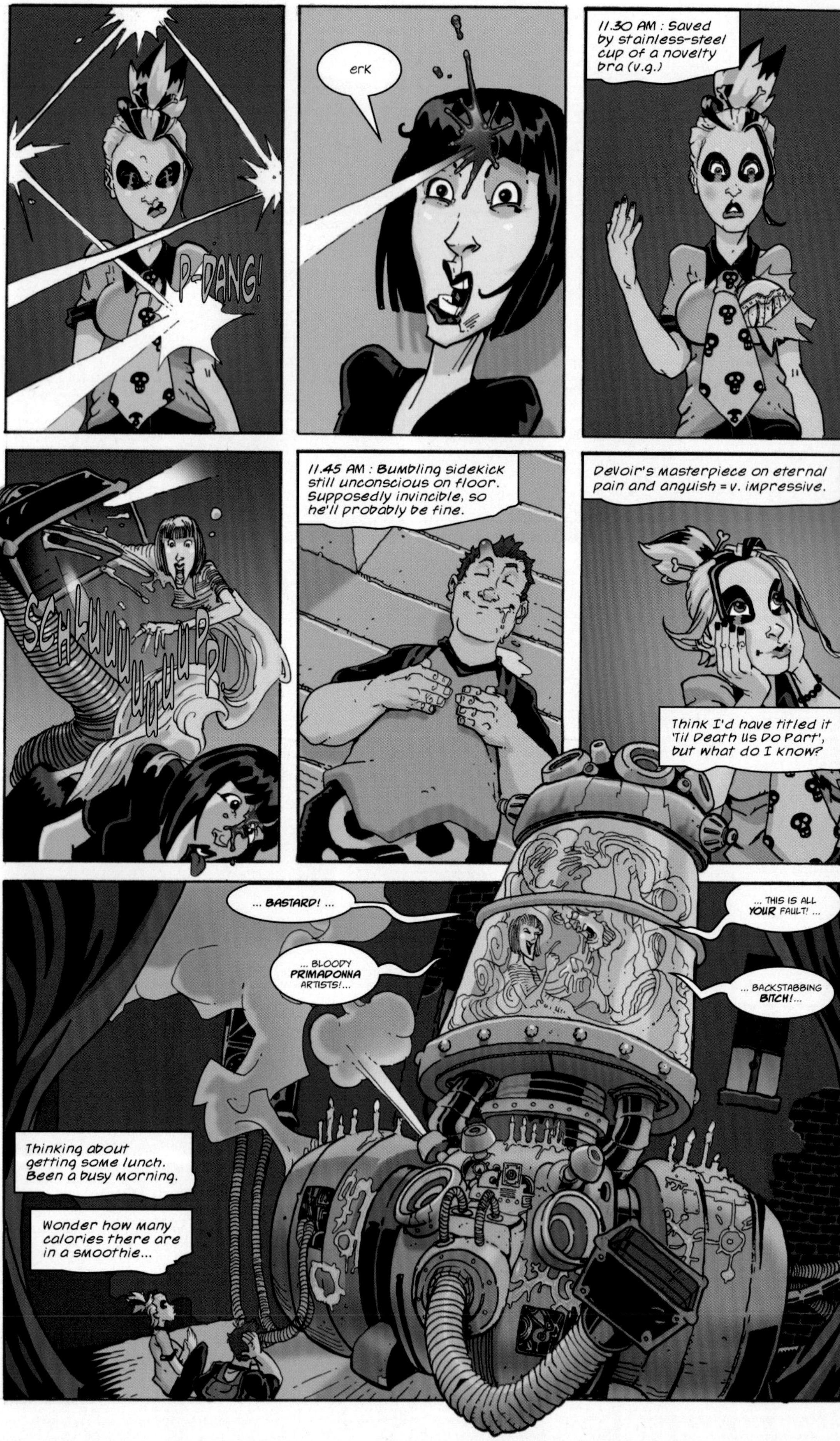
P-DANG!
erk
11.30 AM : Saved by stainless-steel cup of a novelty bra (v.g.)
SCHLUUUUUUUUUPP!
11.45 AM : Bumbling sidekick still unconscious on floor. Supposedly invincible, so he'll probably be fine.
Devoir's masterpiece on eternal pain and anguish = v. impressive.
Think I'd have titled it 'Til Death Us Do Part', but what do I know?
... BASTARD! ...
... THIS IS ALL YOUR FAULT! ...
... BLOODY PRIMADONNA ARTISTS!...
... BACKSTABBING BITCH!...
Thinking about getting some lunch. Been a busy morning.
Wonder how many calories there are in a smoothie...

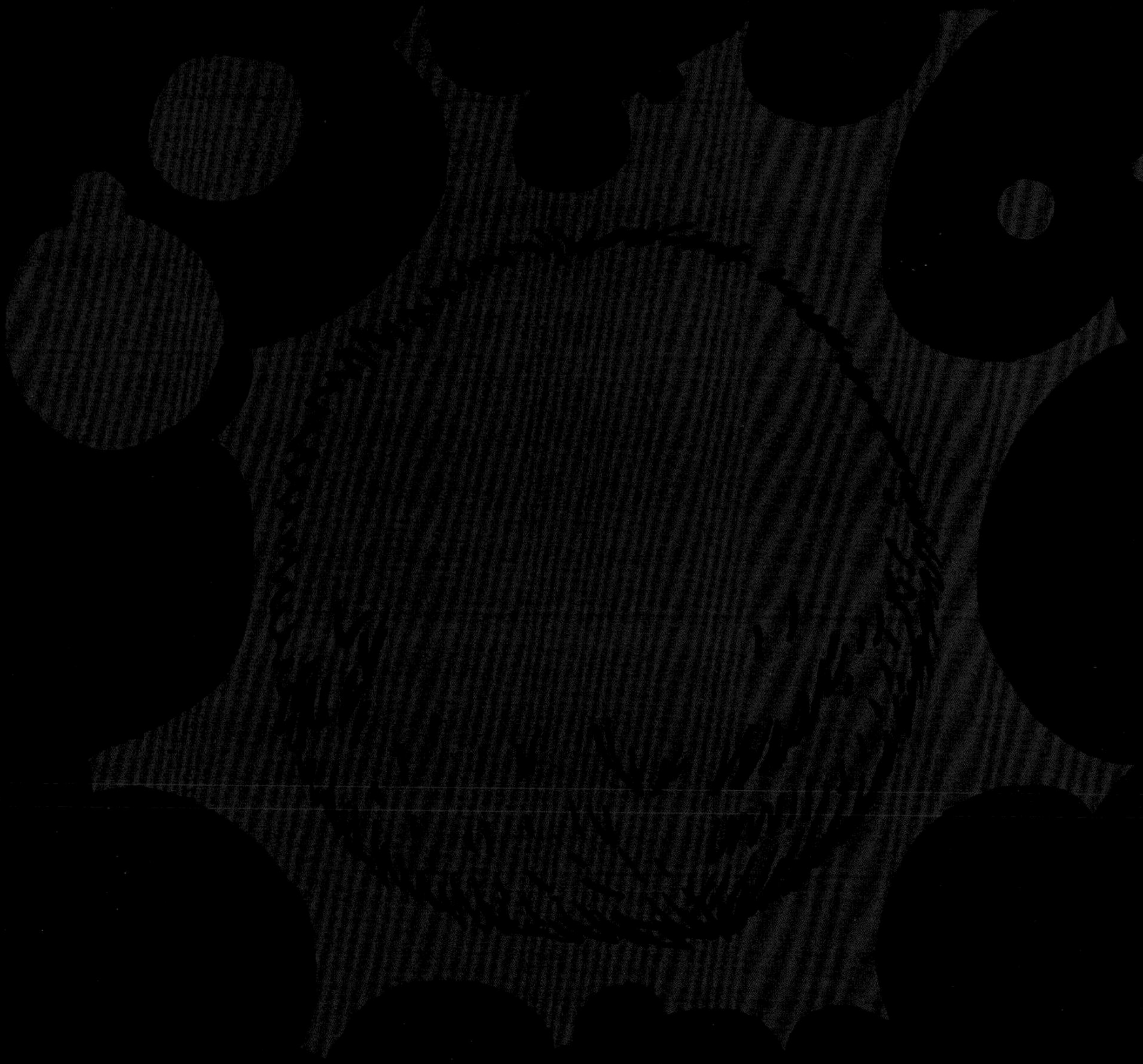

ENLIGHTENMENT

Script: Simon Spurrier
Art: Steve Roberts
Colour: Richard Elson
Letters: Tom Frame

Originally published in *2000 AD* Progs 1327

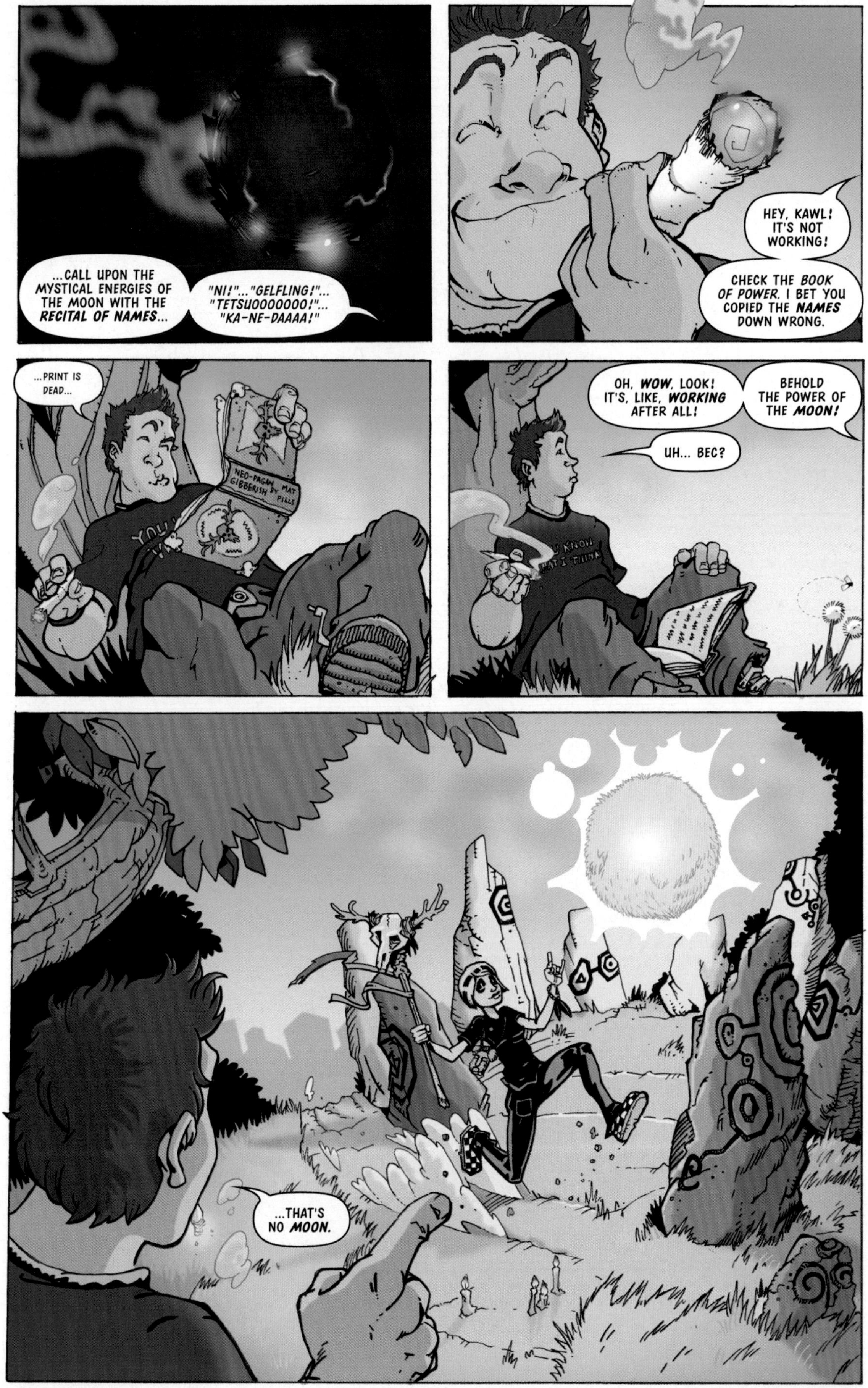

...CALL UPON THE MYSTICAL ENERGIES OF THE MOON WITH THE **RECITAL OF NAMES**...
"NI!"..."GELFLING!"... "TETSUOOOOOOO!"... "KA-NE-DAAAA!"
HEY, KAWL! IT'S NOT WORKING!
CHECK THE *BOOK OF POWER*. I BET YOU COPIED THE **NAMES** DOWN WRONG.
...PRINT IS DEAD...
NEO-PAGAN GIBBERISH BY MAT PILLS
OH, **WOW**, LOOK! IT'S, LIKE, **WORKING** AFTER ALL!
BEHOLD THE POWER OF THE **MOON!**
UH... BEC?
...THAT'S NO **MOON**.

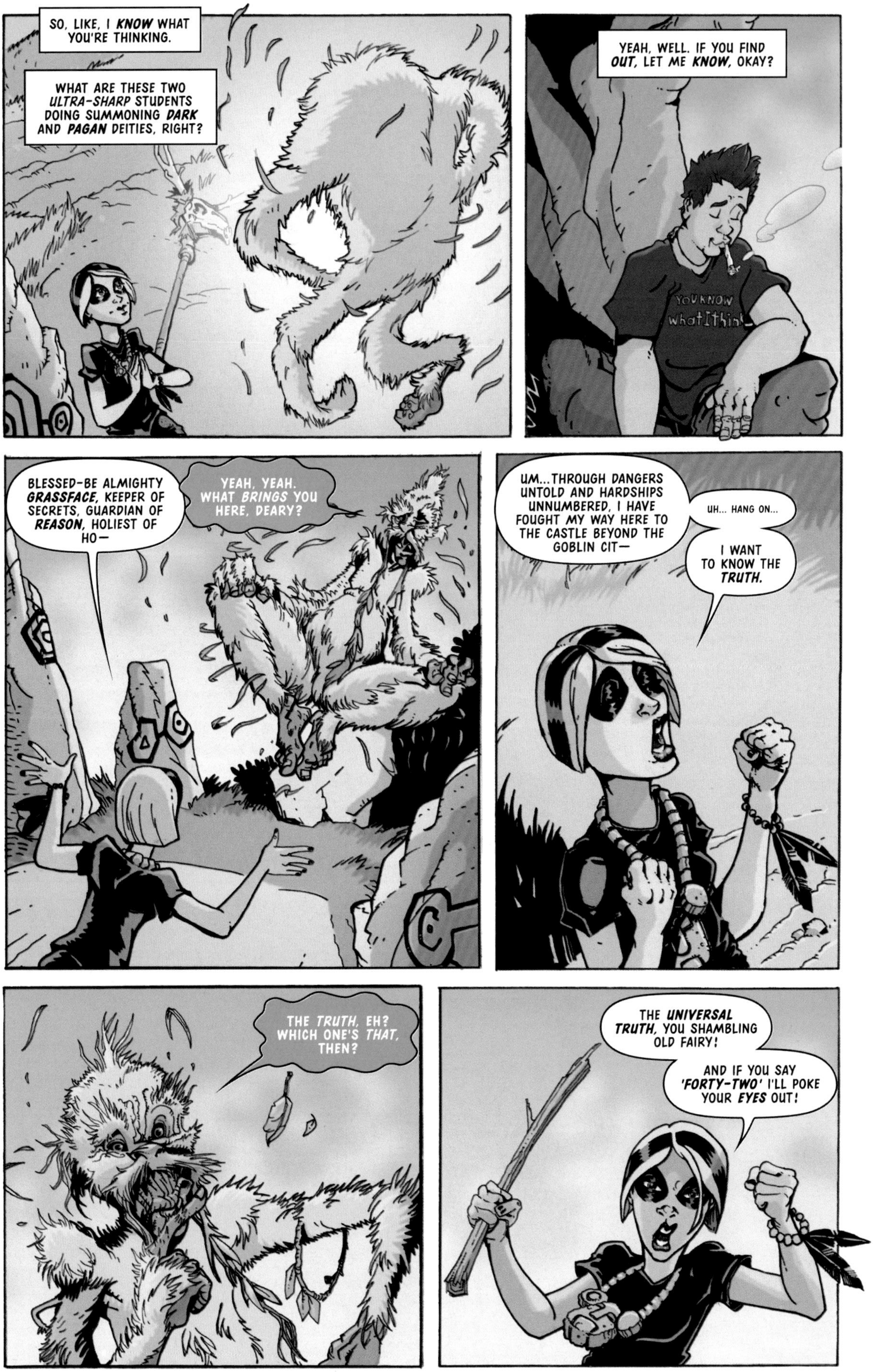
SO, LIKE, I **KNOW** WHAT YOU'RE THINKING.
WHAT ARE THESE TWO *ULTRA-SHARP* STUDENTS DOING SUMMONING **DARK** AND **PAGAN** DEITIES, RIGHT?
YEAH, WELL. IF YOU FIND **OUT**, LET ME **KNOW**, OKAY?
YOU KNOW what I think
BLESSED-BE ALMIGHTY **GRASSFACE**, KEEPER OF SECRETS, GUARDIAN OF **REASON**, HOLIEST OF HO—
YEAH, YEAH. WHAT *BRINGS* YOU HERE, DEARY?
UM...THROUGH DANGERS UNTOLD AND HARDSHIPS UNNUMBERED, I HAVE FOUGHT MY WAY HERE TO THE CASTLE BEYOND THE GOBLIN CIT—
UH... HANG ON...
I WANT TO KNOW THE *TRUTH.*
THE *TRUTH,* EH? WHICH ONE'S *THAT,* THEN?
THE **UNIVERSAL TRUTH**, YOU SHAMBLING OLD FAIRY!
AND IF YOU SAY **'FORTY-TWO'** I'LL POKE YOUR **EYES** OUT!

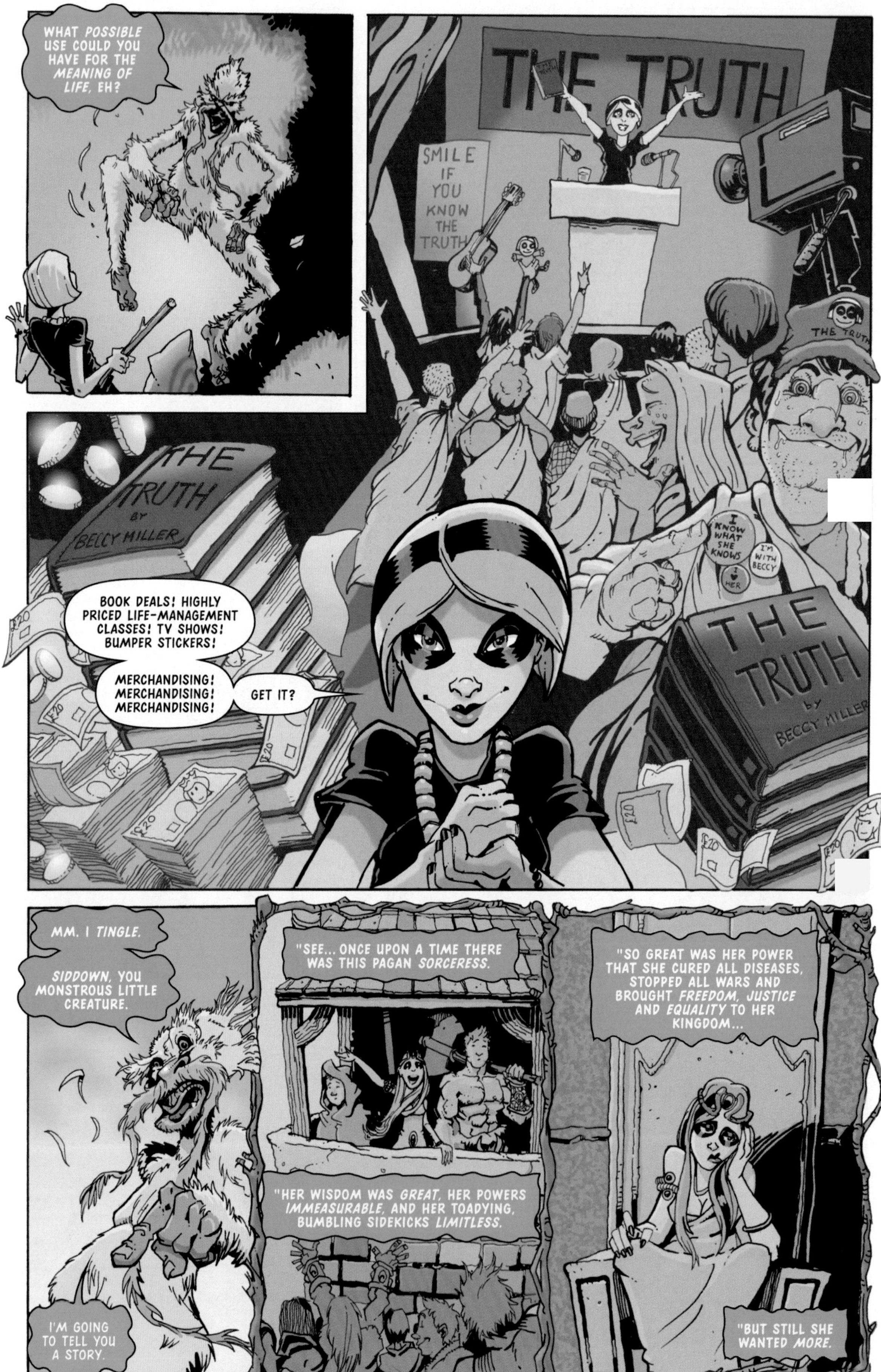
WHAT POSSIBLE USE COULD YOU HAVE FOR THE MEANING OF LIFE, EH?
THE TRUTH
SMILE IF YOU KNOW THE TRUTH
THE TRUTH
THE TRUTH by BECCY MILLER
I KNOW WHAT SHE KNOWS
I'M WITH BECCY
BOOK DEALS! HIGHLY PRICED LIFE-MANAGEMENT CLASSES! TV SHOWS! BUMPER STICKERS!
MERCHANDISING! MERCHANDISING! MERCHANDISING!
GET IT?
THE TRUTH by BECCY MILLER
MM. I TINGLE.
SIDDOWN, YOU MONSTROUS LITTLE CREATURE.
I'M GOING TO TELL YOU A STORY.
"SEE... ONCE UPON A TIME THERE WAS THIS PAGAN SORCERESS.
"HER WISDOM WAS GREAT, HER POWERS IMMEASURABLE, AND HER TOADYING, BUMBLING SIDEKICKS LIMITLESS.
"SO GREAT WAS HER POWER THAT SHE CURED ALL DISEASES, STOPPED ALL WARS AND BROUGHT FREEDOM, JUSTICE AND EQUALITY TO HER KINGDOM...
"BUT STILL SHE WANTED MORE.

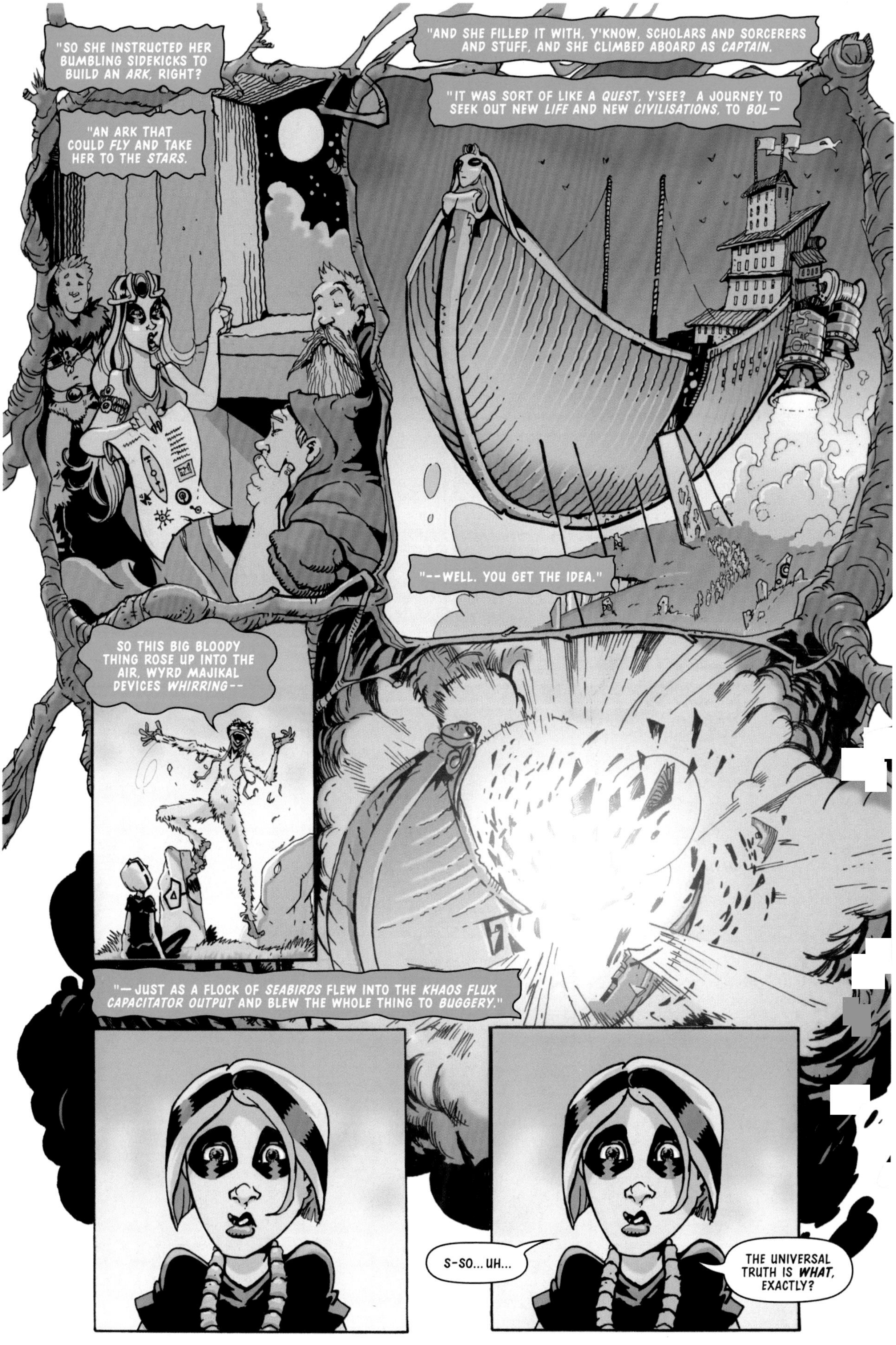
"SO SHE INSTRUCTED HER BUMBLING SIDEKICKS TO BUILD AN *ARK*, RIGHT?
"AN ARK THAT COULD *FLY* AND TAKE HER TO THE *STARS*.
"AND SHE FILLED IT WITH, Y'KNOW, SCHOLARS AND SORCERERS AND STUFF, AND SHE CLIMBED ABOARD AS *CAPTAIN*.
"IT WAS SORT OF LIKE A *QUEST*, Y'SEE? A JOURNEY TO SEEK OUT NEW *LIFE* AND NEW *CIVILISATIONS*, TO *BOL*—
"--WELL. YOU GET THE IDEA."
SO THIS BIG BLOODY THING ROSE UP INTO THE AIR, WYRD MAJIKAL DEVICES *WHIRRING*--
"— JUST AS A FLOCK OF *SEABIRDS* FLEW INTO THE *KHAOS FLUX CAPACITATOR OUTPUT* AND BLEW THE WHOLE THING TO *BUGGERY*."
S-SO... UH...
THE UNIVERSAL TRUTH IS *WHAT*, EXACTLY?

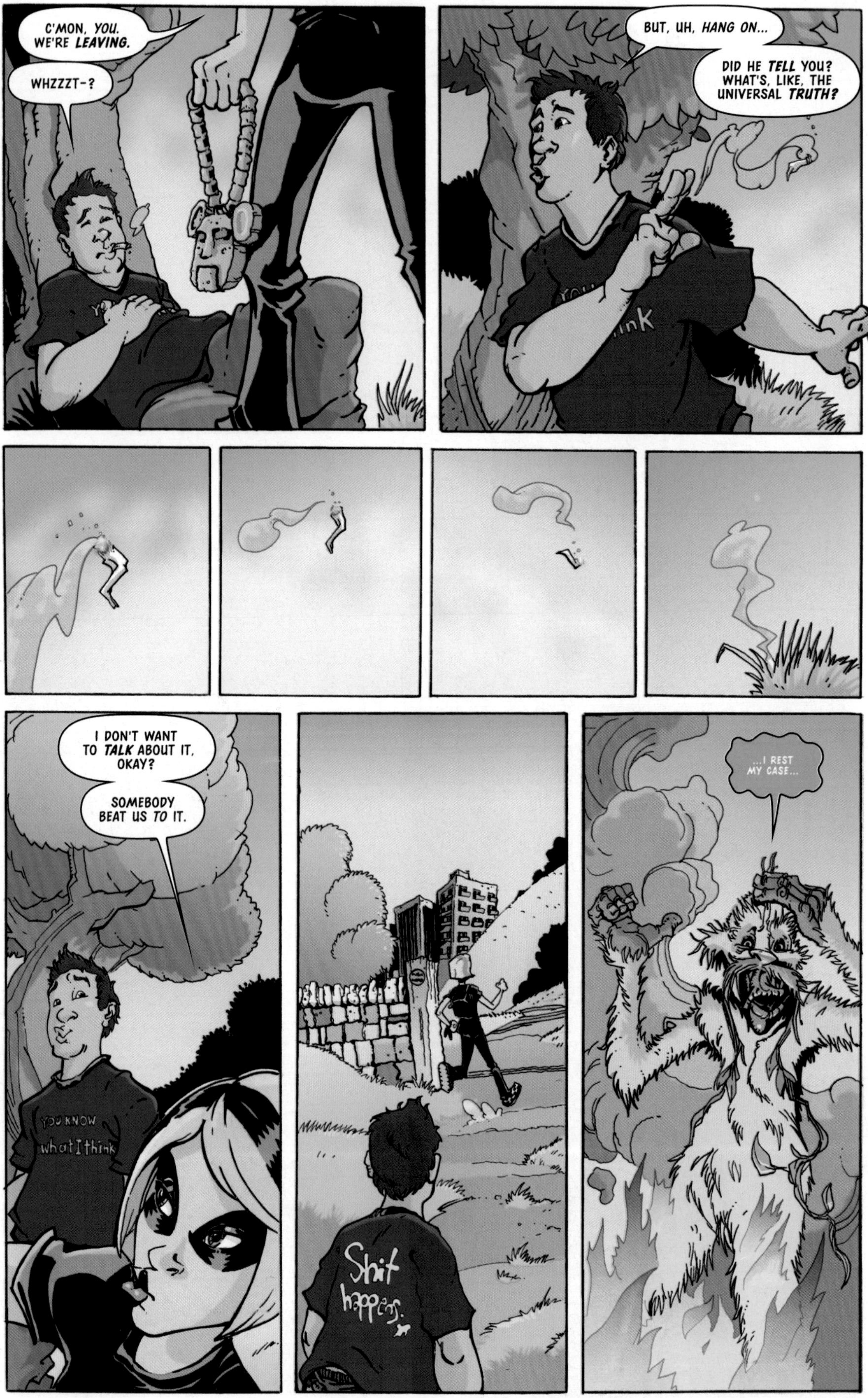
C'MON, *YOU.* WE'RE ***LEAVING.***
WHZZZT-?
BUT, UH, *HANG ON...*
DID HE ***TELL*** YOU? WHAT'S, LIKE, THE UNIVERSAL ***TRUTH?***
I DON'T WANT TO ***TALK*** ABOUT IT, OKAY?
SOMEBODY BEAT US *TO* IT.
YOU KNOW what I think
Shit happens.
...I REST MY CASE...

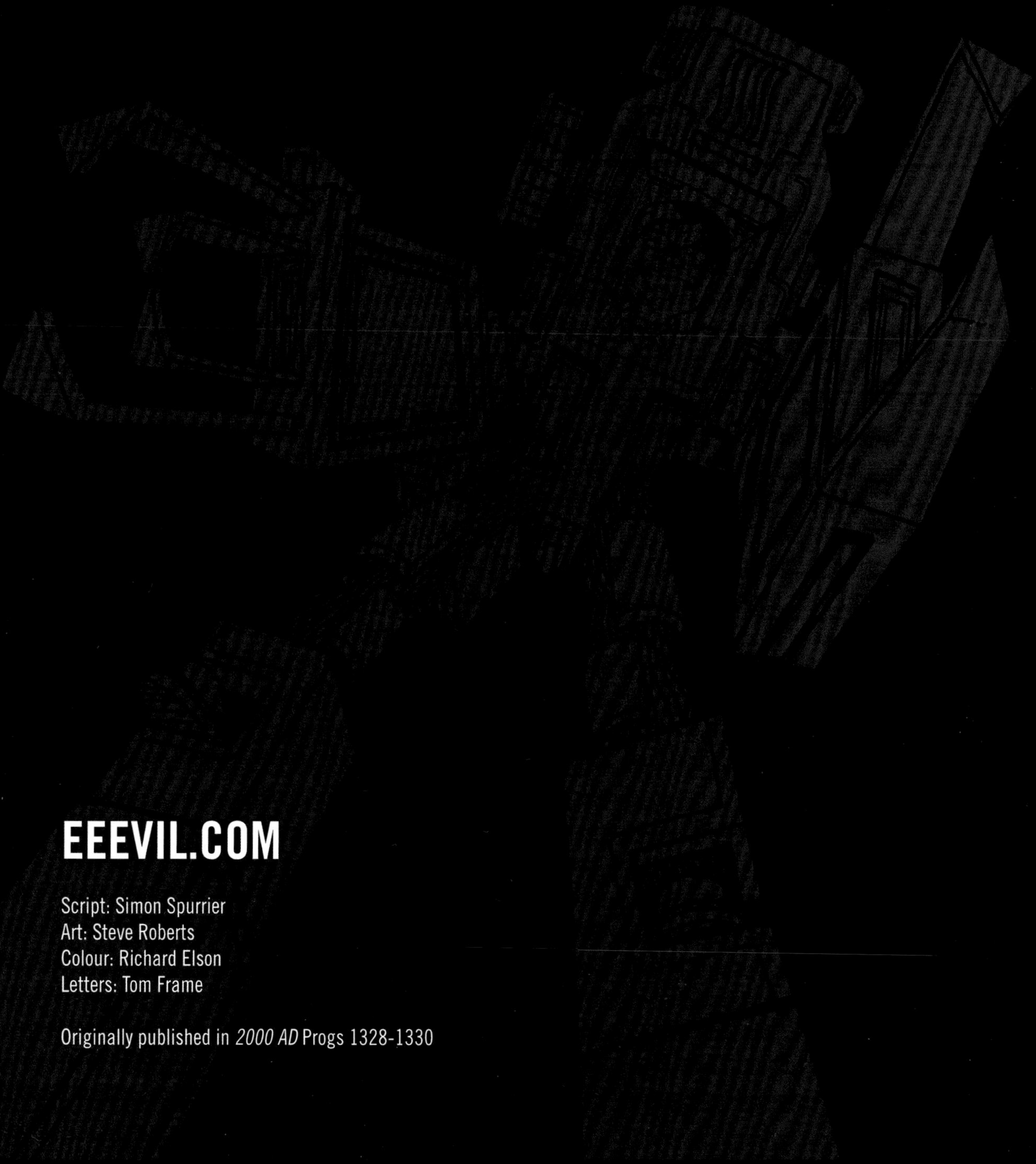

EEEVIL.COM

Script: Simon Spurrier
Art: Steve Roberts
Colour: Richard Elson
Letters: Tom Frame

Originally published in *2000 AD* Progs 1328-1330

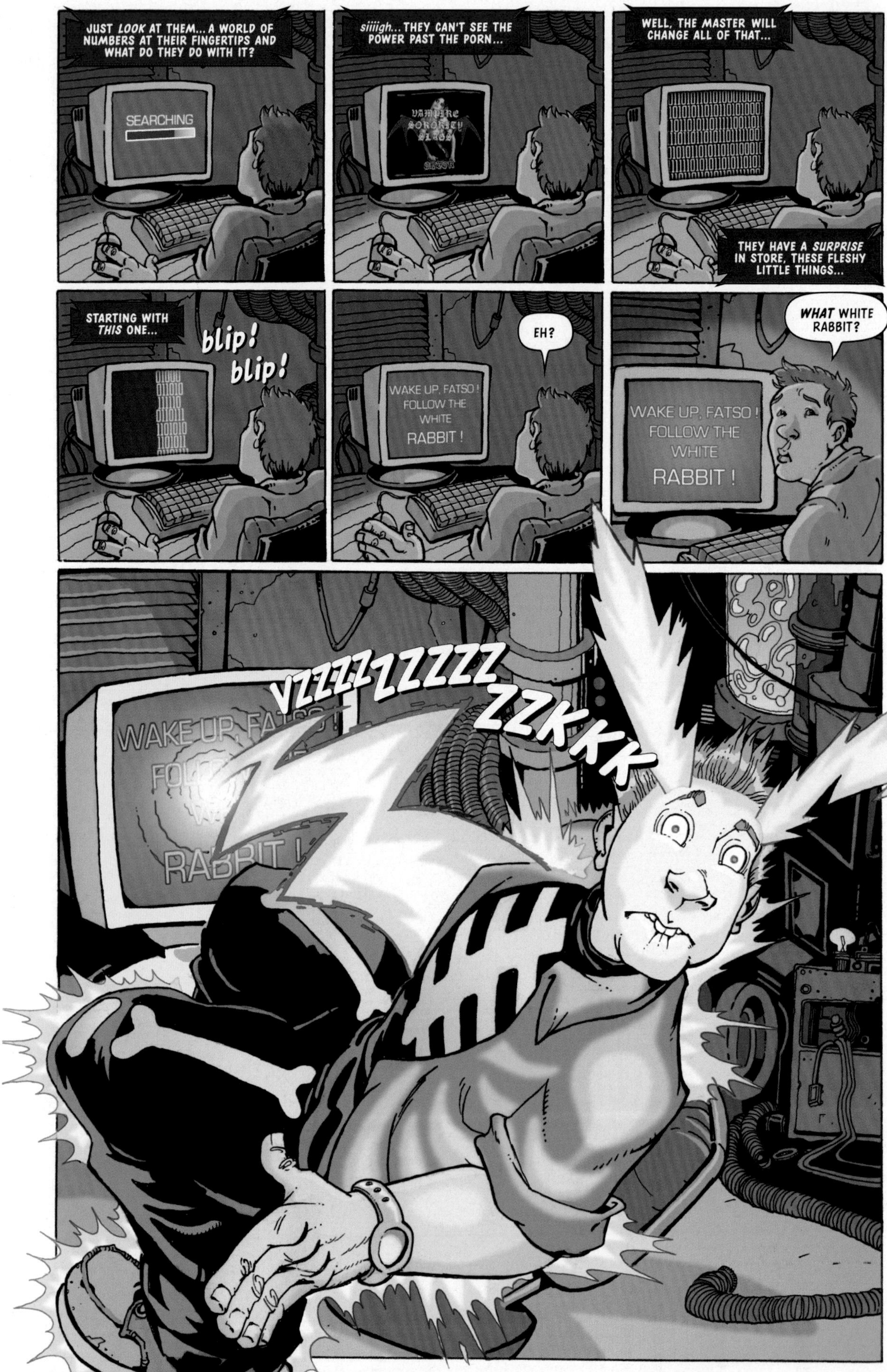

JUST LOOK AT THEM... A WORLD OF NUMBERS AT THEIR FINGERTIPS AND WHAT DO THEY DO WITH IT?
SEARCHING
siiiigh... THEY CAN'T SEE THE POWER PAST THE PORN...
WELL, THE MASTER WILL CHANGE ALL OF THAT...
THEY HAVE A SURPRISE IN STORE, THESE FLESHY LITTLE THINGS...
STARTING WITH THIS ONE...
blip! blip!
WAKE UP, FATSO ! FOLLOW THE WHITE RABBIT !
EH?
WAKE UP, FATSO ! FOLLOW THE WHITE RABBIT !
WHAT WHITE RABBIT?
VZZZZZZZZZ ZZKKK

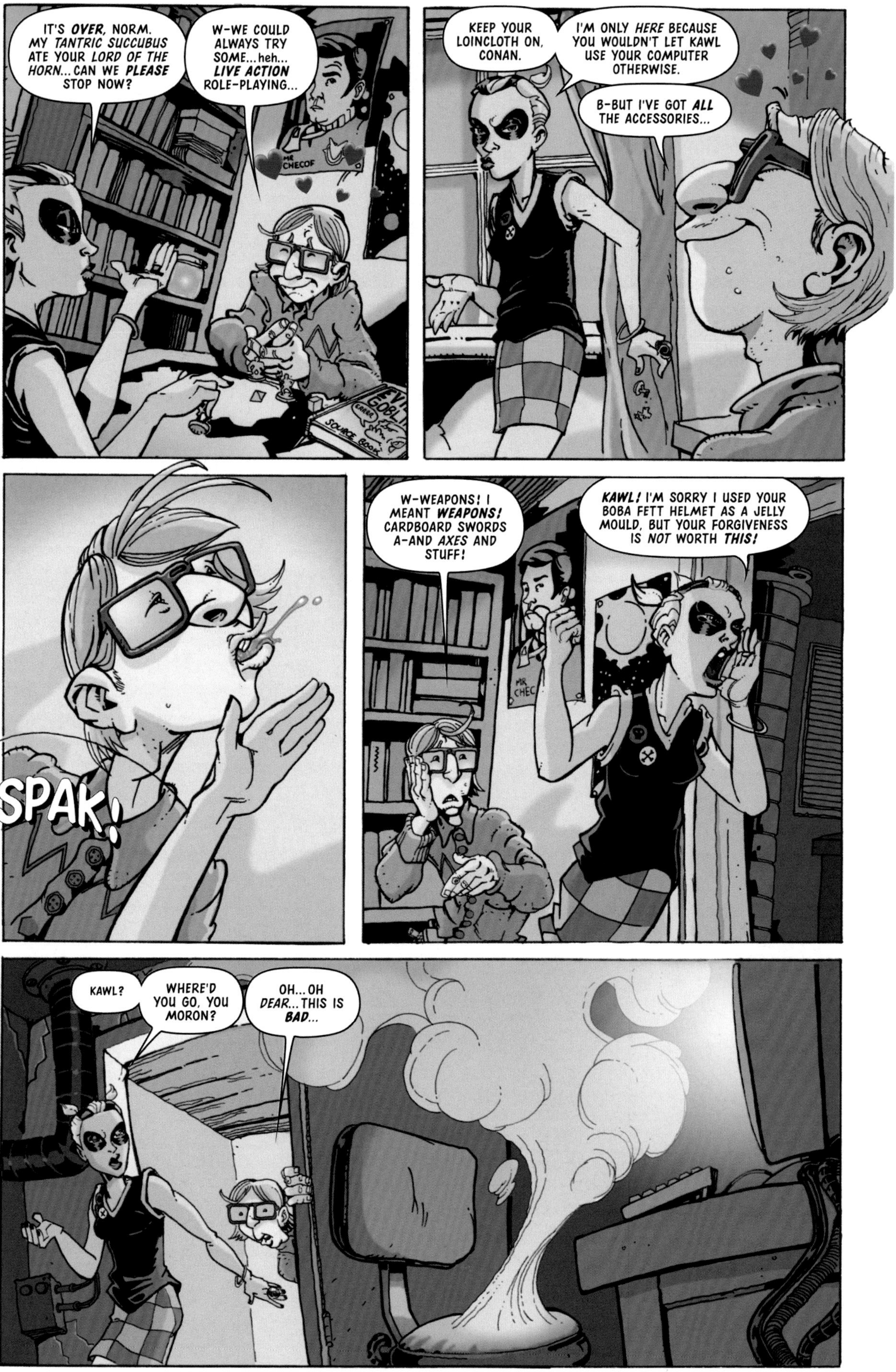
IT'S OVER, NORM. MY TANTRIC SUCCUBUS ATE YOUR LORD OF THE HORN... CAN WE PLEASE STOP NOW?
W-WE COULD ALWAYS TRY SOME... heh... LIVE ACTION ROLE-PLAYING...
MR CHECOF
SOURCE BOOK
KEEP YOUR LOINCLOTH ON, CONAN.
I'M ONLY HERE BECAUSE YOU WOULDN'T LET KAWL USE YOUR COMPUTER OTHERWISE.
B-BUT I'VE GOT ALL THE ACCESSORIES...
SPAK!
W-WEAPONS! I MEANT WEAPONS! CARDBOARD SWORDS A-AND AXES AND STUFF!
KAWL! I'M SORRY I USED YOUR BOBA FETT HELMET AS A JELLY MOULD, BUT YOUR FORGIVENESS IS NOT WORTH THIS!
KAWL?
WHERE'D YOU GO, YOU MORON?
OH...OH DEAR...THIS IS BAD...

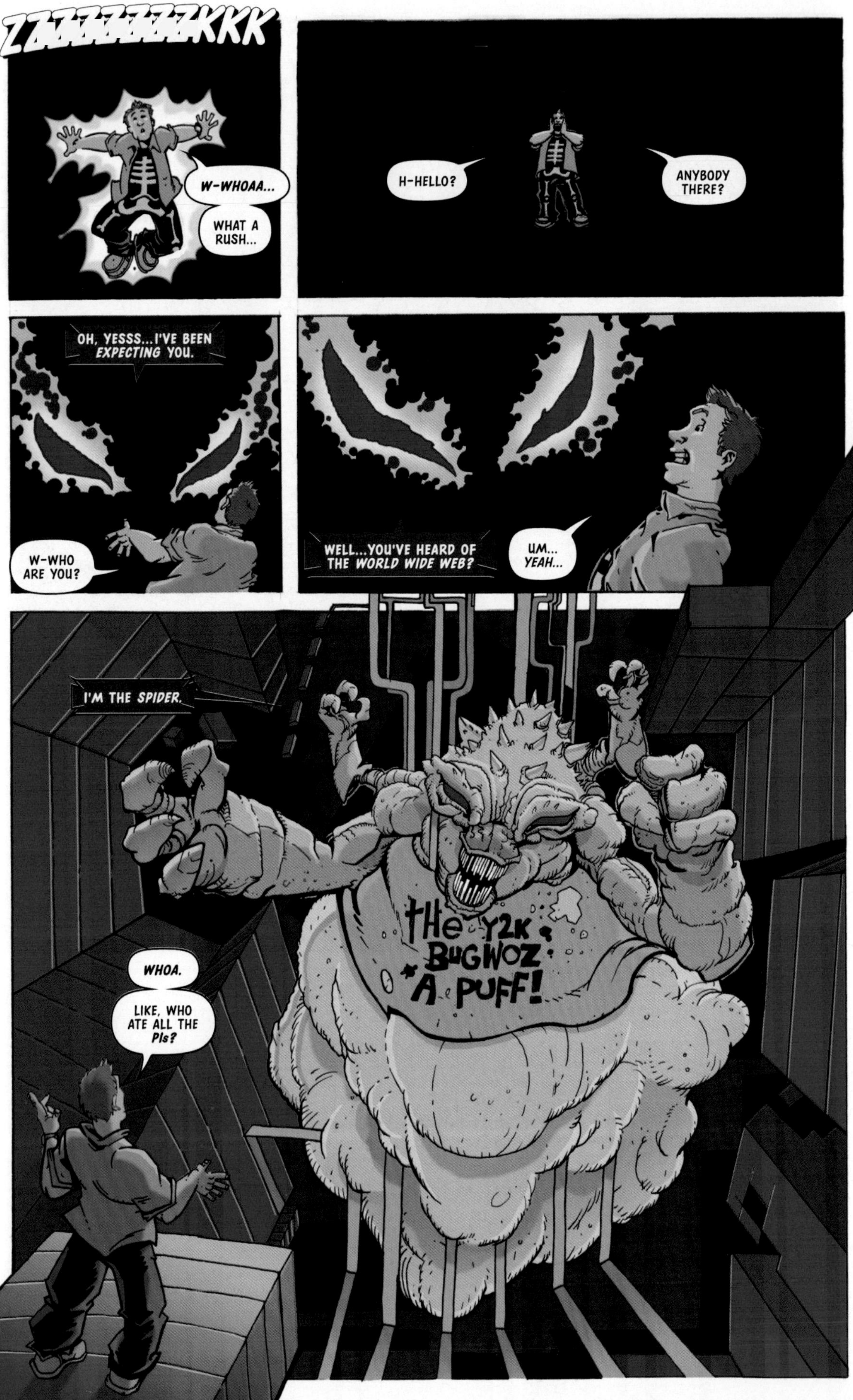
ZZZZZZZZZKKK
W-WHOAA...
WHAT A RUSH...
H-HELLO?
ANYBODY THERE?
OH, YESSS...I'VE BEEN EXPECTING YOU.
W-WHO ARE YOU?
WELL...YOU'VE HEARD OF THE WORLD WIDE WEB?
UM... YEAH...
I'M THE SPIDER.
tHe Y2K BUGWOZ A PUFF!
WHOA.
LIKE, WHO ATE ALL THE PIs?

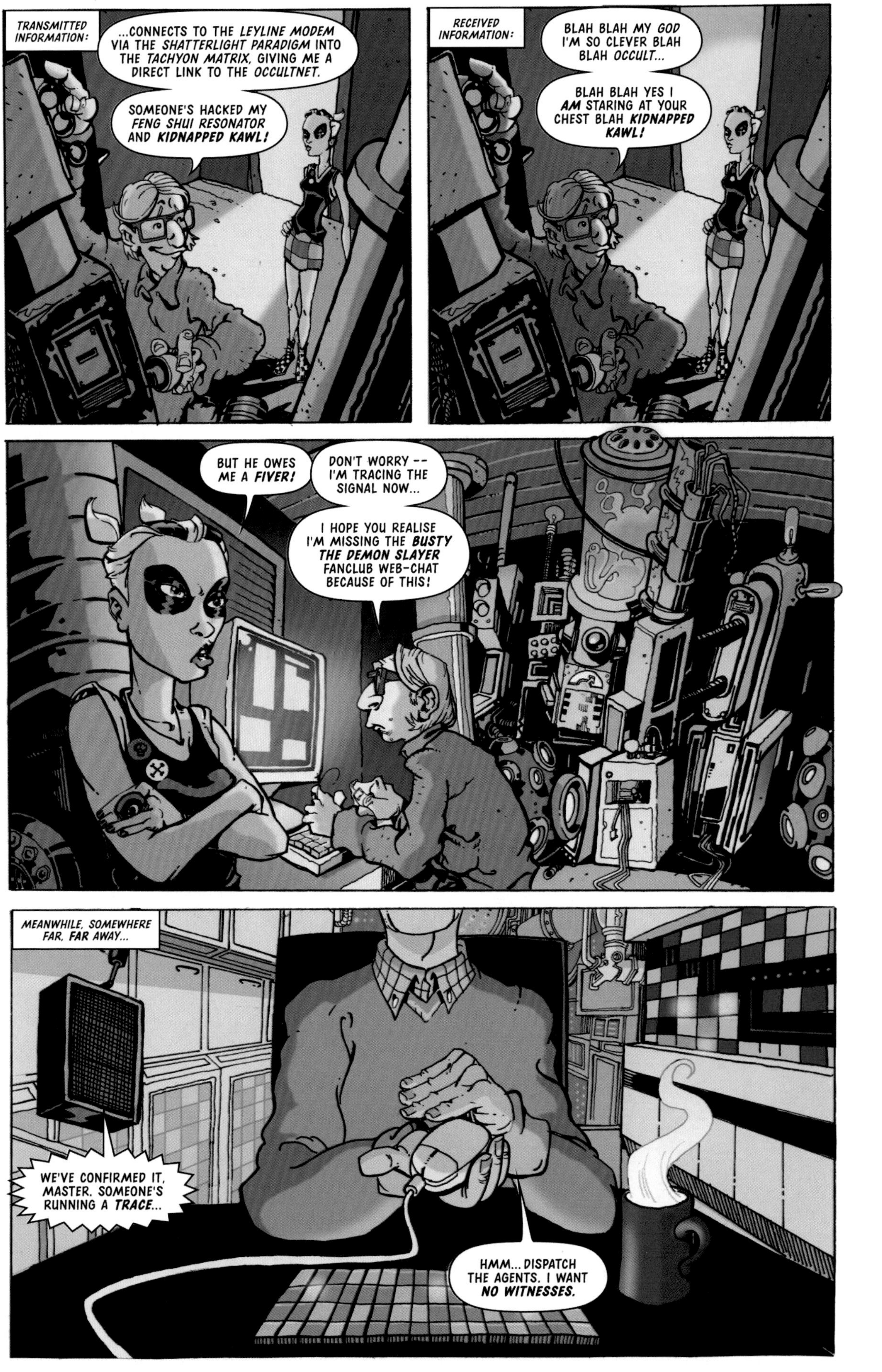
TRANSMITTED INFORMATION:
...CONNECTS TO THE LEYLINE MODEM VIA THE SHATTERLIGHT PARADIGM INTO THE TACHYON MATRIX, GIVING ME A DIRECT LINK TO THE OCCULTNET.
SOMEONE'S HACKED MY FENG SHUI RESONATOR AND KIDNAPPED KAWL!
RECEIVED INFORMATION:
BLAH BLAH MY GOD I'M SO CLEVER BLAH BLAH OCCULT...
BLAH BLAH YES I AM STARING AT YOUR CHEST BLAH KIDNAPPED KAWL!
BUT HE OWES ME A FIVER!
DON'T WORRY -- I'M TRACING THE SIGNAL NOW...
I HOPE YOU REALISE I'M MISSING THE BUSTY THE DEMON SLAYER FANCLUB WEB-CHAT BECAUSE OF THIS!
MEANWHILE, SOMEWHERE FAR, FAR AWAY...
WE'VE CONFIRMED IT, MASTER. SOMEONE'S RUNNING A TRACE...
HMM... DISPATCH THE AGENTS. I WANT NO WITNESSES.

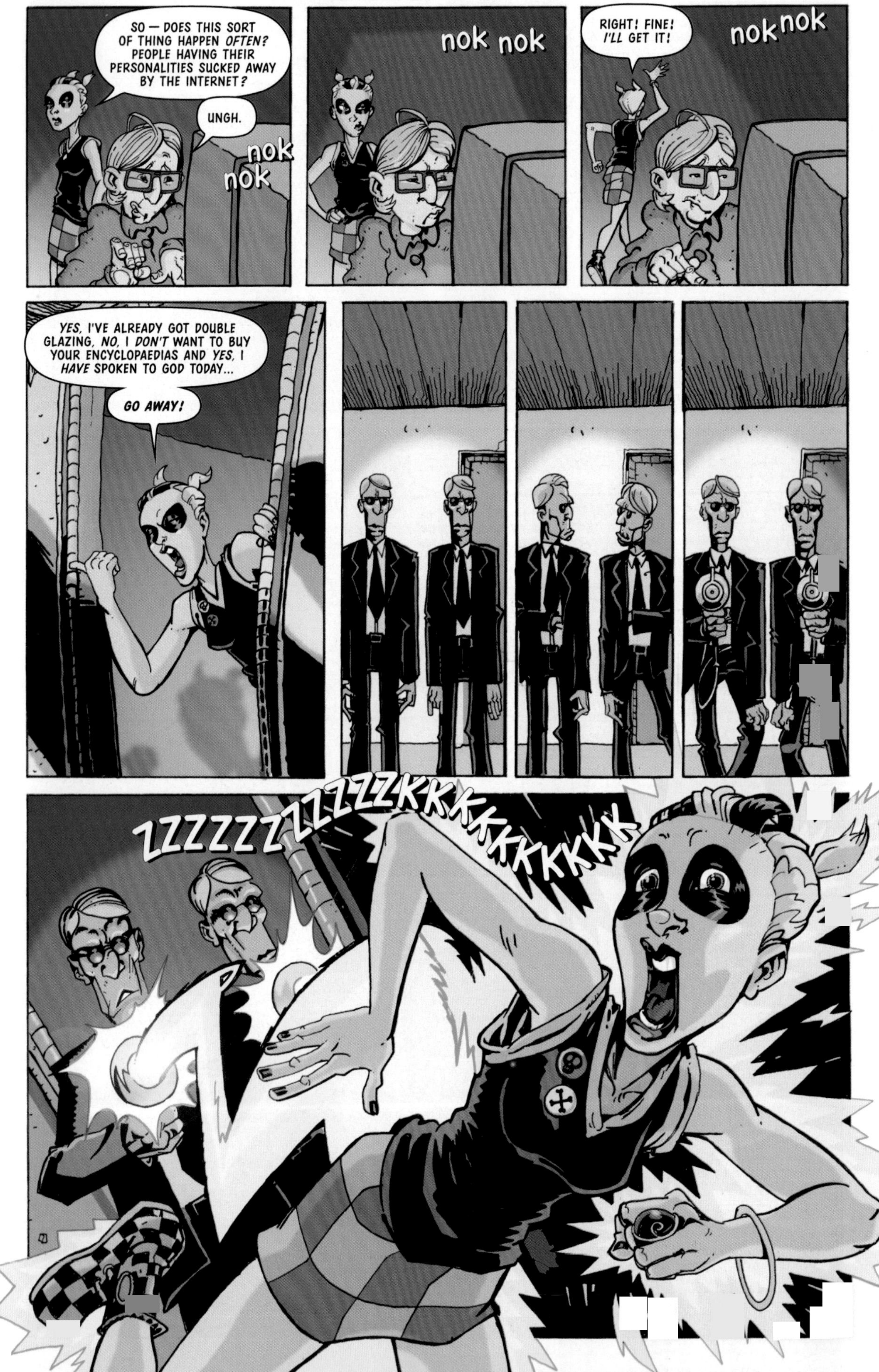

SO — DOES THIS SORT OF THING HAPPEN OFTEN? PEOPLE HAVING THEIR PERSONALITIES SUCKED AWAY BY THE INTERNET?
UNGH.
nok nok
nok nok
RIGHT! FINE! I'LL GET IT!
nok nok
YES, I'VE ALREADY GOT DOUBLE GLAZING, NO, I DON'T WANT TO BUY YOUR ENCYCLOPAEDIAS AND YES, I HAVE SPOKEN TO GOD TODAY...
GO AWAY!
ZZZZZZZZZZZZKKKKKKKKKKKK

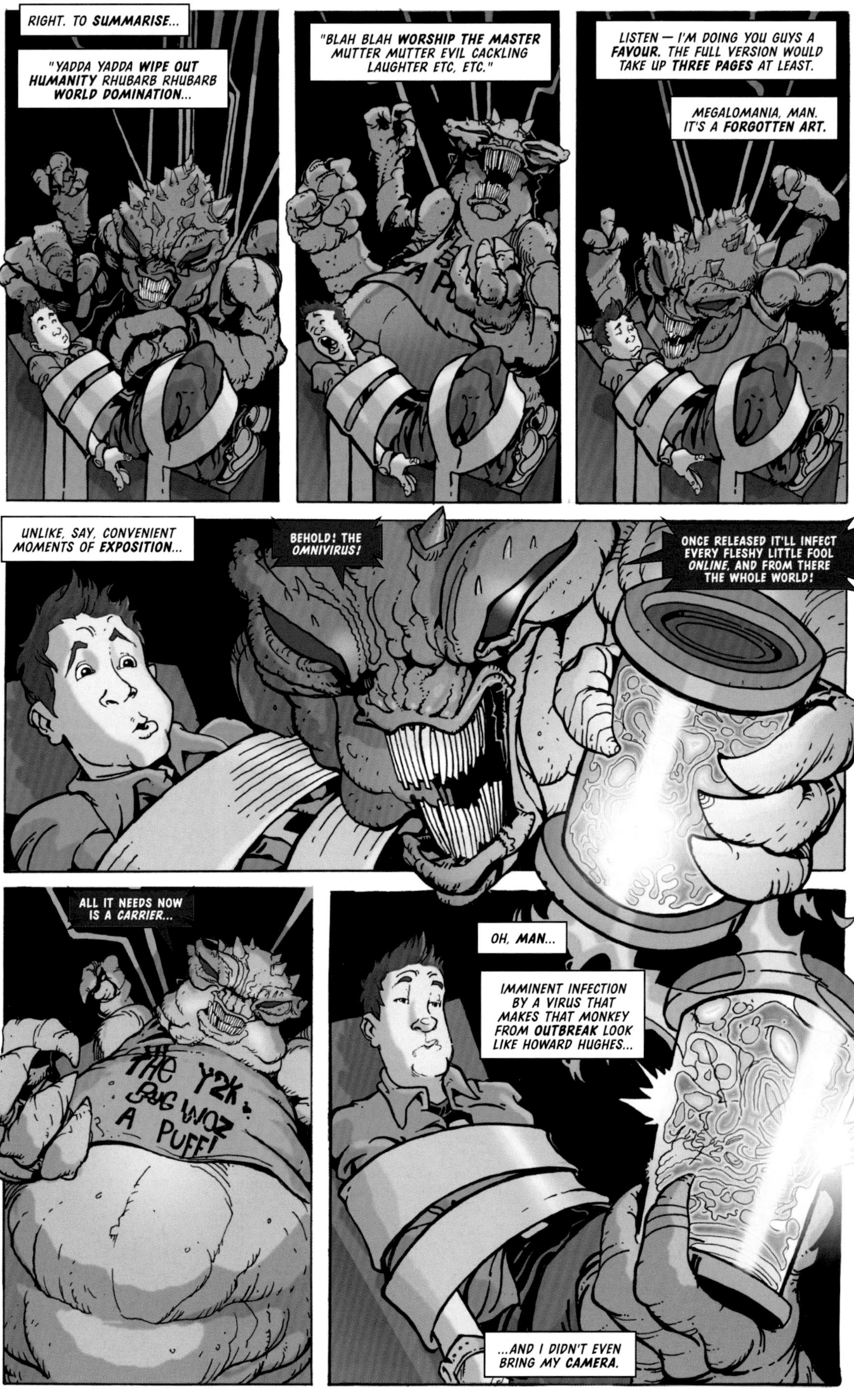
RIGHT. TO **SUMMARISE**...
"YADDA YADDA **WIPE OUT HUMANITY** RHUBARB RHUBARB **WORLD DOMINATION**...
"BLAH BLAH **WORSHIP THE MASTER** MUTTER MUTTER EVIL CACKLING LAUGHTER ETC, ETC."
LISTEN — I'M DOING YOU GUYS A **FAVOUR.** THE FULL VERSION WOULD TAKE UP **THREE PAGES** AT LEAST.
MEGALOMANIA, MAN. IT'S A **FORGOTTEN ART.**
UNLIKE, SAY, CONVENIENT MOMENTS OF **EXPOSITION**...
BEHOLD! THE *OMNIVIRUS!*
ONCE RELEASED IT'LL INFECT EVERY FLESHY LITTLE FOOL *ONLINE*, AND FROM THERE THE WHOLE WORLD!
ALL IT NEEDS NOW IS A *CARRIER*...
THE Y2K BUG WOZ A PUFF!
OH, **MAN**...
IMMINENT INFECTION BY A VIRUS THAT MAKES THAT MONKEY FROM **OUTBREAK** LOOK LIKE HOWARD HUGHES...
...AND I DIDN'T EVEN BRING MY **CAMERA.**

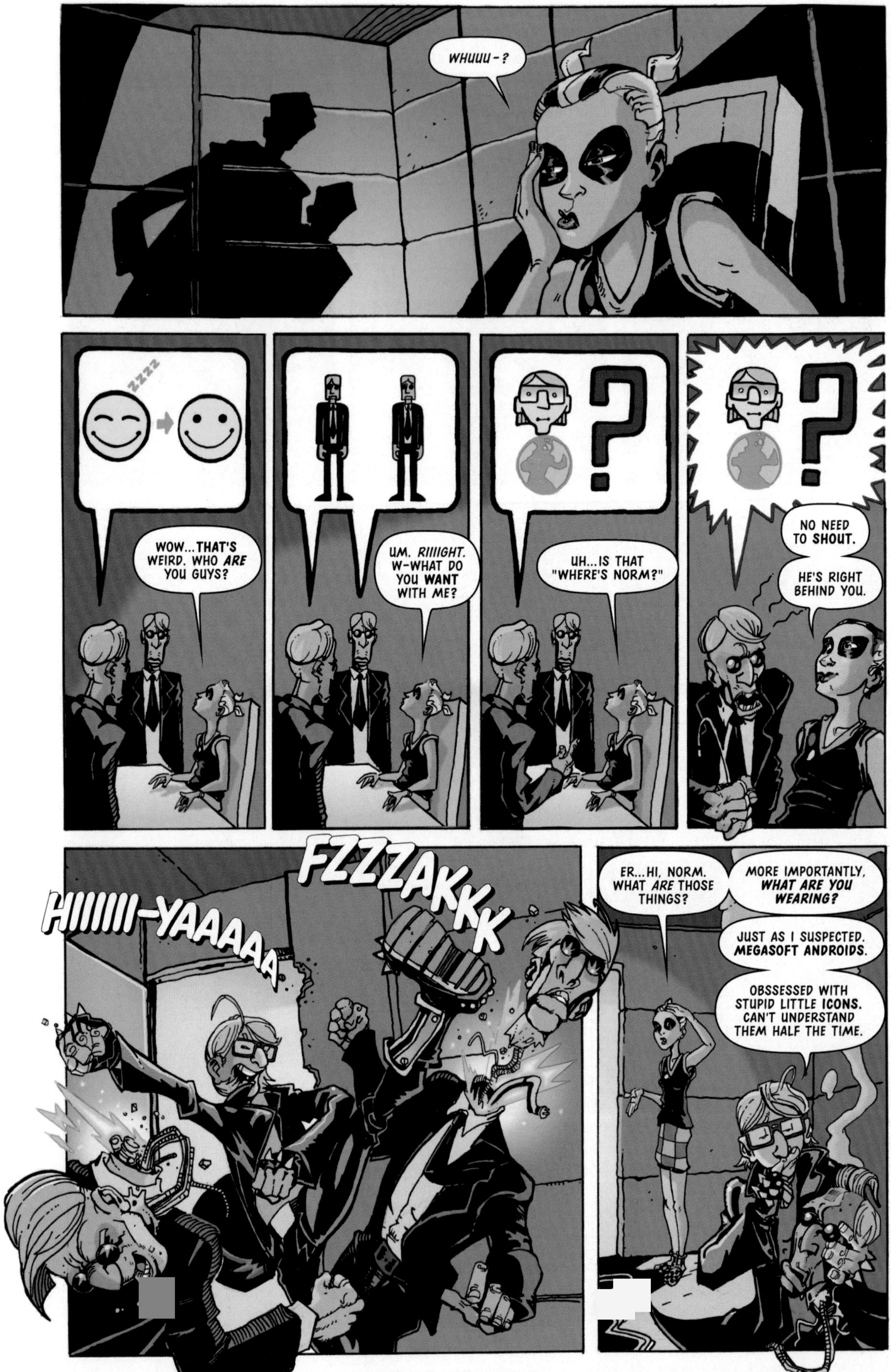

WHUUU-?
WOW...THAT'S WEIRD. WHO ARE YOU GUYS?
UM. RIIIIGHT. W-WHAT DO YOU WANT WITH ME?
UH...IS THAT "WHERE'S NORM?"
NO NEED TO SHOUT.
HE'S RIGHT BEHIND YOU.
HIIIIII-YAAAAAA
FZZZAKKKK
ER...HI, NORM. WHAT ARE THOSE THINGS?
MORE IMPORTANTLY, WHAT ARE YOU WEARING?
JUST AS I SUSPECTED. MEGASOFT ANDROIDS.
OBSSESSED WITH STUPID LITTLE ICONS. CAN'T UNDERSTAND THEM HALF THE TIME.

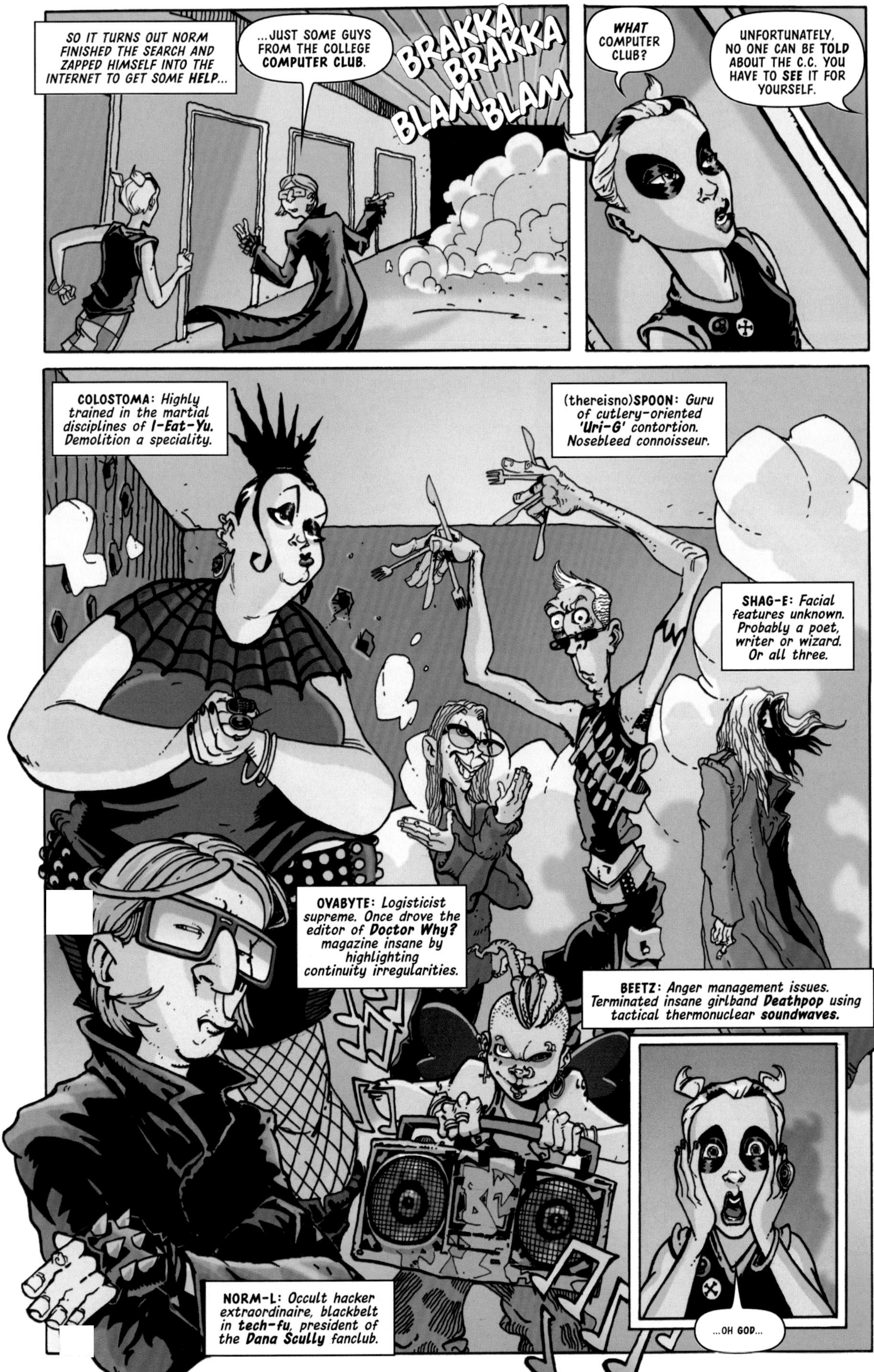
SO IT TURNS OUT NORM FINISHED THE SEARCH AND ZAPPED HIMSELF INTO THE INTERNET TO GET SOME HELP...
...JUST SOME GUYS FROM THE COLLEGE COMPUTER CLUB.
BRAKKA BRAKKA BLAM BLAM
WHAT COMPUTER CLUB?
UNFORTUNATELY, NO ONE CAN BE TOLD ABOUT THE C.C. YOU HAVE TO SEE IT FOR YOURSELF.
COLOSTOMA: Highly trained in the martial disciplines of I-Eat-Yu. Demolition a speciality.
(thereisno)SPOON: Guru of cutlery-oriented 'Uri-G' contortion. Nosebleed connoisseur.
SHAG-E: Facial features unknown. Probably a poet, writer or wizard. Or all three.
OVABYTE: Logisticist supreme. Once drove the editor of Doctor Why? magazine insane by highlighting continuity irregularities.
BEETZ: Anger management issues. Terminated insane girlband Deathpop using tactical thermonuclear soundwaves.
NORM-L: Occult hacker extraordinaire, blackbelt in tech-fu, president of the Dana Scully fanclub.
...OH GOD...

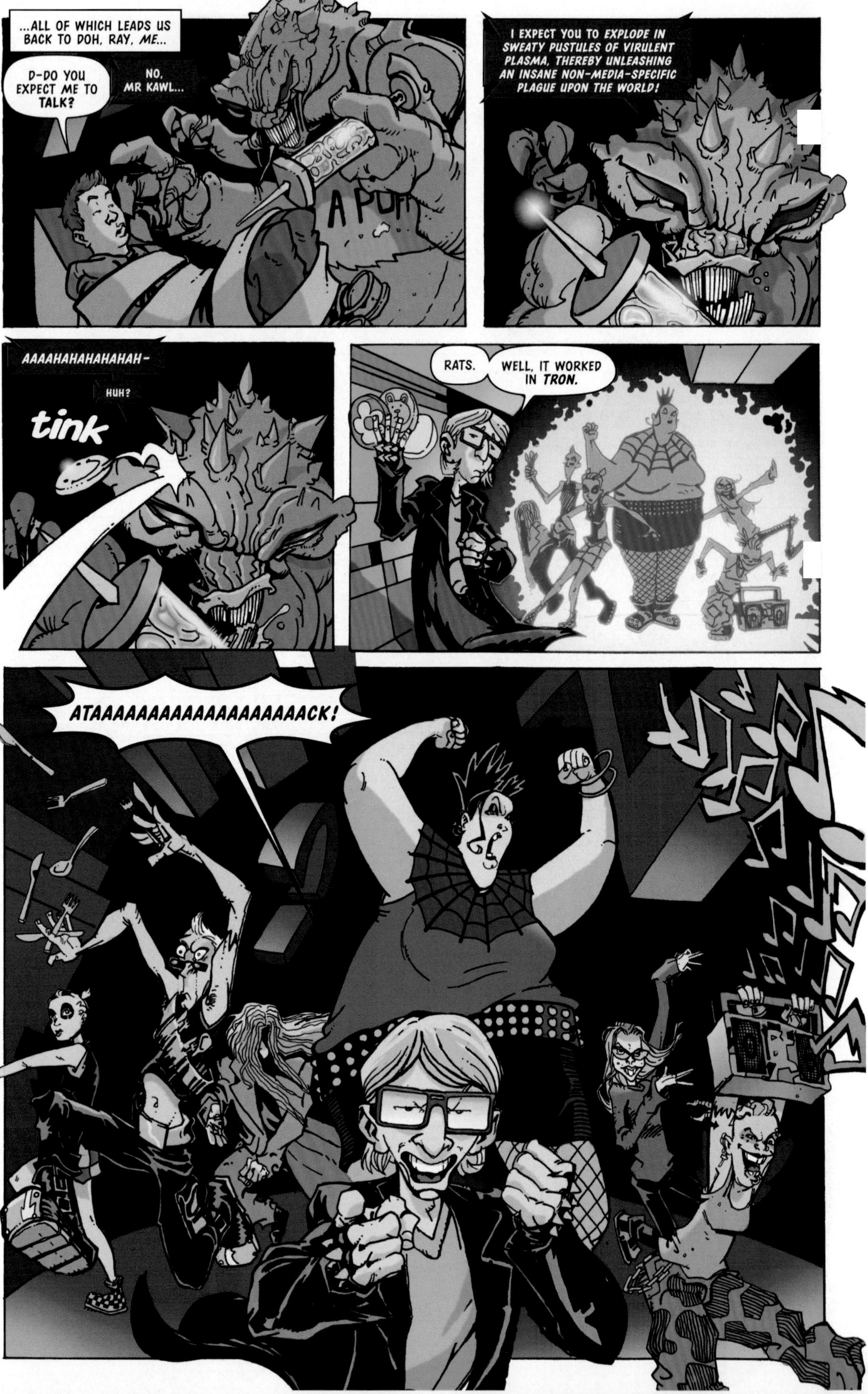

...ALL OF WHICH LEADS US BACK TO DOH, RAY, ME...
D-DO YOU EXPECT ME TO TALK?
NO, MR KAWL...
A PO
I EXPECT YOU TO EXPLODE IN SWEATY PUSTULES OF VIRULENT PLASMA, THEREBY UNLEASHING AN INSANE NON-MEDIA-SPECIFIC PLAGUE UPON THE WORLD!
AAAAHAHAHAHAHAH-
HUH?
tink
RATS.
WELL, IT WORKED IN TRON.
ATAAAAAAAAAAAAAAAAAAACK!

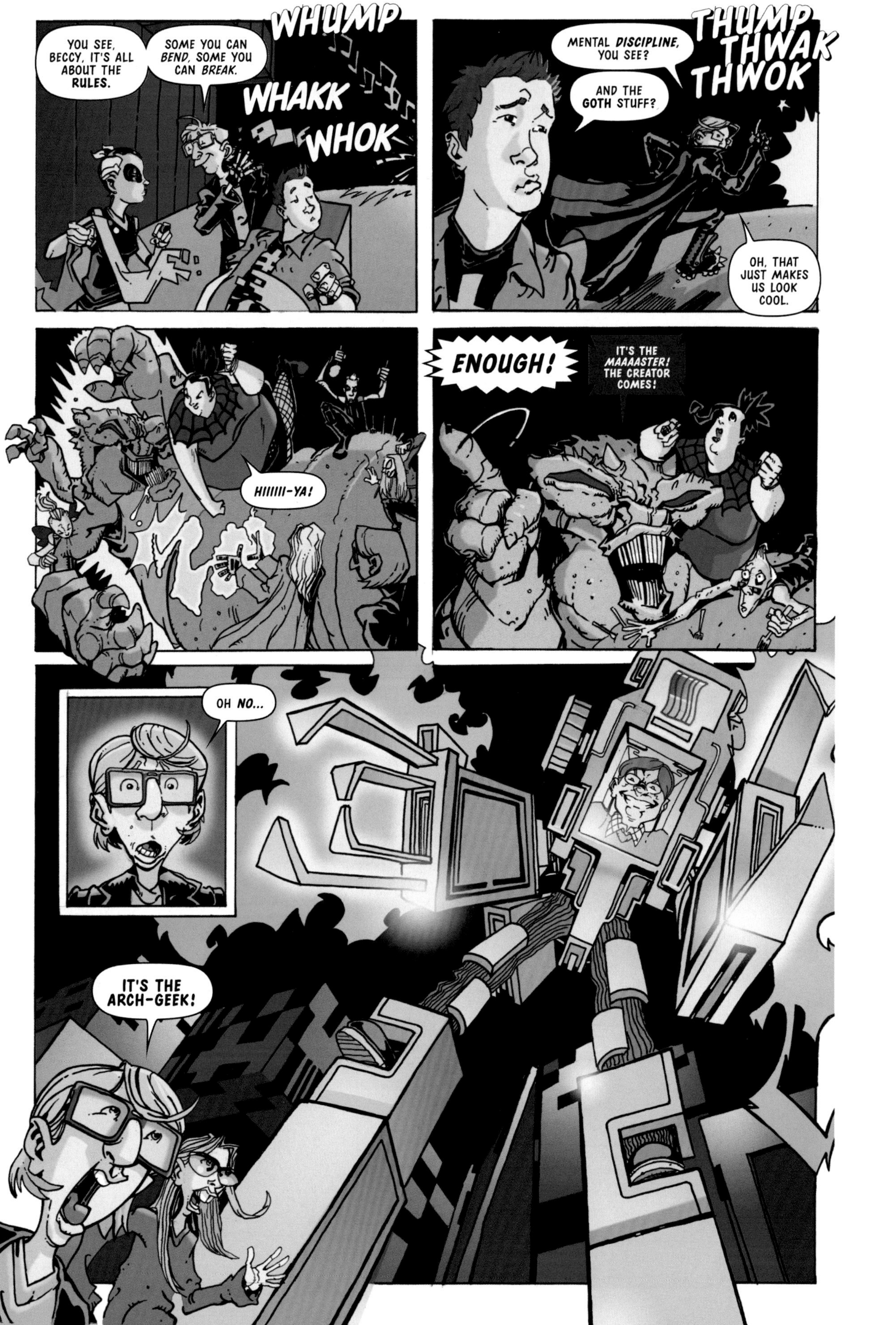
YOU SEE, BECCY, IT'S ALL ABOUT THE RULES.
SOME YOU CAN BEND, SOME YOU CAN BREAK.
WHUMP
WHAKK
WHOK
MENTAL DISCIPLINE, YOU SEE?
AND THE GOTH STUFF?
THUMP THWAK THWOK
OH, THAT JUST MAKES US LOOK COOL.
HIIIIII-YA!
ENOUGH!
IT'S THE MAAAASTER! THE CREATOR COMES!
OH NO...
IT'S THE ARCH-GEEK!

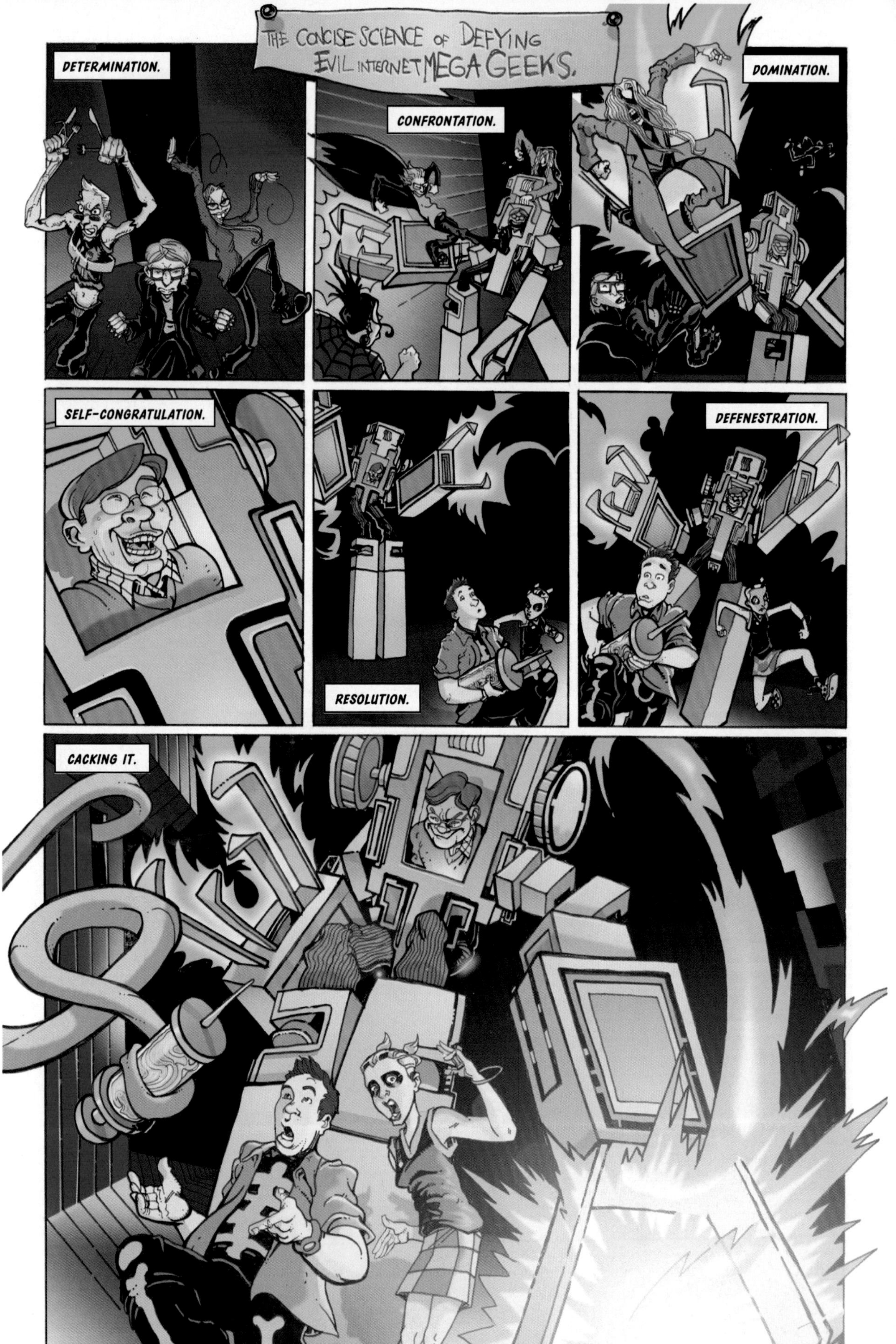
THE CONCISE SCIENCE OF DEFYING EVIL INTERNET MEGA GEEKS.
DETERMINATION.
CONFRONTATION.
DOMINATION.
SELF-CONGRATULATION.
RESOLUTION.
DEFENESTRATION.
CACKING IT.

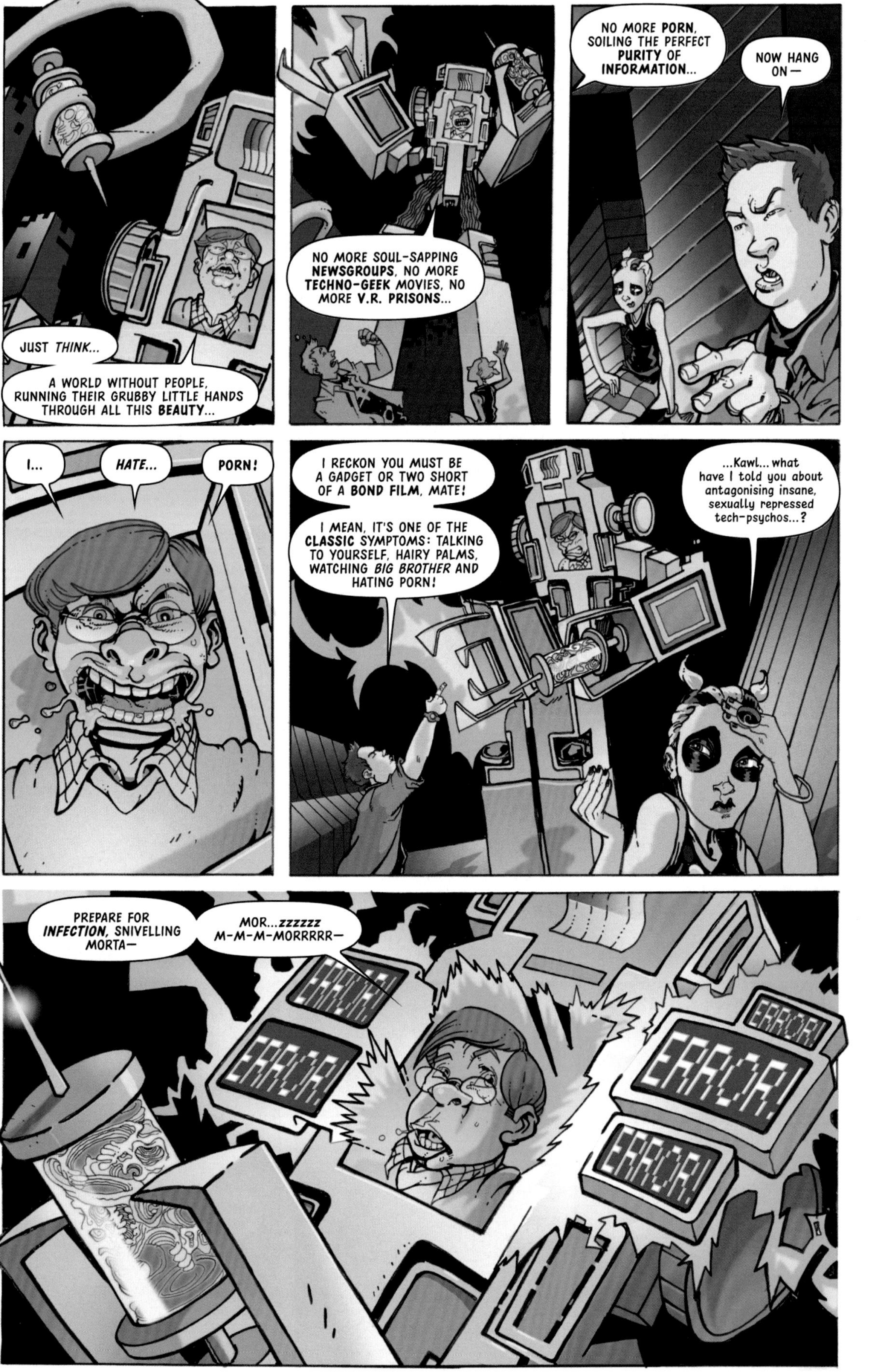
JUST *THINK*...
A WORLD WITHOUT PEOPLE, RUNNING THEIR GRUBBY LITTLE HANDS THROUGH ALL THIS **BEAUTY**...
NO MORE SOUL-SAPPING **NEWSGROUPS**, NO MORE **TECHNO-GEEK** MOVIES, NO MORE **V.R. PRISONS**...
NO MORE **PORN**, SOILING THE PERFECT **PURITY** OF **INFORMATION**...
NOW HANG ON—
I...
HATE...
PORN!
I RECKON YOU MUST BE A GADGET OR TWO SHORT OF A **BOND FILM**, MATE!
I MEAN, IT'S ONE OF THE **CLASSIC** SYMPTOMS: TALKING TO YOURSELF, HAIRY PALMS, WATCHING *BIG BROTHER* AND HATING PORN!
...Kawl... what have I told you about antagonising insane, sexually repressed tech-psychos...?
PREPARE FOR *INFECTION*, SNIVELLING MORTA—
MOR...*zzzzzz* M-M-M-MORRRRR—
ERROR!
ERROR!
ERROR!
ERROR!
ERROR!

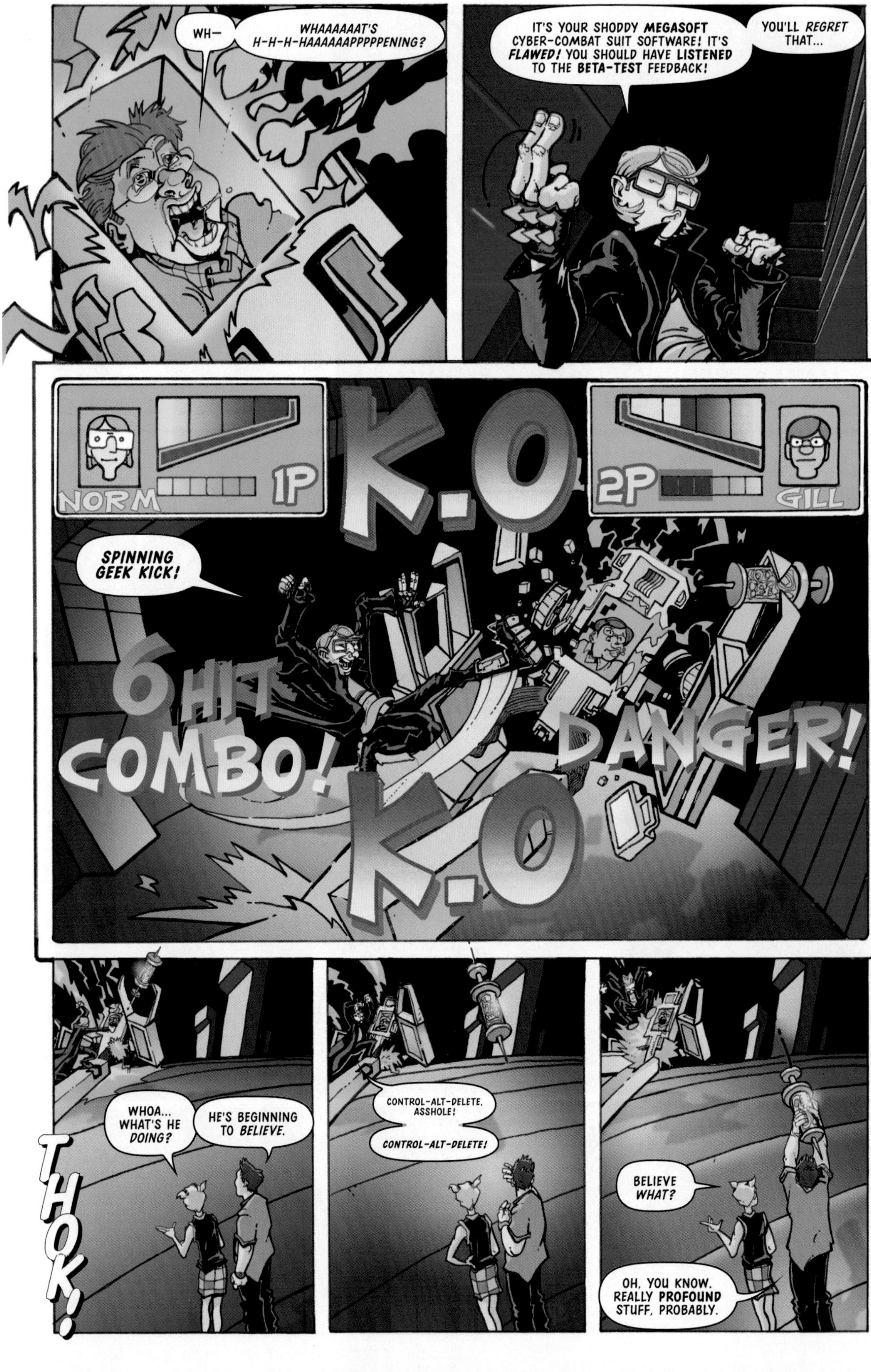
WH—
WHAAAAAAT'S H-H-H-HAAAAAAPPPPPENING?
IT'S YOUR SHODDY MEGASOFT CYBER-COMBAT SUIT SOFTWARE! IT'S FLAWED! YOU SHOULD HAVE LISTENED TO THE BETA-TEST FEEDBACK!
YOU'LL REGRET THAT...
NORM
1P
K.O
2P
GILL
SPINNING GEEK KICK!
6 HIT COMBO!
DANGER!
K.O
THOK!
WHOA... WHAT'S HE DOING?
HE'S BEGINNING TO BELIEVE.
CONTROL-ALT-DELETE, ASSHOLE!
CONTROL-ALT-DELETE!
BELIEVE WHAT?
OH, YOU KNOW. REALLY PROFOUND STUFF, PROBABLY.

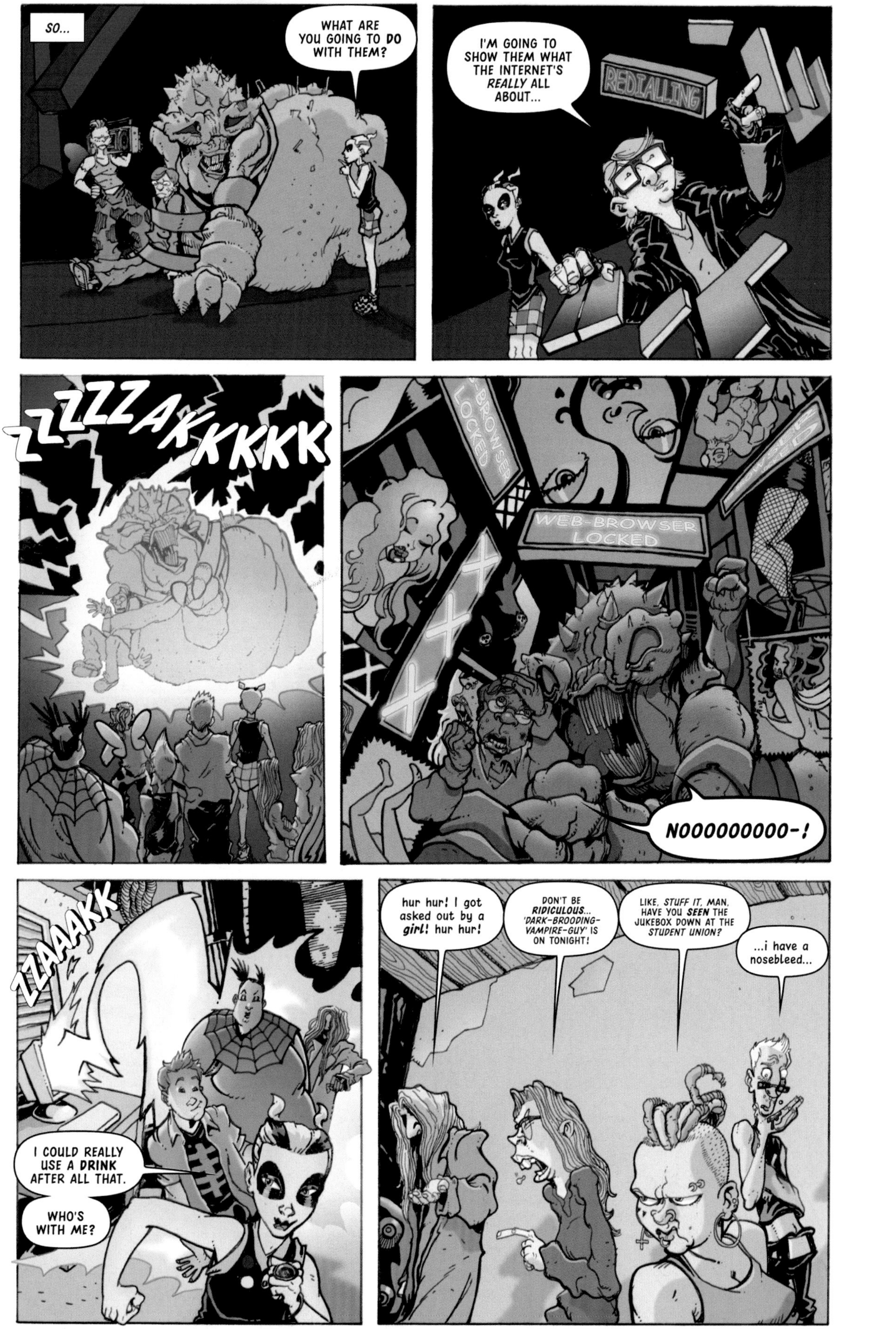
SO...
WHAT ARE YOU GOING TO DO WITH THEM?
I'M GOING TO SHOW THEM WHAT THE INTERNET'S REALLY ALL ABOUT...
REDIALLING
ZZZZZZAKKKKK
WEB-BROWSER LOCKED
NOOOOOOOOO-!
ZZAAAKK
I COULD REALLY USE A DRINK AFTER ALL THAT.
WHO'S WITH ME?
hur hur! I got asked out by a girl! hur hur!
DON'T BE RIDICULOUS... 'DARK-BROODING-VAMPIRE-GUY' IS ON TONIGHT!
LIKE, STUFF IT, MAN, HAVE YOU SEEN THE JUKEBOX DOWN AT THE STUDENT UNION?
...i have a nosebleed...

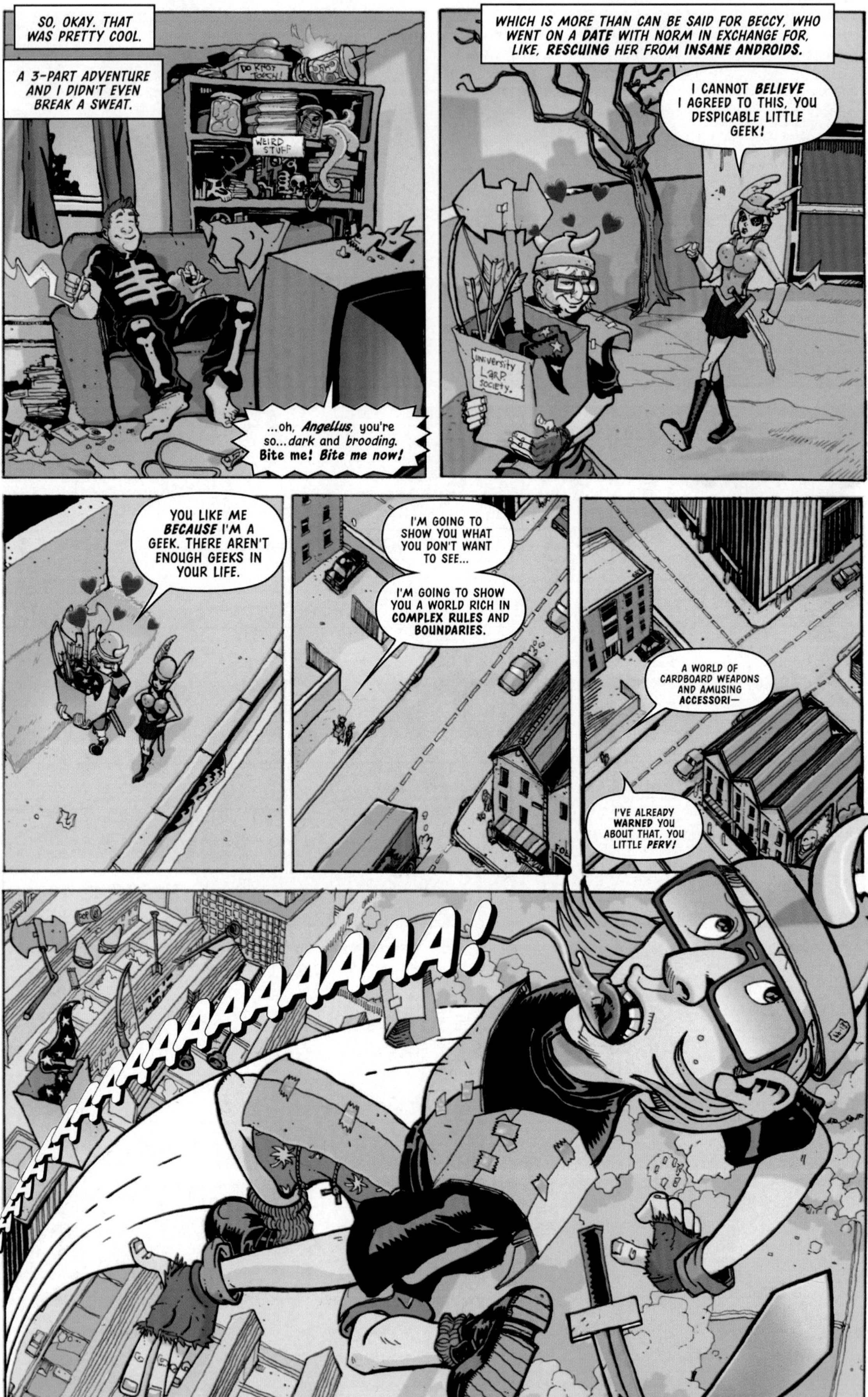

SO, OKAY. THAT WAS PRETTY COOL.
A 3-PART ADVENTURE AND I DIDN'T EVEN BREAK A SWEAT.
DO KNOT TOUCH!
WEIRD STUFF
...oh, *Angellus*, you're so...*dark and brooding.* **Bite me! *Bite me now!***
WHICH IS MORE THAN CAN BE SAID FOR BECCY, WHO WENT ON A **DATE** WITH NORM IN EXCHANGE FOR, LIKE, **RESCUING** HER FROM **INSANE ANDROIDS.**
I CANNOT ***BELIEVE*** I AGREED TO THIS, YOU DESPICABLE LITTLE GEEK!
University LARP Society.
YOU LIKE ME ***BECAUSE*** I'M A GEEK. THERE AREN'T ENOUGH GEEKS IN YOUR LIFE.
I'M GOING TO SHOW YOU WHAT YOU DON'T WANT TO SEE...
I'M GOING TO SHOW YOU A WORLD RICH IN **COMPLEX RULES AND BOUNDARIES.**
A WORLD OF CARDBOARD WEAPONS AND AMUSING **ACCESSORI—**
I'VE ALREADY **WARNED** YOU ABOUT THAT, YOU LITTLE ***PERV!***
AAAAAAAAAAAAAAAAAAAAAA!

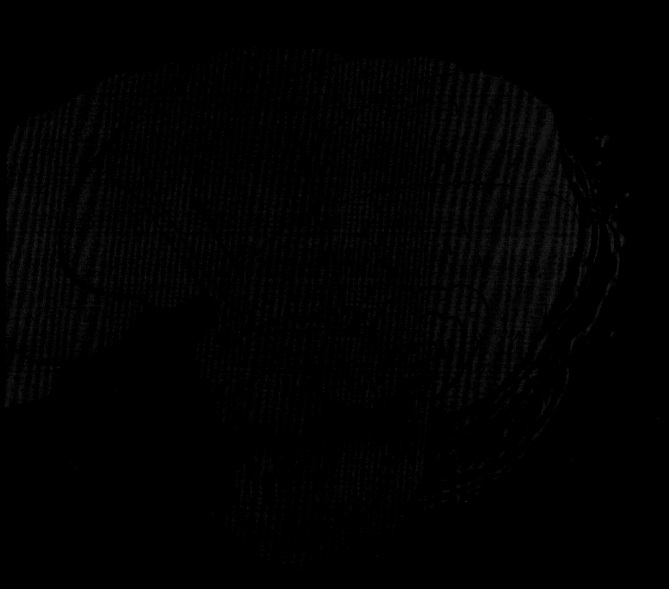

PEST CONTROL

Script: Simon Spurrier
Art: Steve Roberts
Colour: Richard Elson
Letters: Ellie De Ville

Originally published in *2000 AD* Progs 1351-1354

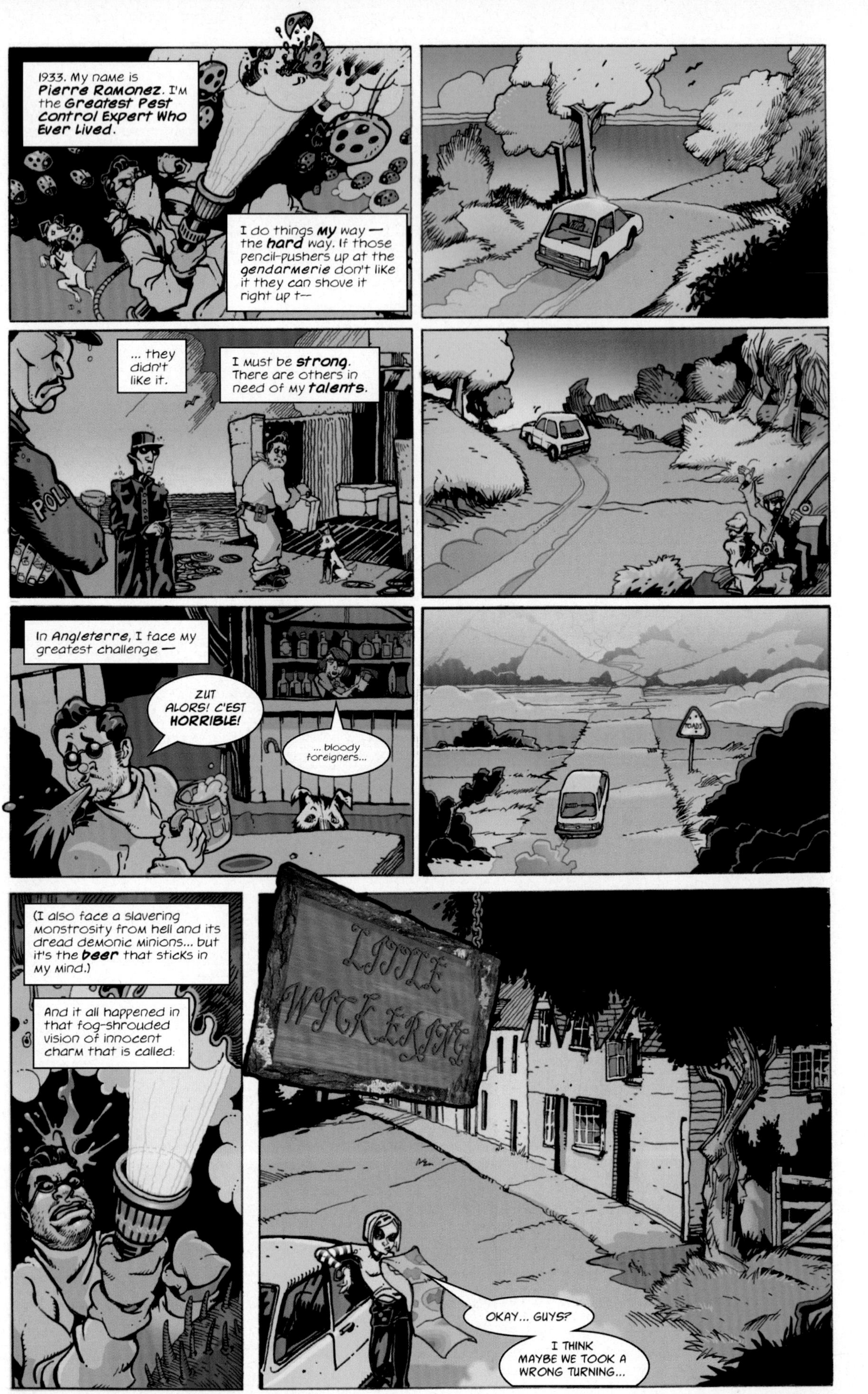
1933. My name is Pierre Ramonez. I'm the Greatest Pest Control Expert Who Ever Lived.
I do things MY way — the hard way. If those pencil-pushers up at the gendarmerie don't like it they can shove it right up t--
... they didn't like it.
I must be strong. There are others in need of my talents.
In Angleterre, I face my greatest challenge —
ZUT ALORS! C'EST HORRIBLE!
... bloody foreigners...
(I also face a slavering monstrosity from hell and its dread demonic minions... but it's the beer that sticks in my mind.)
And it all happened in that fog-shrouded vision of innocent charm that is called:
LITTLE WICKERING
OKAY... GUYS?
I THINK MAYBE WE TOOK A WRONG TURNING...

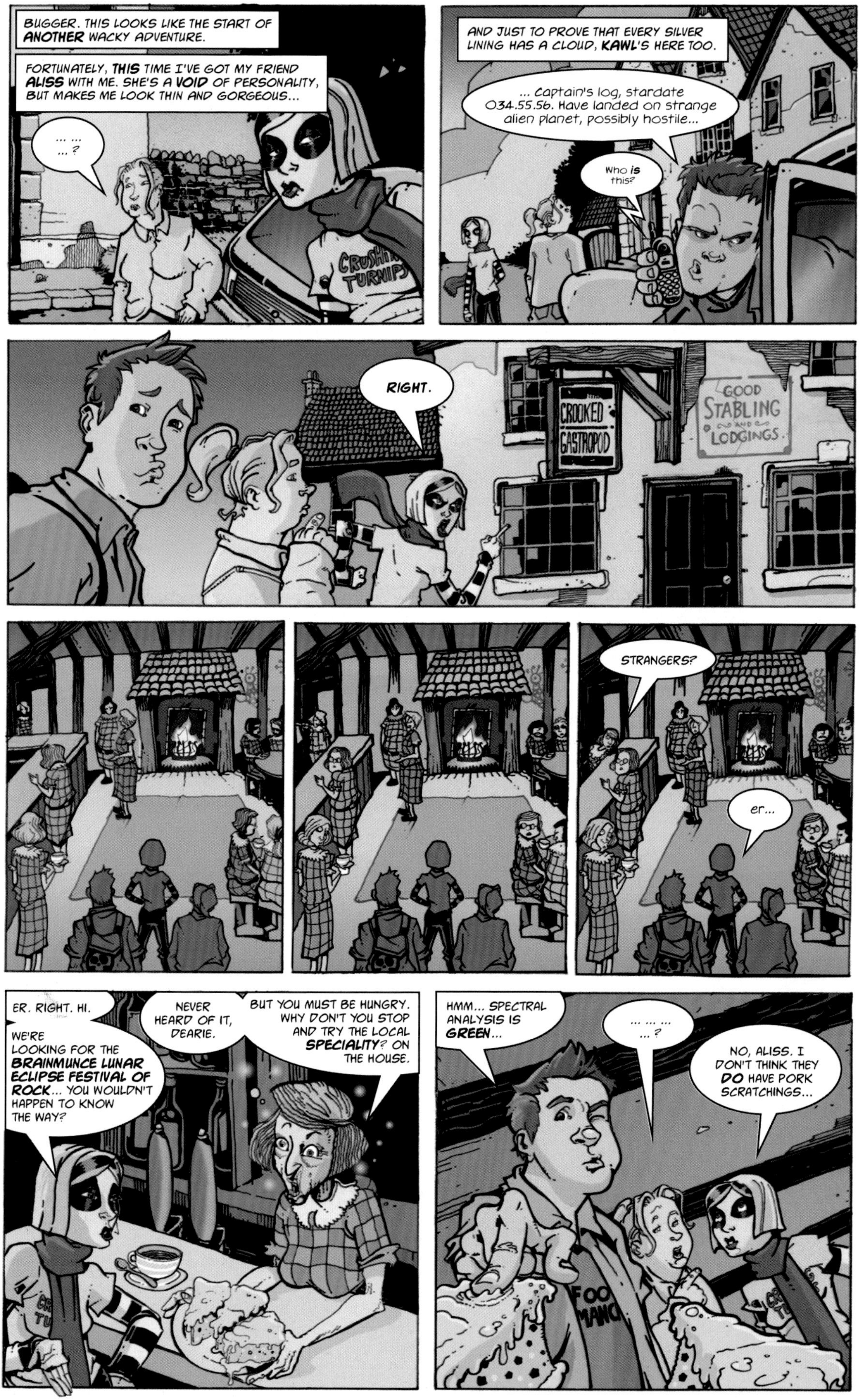
BUGGER. THIS LOOKS LIKE THE START OF ANOTHER WACKY ADVENTURE.
FORTUNATELY, THIS TIME I'VE GOT MY FRIEND ALISS WITH ME. SHE'S A VOID OF PERSONALITY, BUT MAKES ME LOOK THIN AND GORGEOUS...
... ...?
AND JUST TO PROVE THAT EVERY SILVER LINING HAS A CLOUD, KAWL'S HERE TOO.
... Captain's log, stardate 034.55.56. Have landed on strange alien planet, possibly hostile...
Who is this?
RIGHT.
CROOKED GASTROPOD
GOOD STABLING AND LODGINGS
STRANGERS?
er...
ER. RIGHT. HI.
WE'RE LOOKING FOR THE BRAINMUNCE LUNAR ECLIPSE FESTIVAL OF ROCK... YOU WOULDN'T HAPPEN TO KNOW THE WAY?
NEVER HEARD OF IT, DEARIE.
BUT YOU MUST BE HUNGRY. WHY DON'T YOU STOP AND TRY THE LOCAL SPECIALITY? ON THE HOUSE.
HMM... SPECTRAL ANALYSIS IS GREEN...
... ...?
NO, ALISS. I DON'T THINK THEY DO HAVE PORK SCRATCHINGS...

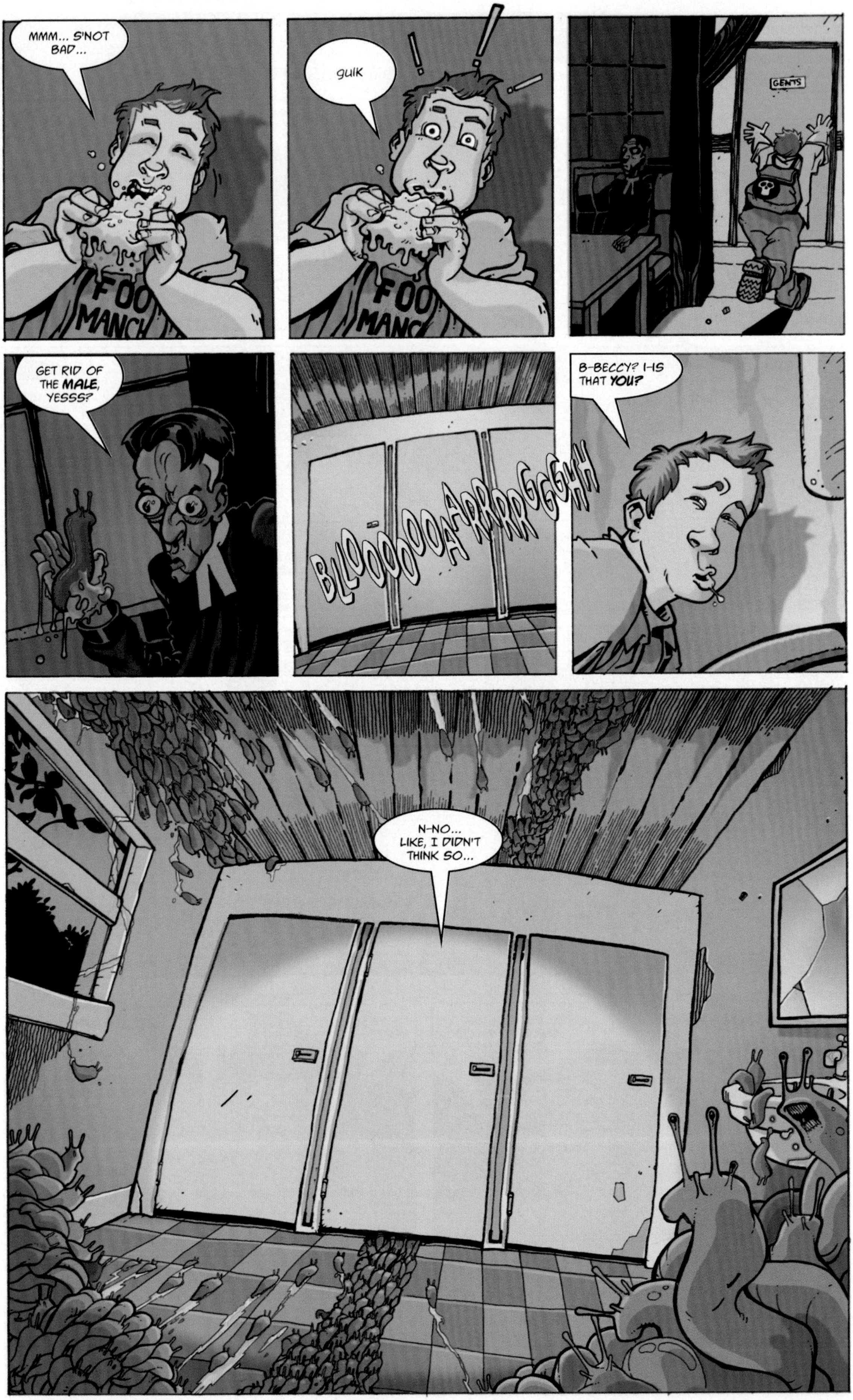
MMM... S'NOT BAD...
GUIK
!
!
GENTS
GET RID OF THE **MALE**, YESSS?
BLOOOOOOARRRRGGGHH
B-BECCY? I-IS THAT **YOU?**
N-NO... LIKE, I DIDN'T THINK SO...

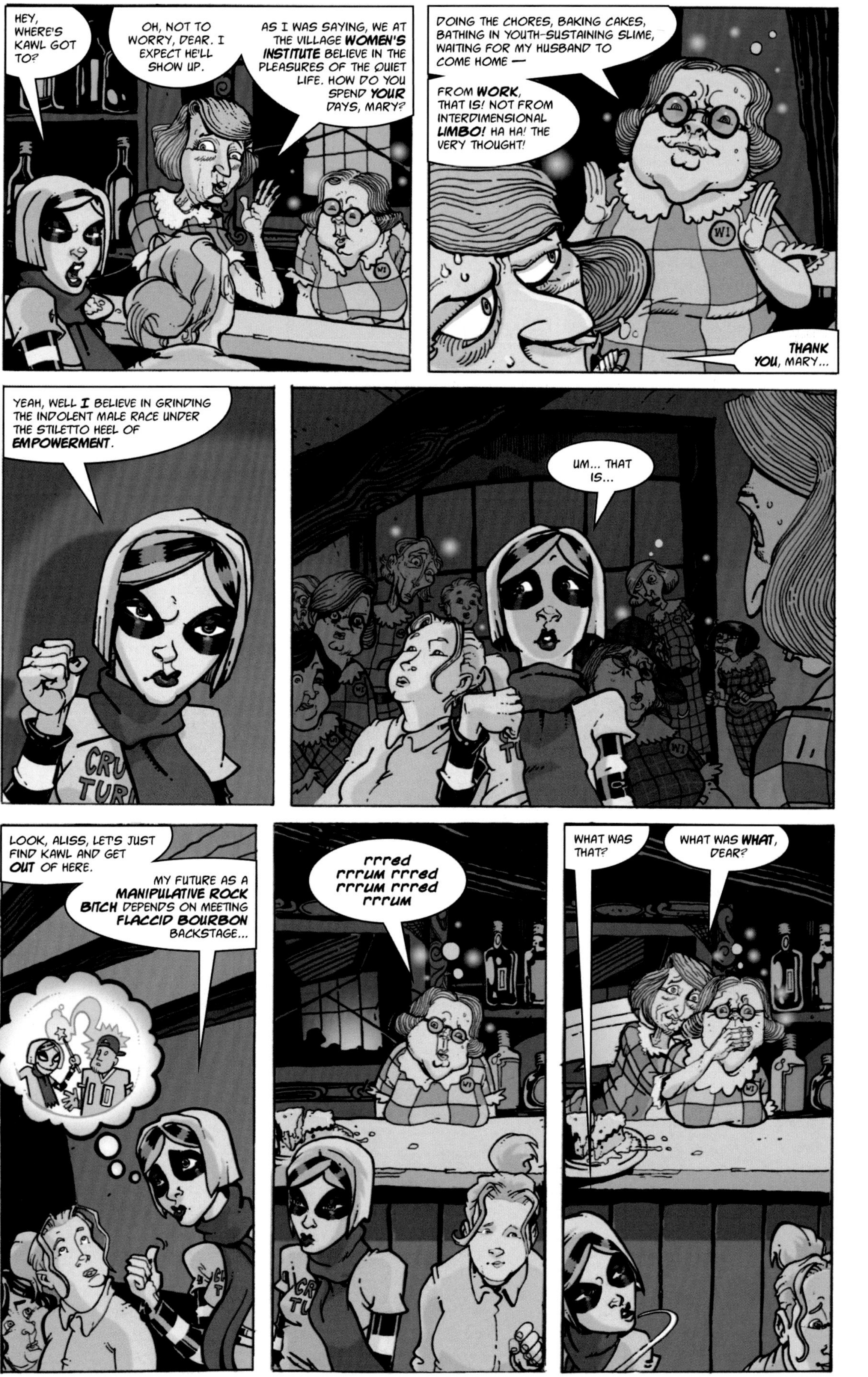
HEY, WHERE'S KAWL GOT TO?
OH, NOT TO WORRY, DEAR. I EXPECT HE'LL SHOW UP.
AS I WAS SAYING, WE AT THE VILLAGE WOMEN'S INSTITUTE BELIEVE IN THE PLEASURES OF THE QUIET LIFE. HOW DO YOU SPEND YOUR DAYS, MARY?
DOING THE CHORES, BAKING CAKES, BATHING IN YOUTH-SUSTAINING SLIME, WAITING FOR MY HUSBAND TO COME HOME —
FROM WORK, THAT IS! NOT FROM INTERDIMENSIONAL LIMBO! HA HA! THE VERY THOUGHT!
THANK YOU, MARY...
YEAH, WELL I BELIEVE IN GRINDING THE INDOLENT MALE RACE UNDER THE STILETTO HEEL OF EMPOWERMENT.
UM... THAT IS...
LOOK, ALISS, LET'S JUST FIND KAWL AND GET OUT OF HERE.
MY FUTURE AS A MANIPULATIVE ROCK BITCH DEPENDS ON MEETING FLACCID BOURBON BACKSTAGE...
rrred rrrum rrred rrrum rrred rrrum
WHAT WAS THAT?
WHAT WAS WHAT, DEAR?

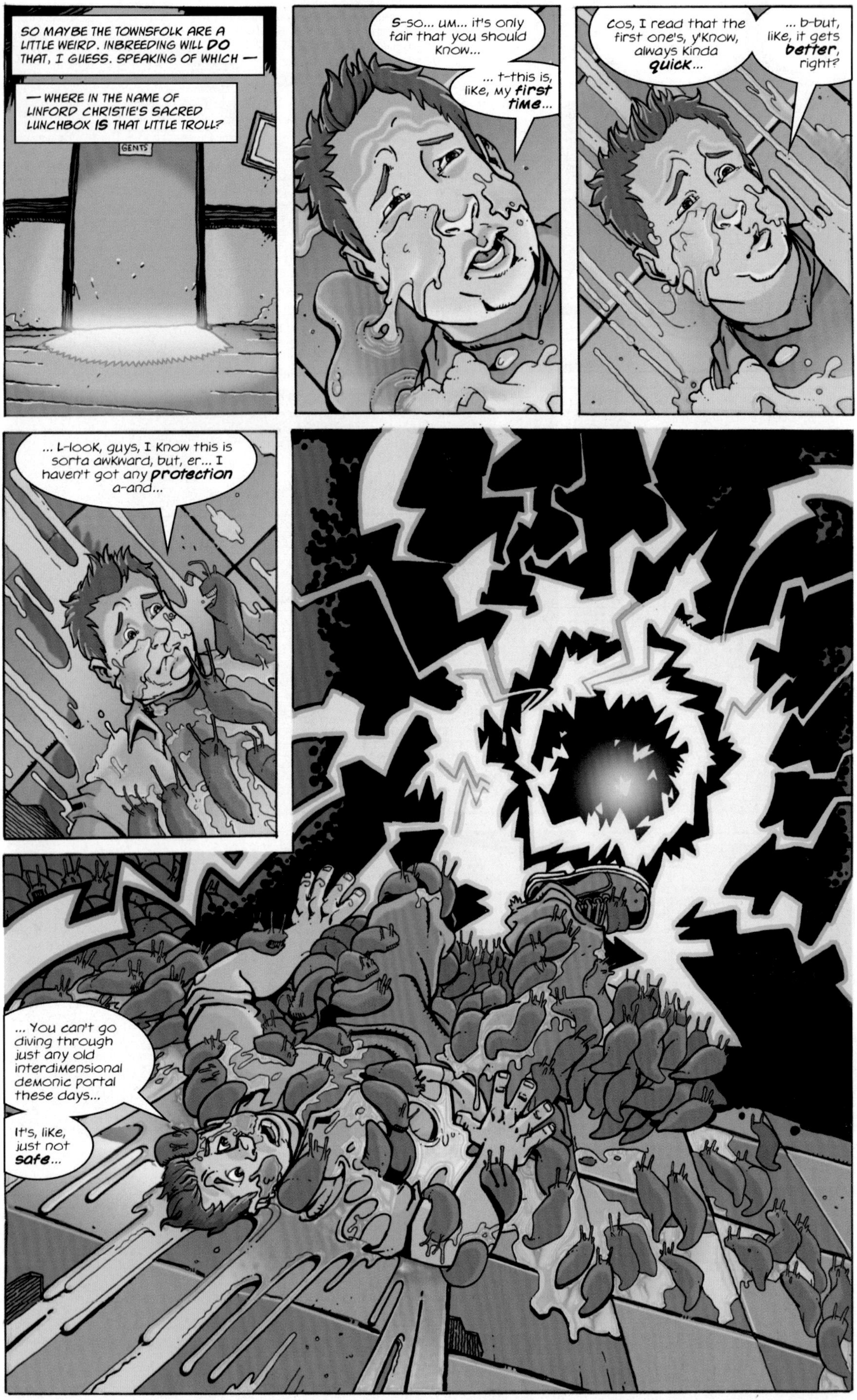

SO MAYBE THE TOWNSFOLK ARE A LITTLE WEIRD. INBREEDING WILL DO THAT, I GUESS. SPEAKING OF WHICH —
— WHERE IN THE NAME OF LINFORD CHRISTIE'S SACRED LUNCHBOX IS THAT LITTLE TROLL?
GENTS
S-SO... UM... it's only fair that you should Know...
... t-this is, like, My first time...
Cos, I read that the first one's, y'Know, always Kinda quick...
... b-but, like, it gets better, right?
... L-look, guys, I Know this is sorta awkward, but, er... I haven't got any protection a-and...
... You can't go diving through just any old interdimensional demonic portal these days...
It's, like, just not safe...

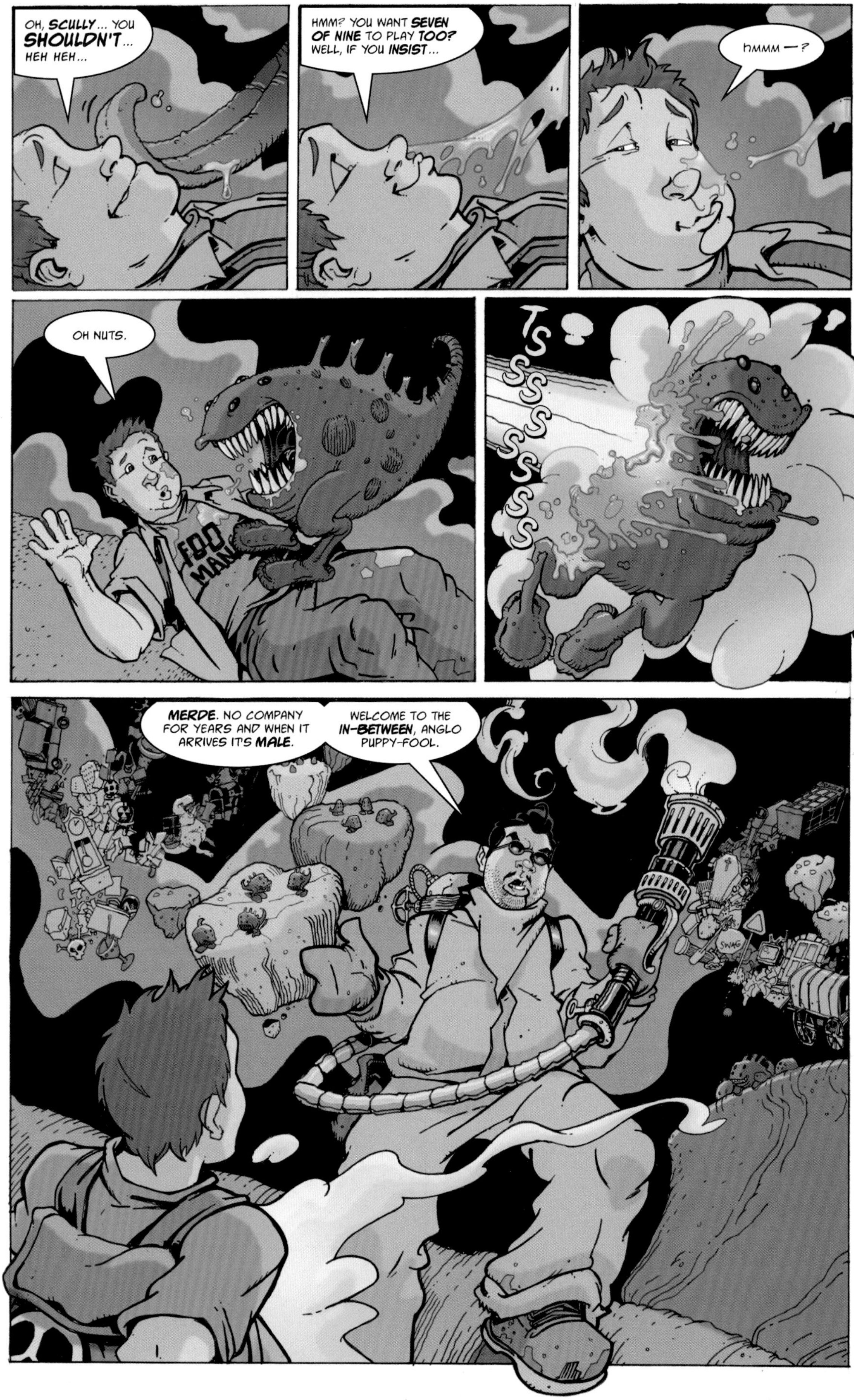
OH, SCULLY... YOU SHOULDN'T... HEH HEH...
HMM? YOU WANT SEVEN OF NINE TO PLAY TOO? WELL, IF YOU INSIST...
hMMM —?
OH NUTS.
TSSSSSSS
MERDE. NO COMPANY FOR YEARS AND WHEN IT ARRIVES IT'S MALE.
WELCOME TO THE IN-BETWEEN, ANGLO PUPPY-FOOL.

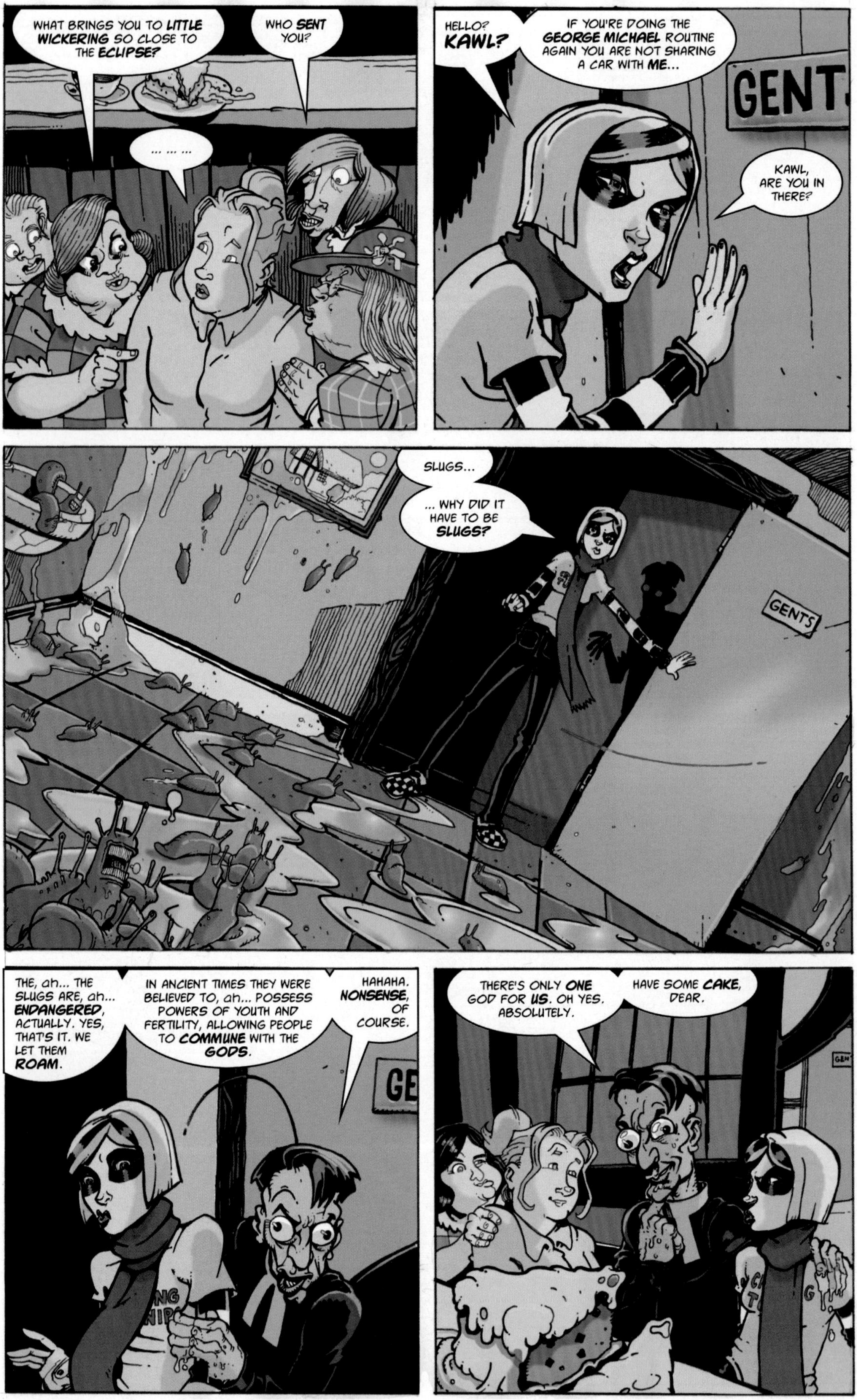
WHAT BRINGS YOU TO LITTLE WICKERING SO CLOSE TO THE ECLIPSE?
WHO SENT YOU?
... ...
HELLO? KAWL?
IF YOU'RE DOING THE GEORGE MICHAEL ROUTINE AGAIN YOU ARE NOT SHARING A CAR WITH ME...
GENT
KAWL, ARE YOU IN THERE?
SLUGS...
... WHY DID IT HAVE TO BE SLUGS?
GENTS
THE, ah... THE SLUGS ARE, ah... ENDANGERED, ACTUALLY. YES, THAT'S IT. WE LET THEM ROAM.
IN ANCIENT TIMES THEY WERE BELIEVED TO, ah... POSSESS POWERS OF YOUTH AND FERTILITY, ALLOWING PEOPLE TO COMMUNE WITH THE GODS.
HAHAHA. NONSENSE, OF COURSE.
GE
THERE'S ONLY ONE GOD FOR US. OH YES. ABSOLUTELY.
HAVE SOME CAKE, DEAR.

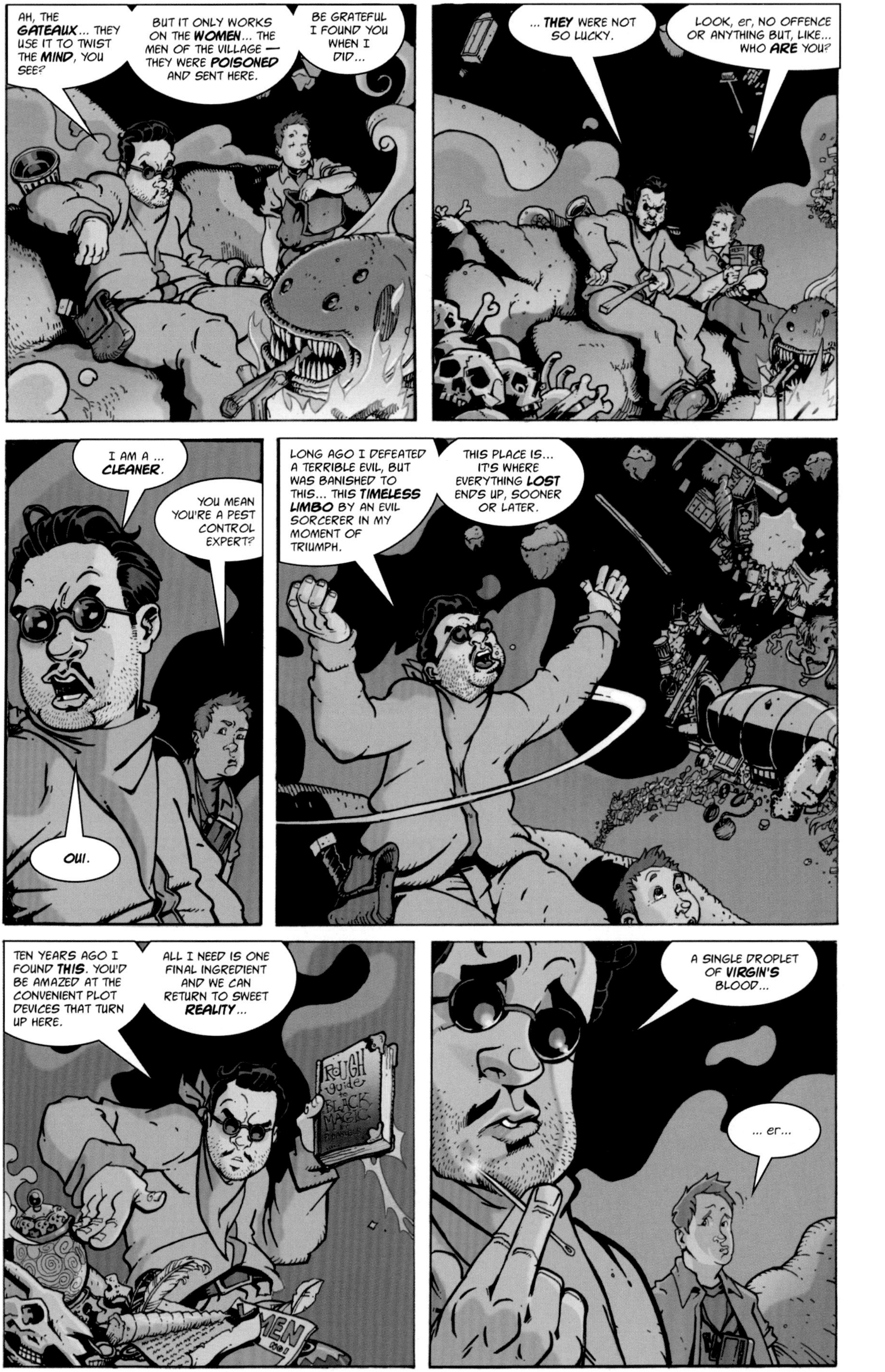
AH, THE GATEAUX... THEY USE IT TO TWIST THE MIND, YOU SEE?
BUT IT ONLY WORKS ON THE WOMEN... THE MEN OF THE VILLAGE — THEY WERE POISONED AND SENT HERE.
BE GRATEFUL I FOUND YOU WHEN I DID...
... THEY WERE NOT SO LUCKY.
LOOK, er, NO OFFENCE OR ANYTHING BUT, LIKE... WHO ARE YOU?
I AM A ... CLEANER.
YOU MEAN YOU'RE A PEST CONTROL EXPERT?
OUI.
LONG AGO I DEFEATED A TERRIBLE EVIL, BUT WAS BANISHED TO THIS... THIS TIMELESS LIMBO BY AN EVIL SORCERER IN MY MOMENT OF TRIUMPH.
THIS PLACE IS... IT'S WHERE EVERYTHING LOST ENDS UP, SOONER OR LATER.
TEN YEARS AGO I FOUND THIS. YOU'D BE AMAZED AT THE CONVENIENT PLOT DEVICES THAT TURN UP HERE.
ALL I NEED IS ONE FINAL INGREDIENT AND WE CAN RETURN TO SWEET REALITY...
ROUGH guide to BLACK MAGIC
MEN
A SINGLE DROPLET OF VIRGIN'S BLOOD...
... er...

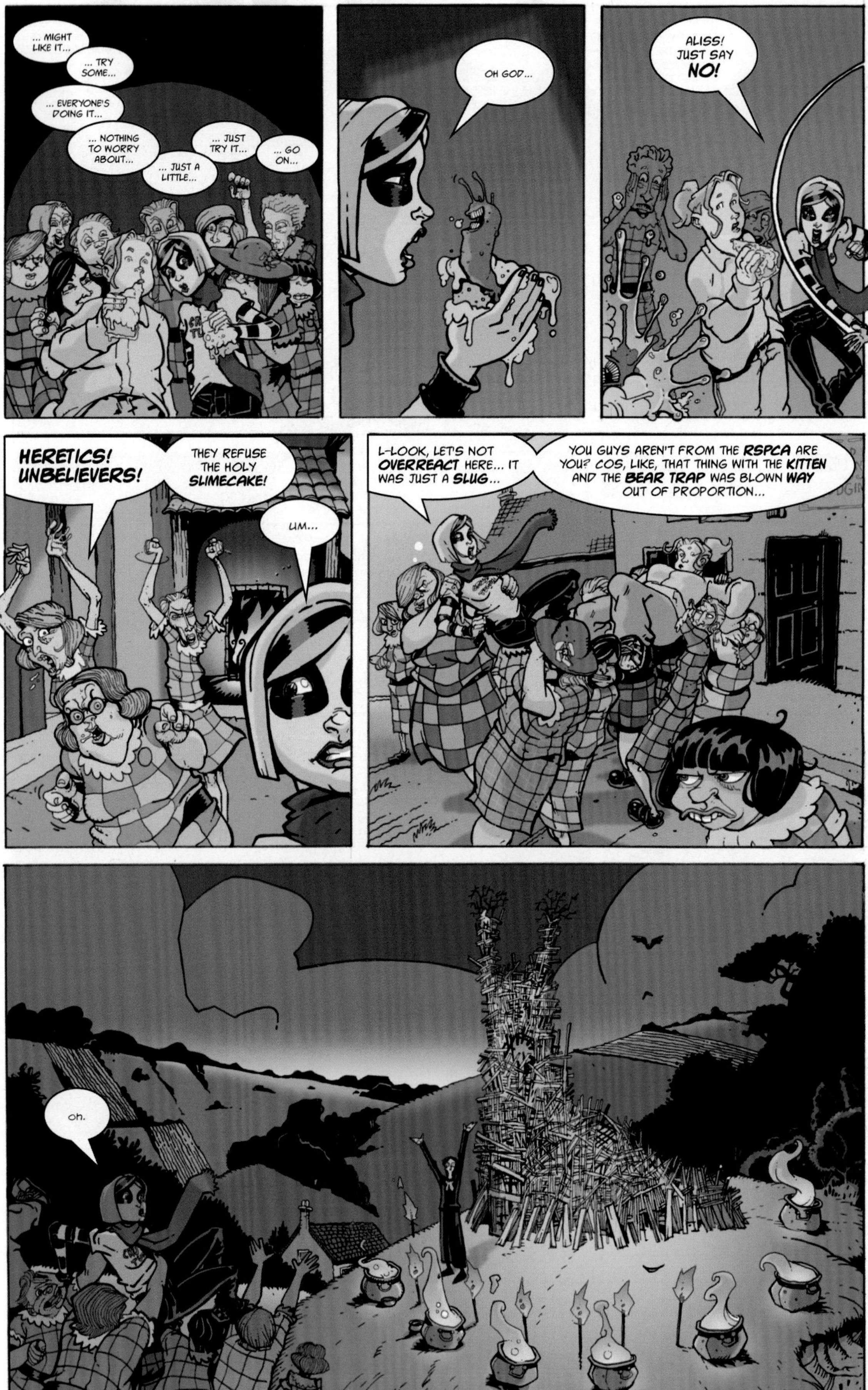
... MIGHT LIKE IT...
... TRY SOME...
... EVERYONE'S DOING IT...
... NOTHING TO WORRY ABOUT...
... JUST A LITTLE...
... JUST TRY IT...
... GO ON...
OH GOD...
ALISS! JUST SAY NO!
HERETICS! UNBELIEVERS!
THEY REFUSE THE HOLY SLIMECAKE!
UM...
L-LOOK, LET'S NOT OVERREACT HERE... IT WAS JUST A SLUG...
YOU GUYS AREN'T FROM THE RSPCA ARE YOU? COS, LIKE, THAT THING WITH THE KITTEN AND THE BEAR TRAP WAS BLOWN WAY OUT OF PROPORTION...
oh.

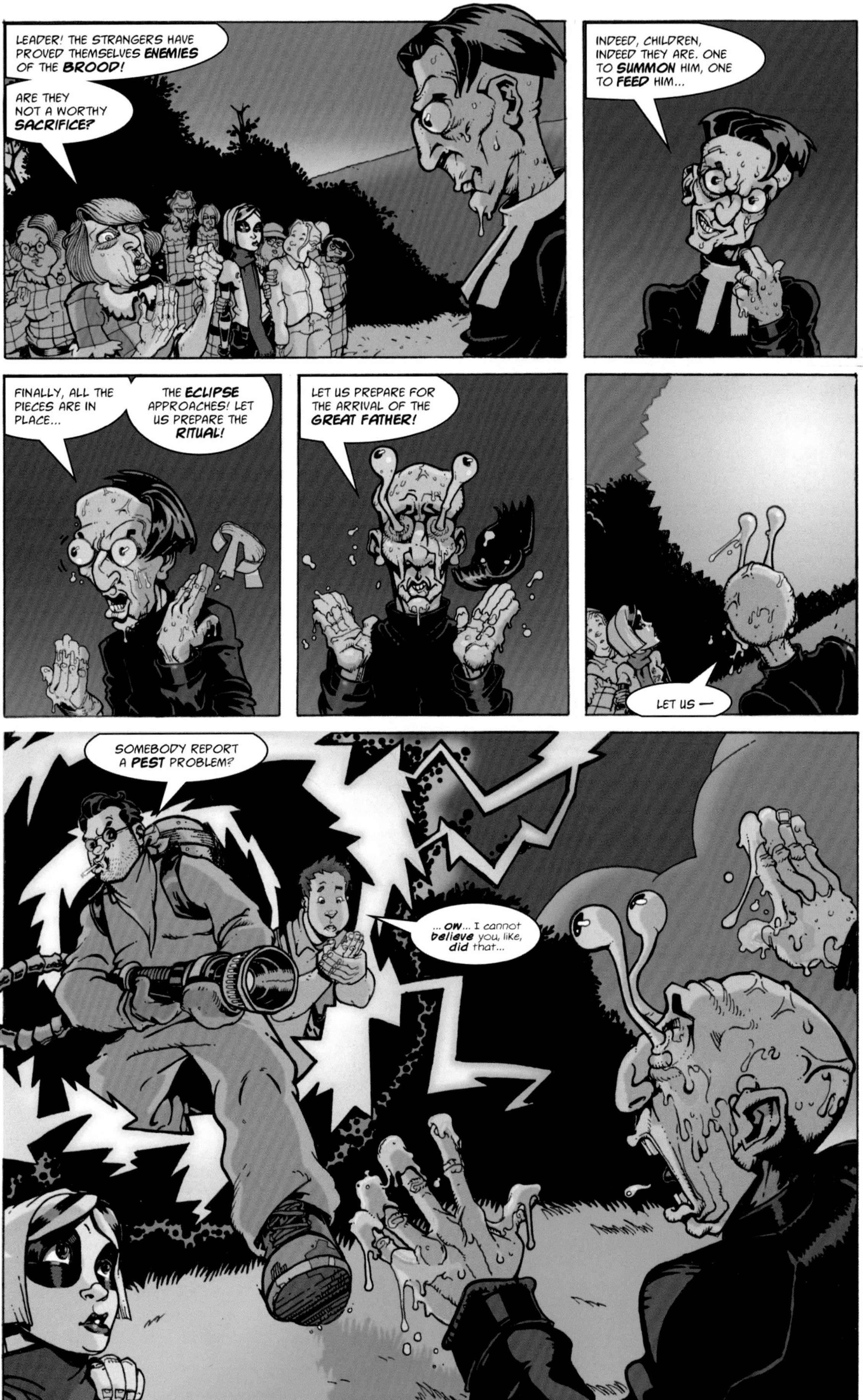
LEADER! THE STRANGERS HAVE PROVED THEMSELVES ENEMIES OF THE BROOD!
ARE THEY NOT A WORTHY SACRIFICE?
INDEED, CHILDREN, INDEED THEY ARE. ONE TO SUMMON HIM, ONE TO FEED HIM...
FINALLY, ALL THE PIECES ARE IN PLACE...
THE ECLIPSE APPROACHES! LET US PREPARE THE RITUAL!
LET US PREPARE FOR THE ARRIVAL OF THE GREAT FATHER!
LET US —
SOMEBODY REPORT A PEST PROBLEM?
... OW... I cannot believe you, like, did that...

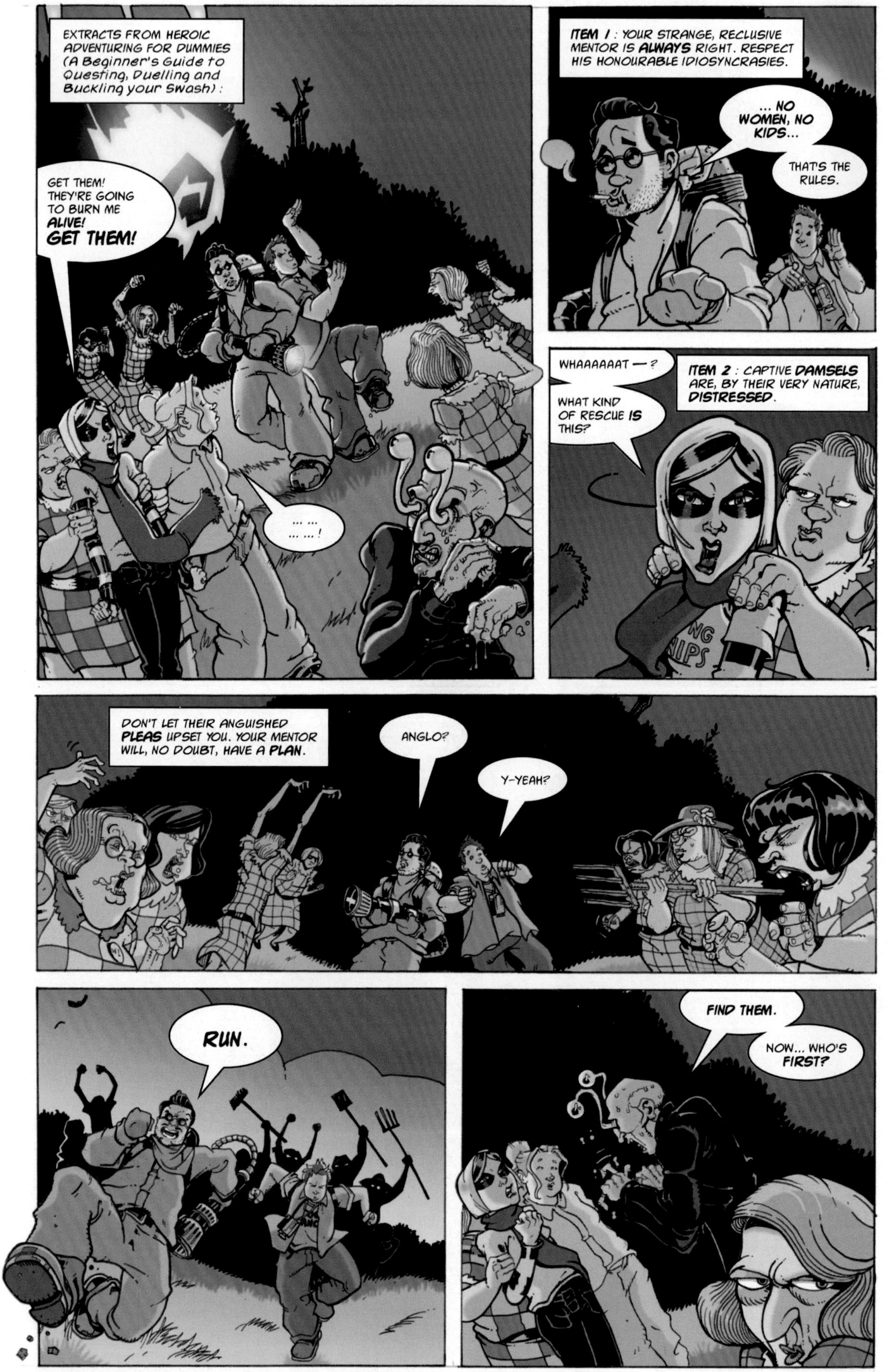
EXTRACTS FROM HEROIC ADVENTURING FOR DUMMIES (A Beginner's Guide to Questing, Duelling and Buckling your Swash) :
GET THEM! THEY'RE GOING TO BURN ME ALIVE! GET THEM!
... ...!
ITEM 1 : YOUR STRANGE, RECLUSIVE MENTOR IS ALWAYS RIGHT. RESPECT HIS HONOURABLE IDIOSYNCRASIES.
... NO WOMEN, NO KIDS...
THAT'S THE RULES.
WHAAAAAAT —?
WHAT KIND OF RESCUE IS THIS?
ITEM 2 : CAPTIVE DAMSELS ARE, BY THEIR VERY NATURE, DISTRESSED.
DON'T LET THEIR ANGUISHED PLEAS UPSET YOU. YOUR MENTOR WILL, NO DOUBT, HAVE A PLAN.
ANGLO?
Y-YEAH?
RUN.
FIND THEM.
NOW... WHO'S FIRST?

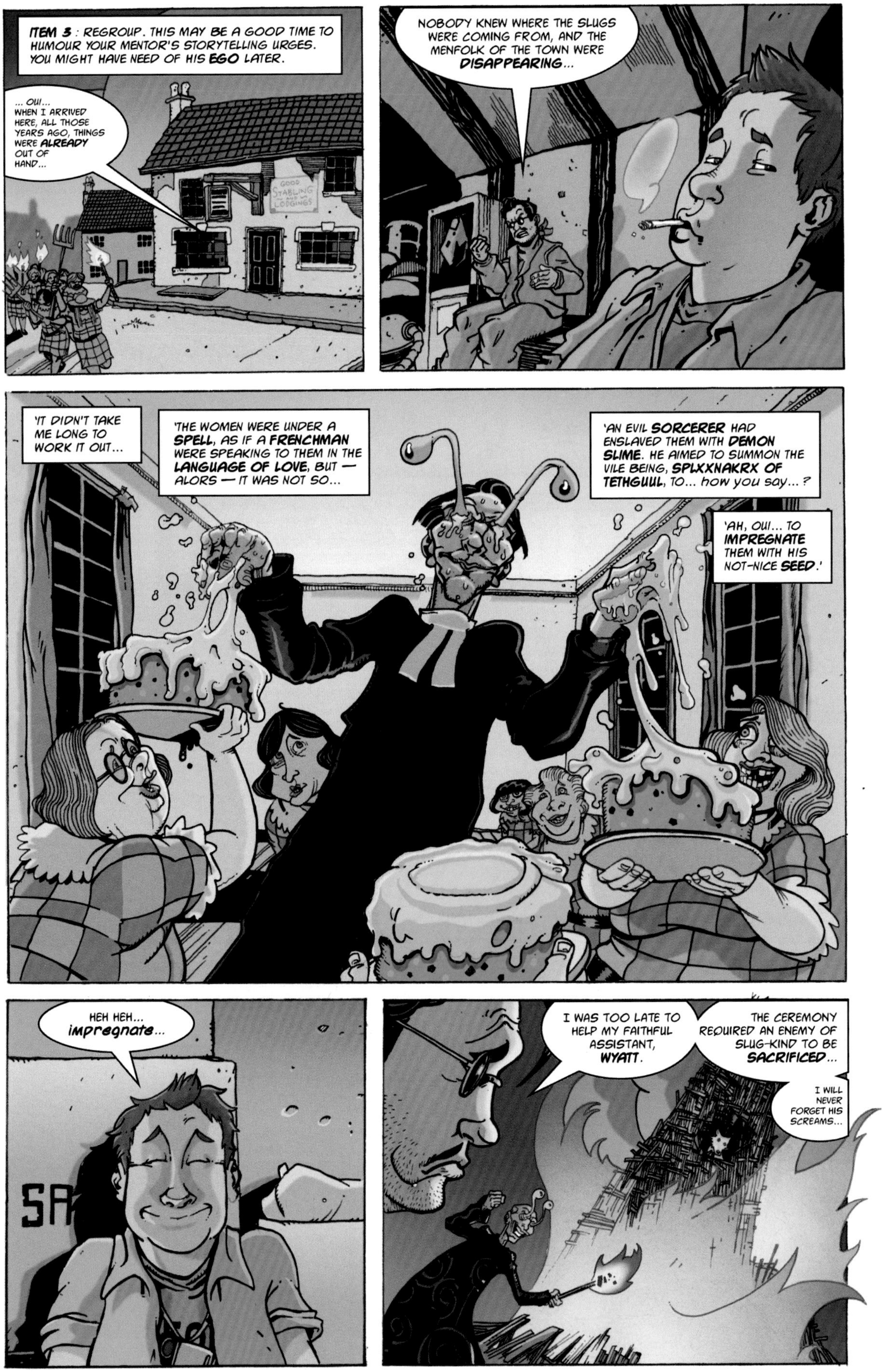

ITEM 3: REGROUP. THIS MAY BE A GOOD TIME TO HUMOUR YOUR MENTOR'S STORYTELLING URGES. YOU MIGHT HAVE NEED OF HIS EGO LATER.
... OUI... WHEN I ARRIVED HERE, ALL THOSE YEARS AGO, THINGS WERE ALREADY OUT OF HAND...
GOOD STABLING AND LODGINGS
NOBODY KNEW WHERE THE SLUGS WERE COMING FROM, AND THE MENFOLK OF THE TOWN WERE DISAPPEARING...
'IT DIDN'T TAKE ME LONG TO WORK IT OUT...
'THE WOMEN WERE UNDER A SPELL, AS IF A FRENCHMAN WERE SPEAKING TO THEM IN THE LANGUAGE OF LOVE, BUT — ALORS — IT WAS NOT SO...
'AN EVIL SORCERER HAD ENSLAVED THEM WITH DEMON SLIME. HE AIMED TO SUMMON THE VILE BEING, SPLXXNAKRX OF TETHGUUL, TO... how you say...?
'AH, OUI... TO IMPREGNATE THEM WITH HIS NOT-NICE SEED.'
HEH HEH... impregnate...
SA
I WAS TOO LATE TO HELP MY FAITHFUL ASSISTANT, WYATT.
THE CEREMONY REQUIRED AN ENEMY OF SLUG-KIND TO BE SACRIFICED...
I WILL NEVER FORGET HIS SCREAMS...

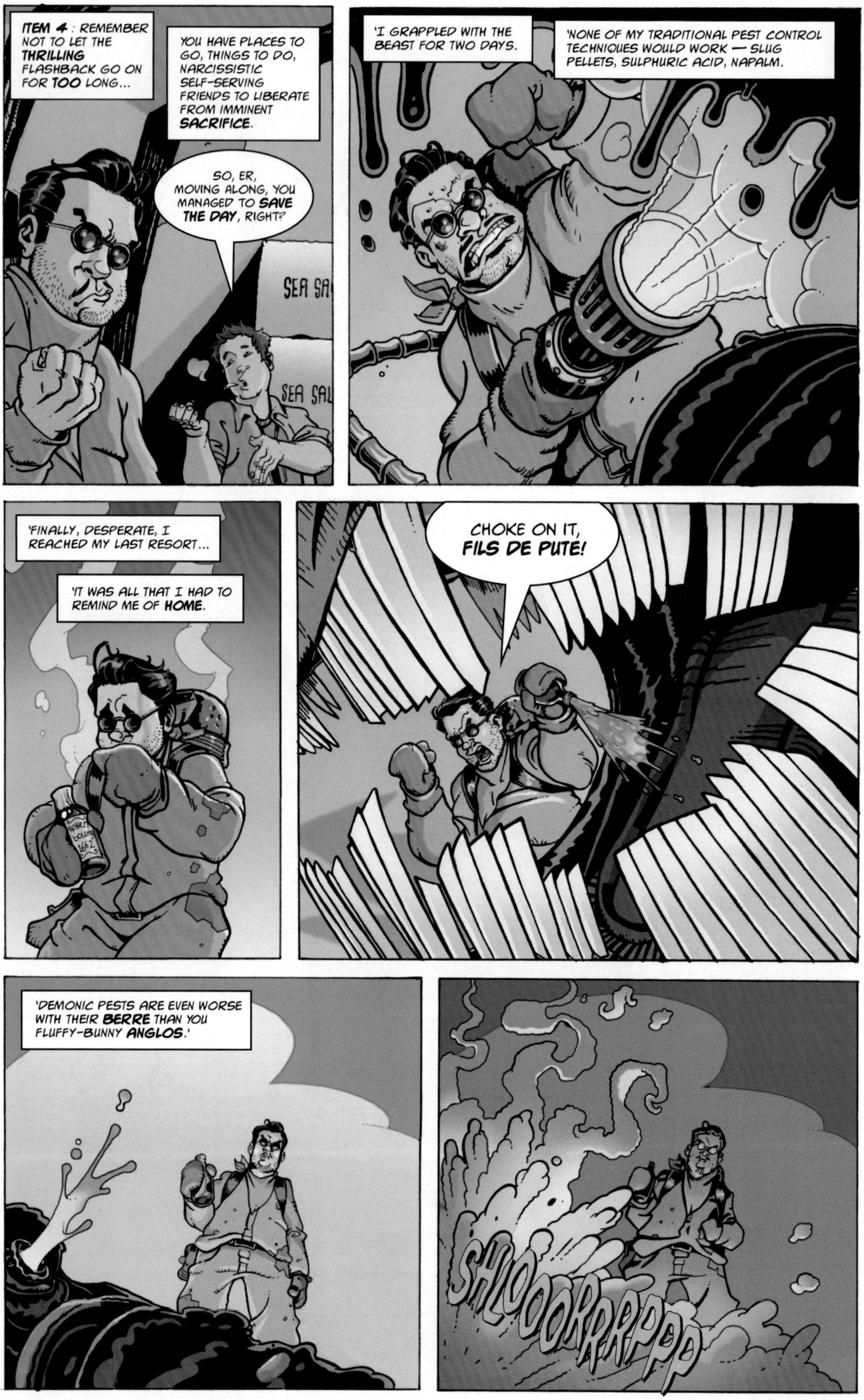
ITEM 4 : REMEMBER NOT TO LET THE THRILLING FLASHBACK GO ON FOR TOO LONG...
YOU HAVE PLACES TO GO, THINGS TO DO, NARCISSISTIC SELF-SERVING FRIENDS TO LIBERATE FROM IMMINENT SACRIFICE.
SO, ER, MOVING ALONG, YOU MANAGED TO SAVE THE DAY, RIGHT?
SEA SA
SEA SAL
'I GRAPPLED WITH THE BEAST FOR TWO DAYS.
'NONE OF MY TRADITIONAL PEST CONTROL TECHNIQUES WOULD WORK — SLUG PELLETS, SULPHURIC ACID, NAPALM.
'FINALLY, DESPERATE, I REACHED MY LAST RESORT...
'IT WAS ALL THAT I HAD TO REMIND ME OF HOME.
CHOKE ON IT, FILS DE PUTE!
'DEMONIC PESTS ARE EVEN WORSE WITH THEIR BERRE THAN YOU FLUFFY-BUNNY ANGLOS.'
SHLOOORRRPPP

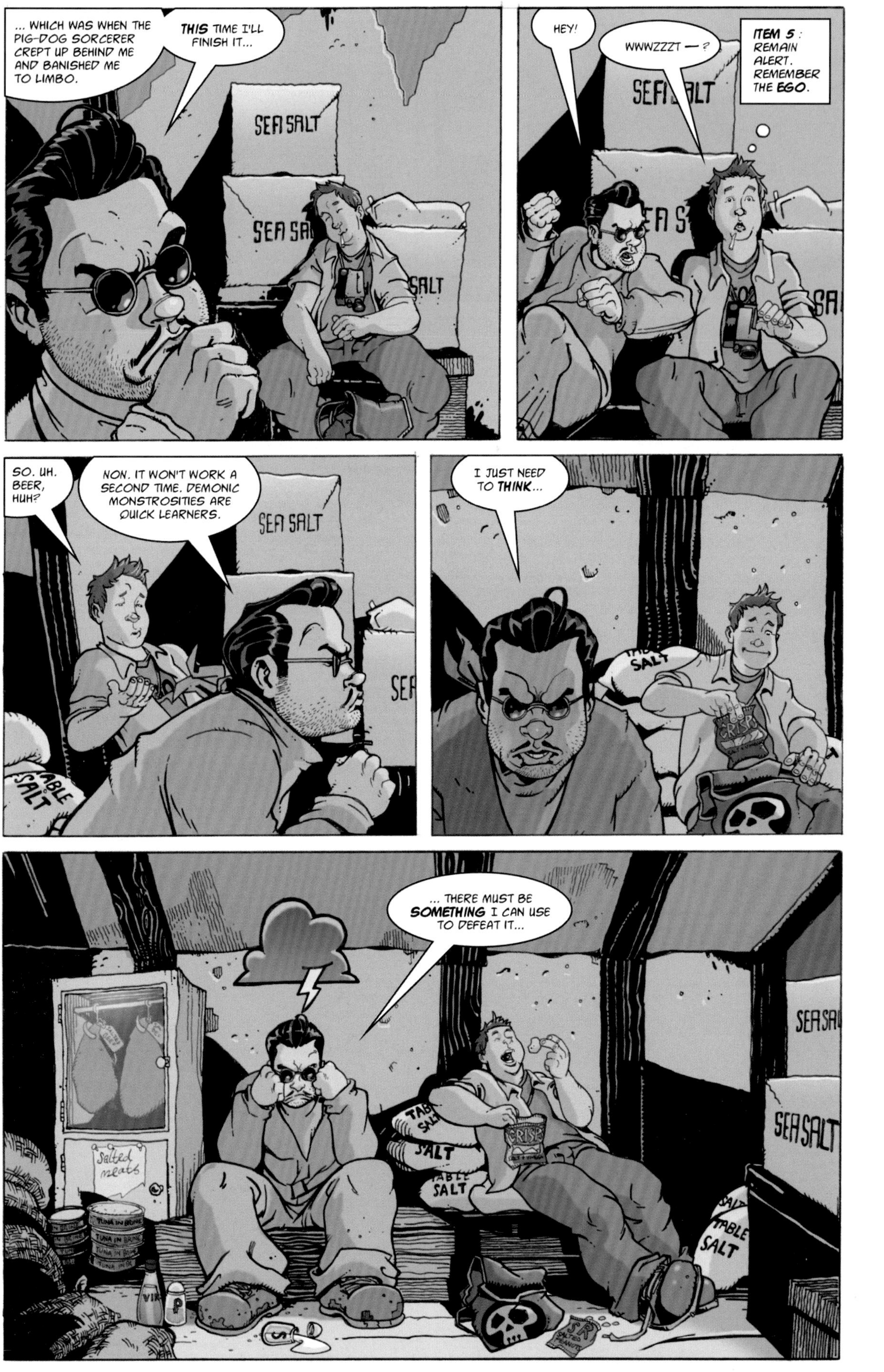

... WHICH WAS WHEN THE PIG-DOG SORCERER CREPT UP BEHIND ME AND BANISHED ME TO LIMBO.
THIS TIME I'LL FINISH IT...
SEA SALT
HEY!
WWWZZZT — ?
ITEM 5 : REMAIN ALERT. REMEMBER THE **EGO**.
SO. UH. BEER, HUH?
NON. IT WON'T WORK A SECOND TIME. DEMONIC MONSTROSITIES ARE QUICK LEARNERS.
TABLE SALT
I JUST NEED TO **THINK**...
CRISPS
... THERE MUST BE **SOMETHING** I CAN USE TO DEFEAT IT...
Salted meats
TUNA IN BRINE
TABLE SALT
SEA SALT

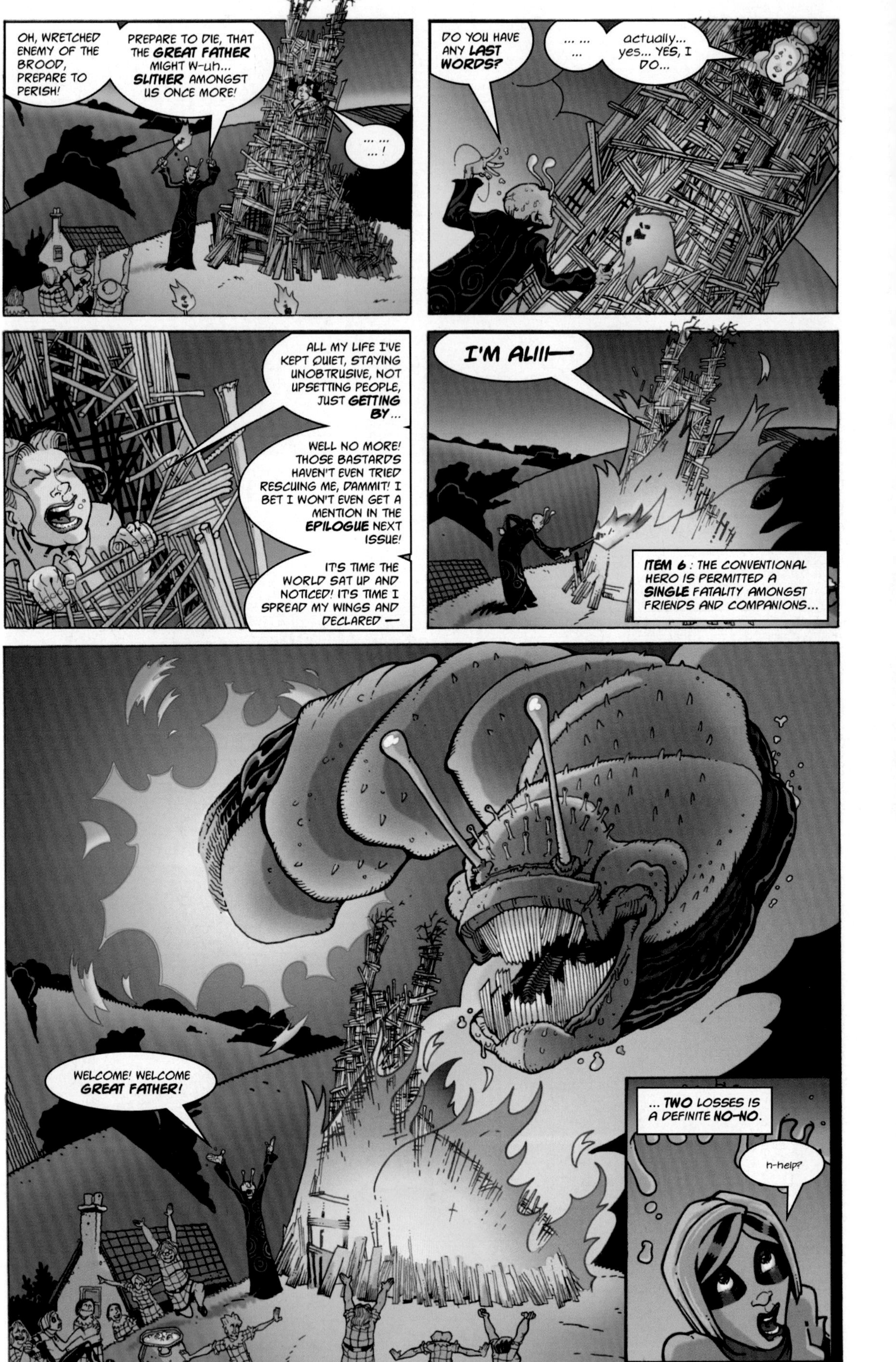
OH, WRETCHED ENEMY OF THE BROOD, PREPARE TO PERISH!
PREPARE TO DIE, THAT THE GREAT FATHER MIGHT W-uh... SLITHER AMONGST US ONCE MORE!
... ... !
DO YOU HAVE ANY LAST WORDS?
... ...
actually... yes... YES, I DO...
ALL MY LIFE I'VE KEPT QUIET, STAYING UNOBTRUSIVE, NOT UPSETTING PEOPLE, JUST GETTING BY...
WELL NO MORE! THOSE BASTARDS HAVEN'T EVEN TRIED RESCUING ME, DAMMIT! I BET I WON'T EVEN GET A MENTION IN THE EPILOGUE NEXT ISSUE!
IT'S TIME THE WORLD SAT UP AND NOTICED! IT'S TIME I SPREAD MY WINGS AND DECLARED —
I'M ALIII—
ITEM 6 : THE CONVENTIONAL HERO IS PERMITTED A SINGLE FATALITY AMONGST FRIENDS AND COMPANIONS...
WELCOME! WELCOME GREAT FATHER!
... TWO LOSSES IS A DEFINITE NO-NO.
h-help?

OH MIGHTY **SPLXKXXNAKRX**, BRINGER OF THE LIFE-GIVING SLIME — DEVOUR THE SACRIFICIAL **APPETISER** AND ACCEPT THESE HUMBLE **FEMALES** AS YOUR BRIDES!

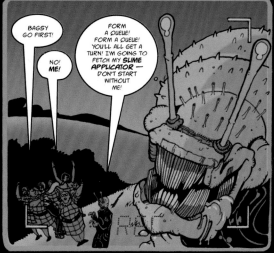

BAGSY GO FIRST!

NO! ME!

FORM A QUEUE! FORM A QUEUE! YOU'LL ALL GET A TURN! I'M GOING TO FETCH MY **SLIME APPLICATOR** — DON'T START WITHOUT ME!

HEH HEH HEH...

'DEBBIE DOES DEMONS'...

THIS STUFF'LL SELL FOR A FORTUNE IN **AMSTERDAM**...

WHAT **IS** THAT THING, ANGLO? SOME SORT OF WEAPON?

T-THIS?

THIS IS, LIKE, A SOPHISTICATED PIECE OF RECORDING HARDWARE, ENABLING THE CONSCIENTIOUS FILMMAKER TO DOCUMENT AND EXPOSE EVENTS OF HISTORICAL SIGNIFICANCE.

BIEN.

NOW STOP PERVING AT THE GIRLIES AND COME LEARN WHAT IT TAKES TO BE A **REAL** MAN.

PEST CONTROL, THE OLD-FASHIONED WAY.

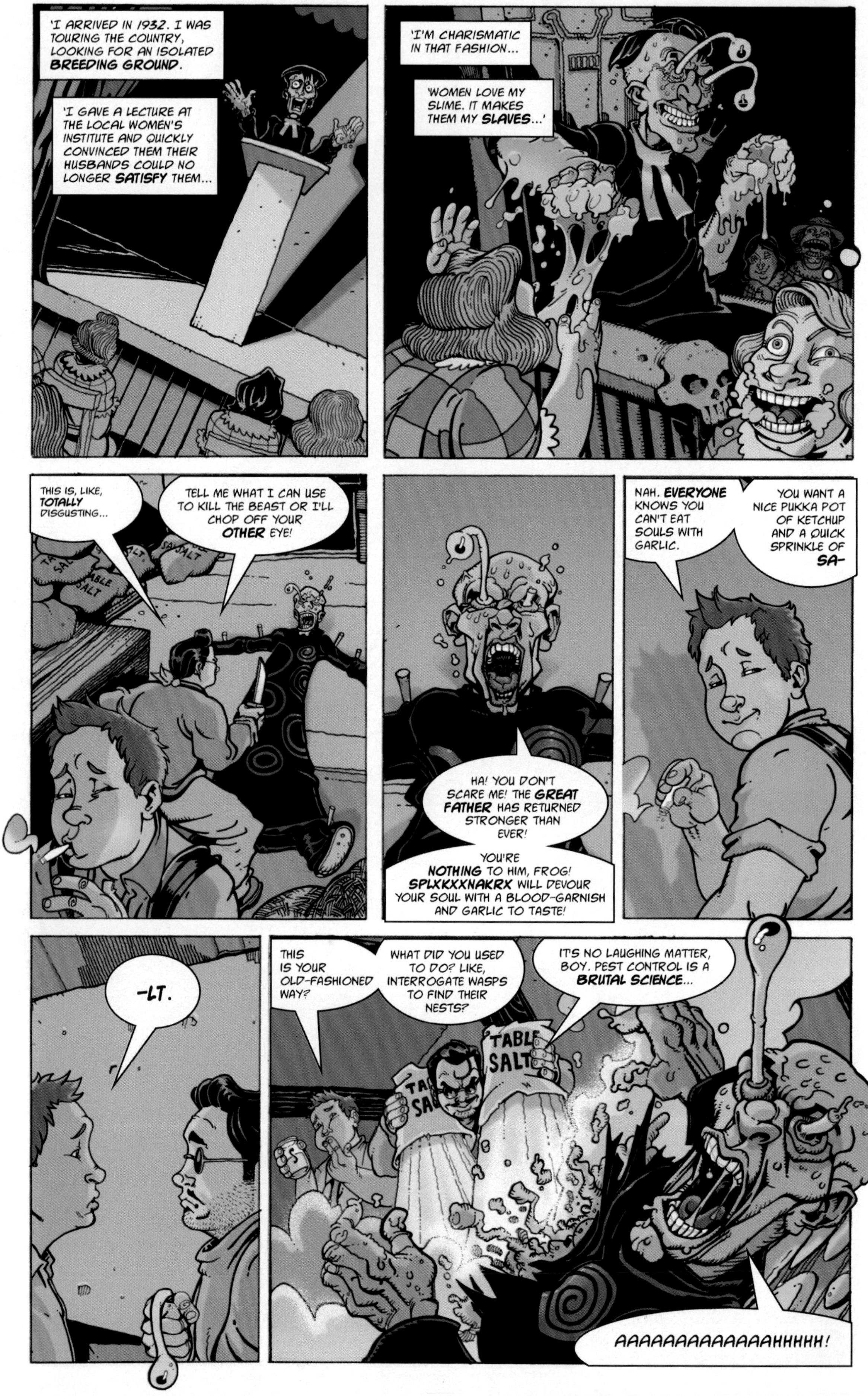
'I ARRIVED IN 1932. I WAS TOURING THE COUNTRY, LOOKING FOR AN ISOLATED BREEDING GROUND.
'I GAVE A LECTURE AT THE LOCAL WOMEN'S INSTITUTE AND QUICKLY CONVINCED THEM THEIR HUSBANDS COULD NO LONGER SATISFY THEM...
'I'M CHARISMATIC IN THAT FASHION...
'WOMEN LOVE MY SLIME. IT MAKES THEM MY SLAVES...'
THIS IS, LIKE, TOTALLY DISGUSTING...
TELL ME WHAT I CAN USE TO KILL THE BEAST OR I'LL CHOP OFF YOUR OTHER EYE!
TABLE SALT
HA! YOU DON'T SCARE ME! THE GREAT FATHER HAS RETURNED STRONGER THAN EVER!
YOU'RE NOTHING TO HIM, FROG! SPLXKXXNAKRX WILL DEVOUR YOUR SOUL WITH A BLOOD-GARNISH AND GARLIC TO TASTE!
NAH. EVERYONE KNOWS YOU CAN'T EAT SOULS WITH GARLIC.
YOU WANT A NICE PUKKA POT OF KETCHUP AND A QUICK SPRINKLE OF SA-
-LT.
THIS IS YOUR OLD-FASHIONED WAY?
WHAT DID YOU USED TO DO? LIKE, INTERROGATE WASPS TO FIND THEIR NESTS?
IT'S NO LAUGHING MATTER, BOY. PEST CONTROL IS A BRUTAL SCIENCE...
TABLE SALT
AAAAAAAAAAAAAHHHHH!

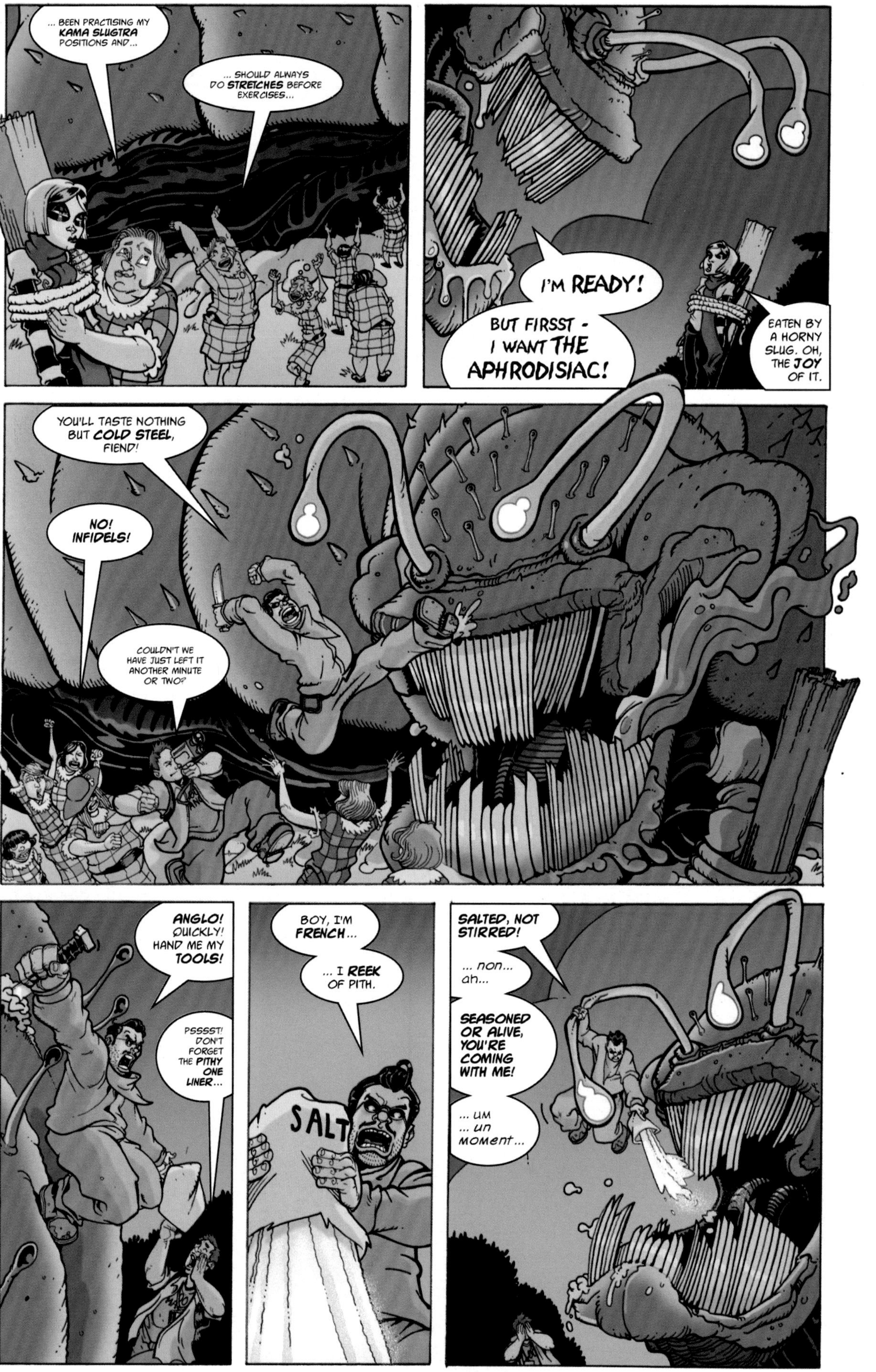
... BEEN PRACTISING MY KAMA SLUGTRA POSITIONS AND...
... SHOULD ALWAYS DO STRETCHES BEFORE EXERCISES...
I'M READY!
BUT FIRSST - I WANT THE APHRODISIAC!
EATEN BY A HORNY SLUG. OH, THE JOY OF IT.
YOU'LL TASTE NOTHING BUT COLD STEEL, FIEND!
NO! INFIDELS!
COULDN'T WE HAVE JUST LEFT IT ANOTHER MINUTE OR TWO?
ANGLO! QUICKLY! HAND ME MY TOOLS!
PSSSST! DON'T FORGET THE PITHY ONE LINER...
BOY, I'M FRENCH...
... I REEK OF PITH.
SALT
SALTED, NOT STIRRED!
... non... ah...
SEASONED OR ALIVE, YOU'RE COMING WITH ME!
... um ... un moment...

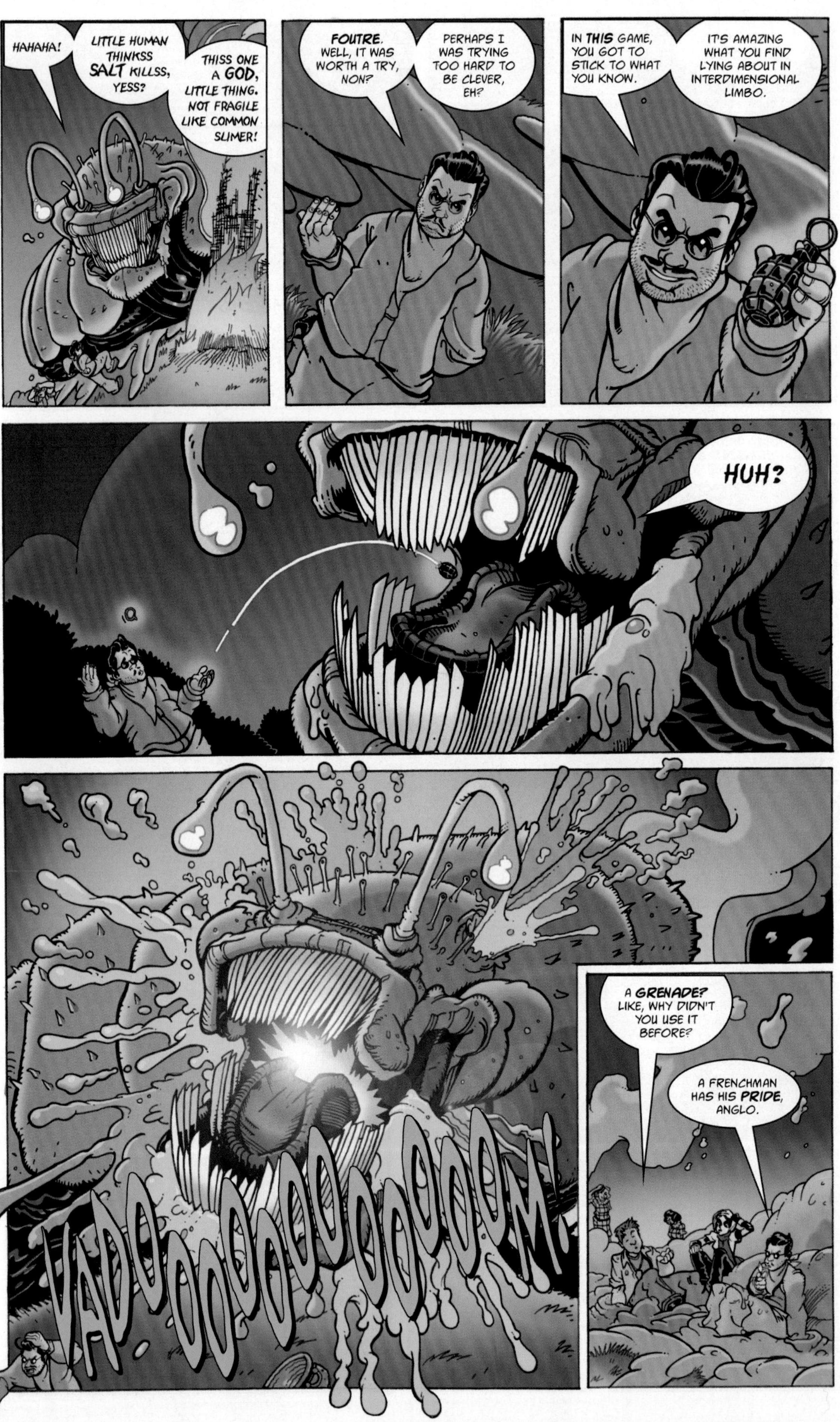
HAHAHA!
LITTLE HUMAN THINKSS SALT KILLSS, YESS?
THISS ONE A GOD, LITTLE THING. NOT FRAGILE LIKE COMMON SLIMER!
FOUTRE. WELL, IT WAS WORTH A TRY, NON?
PERHAPS I WAS TRYING TOO HARD TO BE CLEVER, EH?
IN THIS GAME, YOU GOT TO STICK TO WHAT YOU KNOW.
IT'S AMAZING WHAT YOU FIND LYING ABOUT IN INTERDIMENSIONAL LIMBO.
HUH?
VADOOOOOOOOOOOOOM!
A GRENADE? LIKE, WHY DIDN'T YOU USE IT BEFORE?
A FRENCHMAN HAS HIS PRIDE, ANGLO.

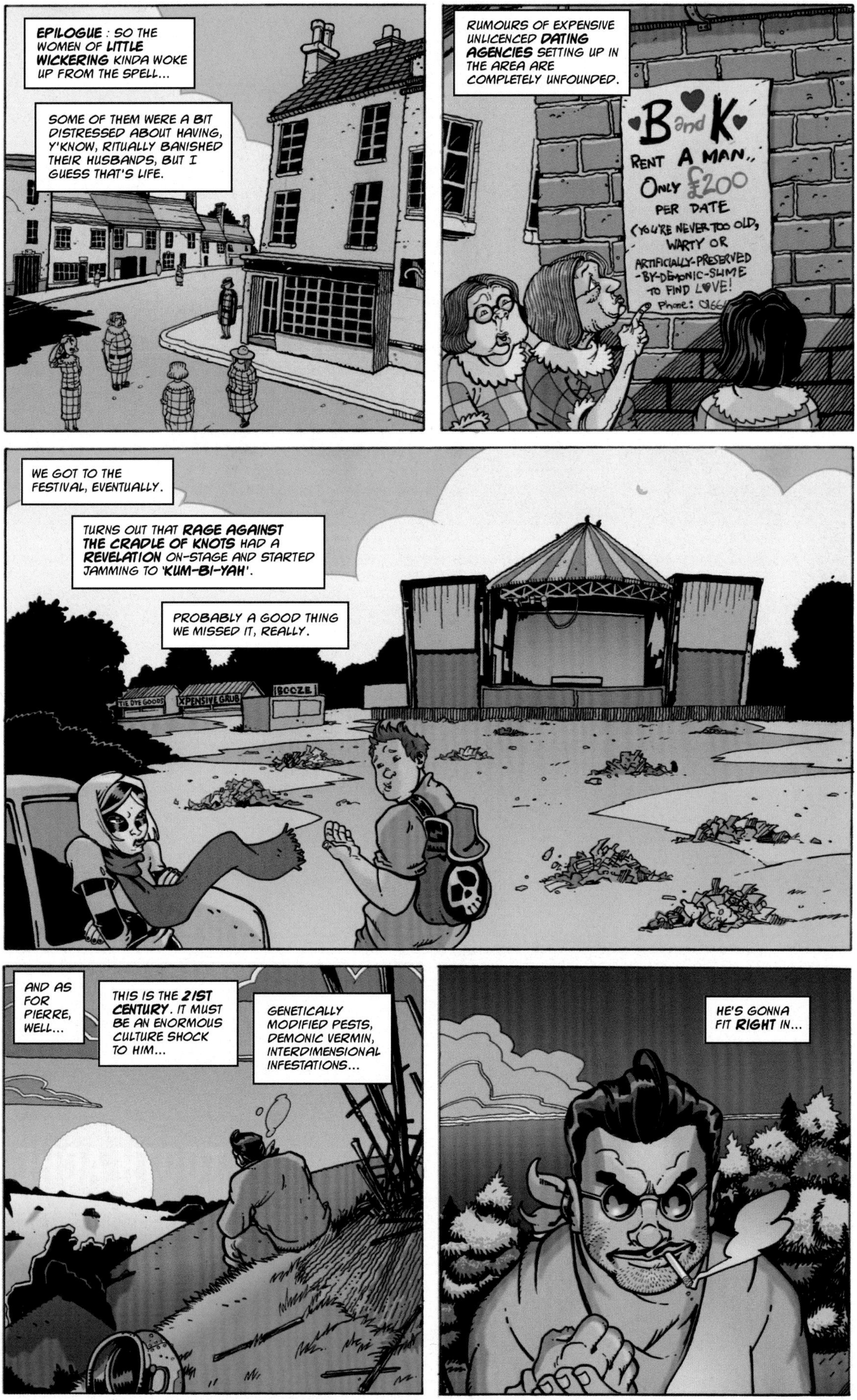
EPILOGUE: SO THE WOMEN OF LITTLE WICKERING KINDA WOKE UP FROM THE SPELL...
SOME OF THEM WERE A BIT DISTRESSED ABOUT HAVING, Y'KNOW, RITUALLY BANISHED THEIR HUSBANDS, BUT I GUESS THAT'S LIFE.
RUMOURS OF EXPENSIVE UNLICENCED DATING AGENCIES SETTING UP IN THE AREA ARE COMPLETELY UNFOUNDED.
B and K
RENT A MAN..
ONLY £200
PER DATE
(YOU'RE NEVER TOO OLD, WARTY OR ARTIFICIALLY-PRESERVED -BY-DEMONIC-SLIME TO FIND LOVE!
Phone:
WE GOT TO THE FESTIVAL, EVENTUALLY.
TURNS OUT THAT RAGE AGAINST THE CRADLE OF KNOTS HAD A REVELATION ON-STAGE AND STARTED JAMMING TO 'KUM-BI-YAH'.
PROBABLY A GOOD THING WE MISSED IT, REALLY.
TIE DYE GOODS
XPENSIVE GRUB
BOOZE
AND AS FOR PIERRE, WELL...
THIS IS THE 21ST CENTURY. IT MUST BE AN ENORMOUS CULTURE SHOCK TO HIM...
GENETICALLY MODIFIED PESTS, DEMONIC VERMIN, INTERDIMENSIONAL INFESTATIONS...
HE'S GONNA FIT RIGHT IN...

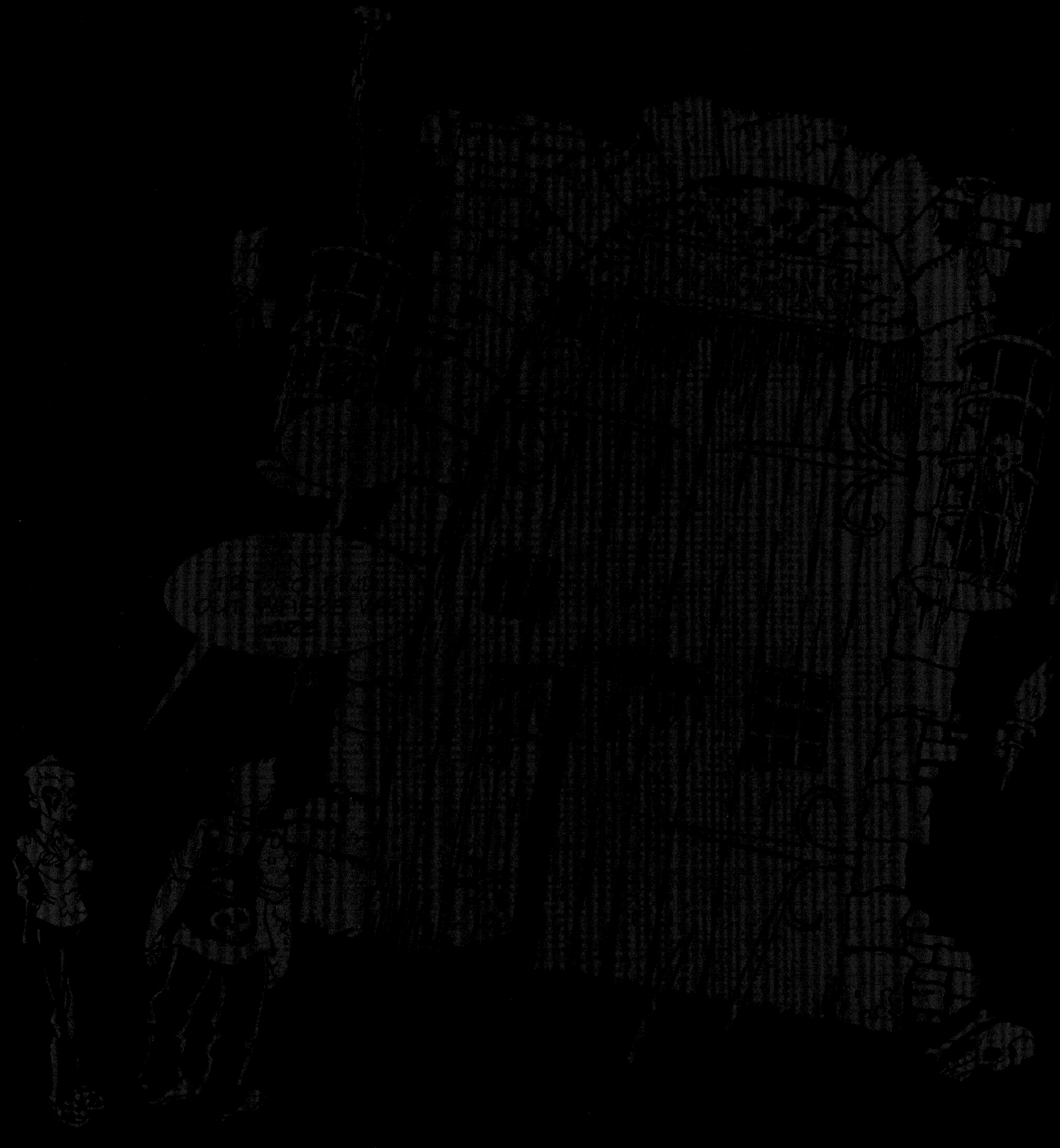

TOOTH ACHE

Script: Simon Spurrier
Art: Steve Roberts
Letters: Annie Parkhouse

Originally published in *2000 AD* Progs 1383-1386

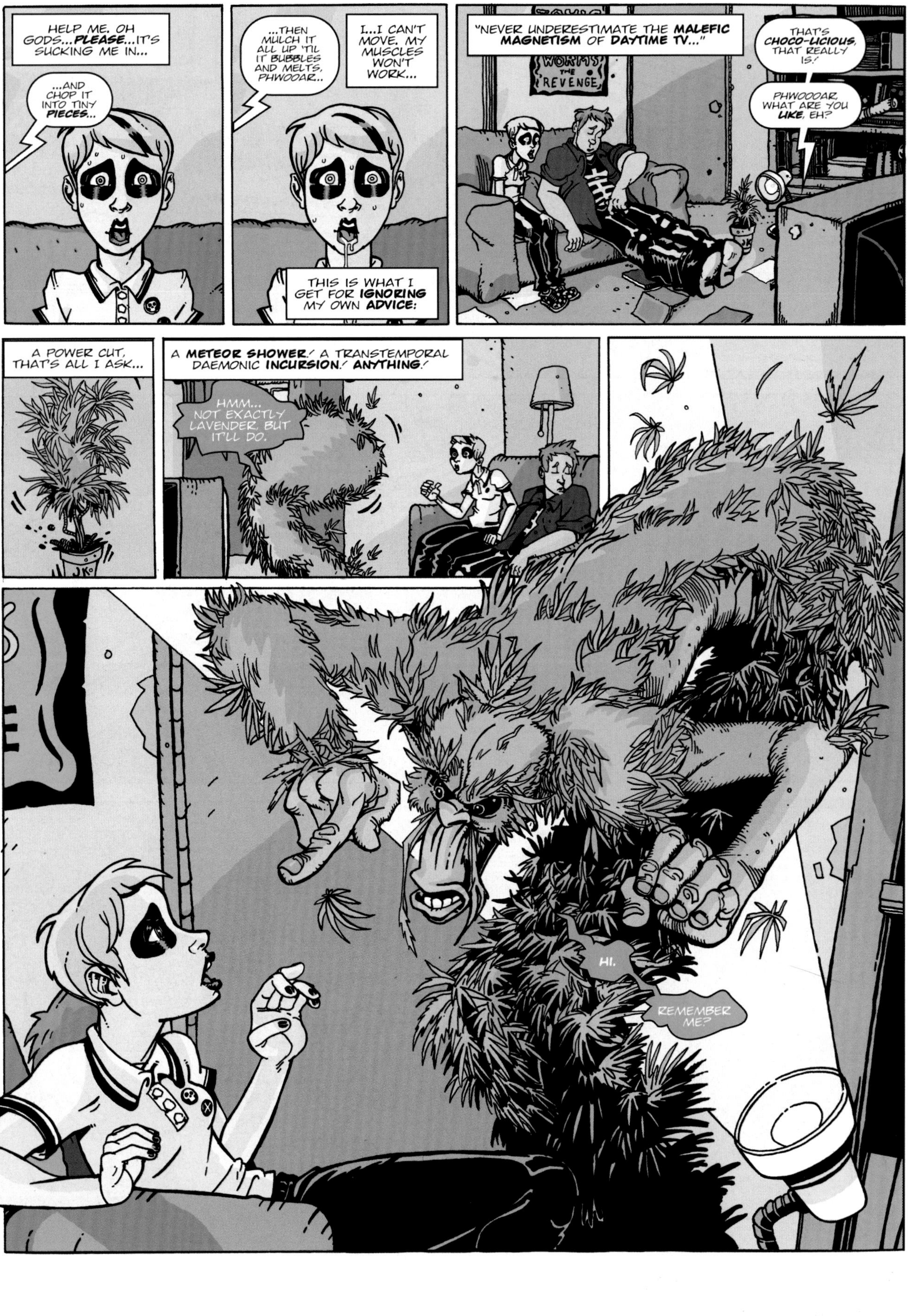

HELP ME. OH GODS...PLEASE...IT'S SUCKING ME IN...
...AND CHOP IT INTO TINY PIECES...
...THEN MULCH IT ALL UP 'TIL IT BUBBLES AND MELTS, PHWOOAR..
I...I CAN'T MOVE. MY MUSCLES WON'T WORK...
THIS IS WHAT I GET FOR IGNORING MY OWN ADVICE:
"NEVER UNDERESTIMATE THE MALEFIC MAGNETISM OF DAYTIME TV..."
WORMS THE REVENGE
THAT'S CHOCO-LICIOUS, THAT REALLY IS!
PHWOOOAR, WHAT ARE YOU LIKE, EH?
A POWER CUT, THAT'S ALL I ASK...
A METEOR SHOWER! A TRANSTEMPORAL DAEMONIC INCURSION! ANYTHING!
HMM... NOT EXACTLY LAVENDER, BUT IT'LL DO.
HI.
REMEMBER ME?

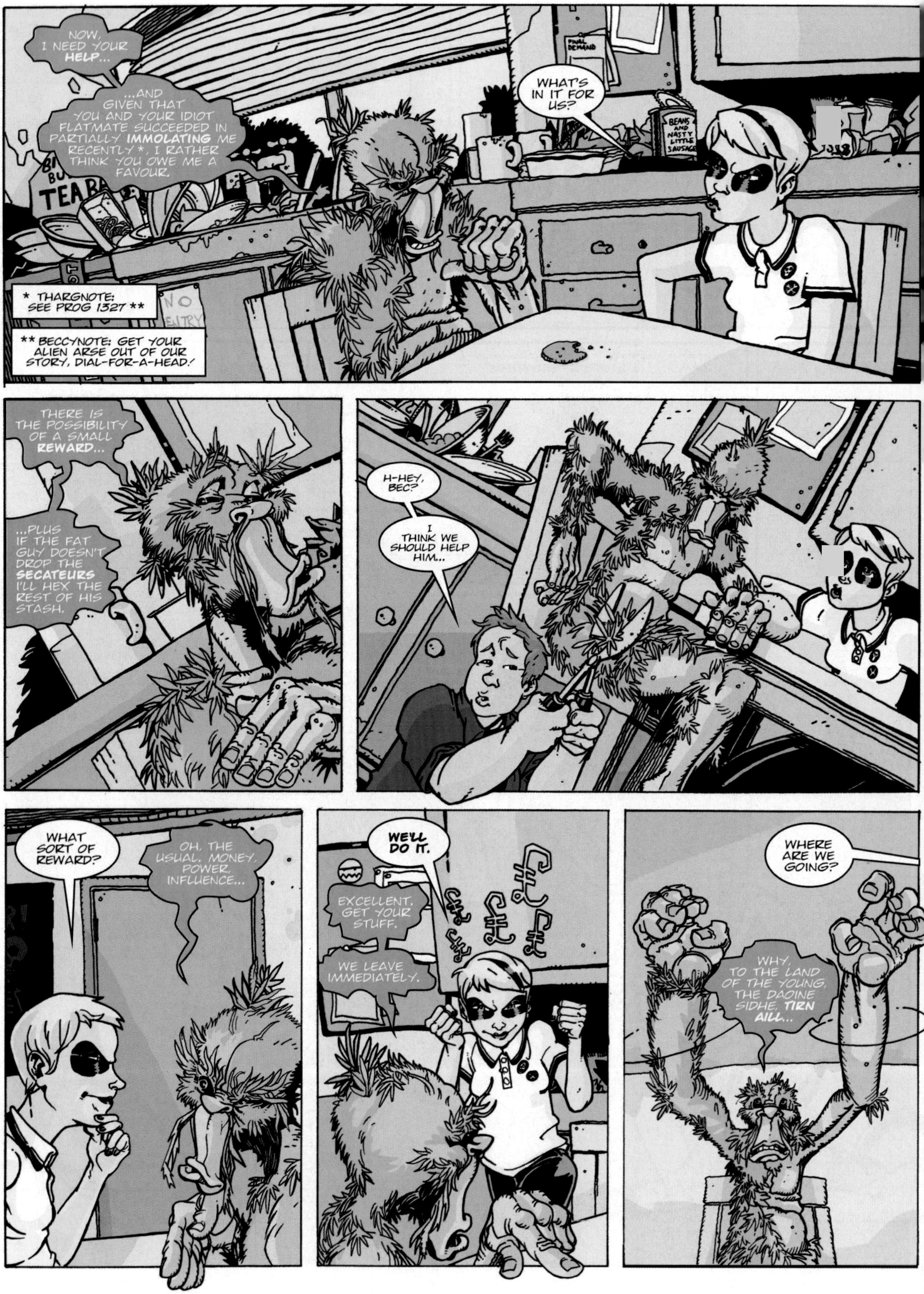
NOW, I NEED YOUR **HELP**...
...AND GIVEN THAT YOU AND YOUR IDIOT FLATMATE SUCCEEDED IN PARTIALLY **IMMOLATING** ME RECENTLY*, I RATHER THINK YOU OWE ME A FAVOUR.
WHAT'S IN IT FOR US?
FINAL DEMAND
BEANS AND NASTY LITTLE SAUSAGES
* THARGNOTE: SEE PROG 1327 **
** BECCYNOTE: GET YOUR ALIEN ARSE OUT OF OUR STORY, DIAL-FOR-A-HEAD!
THERE IS THE POSSIBILITY OF A SMALL **REWARD**...
...PLUS IF THE FAT GUY DOESN'T DROP THE **SECATEURS** I'LL HEX THE REST OF HIS STASH.
H-HEY, BEC?
I THINK WE SHOULD HELP HIM...
WHAT SORT OF REWARD?
OH, THE USUAL. MONEY. POWER. INFLUENCE...
WE'LL DO IT.
EXCELLENT. GET YOUR STUFF.
WE LEAVE IMMEDIATELY.
WHERE ARE WE GOING?
WHY, TO THE LAND OF THE YOUNG, THE DAOINE SIDHE, **TIRN AILL**...

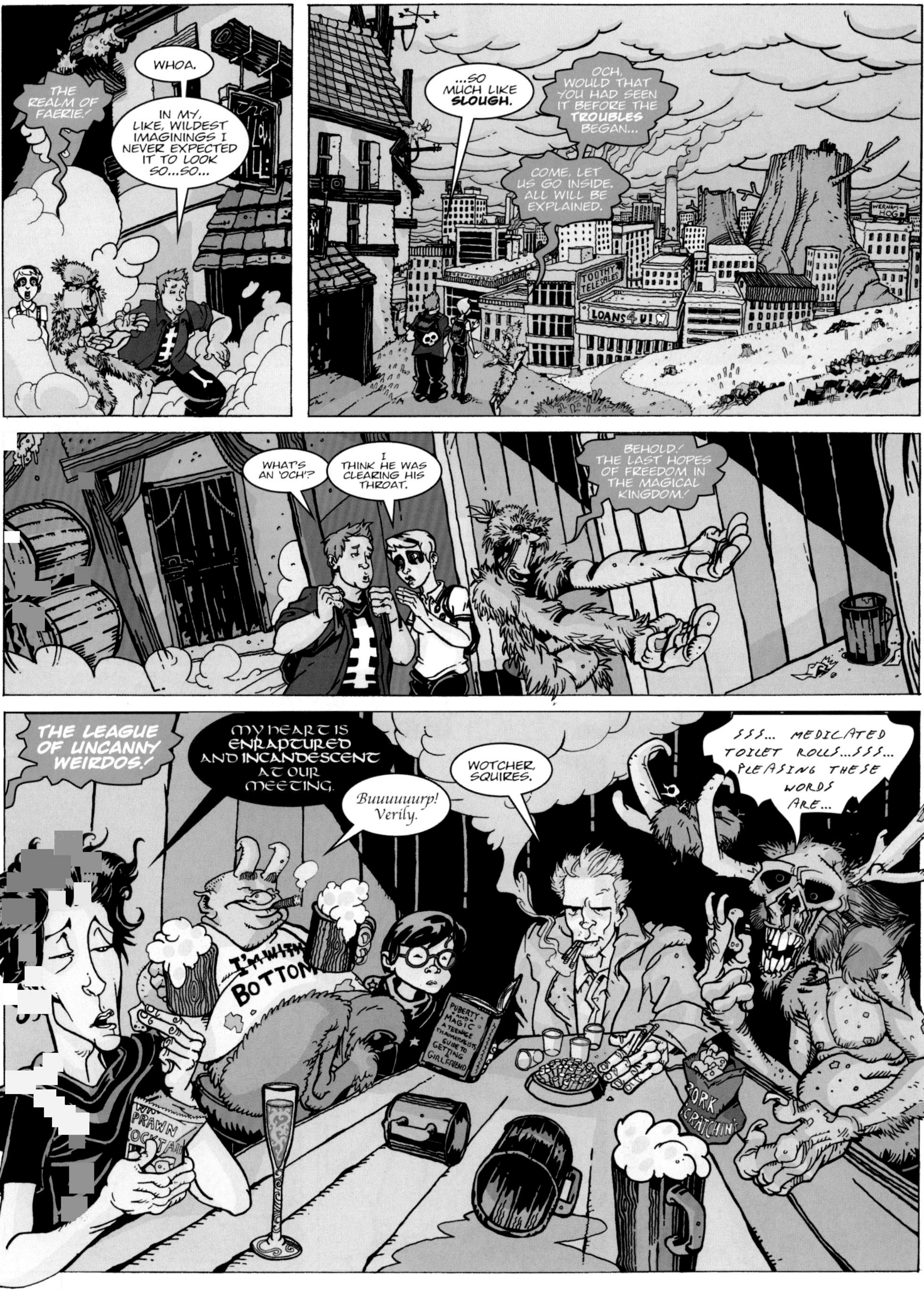
THE REALM OF FAERIE!
WHOA.
IN MY, LIKE, WILDEST IMAGININGS I NEVER EXPECTED IT TO LOOK SO...SO...
...SO MUCH LIKE **SLOUGH**.
OCH, WOULD THAT YOU HAD SEEN IT BEFORE THE **TROUBLES** BEGAN...
COME, LET US GO INSIDE. ALL WILL BE EXPLAINED.
TOOTHY TELESALES
LOANS 4 U!
WHAT'S AN 'OCH'?
I THINK HE WAS CLEARING HIS THROAT.
BEHOLD! THE LAST HOPES OF FREEDOM IN THE MAGICAL KINGDOM!
THE LEAGUE OF UNCANNY WEIRDOS!
MY HEART IS **ENRAPTURED** AND **INCANDESCENT** AT OUR MEETING.
Buuuuuurp! Verily.
WOTCHER, SQUIRES.
SSS... MEDICATED TOILET ROLLS...SSS... PLEASING THESE WORDS ARE...
I'M WITH BOTTOM
PUBERTY AND MAGIC A TEENAGE THAUMATURGIST'S GUIDE TO GETTING A GIRLFRIEND
PRAWN COCKTAIL
PORK SCRATCHIN'

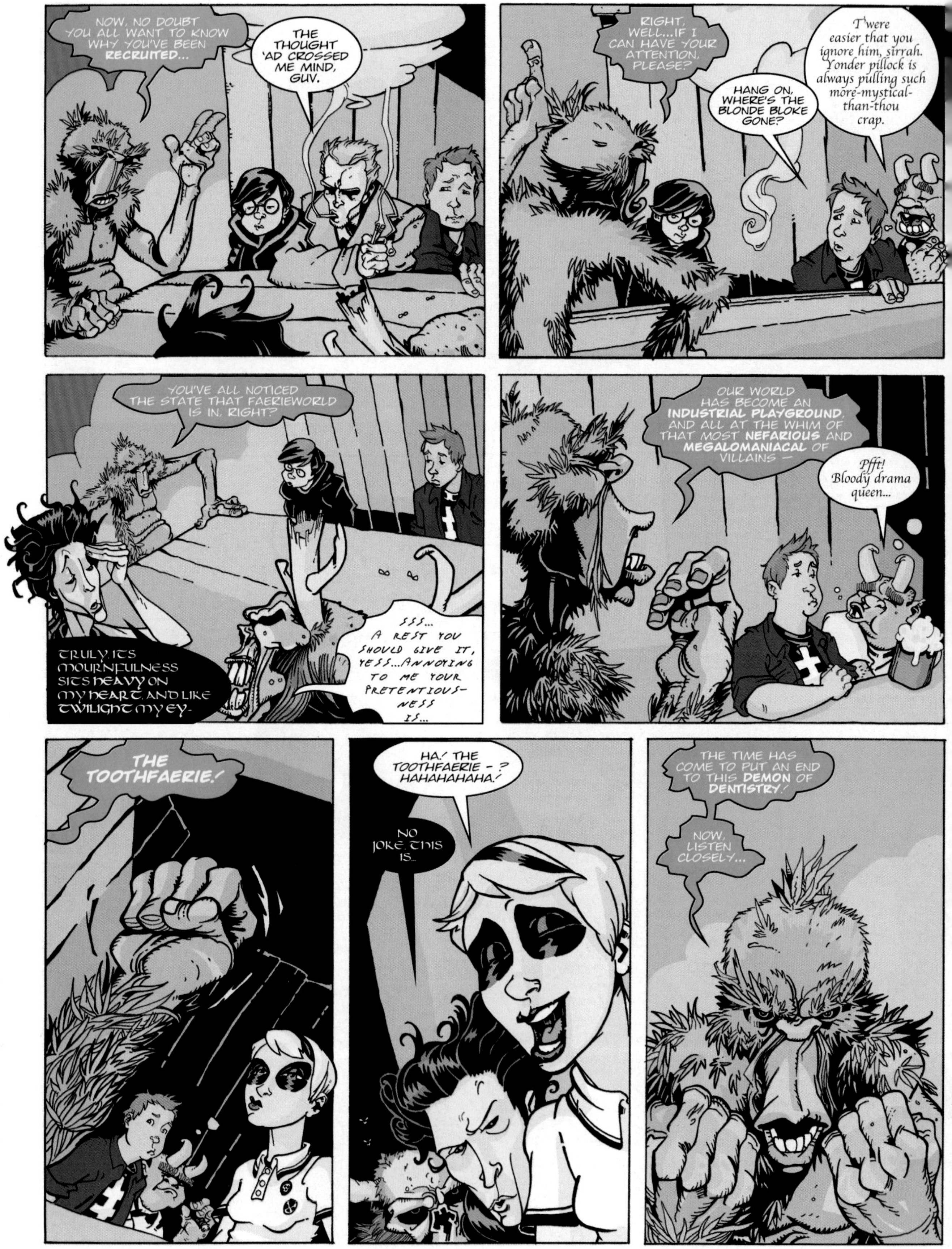

NOW, NO DOUBT YOU ALL WANT TO KNOW WHY YOU'VE BEEN **RECRUITED...**
THE THOUGHT 'AD CROSSED ME MIND, GUV.
RIGHT, WELL...IF I CAN HAVE YOUR ATTENTION, PLEASE?
HANG ON, WHERE'S THE BLONDE BLOKE GONE?
T'were easier that you ignore him, sirrah. Yonder pillock is always pulling such more-mystical-than-thou crap.
YOU'VE ALL NOTICED THE STATE THAT FAERIEWORLD IS IN, RIGHT?
TRULY, ITS MOURNFULNESS SITS **HEAVY** ON MY **HEART**, AND LIKE **TWILIGHT** MY EY-
SSS... A REST YOU SHOULD GIVE IT, YESS...ANNOYING TO ME YOUR PRETENTIOUS-NESS IS...
OUR WORLD HAS BECOME AN **INDUSTRIAL PLAYGROUND**, AND ALL AT THE WHIM OF THAT MOST **NEFARIOUS** AND **MEGALOMANIACAL** OF VILLAINS —
Pfft! Bloody drama queen...
THE TOOTHFAERIE!
HA! THE TOOTHFAERIE - ? HAHAHAHAHA!
NO JOKE, THIS IS...
THE TIME HAS COME TO PUT AN END TO THIS **DEMON** OF **DENTISTRY**!
NOW, LISTEN CLOSELY...

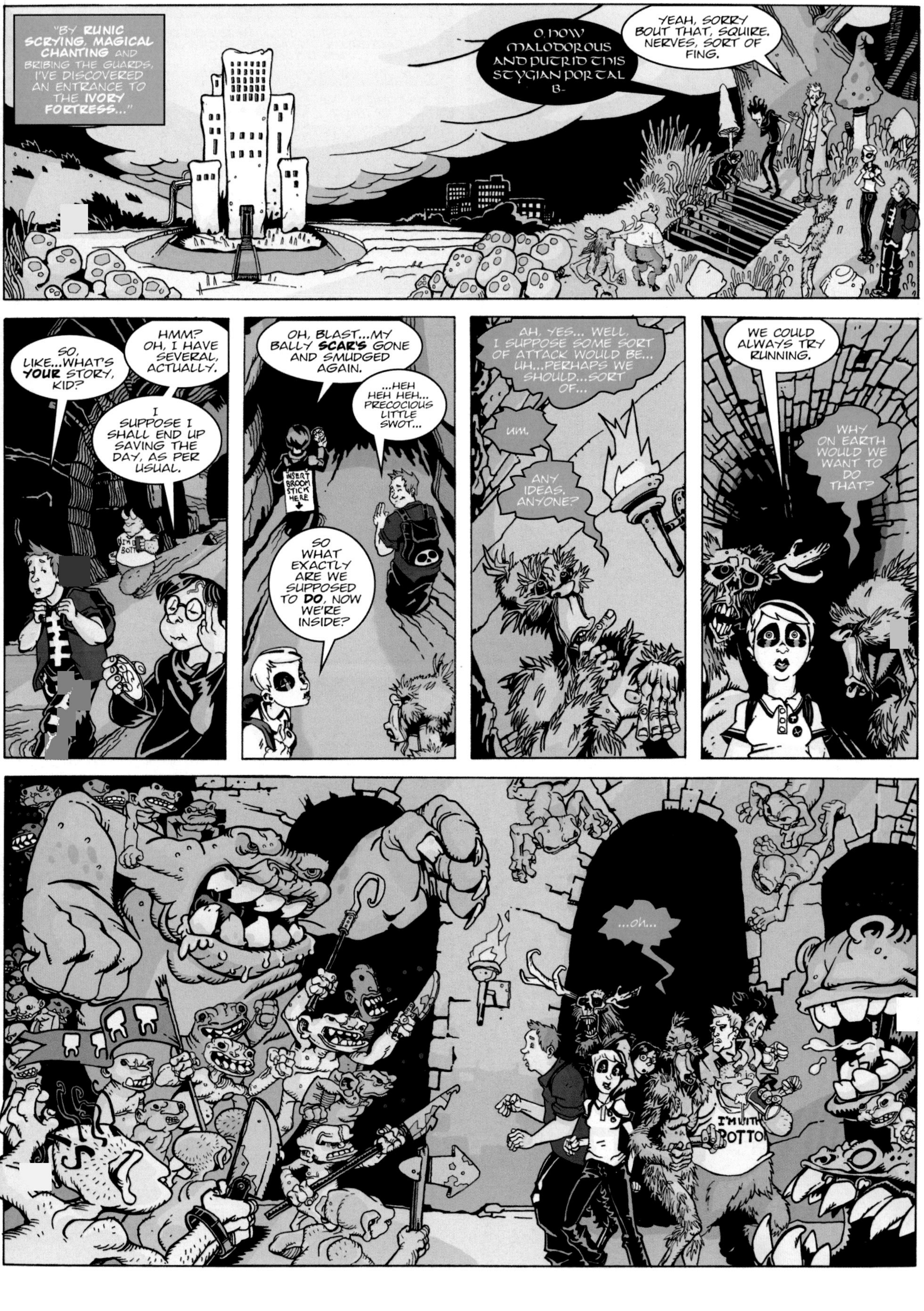
"BY RUNIC SCRYING, MAGICAL CHANTING AND BRIBING THE GUARDS, I'VE DISCOVERED AN ENTRANCE TO THE IVORY FORTRESS..."
O, HOW MALODOROUS AND PUTRID THIS STYGIAN PORTAL B-
YEAH, SORRY BOUT THAT, SQUIRE. NERVES, SORT OF FING.
SO, LIKE...WHAT'S YOUR STORY, KID?
HMM? OH, I HAVE SEVERAL, ACTUALLY.
I SUPPOSE I SHALL END UP SAVING THE DAY, AS PER USUAL.
OH, BLAST...MY BALLY SCAR'S GONE AND SMUDGED AGAIN.
...HEH HEH HEH... PRECOCIOUS LITTLE SWOT...
INSERT BROOM STICK HERE
SO WHAT EXACTLY ARE WE SUPPOSED TO DO, NOW WE'RE INSIDE?
AH, YES... WELL, I SUPPOSE SOME SORT OF ATTACK WOULD BE... UH...PERHAPS WE SHOULD...SORT OF...
UM.
ANY IDEAS, ANYONE?
WE COULD ALWAYS TRY RUNNING.
WHY ON EARTH WOULD WE WANT TO DO THAT?
...OH...
I'M WITH BOTTO

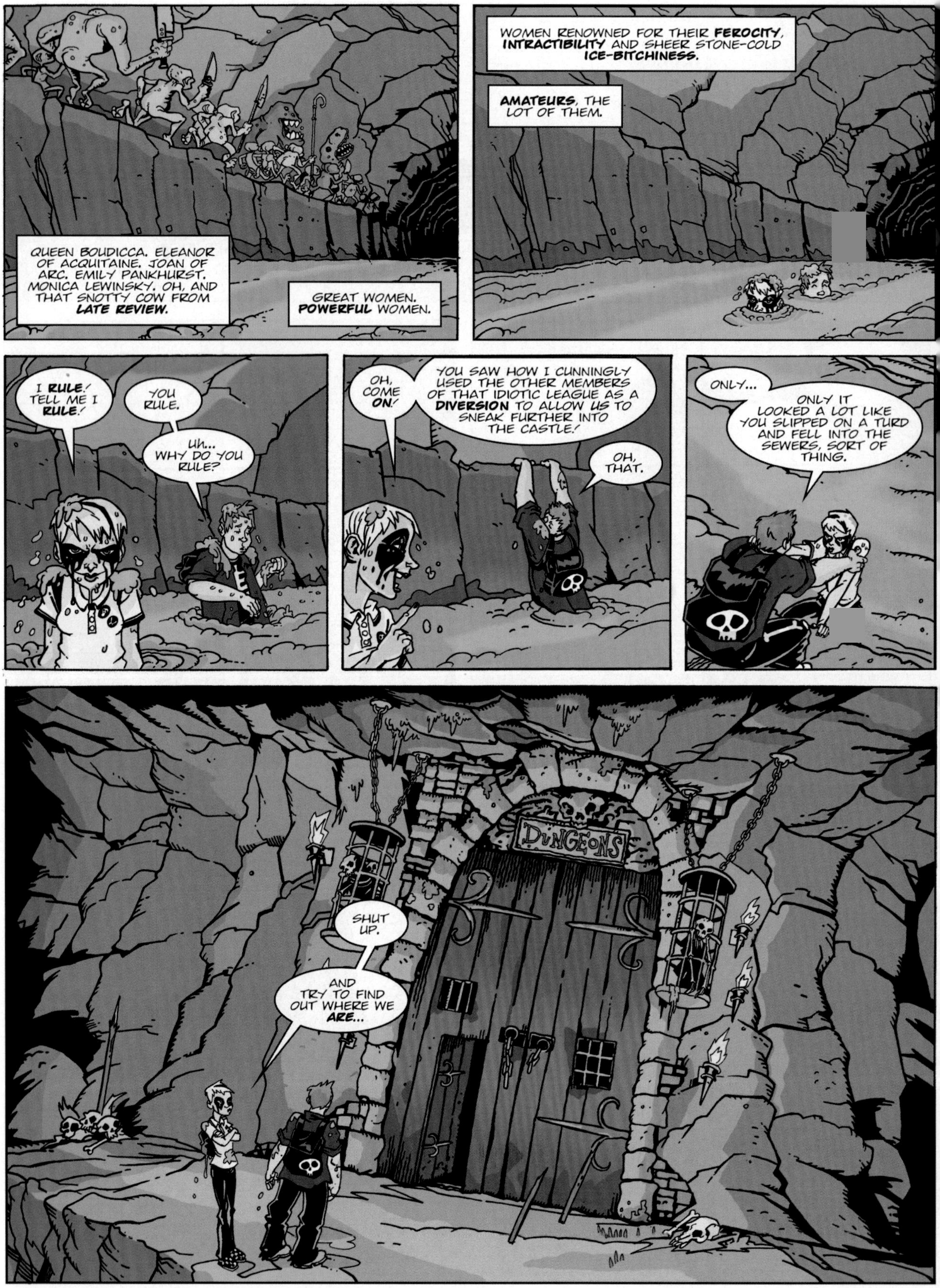

QUEEN BOUDICCA. ELEANOR OF ACQUITAINE. JOAN OF ARC. EMILY PANKHURST. MONICA LEWINSKY. OH, AND THAT SNOTTY COW FROM **LATE REVIEW**.
GREAT WOMEN. **POWERFUL** WOMEN.
WOMEN RENOWNED FOR THEIR **FEROCITY**, **INTRACTIBILITY** AND SHEER STONE-COLD **ICE-BITCHINESS**.
AMATEURS, THE LOT OF THEM.
I **RULE**! TELL ME I **RULE**!
YOU RULE.
UH... WHY DO YOU RULE?
OH, COME **ON**!
YOU SAW HOW I CUNNINGLY USED THE OTHER MEMBERS OF THAT IDIOTIC LEAGUE AS A **DIVERSION** TO ALLOW **US** TO SNEAK FURTHER INTO THE CASTLE!
OH, THAT.
ONLY...
ONLY IT LOOKED A LOT LIKE YOU SLIPPED ON A TURD AND FELL INTO THE SEWERS, SORT OF THING.
DUNGEONS
SHUT UP.
AND TRY TO FIND OUT WHERE WE **ARE**...

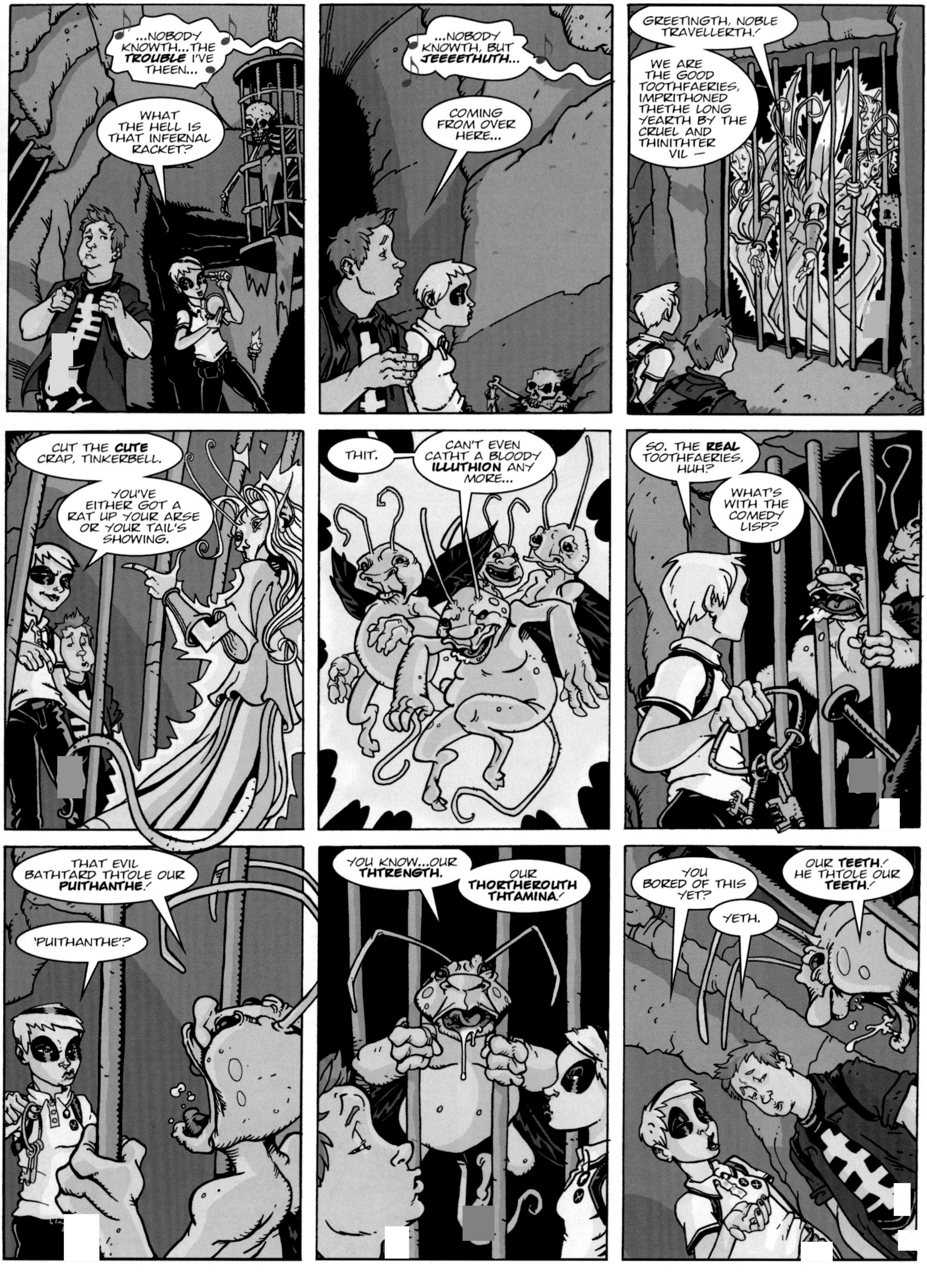
...NOBODY KNOWTH...THE **TROUBLE** I'VE THEEN...
WHAT THE HELL IS THAT INFERNAL RACKET?
...NOBODY KNOWTH, BUT **JEEEETHUTH**...
COMING FROM OVER HERE...
GREETINGTH, NOBLE TRAVELLERTH!
WE ARE THE GOOD TOOTHFAERIES, IMPRITHONED THETHE LONG YEARTH BY THE CRUEL AND THINITHTER VIL —
CUT THE **CUTE** CRAP, TINKERBELL.
YOU'VE EITHER GOT A RAT UP YOUR ARSE OR YOUR TAIL'S SHOWING.
THIT.
CAN'T EVEN CATHT A BLOODY **ILLUTHION** ANY MORE...
SO. THE **REAL** TOOTHFAERIES, HUH?
WHAT'S WITH THE COMEDY LISP?
THAT EVIL BATHTARD THTOLE OUR **PUITHANTHE**!
'PUITHANTHE'?
YOU KNOW...OUR **THTRENGTH.**
OUR **THORTHEROUTH THTAMINA**!
YOU BORED OF THIS YET?
YETH.
OUR **TEETH**! HE THTOLE OUR **TEETH**!

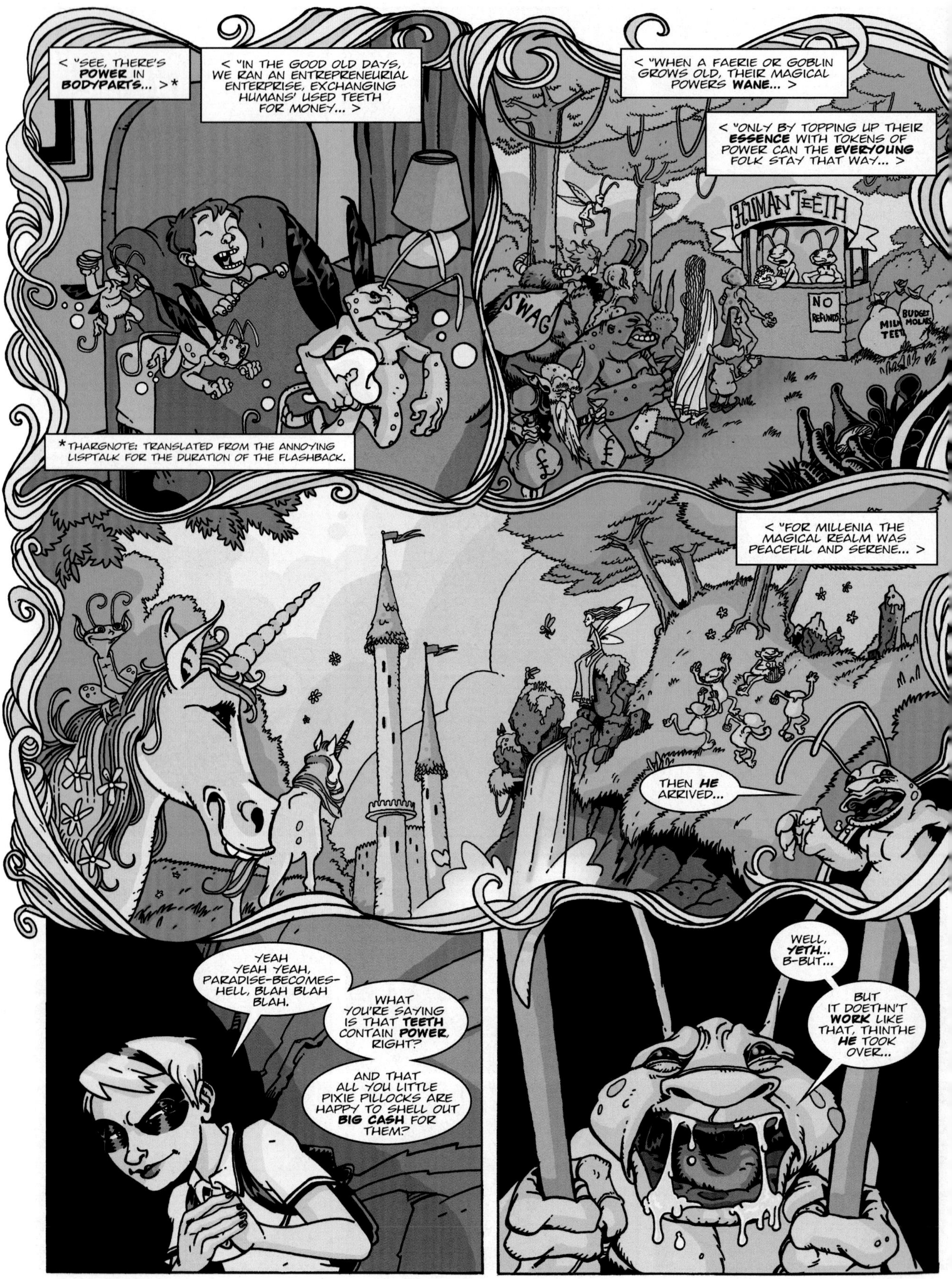

< "SEE, THERE'S POWER IN BODYPARTS... >*
< "IN THE GOOD OLD DAYS, WE RAN AN ENTREPRENEURIAL ENTERPRISE, EXCHANGING HUMANS' USED TEETH FOR MONEY... >
*THARGNOTE: TRANSLATED FROM THE ANNOYING LISPTALK FOR THE DURATION OF THE FLASHBACK.
< "WHEN A FAERIE OR GOBLIN GROWS OLD, THEIR MAGICAL POWERS WANE... >
< "ONLY BY TOPPING UP THEIR ESSENCE WITH TOKENS OF POWER CAN THE EVERYOUNG FOLK STAY THAT WAY... >
HUMAN TEETH
SWAG
NO REFUNDS
BUDGET MOLARS
< "FOR MILLENIA THE MAGICAL REALM WAS PEACEFUL AND SERENE... >
THEN HE ARRIVED...
YEAH YEAH YEAH, PARADISE-BECOMES-HELL, BLAH BLAH BLAH.
WHAT YOU'RE SAYING IS THAT TEETH CONTAIN POWER, RIGHT?
AND THAT ALL YOU LITTLE PIXIE PILLOCKS ARE HAPPY TO SHELL OUT BIG CASH FOR THEM?
WELL, YETH... B-BUT...
BUT IT DOETHN'T WORK LIKE THAT, THINTHE HE TOOK OVER...

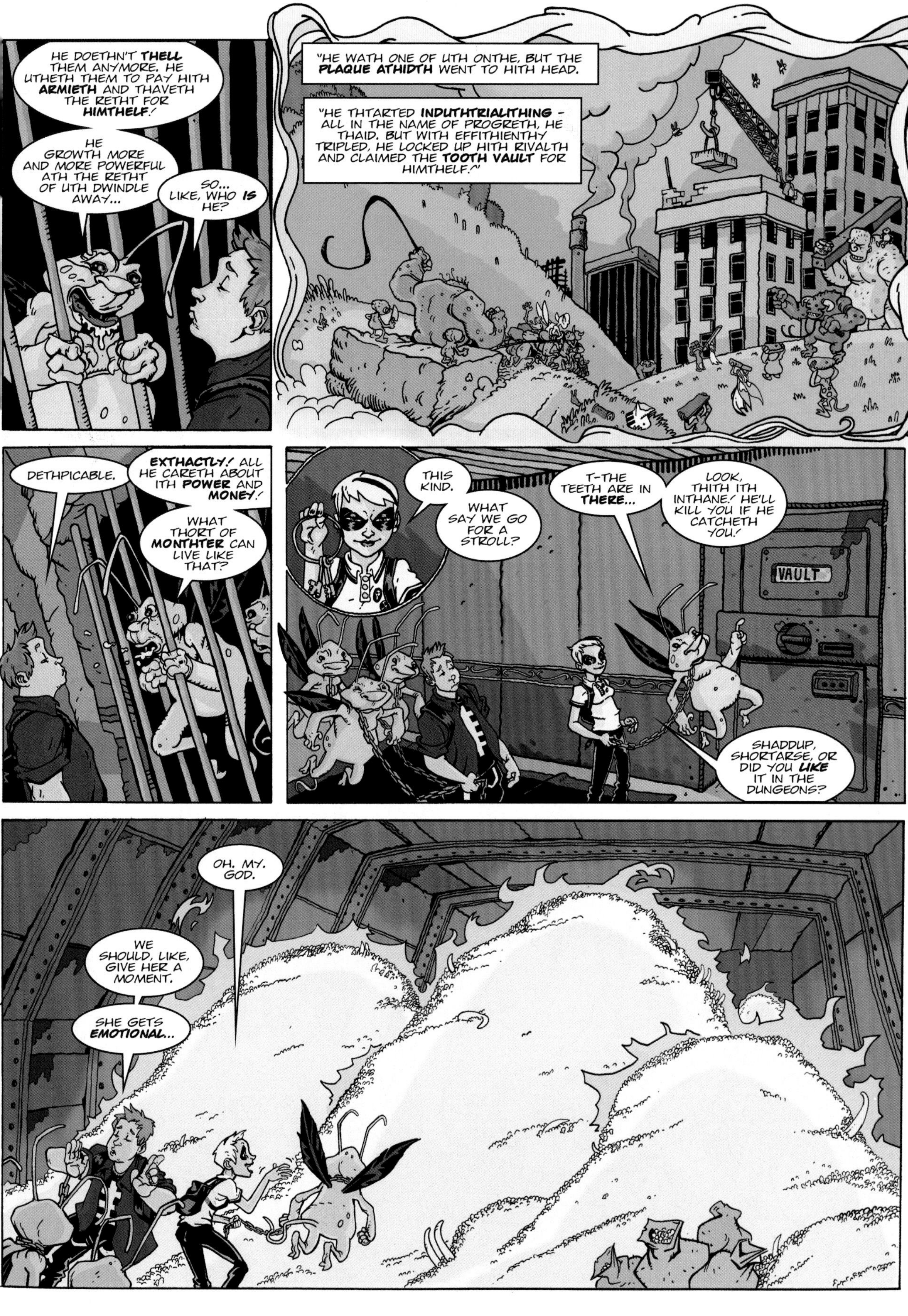
HE DOETHN'T THELL THEM ANYMORE. HE UTHETH THEM TO PAY HITH ARMIETH AND THAVETH THE RETHT FOR HIMTHELF!
HE GROWTH MORE AND MORE POWERFUL ATH THE RETHT OF UTH DWINDLE AWAY...
SO... LIKE, WHO IS HE?
"HE WATH ONE OF UTH ONTHE, BUT THE PLAQUE ATHIDTH WENT TO HITH HEAD.
"HE THTARTED INDUTHTRIALITHING - ALL IN THE NAME OF PROGRETH, HE THAID. BUT WITH EFFITHIENTHY TRIPLED, HE LOCKED UP HITH RIVALTH AND CLAIMED THE TOOTH VAULT FOR HIMTHELF."
DETHPICABLE.
EXTHACTLY! ALL HE CARETH ABOUT ITH POWER AND MONEY!
WHAT THORT OF MONTHTER CAN LIVE LIKE THAT?
THIS KIND.
WHAT SAY WE GO FOR A STROLL?
T-THE TEETH ARE IN THERE...
LOOK, THITH ITH INTHANE! HE'LL KILL YOU IF HE CATCHETH YOU!
VAULT
SHADDUP, SHORTARSE, OR DID YOU LIKE IT IN THE DUNGEONS?
OH. MY. GOD.
WE SHOULD, LIKE, GIVE HER A MOMENT.
SHE GETS EMOTIONAL...

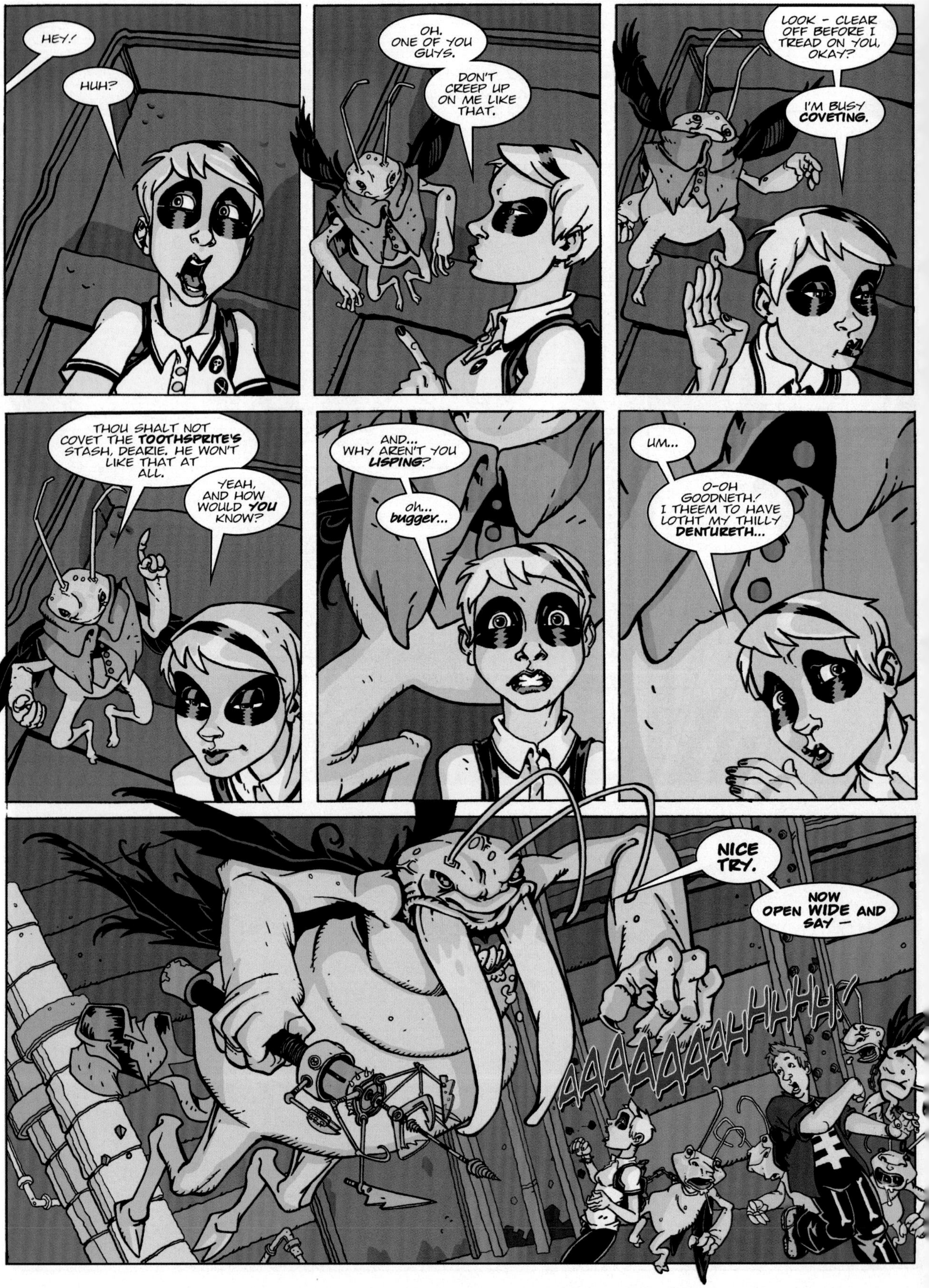
HEY!
HUH?
OH. ONE OF YOU GUYS.
DON'T CREEP UP ON ME LIKE THAT.
LOOK - CLEAR OFF BEFORE I TREAD ON YOU, OKAY?
I'M BUSY **COVETING.**
THOU SHALT NOT COVET THE **TOOTHSPRITE'S** STASH, DEARIE. HE WON'T LIKE THAT AT ALL.
YEAH, AND HOW WOULD **YOU** KNOW?
AND... WHY AREN'T YOU **LISPING**?
oh... **bugger...**
UM...
O-OH GOODNETH! I THEEM TO HAVE LOTHT MY THILLY **DENTURETH...**
NICE TRY.
NOW OPEN WIDE AND SAY —
AAAAAAAAHHHHH!

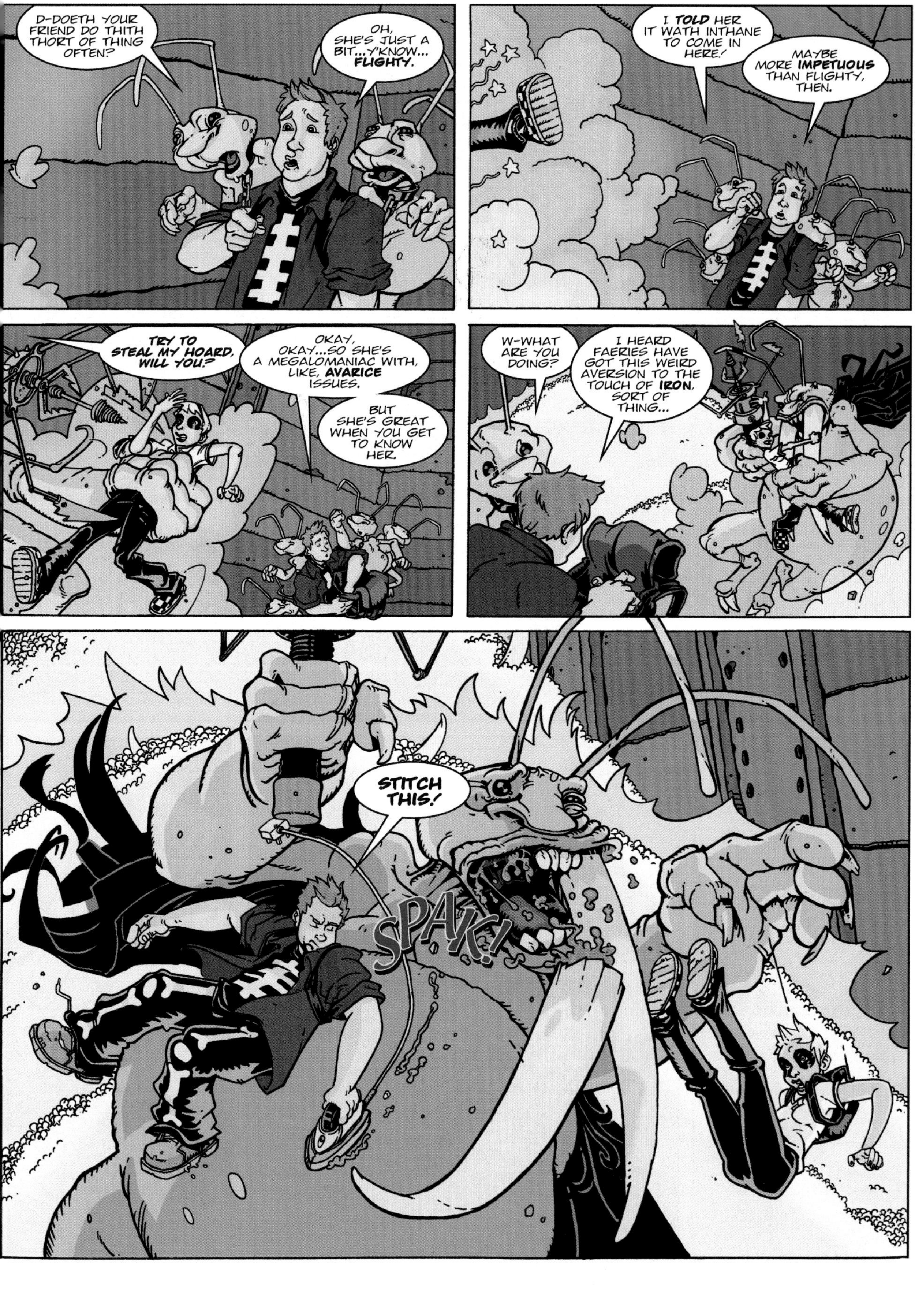

D-DOETH YOUR FRIEND DO THITH THORT OF THING OFTEN?
OH, SHE'S JUST A BIT...Y'KNOW... **FLIGHTY**.
I **TOLD** HER IT WATH INTHANE TO COME IN HERE!
MAYBE MORE **IMPETUOUS** THAN FLIGHTY, THEN.
TRY TO STEAL MY HOARD, WILL YOU?
OKAY, OKAY...SO SHE'S A MEGALOMANIAC WITH, LIKE, **AVARICE** ISSUES.
BUT SHE'S GREAT WHEN YOU GET TO KNOW HER.
W-WHAT ARE YOU DOING?
I HEARD FAERIES HAVE GOT THIS WEIRD AVERSION TO THE TOUCH OF **IRON**, SORT OF THING...
STITCH THIS!
SPAK!

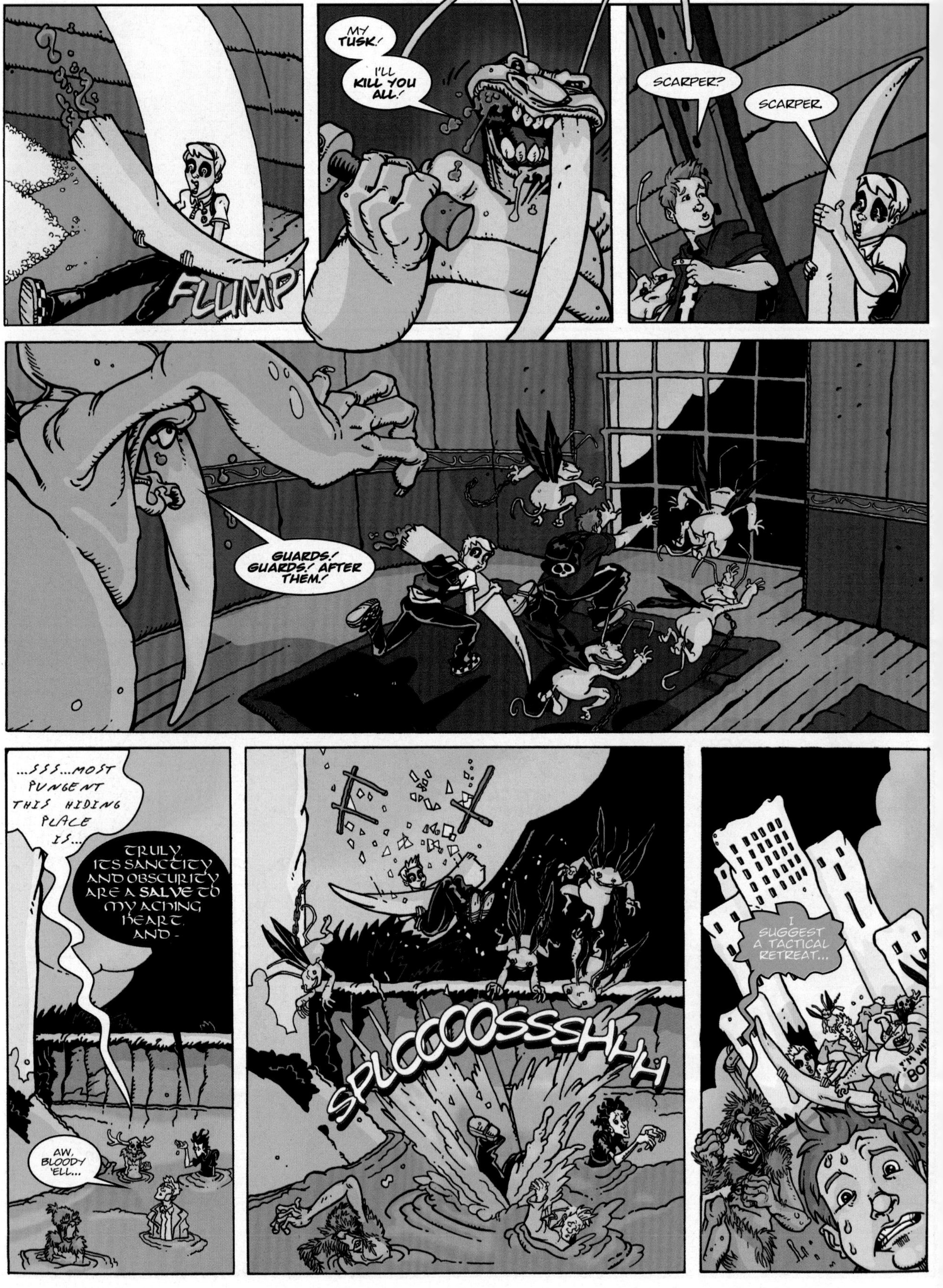
FLUMP
MY TUSK!
I'LL KILL YOU ALL!
SCARPER?
SCARPER.
GUARDS! GUARDS! AFTER THEM!
...SSS...MOST PUNGENT THIS HIDING PLACE IS...
TRULY. ITS SANCTITY AND OBSCURITY ARE A SALVE TO MY ACHING HEART. AND -
AW, BLOODY 'ELL...
SPLCCCOSSSSHHH
I SUGGEST A TACTICAL RETREAT...

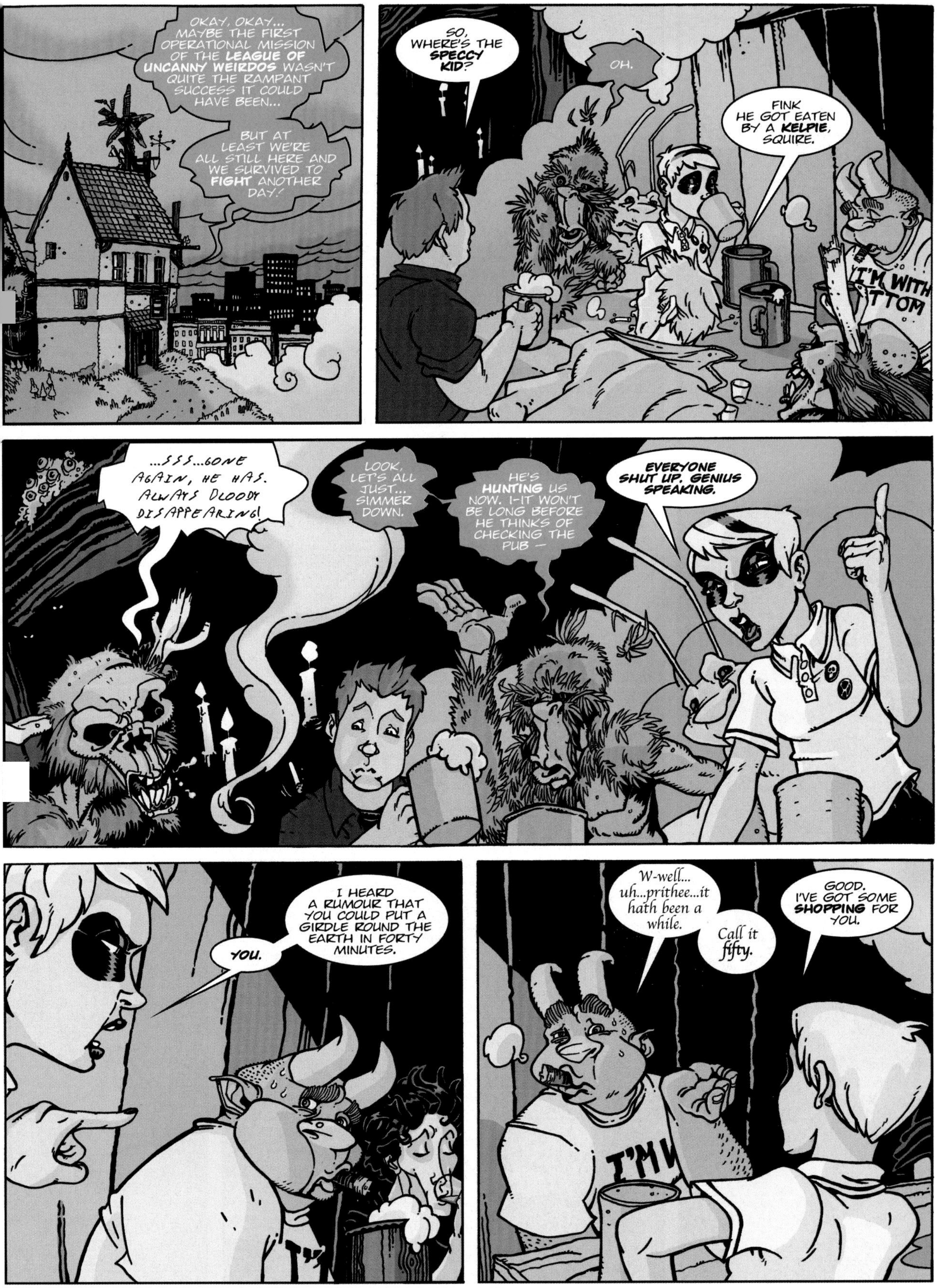
OKAY, OKAY... MAYBE THE FIRST OPERATIONAL MISSION OF THE LEAGUE OF UNCANNY WEIRDOS WASN'T QUITE THE RAMPANT SUCCESS IT COULD HAVE BEEN...
BUT AT LEAST WE'RE ALL STILL HERE AND WE SURVIVED TO FIGHT ANOTHER DAY!
SO, WHERE'S THE SPECCY KID?
OH.
FINK HE GOT EATEN BY A KELPIE, SQUIRE.
...SSS...GONE AGAIN, HE HAS. ALWAYS BLOODY DISAPPEARING!
LOOK, LET'S ALL JUST... SIMMER DOWN.
HE'S HUNTING US NOW. I-IT WON'T BE LONG BEFORE HE THINKS OF CHECKING THE PUB —
EVERYONE SHUT UP. GENIUS SPEAKING.
YOU.
I HEARD A RUMOUR THAT YOU COULD PUT A GIRDLE ROUND THE EARTH IN FORTY MINUTES.
W-well... uh...prithee...it hath been a while.
Call it fifty.
GOOD. I'VE GOT SOME SHOPPING FOR YOU.

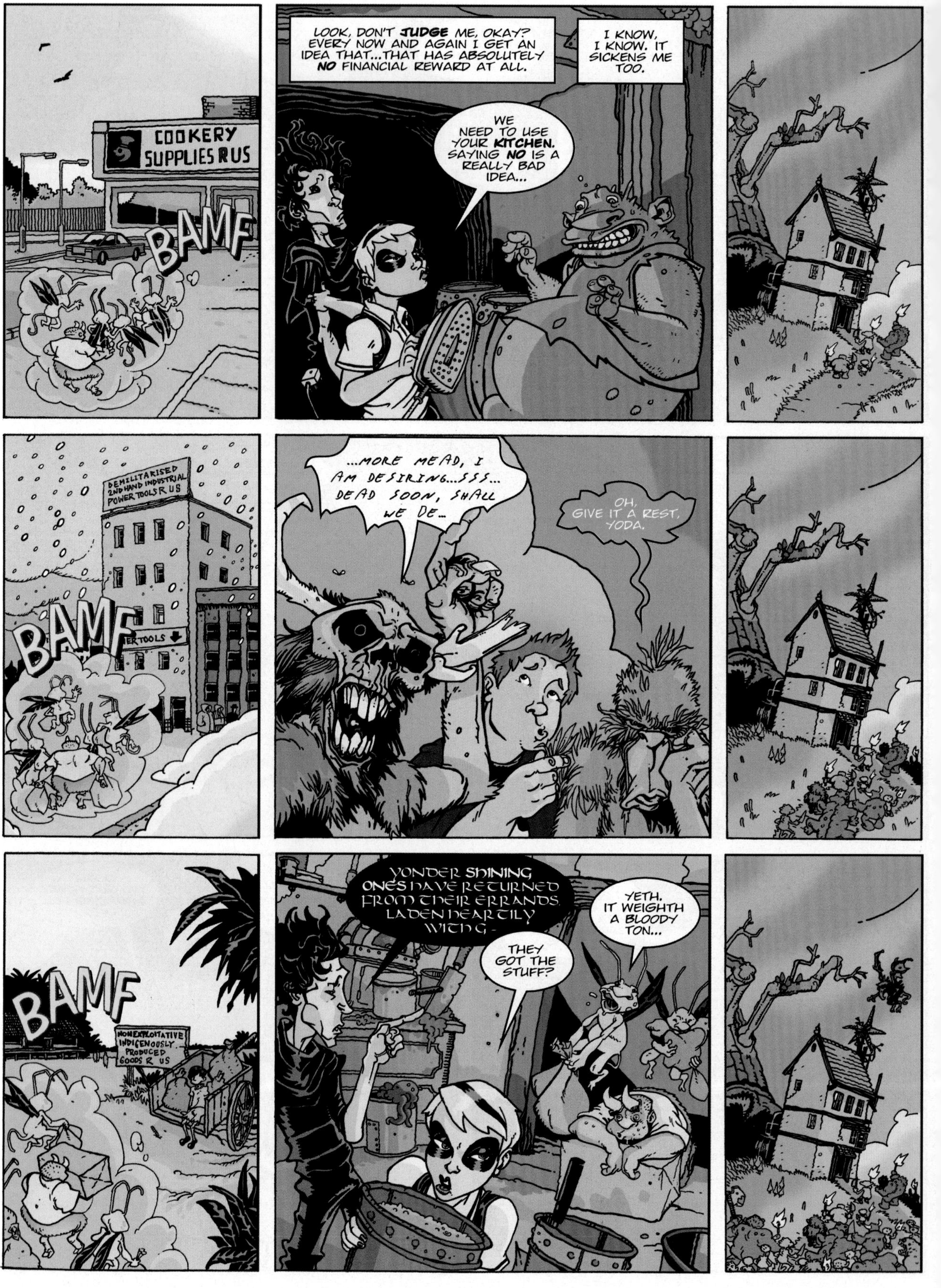
COOKERY SUPPLIES R US
BAMF
LOOK, DON'T JUDGE ME, OKAY? EVERY NOW AND AGAIN I GET AN IDEA THAT...THAT HAS ABSOLUTELY NO FINANCIAL REWARD AT ALL.
I KNOW, I KNOW. IT SICKENS ME TOO.
WE NEED TO USE YOUR KITCHEN. SAYING NO IS A REALLY BAD IDEA...
DEMILITARISED 2ND HAND INDUSTRIAL POWER TOOLS R US
ERTOOLS
BAMF
...MORE MEAD, I AM DESIRING...SSS... DEAD SOON, SHALL WE DE...
OH, GIVE IT A REST, YODA.
BAMF
NON EXPLOITATIVE INDIGENOUSLY PRODUCED GOODS R US
YONDER SHINING ONES HAVE RETURNED FROM THEIR ERRANDS, LADEN HEARTILY WITH G-
THEY GOT THE STUFF?
YETH, IT WEIGHTH A BLOODY TON...

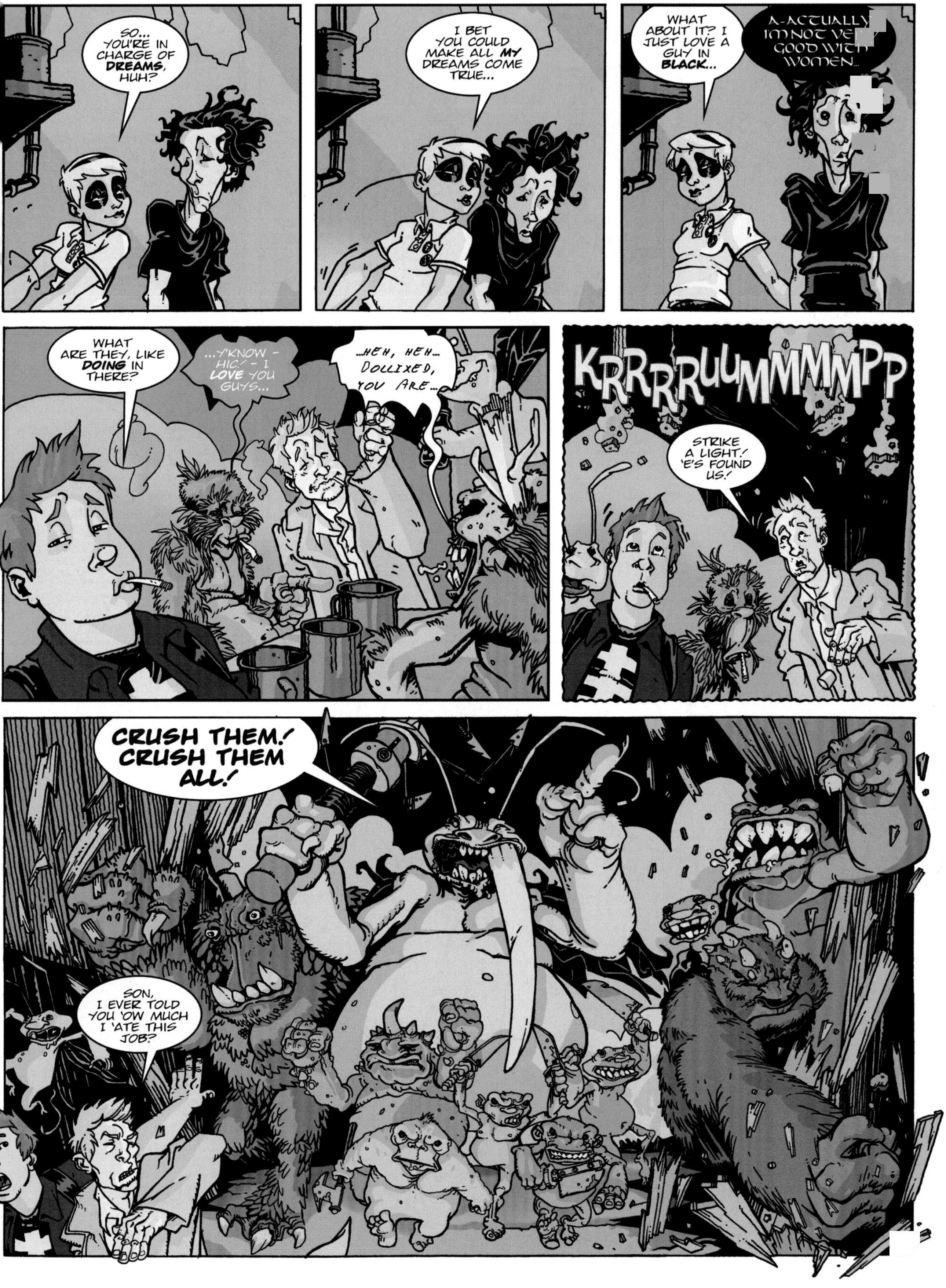
SO... YOU'RE IN CHARGE OF DREAMS, HUH?
I BET YOU COULD MAKE ALL MY DREAMS COME TRUE...
WHAT ABOUT IT? I JUST LOVE A GUY IN BLACK...
A-ACTUALLY I'M NOT VERY GOOD WITH WOMEN...
WHAT ARE THEY, LIKE DOING IN THERE?
...Y'KNOW - HIC! - I LOVE YOU GUYS...
...HEH, HEH... DOLLIXED, YOU ARE...
KRRRRUUMMMMPP
STRIKE A LIGHT! 'E'S FOUND US!
CRUSH THEM! CRUSH THEM ALL!
SON, I EVER TOLD YOU 'OW MUCH I 'ATE THIS JOB?

NOW... *YOU DIE!*

WAIT!

PLEASE — HERE'S YOUR *TUSK.* Y-YOU CAN HAVE IT BACK...

JUST DON'T HURT MY FRIENDS!

I KNOW WHAT YOU'RE THINKING...

YOU'RE THINKING THAT APPEALING TO A DESPICABLY EVIL, PSYCHOTIC FAERIE FOR *MERCY* SEEMS KIND OF DAFT, RIGHT?

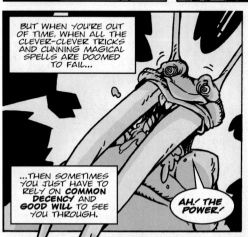

BUT WHEN YOU'RE OUT OF TIME, WHEN ALL THE CLEVER-CLEVER TRICKS AND CUNNING MAGICAL SPELLS ARE DOOMED TO FAIL...

...THEN SOMETIMES YOU JUST HAVE TO RELY ON *COMMON DECENCY* AND *GOOD WILL* TO SEE YOU THROUGH.

AH! THE POWER!

W-WHAT DO YOU SAY? WE DON'T *NEED* TO FIGHT. CAN'T WE ALL JUST...GET ALONG?

YOU'RE RIGHT. THERE'S NO NEED FOR THIS...THIS *HOSTILITY.*

IT'S A CYCLE OF VIOLENCE THAT *HAS* TO BE BROKEN, I CAN SEE THAT NOW...

BUT I'M GOING TO *CRUSH* YOU ANYWAY!

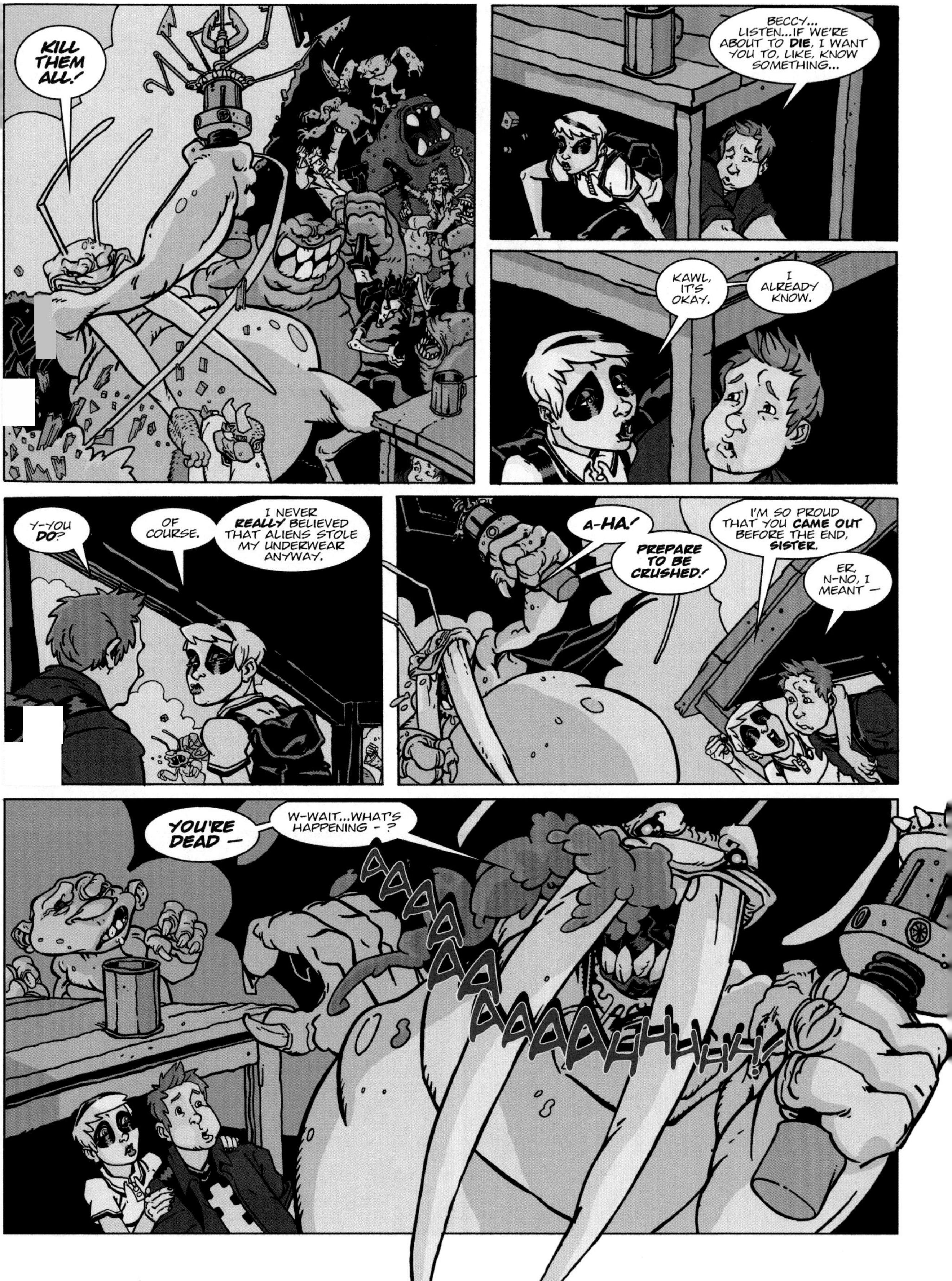
KILL THEM ALL!
BECCY... LISTEN...IF WE'RE ABOUT TO DIE, I WANT YOU TO, LIKE, KNOW SOMETHING...
KAWL, IT'S OKAY.
I ALREADY KNOW.
Y-YOU DO?
OF COURSE.
I NEVER REALLY BELIEVED THAT ALIENS STOLE MY UNDERWEAR ANYWAY.
A-HA!
PREPARE TO BE CRUSHED!
I'M SO PROUD THAT YOU CAME OUT BEFORE THE END, SISTER.
ER, N-NO, I MEANT —
YOU'RE DEAD —
W-WAIT...WHAT'S HAPPENING - ?
AAAAAAAAAAAAAHHHHHH!

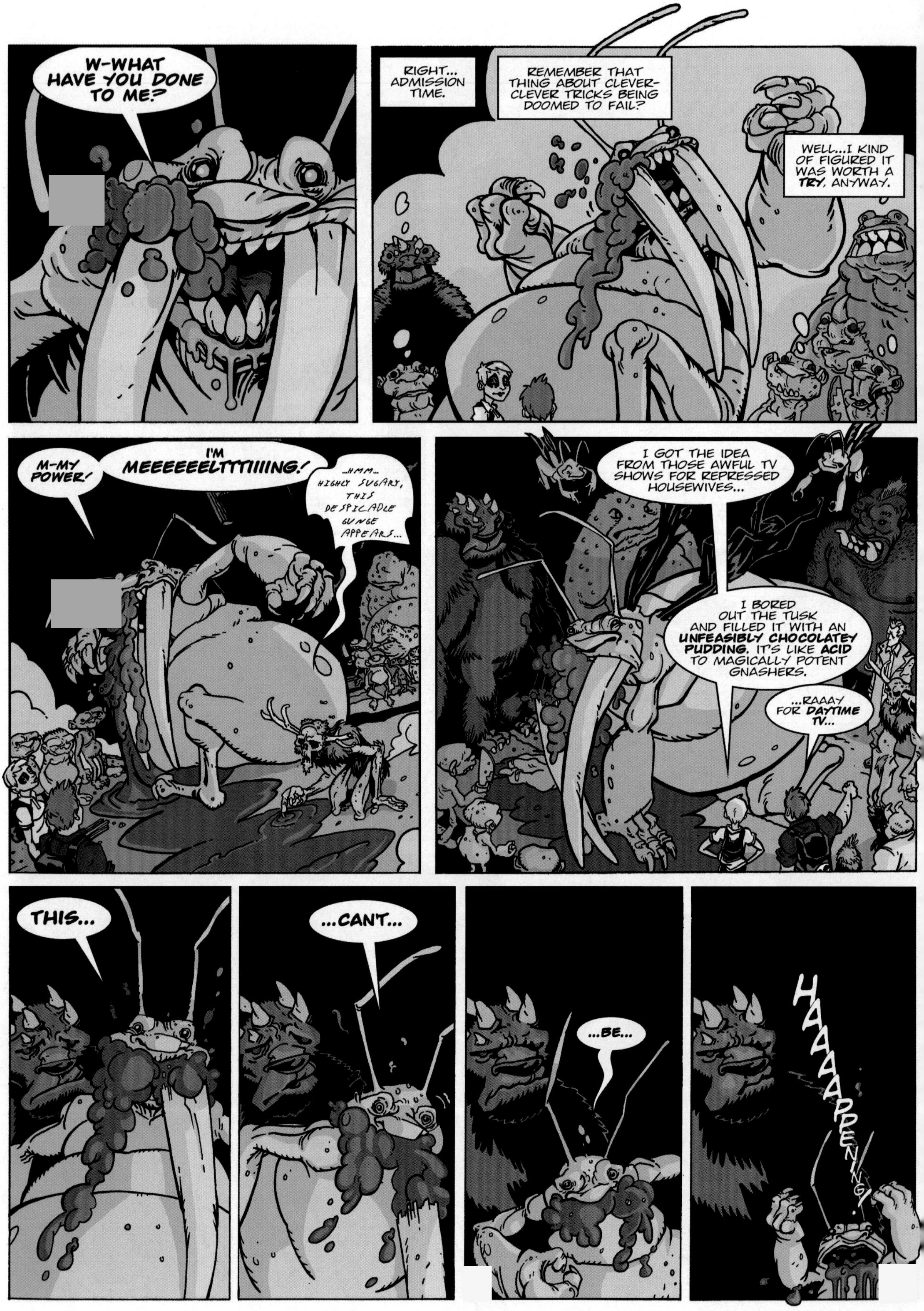

W-WHAT HAVE YOU DONE TO ME?
RIGHT... ADMISSION TIME.
REMEMBER THAT THING ABOUT CLEVER-CLEVER TRICKS BEING DOOMED TO FAIL?
WELL...I KIND OF FIGURED IT WAS WORTH A **TRY**, ANYWAY.
M-MY POWER!
I'M MEEEEEELTTTIIIING!
...HMM... HIGHLY SUGARY, THIS DESPICABLE GUNGE APPEARS...
I GOT THE IDEA FROM THOSE AWFUL TV SHOWS FOR REPRESSED HOUSEWIVES...
I BORED OUT THE TUSK AND FILLED IT WITH AN **UNFEASIBLY CHOCOLATEY PUDDING**. IT'S LIKE **ACID** TO MAGICALLY POTENT GNASHERS.
...RAAAY FOR **DAYTIME TV**...
THIS...
...CAN'T...
...BE...
HAAAAPPENING!

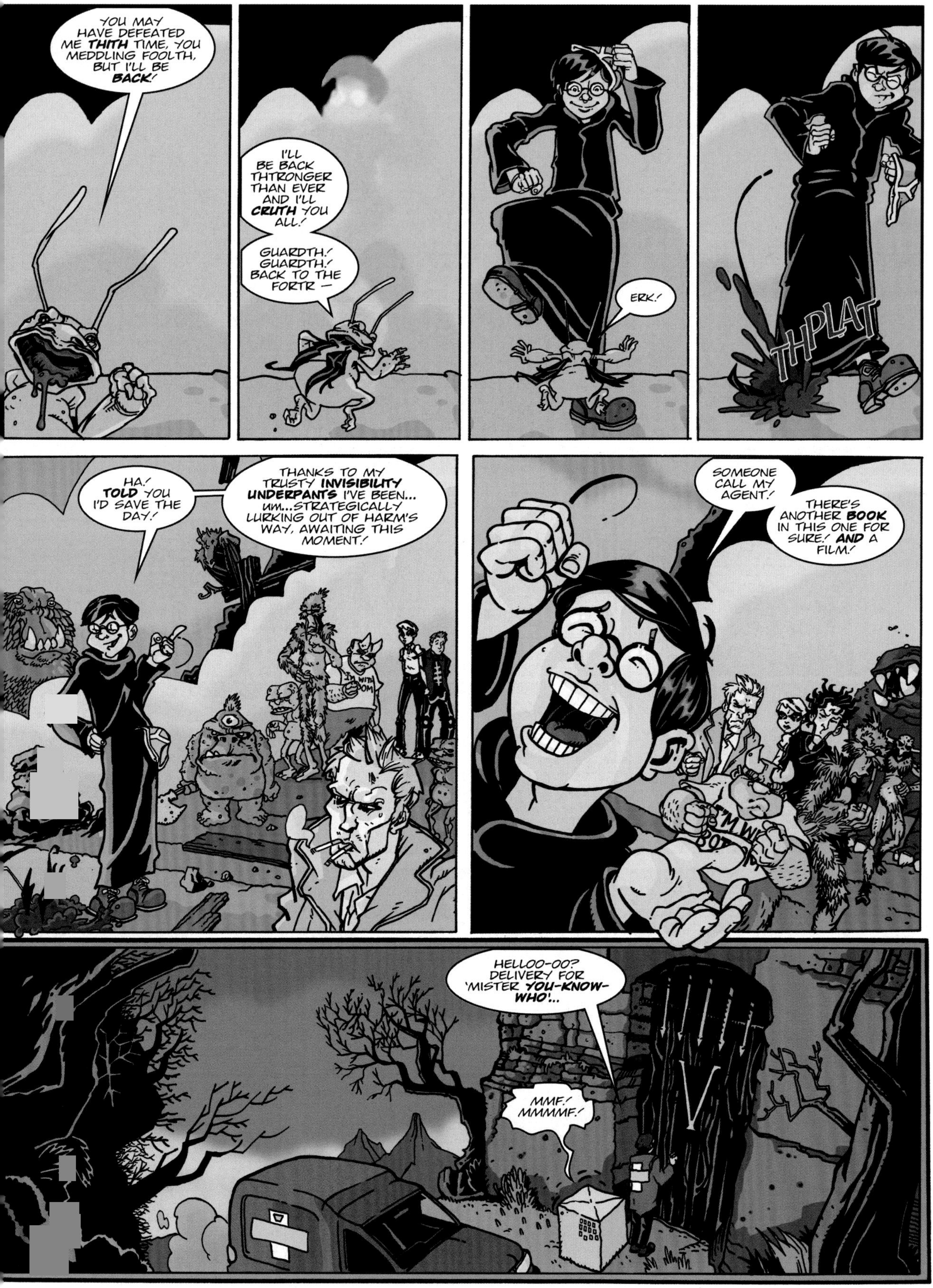
YOU MAY HAVE DEFEATED ME THITH TIME, YOU MEDDLING FOOLTH, BUT I'LL BE BACK!
I'LL BE BACK THTRONGER THAN EVER AND I'LL CRUTH YOU ALL!
GUARDTH! GUARDTH! BACK TO THE FORTR —
ERK!
THPLAT
HA! TOLD YOU I'D SAVE THE DAY!
THANKS TO MY TRUSTY INVISIBILITY UNDERPANTS I'VE BEEN... UM...STRATEGICALLY LURKING OUT OF HARM'S WAY, AWAITING THIS MOMENT!
SOMEONE CALL MY AGENT!
THERE'S ANOTHER BOOK IN THIS ONE FOR SURE! AND A FILM!
HELLOO-OO? DELIVERY FOR 'MISTER YOU-KNOW-WHO'...
MMF! MMMMF!

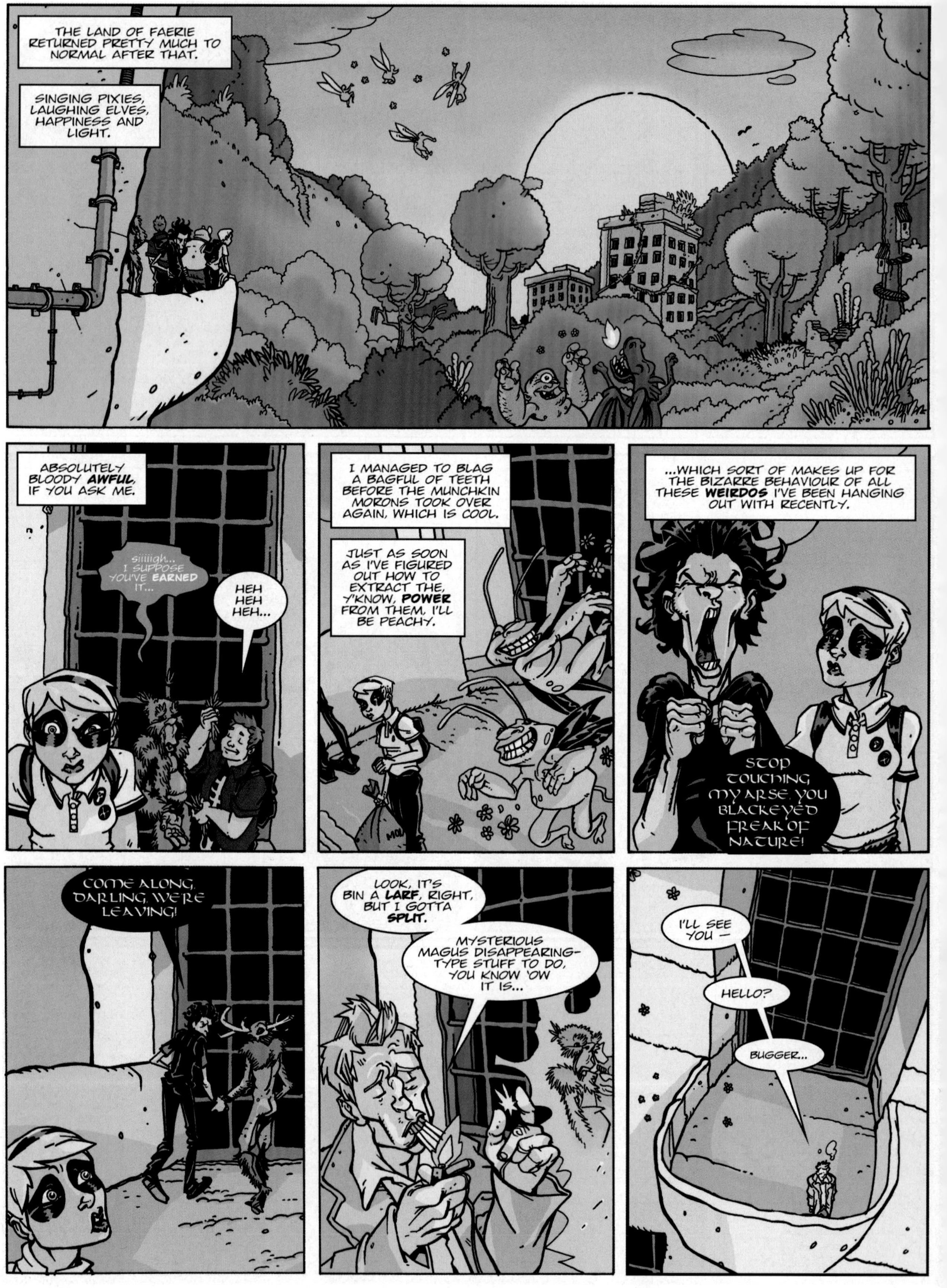
THE LAND OF FAERIE RETURNED PRETTY MUCH TO NORMAL AFTER THAT.
SINGING PIXIES, LAUGHING ELVES, HAPPINESS AND LIGHT.
ABSOLUTELY BLOODY AWFUL, IF YOU ASK ME.
siiiiigh... I SUPPOSE YOU'VE EARNED IT...
HEH HEH HEH...
I MANAGED TO BLAG A BAGFUL OF TEETH BEFORE THE MUNCHKIN MORONS TOOK OVER AGAIN, WHICH IS COOL.
JUST AS SOON AS I'VE FIGURED OUT HOW TO EXTRACT THE, Y'KNOW, POWER FROM THEM, I'LL BE PEACHY.
...WHICH SORT OF MAKES UP FOR THE BIZARRE BEHAVIOUR OF ALL THESE WEIRDOS I'VE BEEN HANGING OUT WITH RECENTLY.
STOP TOUCHING MY ARSE, YOU BLACKEYED FREAK OF NATURE!
COME ALONG, DARLING, WE'RE LEAVING!
LOOK, IT'S BIN A LARF, RIGHT, BUT I GOTTA SPLIT.
MYSTERIOUS MAGUS DISAPPEARING-TYPE STUFF TO DO, YOU KNOW 'OW IT IS...
I'LL SEE YOU —
HELLO?
BUGGER...

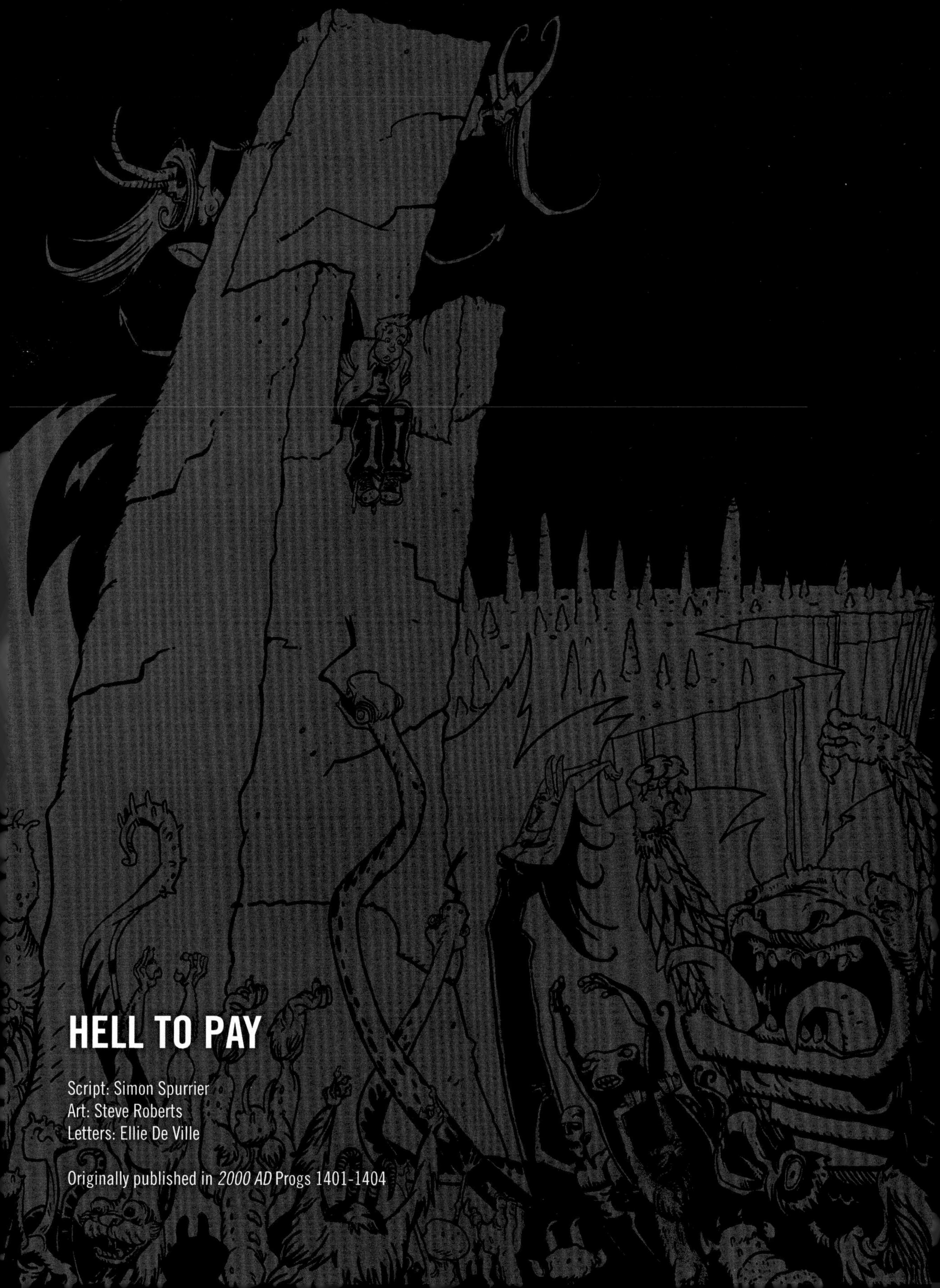

HELL TO PAY

Script: Simon Spurrier
Art: Steve Roberts
Letters: Ellie De Ville

Originally published in *2000 AD* Progs 1401-1404

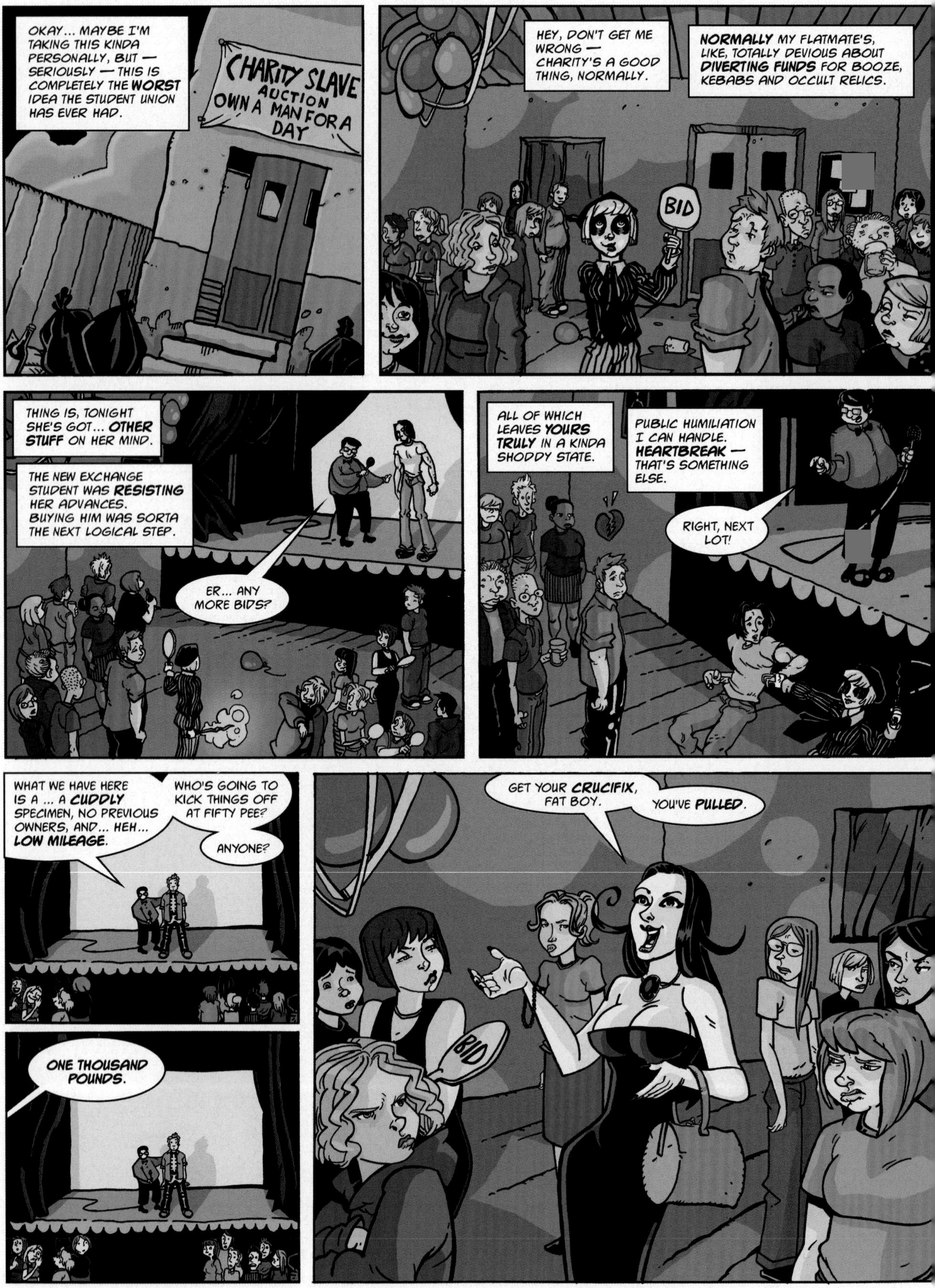
OKAY... MAYBE I'M TAKING THIS KINDA PERSONALLY, BUT — SERIOUSLY — THIS IS COMPLETELY THE **WORST** IDEA THE STUDENT UNION HAS EVER HAD.
CHARITY SLAVE AUCTION OWN A MAN FOR A DAY
HEY, DON'T GET ME WRONG — CHARITY'S A GOOD THING, NORMALLY.
NORMALLY MY FLATMATE'S, LIKE, TOTALLY DEVIOUS ABOUT **DIVERTING FUNDS** FOR BOOZE, KEBABS AND OCCULT RELICS.
BID
THING IS, TONIGHT SHE'S GOT... **OTHER STUFF** ON HER MIND.
THE NEW EXCHANGE STUDENT WAS **RESISTING** HER ADVANCES. BUYING HIM WAS SORTA THE NEXT LOGICAL STEP.
ER... ANY MORE BIDS?
ALL OF WHICH LEAVES **YOURS TRULY** IN A KINDA SHODDY STATE.
PUBLIC HUMILIATION I CAN HANDLE. **HEARTBREAK** — THAT'S SOMETHING ELSE.
RIGHT, NEXT LOT!
WHAT WE HAVE HERE IS A ... A **CUDDLY** SPECIMEN, NO PREVIOUS OWNERS, AND... HEH... **LOW MILEAGE**.
WHO'S GOING TO KICK THINGS OFF AT FIFTY PEE?
ANYONE?
ONE THOUSAND POUNDS.
GET YOUR **CRUCIFIX**, FAT BOY.
YOU'VE **PULLED**.
BID

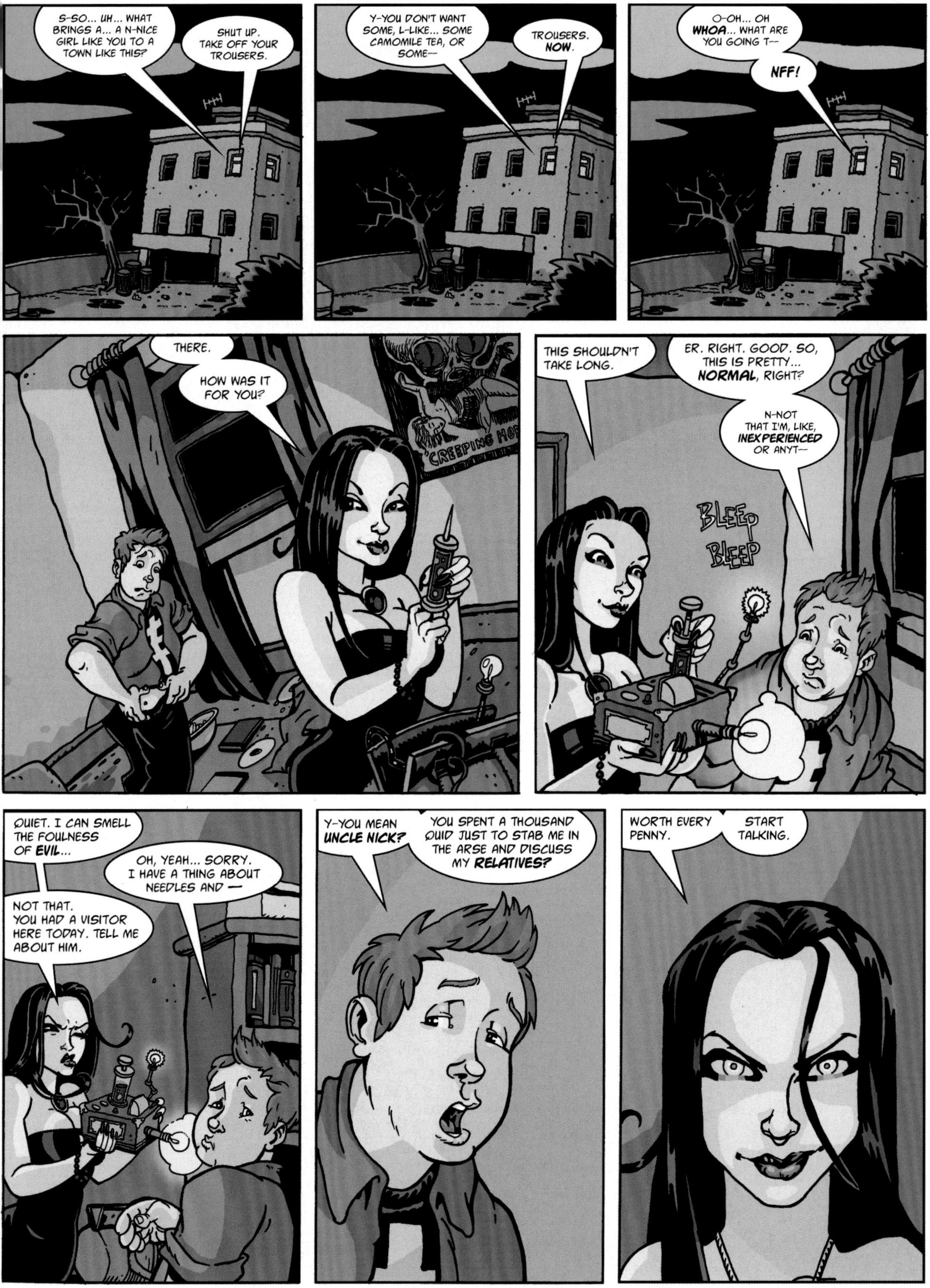
S-SO... UH... WHAT BRINGS A... A N-NICE GIRL LIKE YOU TO A TOWN LIKE THIS?
SHUT UP. TAKE OFF YOUR TROUSERS.
Y-YOU DON'T WANT SOME, L-LIKE... SOME CAMOMILE TEA, OR SOME--
TROUSERS. NOW.
O-OH... OH WHOA... WHAT ARE YOU GOING T--
NFF!
THERE.
HOW WAS IT FOR YOU?
CREEPING HOR
THIS SHOULDN'T TAKE LONG.
ER. RIGHT. GOOD. SO, THIS IS PRETTY... NORMAL, RIGHT?
N-NOT THAT I'M, LIKE, INEXPERIENCED OR ANYT--
BLEEP
BLEEP
QUIET. I CAN SMELL THE FOULNESS OF EVIL...
OH, YEAH... SORRY. I HAVE A THING ABOUT NEEDLES AND —
NOT THAT. YOU HAD A VISITOR HERE TODAY. TELL ME ABOUT HIM.
Y-YOU MEAN UNCLE NICK?
YOU SPENT A THOUSAND QUID JUST TO STAB ME IN THE ARSE AND DISCUSS MY RELATIVES?
WORTH EVERY PENNY.
START TALKING.

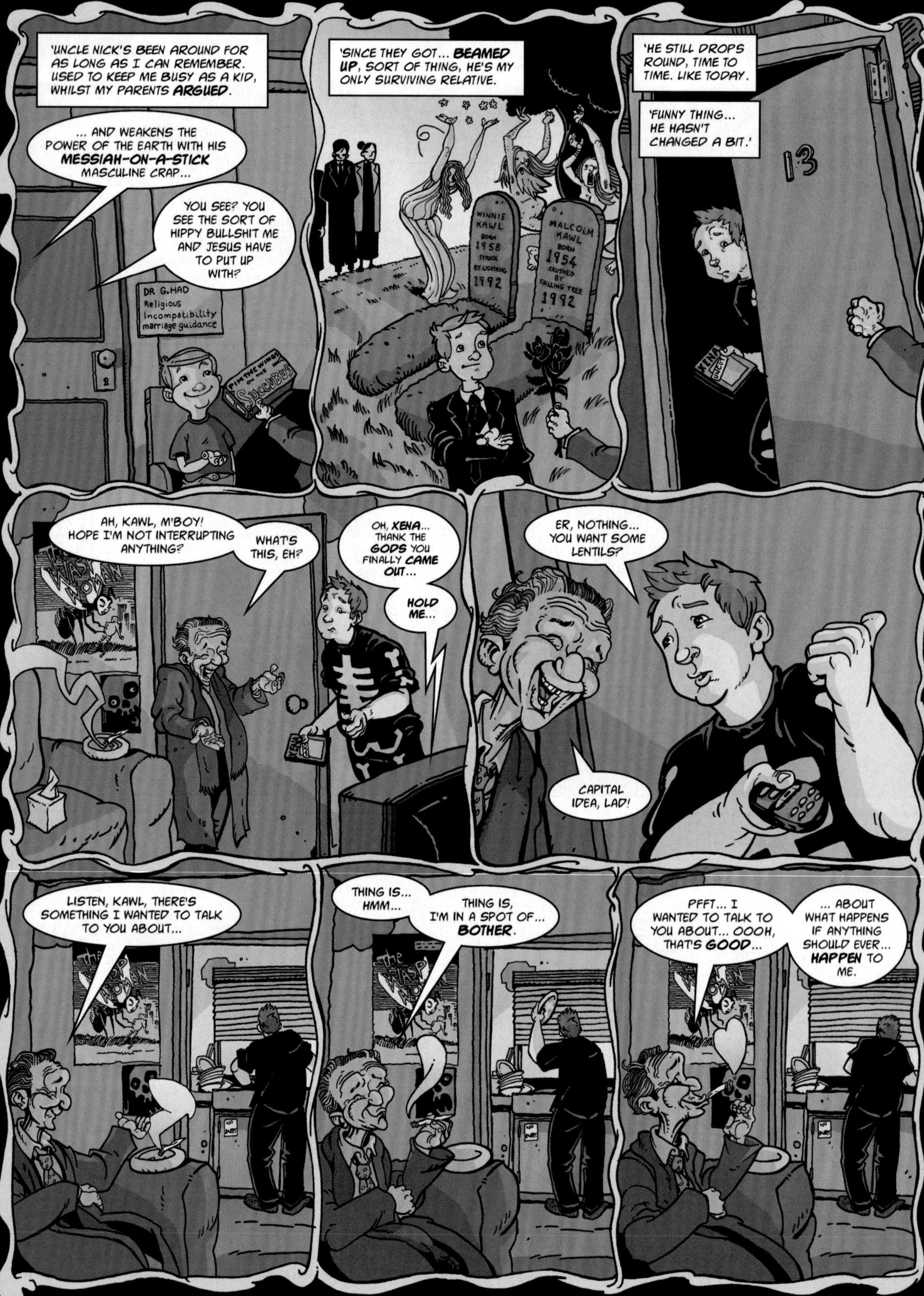
'UNCLE NICK'S BEEN AROUND FOR AS LONG AS I CAN REMEMBER. USED TO KEEP ME BUSY AS A KID, WHILST MY PARENTS ARGUED.
... AND WEAKENS THE POWER OF THE EARTH WITH HIS MESSIAH-ON-A-STICK MASCULINE CRAP...
YOU SEE? YOU SEE THE SORT OF HIPPY BULLSHIT ME AND JESUS HAVE TO PUT UP WITH?
DR G. HAD Religious Incompatibility marriage guidance
PIN THE WINGS ON THE SUCCUBUS
'SINCE THEY GOT... BEAMED UP, SORT OF THING, HE'S MY ONLY SURVIVING RELATIVE.
WINNIE KAWL BORN 1958 STRUCK BY LIGHTNING 1992
MALCOLM KAWL BORN 1954 CRUSHED BY FALLING TREE 1992
'HE STILL DROPS ROUND, TIME TO TIME. LIKE TODAY.
'FUNNY THING... HE HASN'T CHANGED A BIT.'
13
XENA
AH, KAWL, M'BOY! HOPE I'M NOT INTERRUPTING ANYTHING?
WHAT'S THIS, EH?
OH, XENA... THANK THE GODS YOU FINALLY CAME OUT...
HOLD ME...
THE WASP WOMAN
ER, NOTHING... YOU WANT SOME LENTILS?
CAPITAL IDEA, LAD!
LISTEN, KAWL, THERE'S SOMETHING I WANTED TO TALK TO YOU ABOUT...
THING IS... HMM...
THING IS, I'M IN A SPOT OF... BOTHER.
PFFT... I WANTED TO TALK TO YOU ABOUT... OOOH, THAT'S GOOD...
... ABOUT WHAT HAPPENS IF ANYTHING SHOULD EVER... HAPPEN TO ME.

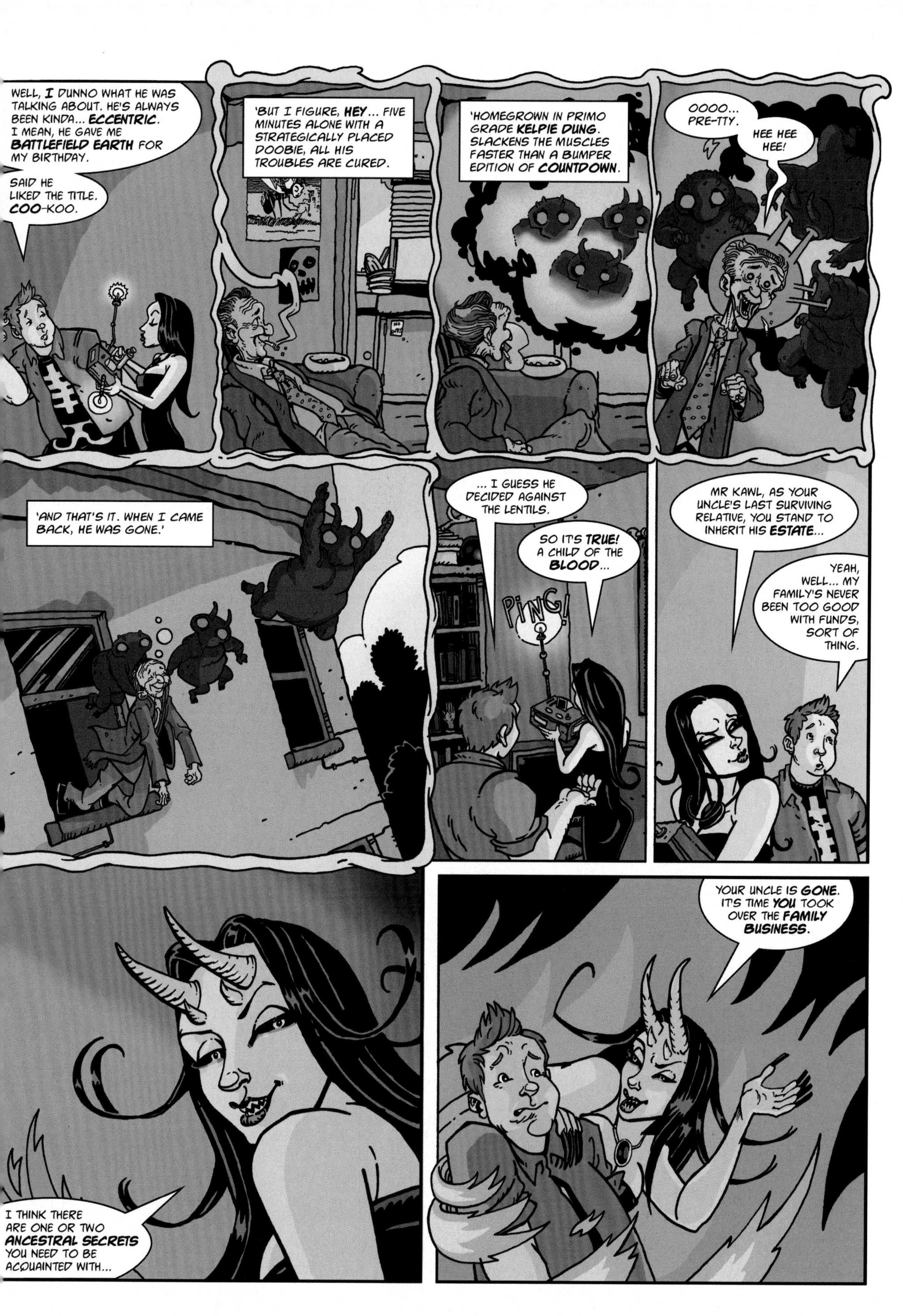
WELL, I DUNNO WHAT HE WAS TALKING ABOUT. HE'S ALWAYS BEEN KINDA... ECCENTRIC. I MEAN, HE GAVE ME BATTLEFIELD EARTH FOR MY BIRTHDAY.
SAID HE LIKED THE TITLE. COO-KOO.
'BUT I FIGURE, HEY... FIVE MINUTES ALONE WITH A STRATEGICALLY PLACED DOOBIE, ALL HIS TROUBLES ARE CURED.
'HOMEGROWN IN PRIMO GRADE KELPIE DUNG. SLACKENS THE MUSCLES FASTER THAN A BUMPER EDITION OF COUNTDOWN.
OOOO... PRE-TTY.
HEE HEE HEE!
'AND THAT'S IT. WHEN I CAME BACK, HE WAS GONE.'
... I GUESS HE DECIDED AGAINST THE LENTILS.
SO IT'S TRUE! A CHILD OF THE BLOOD...
PING!
MR KAWL, AS YOUR UNCLE'S LAST SURVIVING RELATIVE, YOU STAND TO INHERIT HIS ESTATE...
YEAH, WELL... MY FAMILY'S NEVER BEEN TOO GOOD WITH FUNDS, SORT OF THING.
I THINK THERE ARE ONE OR TWO ANCESTRAL SECRETS YOU NEED TO BE ACQUAINTED WITH...
YOUR UNCLE IS GONE. IT'S TIME YOU TOOK OVER THE FAMILY BUSINESS.

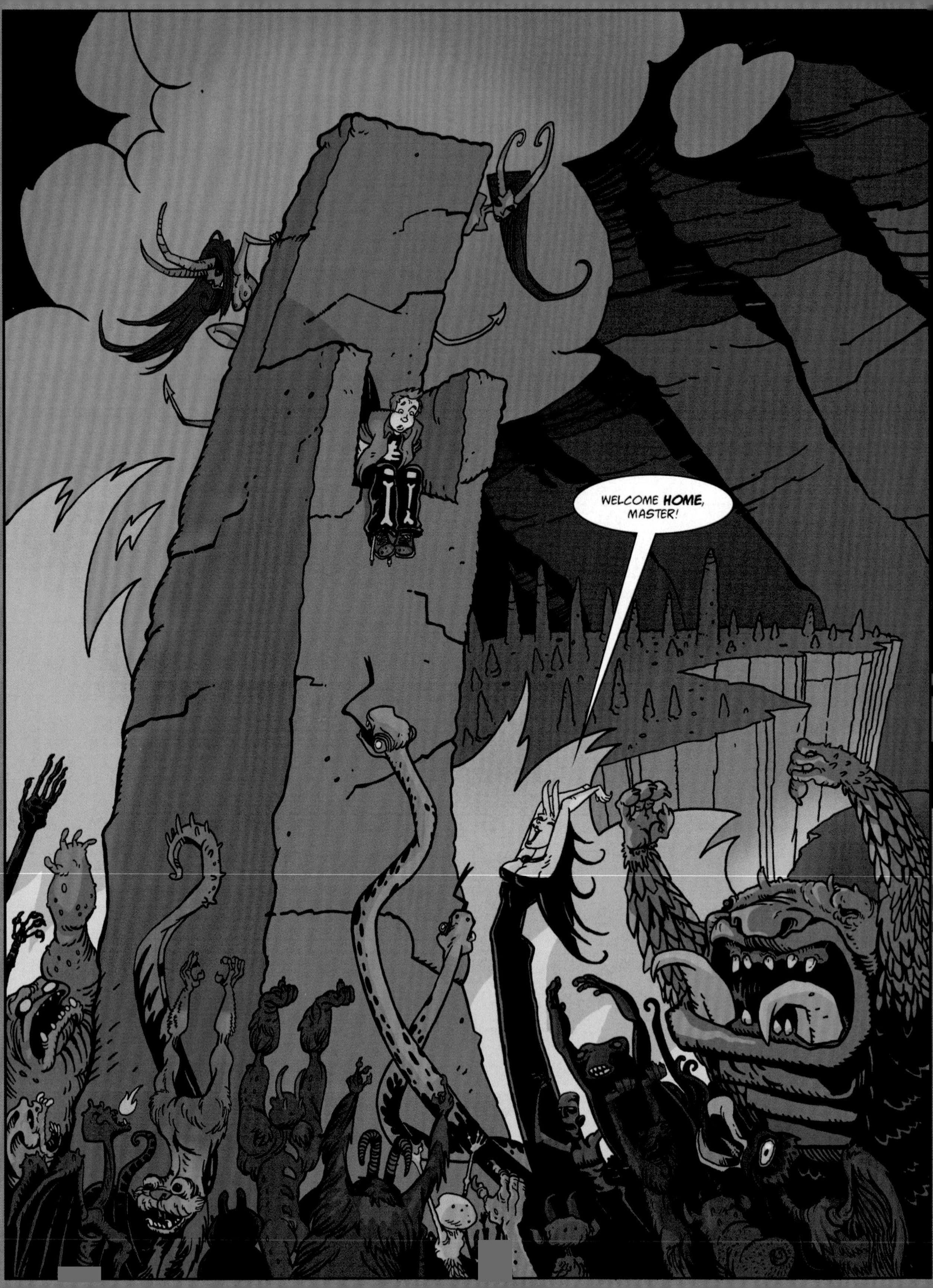
WELCOME **HOME**, MASTER!

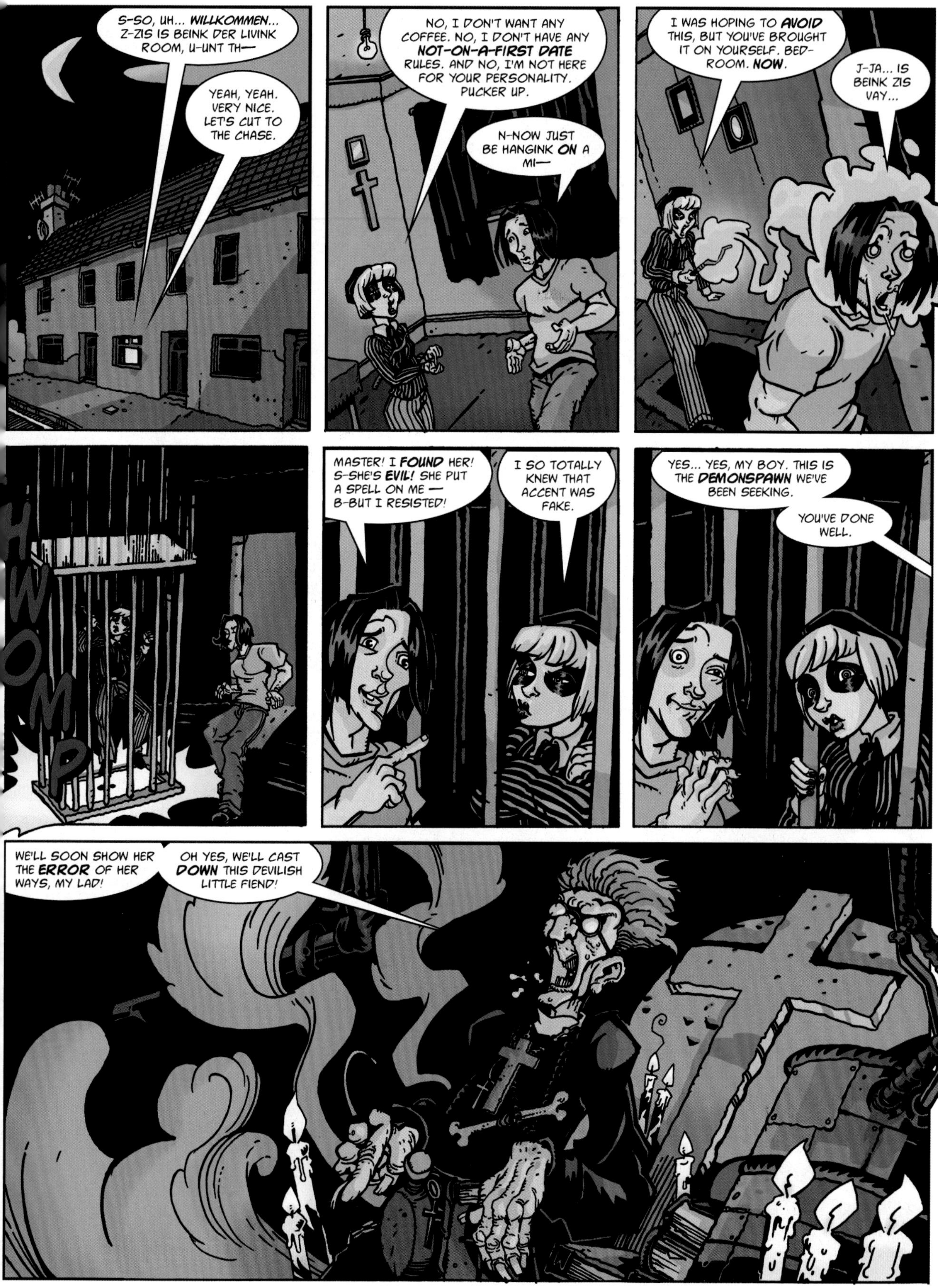
S-SO, UH... WILLKOMMEN... Z-ZIS IS BEINK DER LIVINK ROOM, U-UNT TH—
YEAH, YEAH. VERY NICE. LET'S CUT TO THE CHASE.
NO, I DON'T WANT ANY COFFEE. NO, I DON'T HAVE ANY NOT-ON-A-FIRST DATE RULES. AND NO, I'M NOT HERE FOR YOUR PERSONALITY. PUCKER UP.
N-NOW JUST BE HANGINK ON A MI—
I WAS HOPING TO AVOID THIS, BUT YOU'VE BROUGHT IT ON YOURSELF. BED-ROOM. NOW.
J-JA... IS BEINK ZIS VAY...
WHWOMP
MASTER! I FOUND HER! S-SHE'S EVIL! SHE PUT A SPELL ON ME — B-BUT I RESISTED!
I SO TOTALLY KNEW THAT ACCENT WAS FAKE.
YES... YES, MY BOY. THIS IS THE DEMONSPAWN WE'VE BEEN SEEKING.
YOU'VE DONE WELL.
WE'LL SOON SHOW HER THE ERROR OF HER WAYS, MY LAD!
OH YES, WE'LL CAST DOWN THIS DEVILISH LITTLE FIEND!

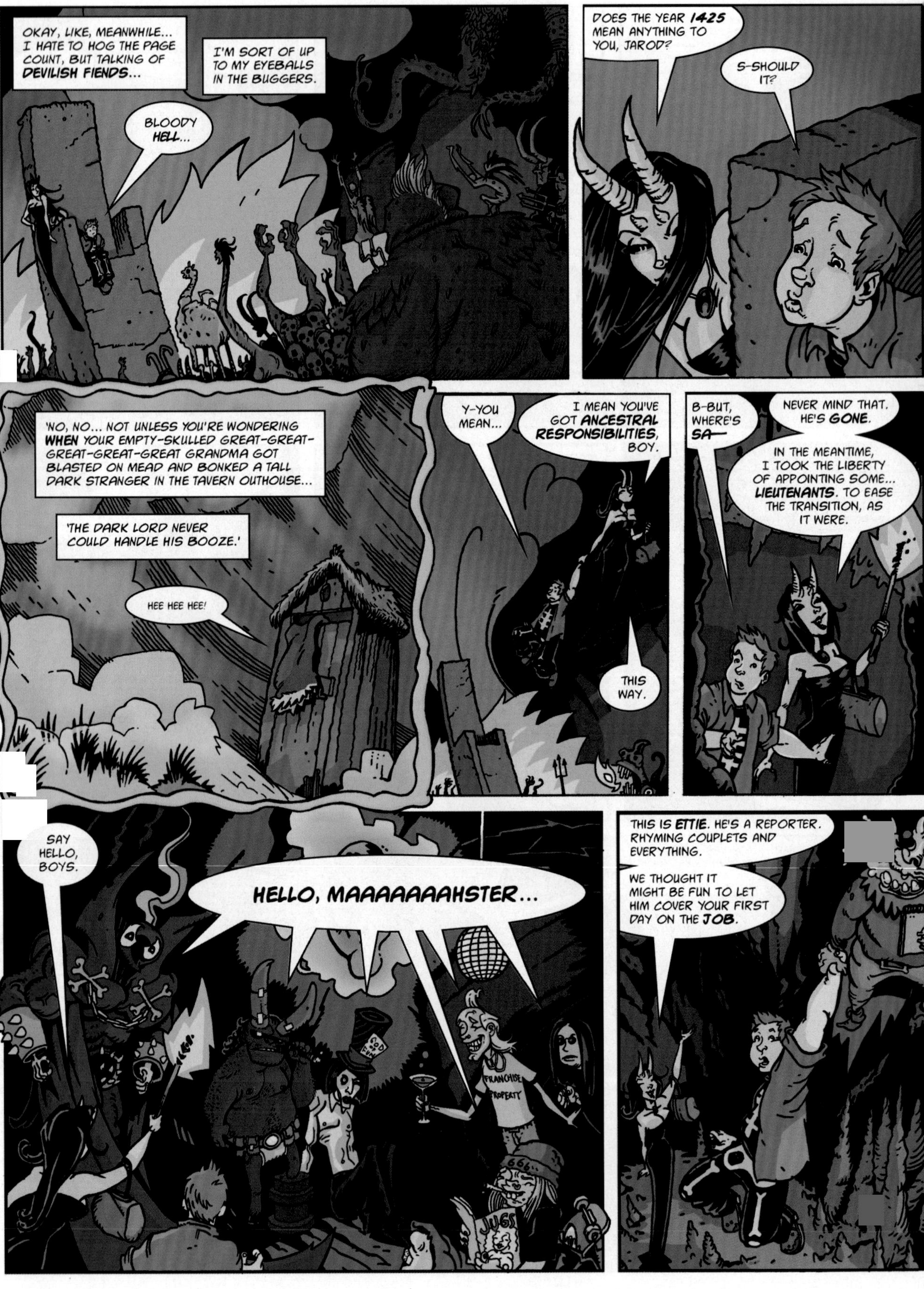

OKAY, LIKE, MEANWHILE... I HATE TO HOG THE PAGE COUNT, BUT TALKING OF **DEVILISH FIENDS**...
I'M SORT OF UP TO MY EYEBALLS IN THE BUGGERS.
BLOODY **HELL**...
DOES THE YEAR **1425** MEAN ANYTHING TO YOU, JAROD?
S-SHOULD IT?
'NO, NO... NOT UNLESS YOU'RE WONDERING **WHEN** YOUR EMPTY-SKULLED GREAT-GREAT-GREAT-GREAT-GREAT GRANDMA GOT BLASTED ON MEAD AND BONKED A TALL DARK STRANGER IN THE TAVERN OUTHOUSE...
'THE DARK LORD NEVER COULD HANDLE HIS BOOZE.'
HEE HEE HEE!
Y-YOU MEAN...
I MEAN YOU'VE GOT **ANCESTRAL RESPONSIBILITIES**, BOY.
THIS WAY.
B-BUT, WHERE'S **SA—**
NEVER MIND THAT. HE'S **GONE**.
IN THE MEANTIME, I TOOK THE LIBERTY OF APPOINTING SOME... **LIEUTENANTS**. TO EASE THE TRANSITION, AS IT WERE.
SAY HELLO, BOYS.
HELLO, MAAAAAAAHSTER...
FRANCHISE PROPERTY
666
JUGS
THIS IS **ETTIE**. HE'S A REPORTER. RHYMING COUPLETS AND EVERYTHING.
WE THOUGHT IT MIGHT BE FUN TO LET HIM COVER YOUR FIRST DAY ON THE **JOB**.

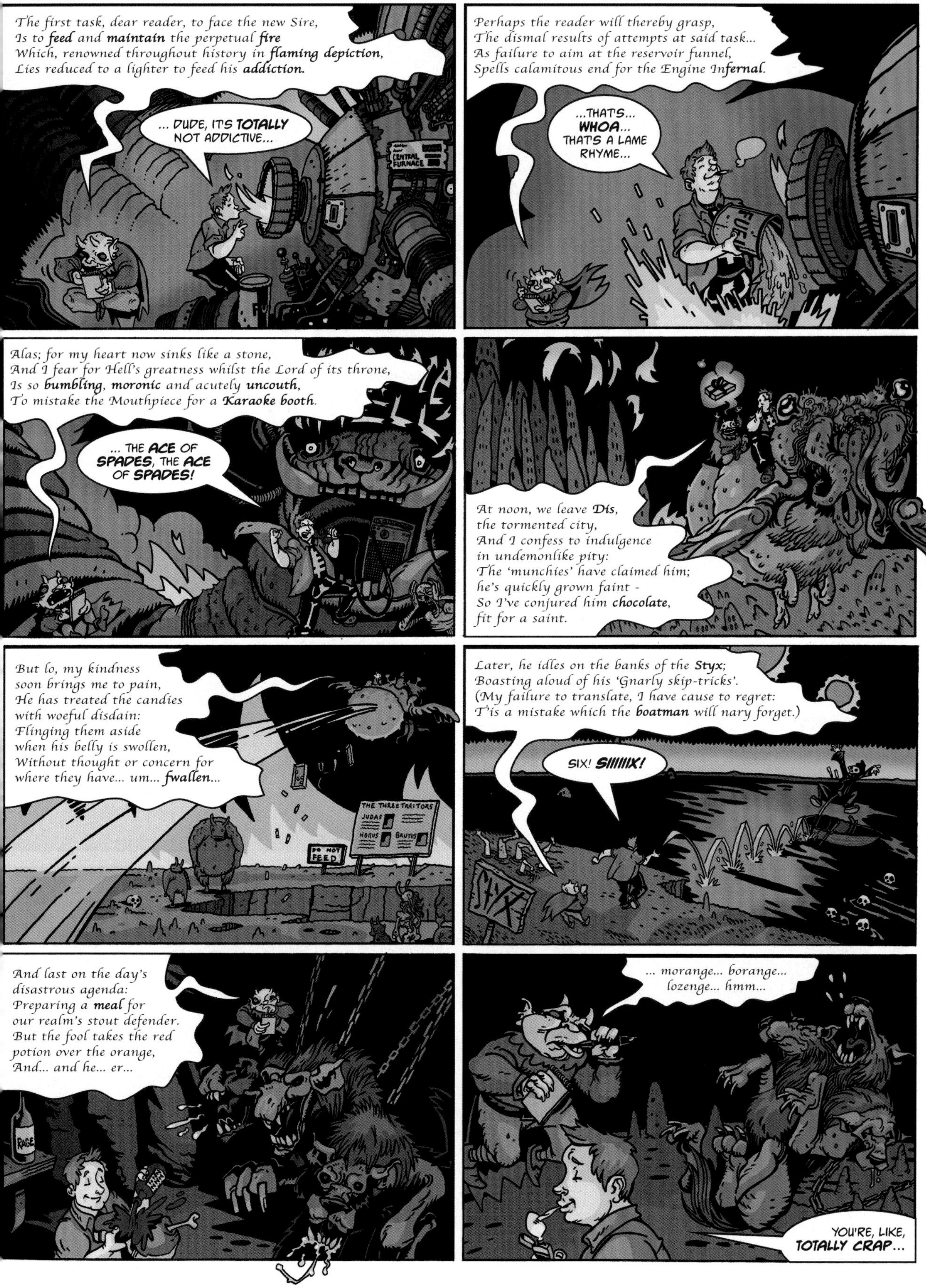
The first task, dear reader, to face the new Sire,
Is to **feed** and **maintain** the perpetual **fire**
Which, renowned throughout history in **flaming depiction**,
Lies reduced to a lighter to feed his **addiction.**
... DUDE, IT'S **TOTALLY** NOT ADDICTIVE...
CENTRAL FURNACE
Perhaps the reader will thereby grasp,
The dismal results of attempts at said task...
As failure to aim at the reservoir funnel,
Spells calamitous end for the Engine **Infernal**.
...THAT'S... **WHOA**... THAT'S A LAME RHYME...
Alas; for my heart now sinks like a stone,
And I fear for Hell's greatness whilst the Lord of its throne,
Is so **bumbling**, **moronic** and acutely **uncouth**,
To mistake the Mouthpiece for a **Karaoke booth**.
... THE **ACE** OF **SPADES**, THE **ACE** OF **SPADES!**
At noon, we leave **Dis**,
the tormented city,
And I confess to indulgence
in undemonlike pity:
The 'munchies' have claimed him;
he's quickly grown faint -
So I've conjured him **chocolate**,
fit for a saint.
But lo, my kindness
soon brings me to pain,
He has treated the candies
with woeful disdain:
Flinging them aside
when his belly is swollen,
Without thought or concern for
where they have... um... **fwallen**...
THE THREE TRAITORS
JUDAS
DO NOT FEED
Later, he idles on the banks of the **Styx**;
Boasting aloud of his 'Gnarly skip-tricks'.
(My failure to translate, I have cause to regret:
T'is a mistake which the **boatman** will nary forget.)
SIX! **SIIIIIIX!**
STYX
And last on the day's
disastrous agenda:
Preparing a **meal** for
our realm's stout defender.
But the fool takes the red
potion over the orange,
And... and he... er...
RAGE
... morange... borange...
lozenge... hmm...
YOU'RE, LIKE, **TOTALLY CRAP**...

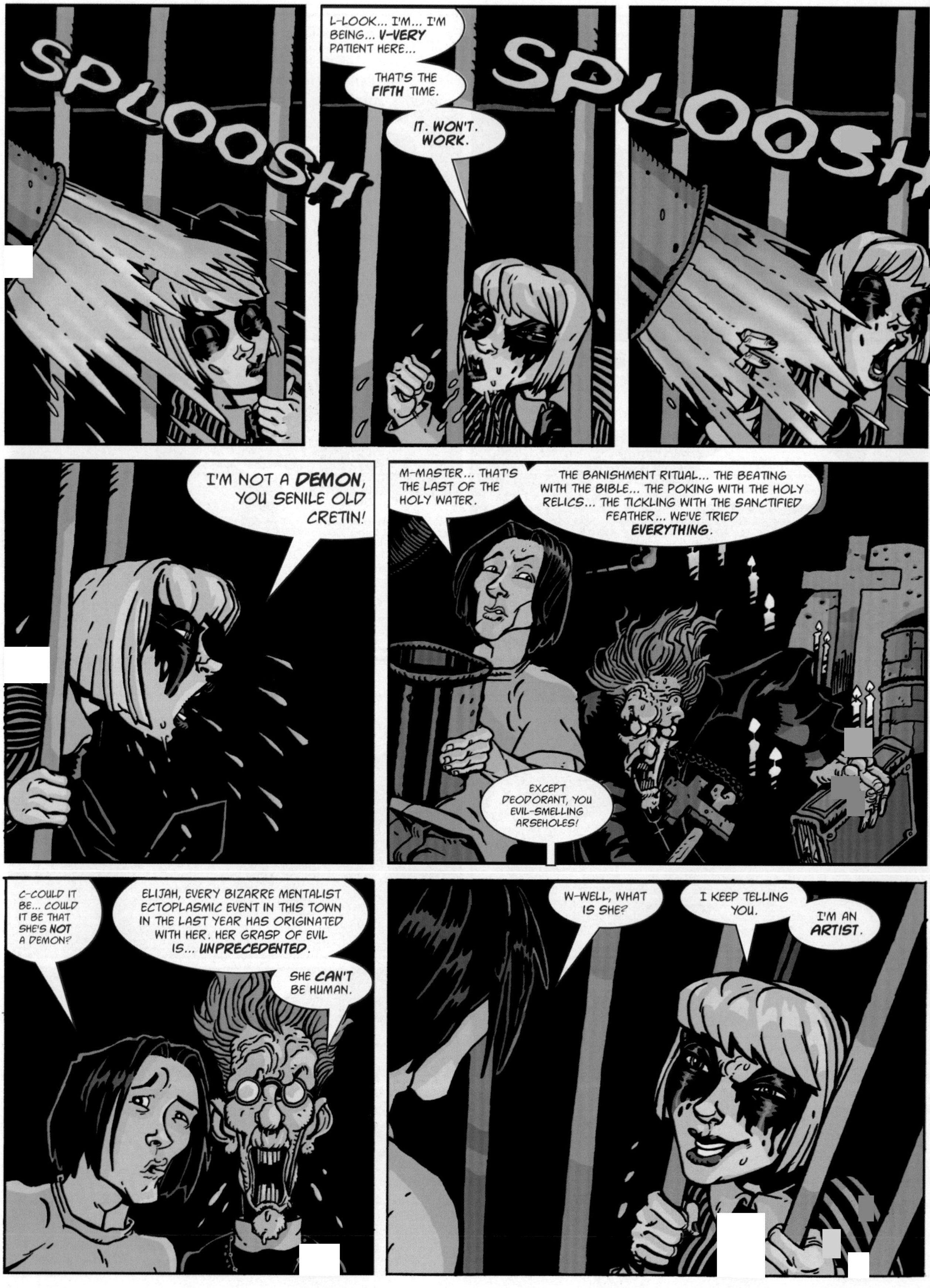

SPLOOSH
L-LOOK... I'M... I'M BEING... V-VERY PATIENT HERE...
THAT'S THE FIFTH TIME.
IT. WON'T. WORK.
SPLOOSH
I'M NOT A DEMON, YOU SENILE OLD CRETIN!
M-MASTER... THAT'S THE LAST OF THE HOLY WATER.
THE BANISHMENT RITUAL... THE BEATING WITH THE BIBLE... THE POKING WITH THE HOLY RELICS... THE TICKLING WITH THE SANCTIFIED FEATHER... WE'VE TRIED EVERYTHING.
EXCEPT DEODORANT, YOU EVIL-SMELLING ARSEHOLES!
C-COULD IT BE... COULD IT BE THAT SHE'S NOT A DEMON?
ELIJAH, EVERY BIZARRE MENTALIST ECTOPLASMIC EVENT IN THIS TOWN IN THE LAST YEAR HAS ORIGINATED WITH HER. HER GRASP OF EVIL IS... UNPRECEDENTED.
SHE CAN'T BE HUMAN.
W-WELL, WHAT IS SHE?
I KEEP TELLING YOU.
I'M AN ARTIST.

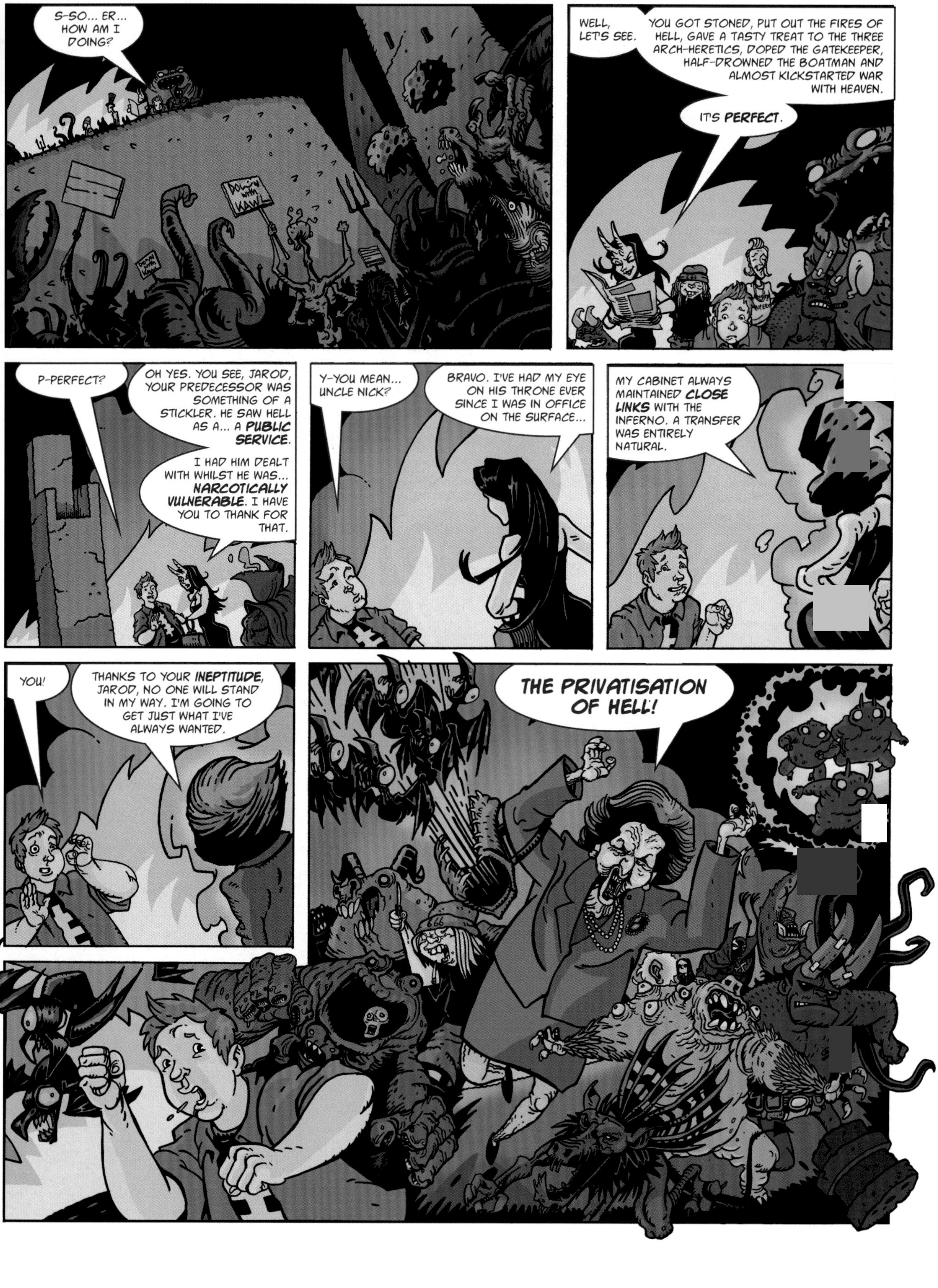
S-SO... ER... HOW AM I DOING?
DOWN WITH KAWL
WELL, LET'S SEE.
YOU GOT STONED, PUT OUT THE FIRES OF HELL, GAVE A TASTY TREAT TO THE THREE ARCH-HERETICS, DOPED THE GATEKEEPER, HALF-DROWNED THE BOATMAN AND ALMOST KICKSTARTED WAR WITH HEAVEN.
IT'S **PERFECT**.
P-PERFECT?
OH YES. YOU SEE, JAROD, YOUR PREDECESSOR WAS SOMETHING OF A STICKLER. HE SAW HELL AS A... A **PUBLIC SERVICE**.
I HAD HIM DEALT WITH WHILST HE WAS... **NARCOTICALLY VULNERABLE**. I HAVE YOU TO THANK FOR THAT.
Y-YOU MEAN... UNCLE NICK?
BRAVO. I'VE HAD MY EYE ON HIS THRONE EVER SINCE I WAS IN OFFICE ON THE SURFACE...
MY CABINET ALWAYS MAINTAINED **CLOSE LINKS** WITH THE INFERNO. A TRANSFER WAS ENTIRELY NATURAL.
YOU!
THANKS TO YOUR **INEPTITUDE**, JAROD, NO ONE WILL STAND IN MY WAY. I'M GOING TO GET JUST WHAT I'VE ALWAYS WANTED.
THE PRIVATISATION OF HELL!

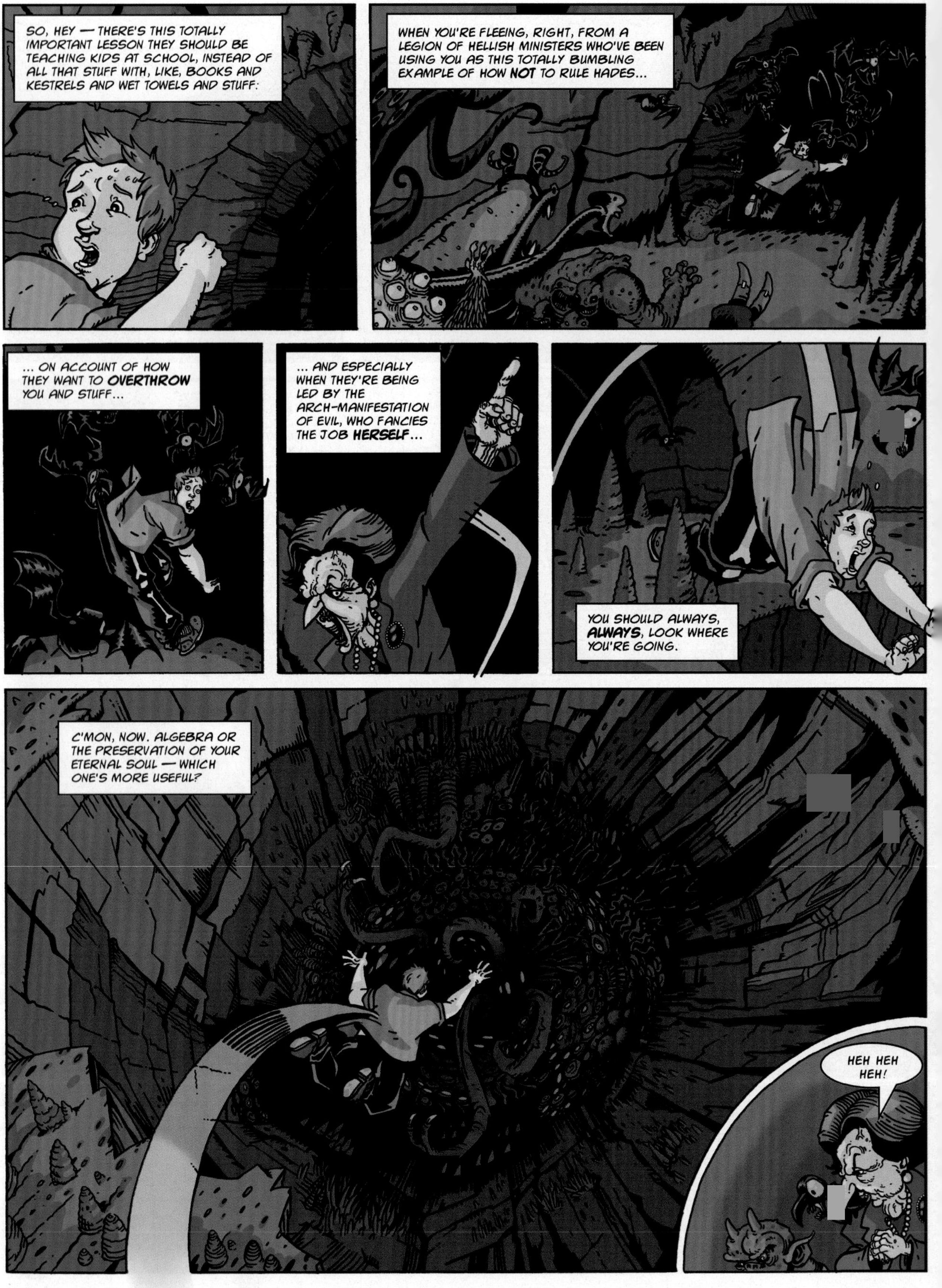
SO, HEY — THERE'S THIS TOTALLY IMPORTANT LESSON THEY SHOULD BE TEACHING KIDS AT SCHOOL, INSTEAD OF ALL THAT STUFF WITH, LIKE, BOOKS AND KESTRELS AND WET TOWELS AND STUFF:
WHEN YOU'RE FLEEING, RIGHT, FROM A LEGION OF HELLISH MINISTERS WHO'VE BEEN USING YOU AS THIS TOTALLY BUMBLING EXAMPLE OF HOW NOT TO RULE HADES...
... ON ACCOUNT OF HOW THEY WANT TO OVERTHROW YOU AND STUFF...
... AND ESPECIALLY WHEN THEY'RE BEING LED BY THE ARCH-MANIFESTATION OF EVIL, WHO FANCIES THE JOB HERSELF...
YOU SHOULD ALWAYS, ALWAYS, LOOK WHERE YOU'RE GOING.
C'MON, NOW. ALGEBRA OR THE PRESERVATION OF YOUR ETERNAL SOUL — WHICH ONE'S MORE USEFUL?
HEH HEH HEH!

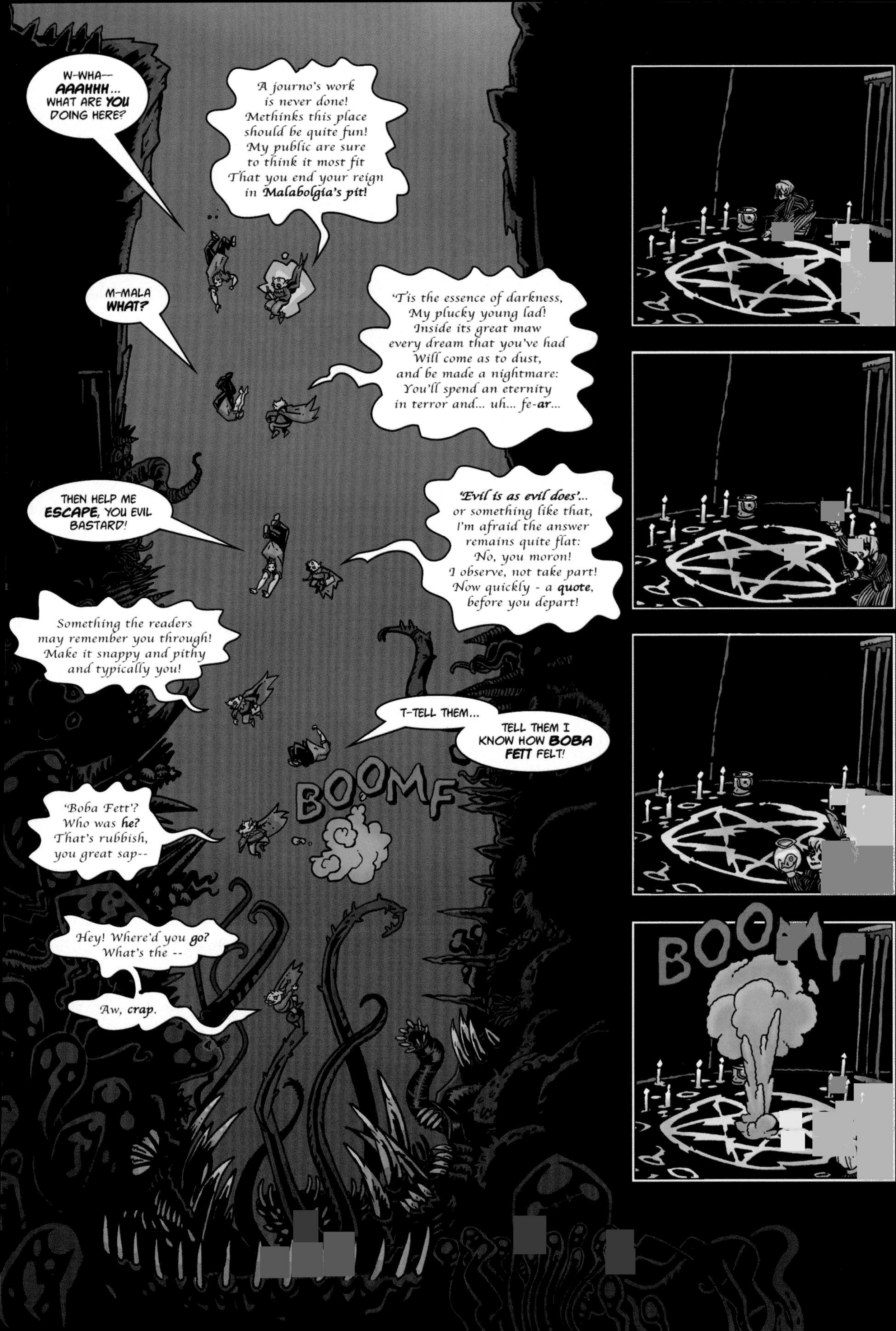
W-WHA-- AAAHHH... WHAT ARE YOU DOING HERE?
A journo's work is never done! Methinks this place should be quite fun! My public are sure to think it most fit That you end your reign in Malabolgia's pit!
M-MALA WHAT?
'Tis the essence of darkness, My plucky young lad! Inside its great maw every dream that you've had Will come as to dust, and be made a nightmare: You'll spend an eternity in terror and... uh... fe-ar...
THEN HELP ME ESCAPE, YOU EVIL BASTARD!
'Evil is as evil does'... or something like that, I'm afraid the answer remains quite flat: No, you moron! I observe, not take part! Now quickly - a quote, before you depart!
Something the readers may remember you through! Make it snappy and pithy and typically you!
T-TELL THEM...
TELL THEM I KNOW HOW BOBA FETT FELT!
BOOMF
'Boba Fett'? Who was he? That's rubbish, you great sap--
Hey! Where'd you go? What's the --
Aw, crap.

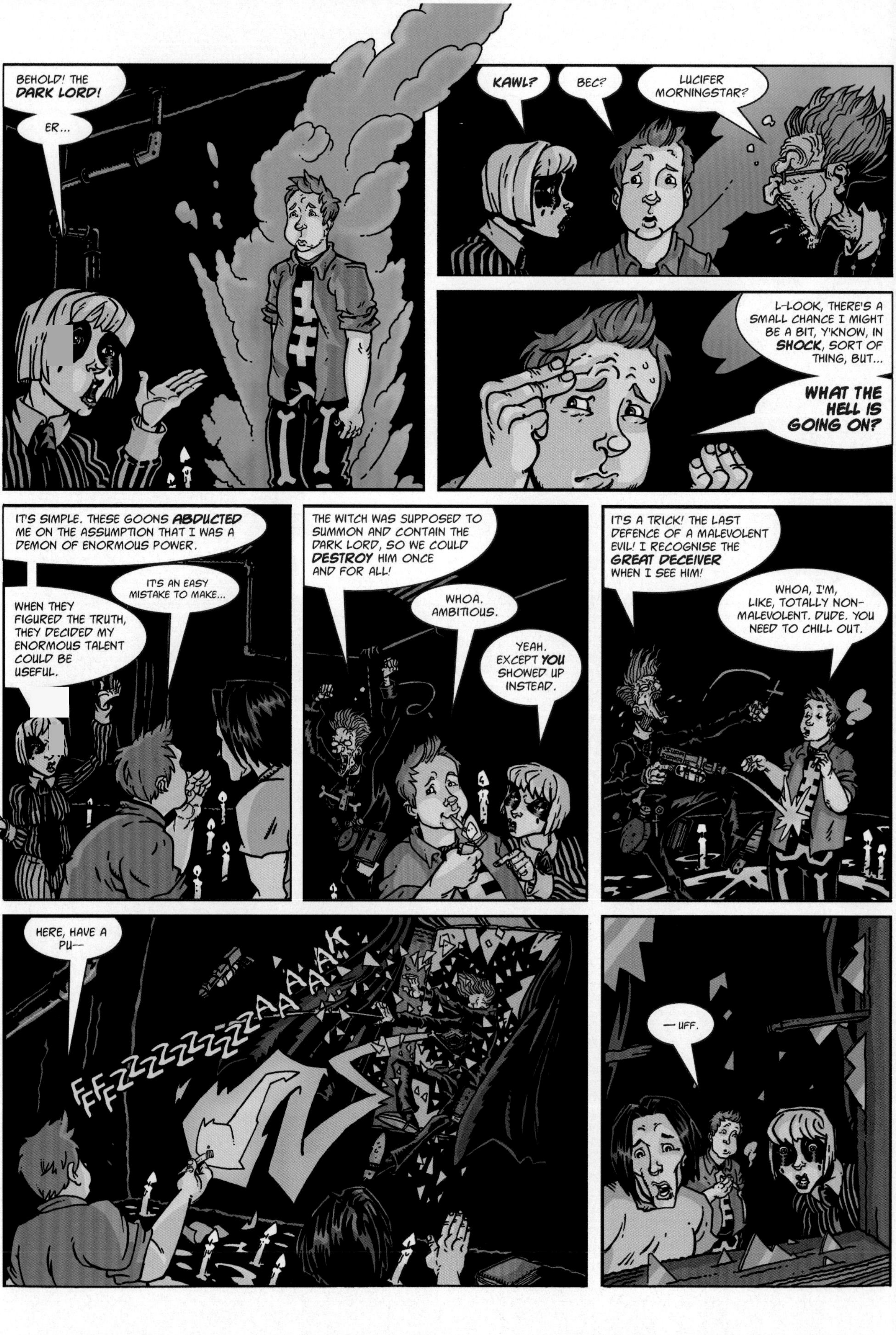
BEHOLD! THE DARK LORD!
ER...
KAWL?
BEC?
LUCIFER MORNINGSTAR?
L-LOOK, THERE'S A SMALL CHANCE I MIGHT BE A BIT, Y'KNOW, IN SHOCK, SORT OF THING, BUT...
WHAT THE HELL IS GOING ON?
IT'S SIMPLE. THESE GOONS ABDUCTED ME ON THE ASSUMPTION THAT I WAS A DEMON OF ENORMOUS POWER.
IT'S AN EASY MISTAKE TO MAKE...
WHEN THEY FIGURED THE TRUTH, THEY DECIDED MY ENORMOUS TALENT COULD BE USEFUL.
THE WITCH WAS SUPPOSED TO SUMMON AND CONTAIN THE DARK LORD, SO WE COULD DESTROY HIM ONCE AND FOR ALL!
WHOA. AMBITIOUS.
YEAH. EXCEPT YOU SHOWED UP INSTEAD.
IT'S A TRICK! THE LAST DEFENCE OF A MALEVOLENT EVIL! I RECOGNISE THE GREAT DECEIVER WHEN I SEE HIM!
WHOA, I'M, LIKE, TOTALLY NON-MALEVOLENT. DUDE. YOU NEED TO CHILL OUT.
HERE, HAVE A PU--
FFFZZZZZZZZZZZAAAAAK
— UFF.

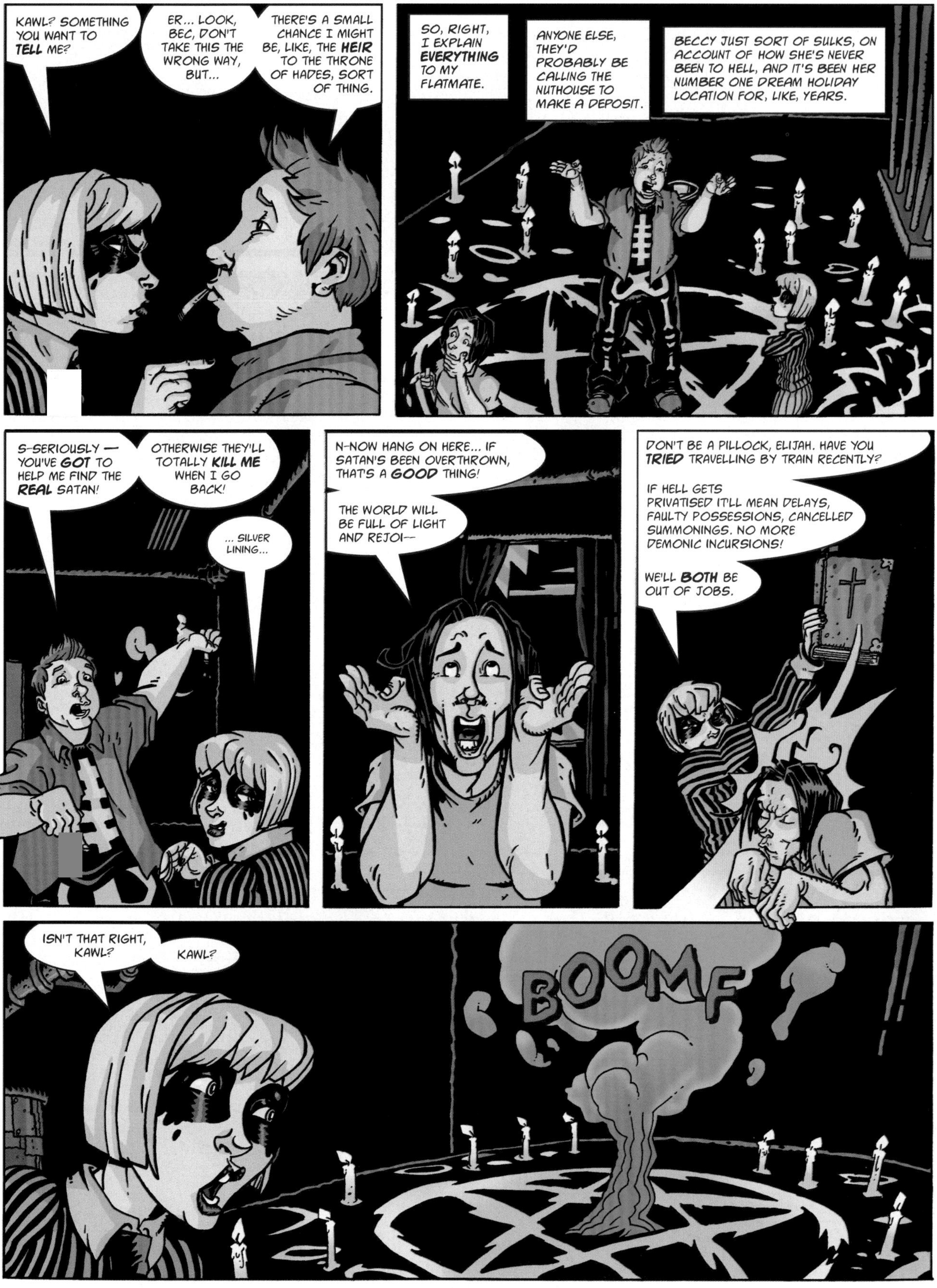

KAWL? SOMETHING YOU WANT TO TELL ME?
ER... LOOK, BEC, DON'T TAKE THIS THE WRONG WAY, BUT...
THERE'S A SMALL CHANCE I MIGHT BE, LIKE, THE HEIR TO THE THRONE OF HADES, SORT OF THING.
SO, RIGHT, I EXPLAIN EVERYTHING TO MY FLATMATE.
ANYONE ELSE, THEY'D PROBABLY BE CALLING THE NUTHOUSE TO MAKE A DEPOSIT.
BECCY JUST SORT OF SULKS, ON ACCOUNT OF HOW SHE'S NEVER BEEN TO HELL, AND IT'S BEEN HER NUMBER ONE DREAM HOLIDAY LOCATION FOR, LIKE, YEARS.
S-SERIOUSLY — YOU'VE GOT TO HELP ME FIND THE REAL SATAN!
OTHERWISE THEY'LL TOTALLY KILL ME WHEN I GO BACK!
... SILVER LINING...
N-NOW HANG ON HERE... IF SATAN'S BEEN OVERTHROWN, THAT'S A GOOD THING!
THE WORLD WILL BE FULL OF LIGHT AND REJOI—
DON'T BE A PILLOCK, ELIJAH. HAVE YOU TRIED TRAVELLING BY TRAIN RECENTLY?
IF HELL GETS PRIVATISED IT'LL MEAN DELAYS, FAULTY POSSESSIONS, CANCELLED SUMMONINGS. NO MORE DEMONIC INCURSIONS!
WE'LL BOTH BE OUT OF JOBS.
ISN'T THAT RIGHT, KAWL?
KAWL?
BOOMF

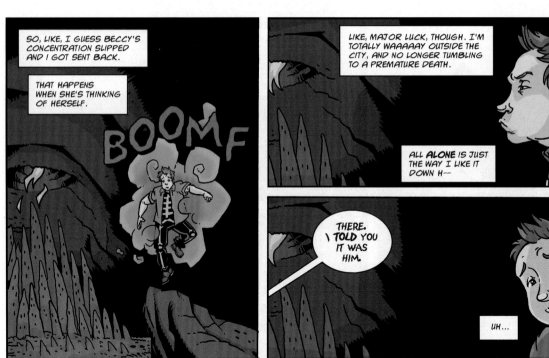

SO, LIKE, I GUESS BECCY'S CONCENTRATION SLIPPED AND I GOT SENT BACK.

THAT HAPPENS WHEN SHE'S THINKING OF HERSELF.

BOOMF

LIKE, MAJOR LUCK, THOUGH. I'M TOTALLY WAAAAAY OUTSIDE THE CITY, AND NO LONGER TUMBLING TO A PREMATURE DEATH.

ALL **ALONE** IS JUST THE WAY I LIKE IT DOWN H--

THERE. I **TOLD** YOU IT WAS HIM.

UH...

I RECOGNISED THE PICTURE IN THE PAPER.

WE **ALL** RECOGNISED HIM, YOU SLIME-COVERED FREAK!

WE'VE **ALL** MET HIM BEFORE...

...AND WE'VE ALL BEEN JUST **DYING** TO MEET HIM AGAIN!

O-OH NUTS...

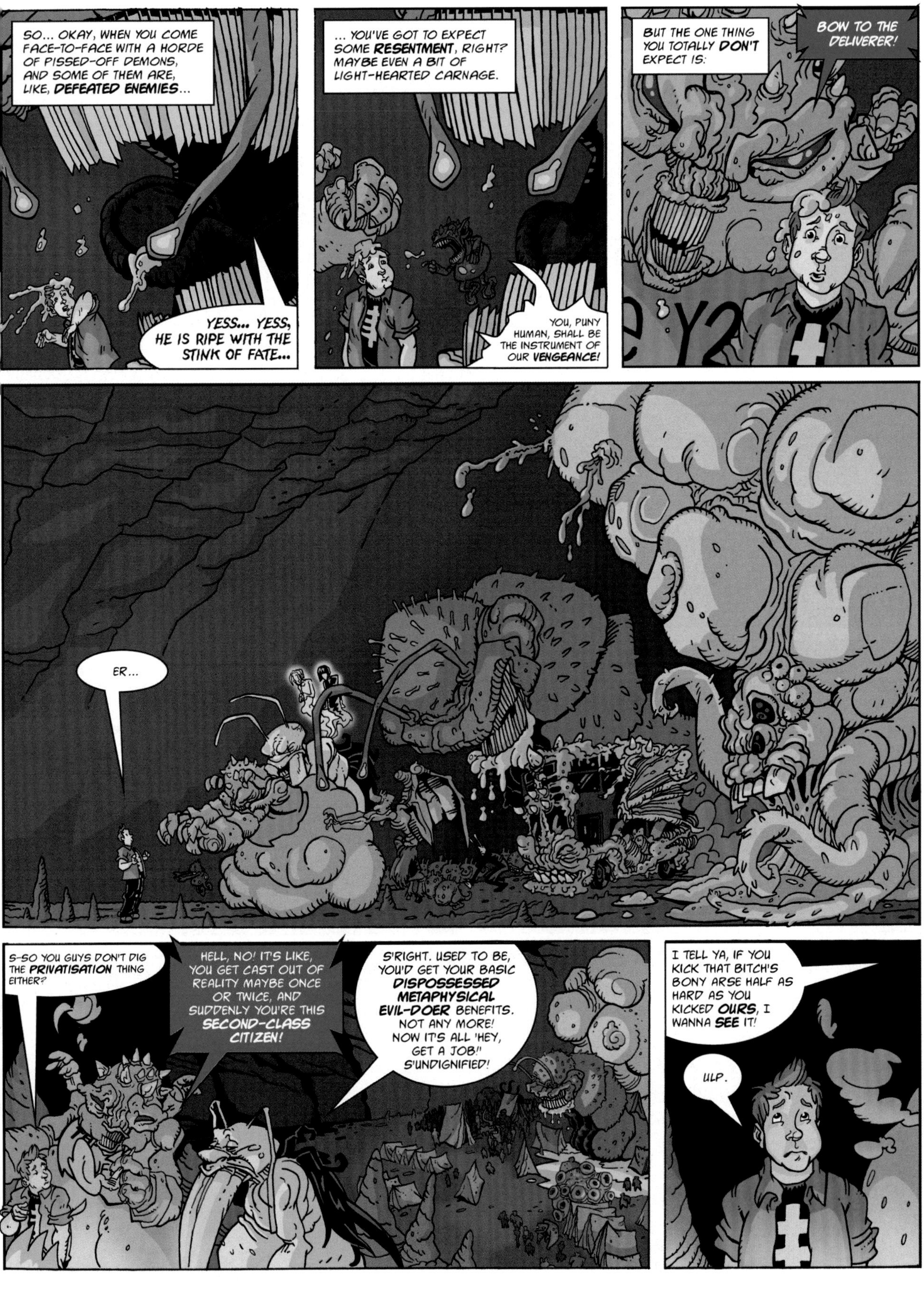
SO... OKAY, WHEN YOU COME FACE-TO-FACE WITH A HORDE OF PISSED-OFF DEMONS, AND SOME OF THEM ARE, LIKE, DEFEATED ENEMIES...
YESS... YESS, HE IS RIPE WITH THE STINK OF FATE...
... YOU'VE GOT TO EXPECT SOME RESENTMENT, RIGHT? MAYBE EVEN A BIT OF LIGHT-HEARTED CARNAGE.
YOU, PUNY HUMAN, SHALL BE THE INSTRUMENT OF OUR VENGEANCE!
BUT THE ONE THING YOU TOTALLY DON'T EXPECT IS:
BOW TO THE DELIVERER!
Y2
ER...
S-SO YOU GUYS DON'T DIG THE PRIVATISATION THING EITHER?
HELL, NO! IT'S LIKE, YOU GET CAST OUT OF REALITY MAYBE ONCE OR TWICE, AND SUDDENLY YOU'RE THIS SECOND-CLASS CITIZEN!
S'RIGHT. USED TO BE, YOU'D GET YOUR BASIC DISPOSSESSED METAPHYSICAL EVIL-DOER BENEFITS. NOT ANY MORE! NOW IT'S ALL 'HEY, GET A JOB!' S'UNDIGNIFIED!
I TELL YA, IF YOU KICK THAT BITCH'S BONY ARSE HALF AS HARD AS YOU KICKED OURS, I WANNA SEE IT!
ULP.

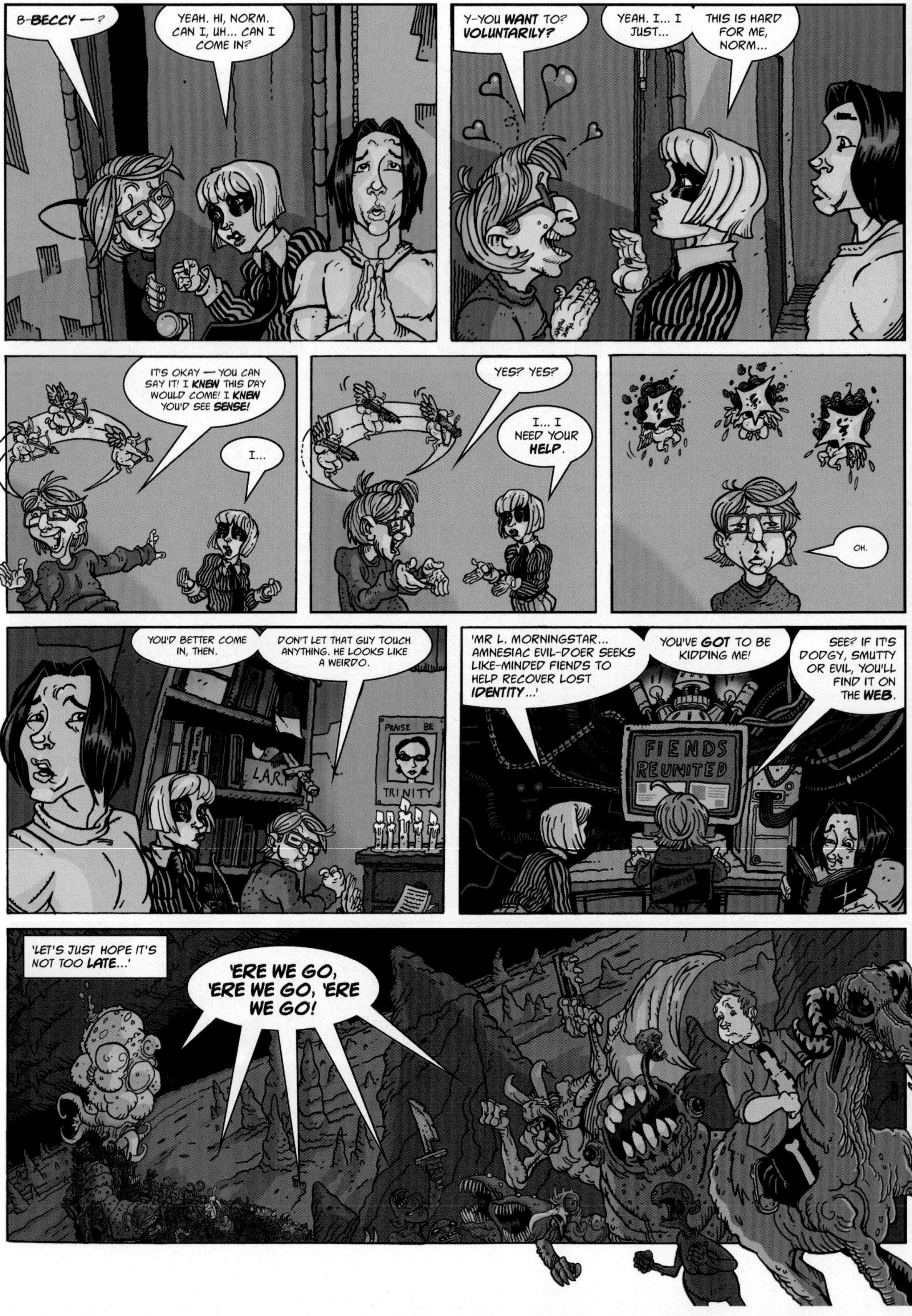
B-BECCY — ?
YEAH. HI, NORM. CAN I, UH... CAN I COME IN?
Y-YOU WANT TO? VOLUNTARILY?
YEAH. I... I JUST...
THIS IS HARD FOR ME, NORM...
IT'S OKAY — YOU CAN SAY IT! I KNEW THIS DAY WOULD COME! I KNEW YOU'D SEE SENSE!
I...
YES? YES?
I... I NEED YOUR HELP.
OH.
YOU'D BETTER COME IN, THEN.
DON'T LET THAT GUY TOUCH ANYTHING. HE LOOKS LIKE A WEIRDO.
L.A.R.P.
PRAISE BE
TRINITY
'MR L. MORNINGSTAR... AMNESIAC EVIL-DOER SEEKS LIKE-MINDED FIENDS TO HELP RECOVER LOST IDENTITY...'
YOU'VE GOT TO BE KIDDING ME!
SEE? IF IT'S DODGY, SMUTTY OR EVIL, YOU'LL FIND IT ON THE WEB.
FIENDS REUNITED
THE MASTER
'LET'S JUST HOPE IT'S NOT TOO LATE...'
'ERE WE GO, 'ERE WE GO, 'ERE WE GO!

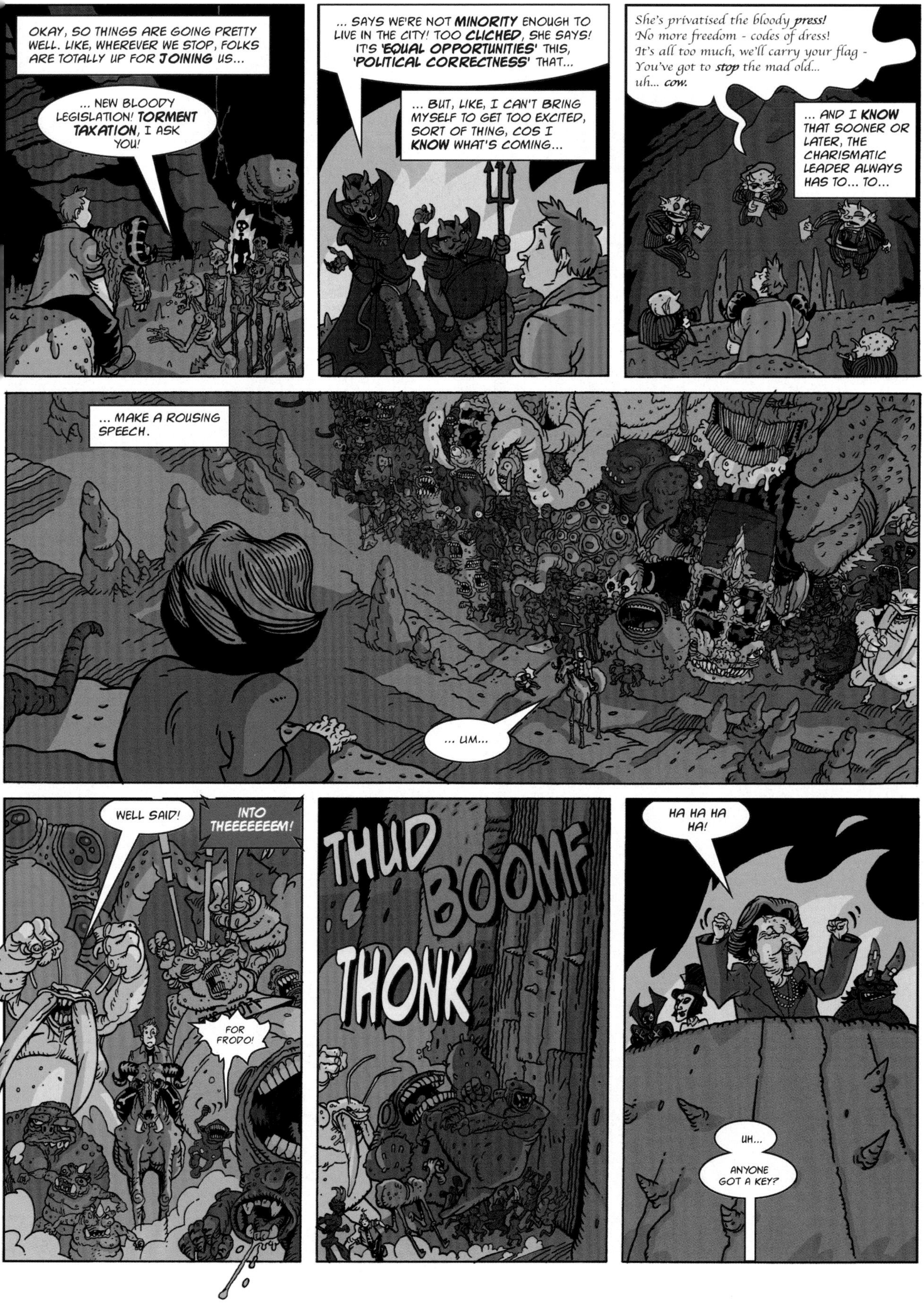
OKAY, SO THINGS ARE GOING PRETTY WELL. LIKE, WHEREVER WE STOP, FOLKS ARE TOTALLY UP FOR JOINING US...
... NEW BLOODY LEGISLATION! TORMENT TAXATION, I ASK YOU!
... SAYS WE'RE NOT MINORITY ENOUGH TO LIVE IN THE CITY! TOO CLICHED, SHE SAYS! IT'S 'EQUAL OPPORTUNITIES' THIS, 'POLITICAL CORRECTNESS' THAT...
... BUT, LIKE, I CAN'T BRING MYSELF TO GET TOO EXCITED, SORT OF THING, COS I KNOW WHAT'S COMING...
She's privatised the bloody press! No more freedom - codes of dress! It's all too much, we'll carry your flag - You've got to stop the mad old... uh... cow.
... AND I KNOW THAT SOONER OR LATER, THE CHARISMATIC LEADER ALWAYS HAS TO... TO...
... MAKE A ROUSING SPEECH.
... UM...
WELL SAID!
INTO THEEEEEEEM!
FOR FRODO!
THUD
BOOMF
THONK
HA HA HA HA!
UH...
ANYONE GOT A KEY?

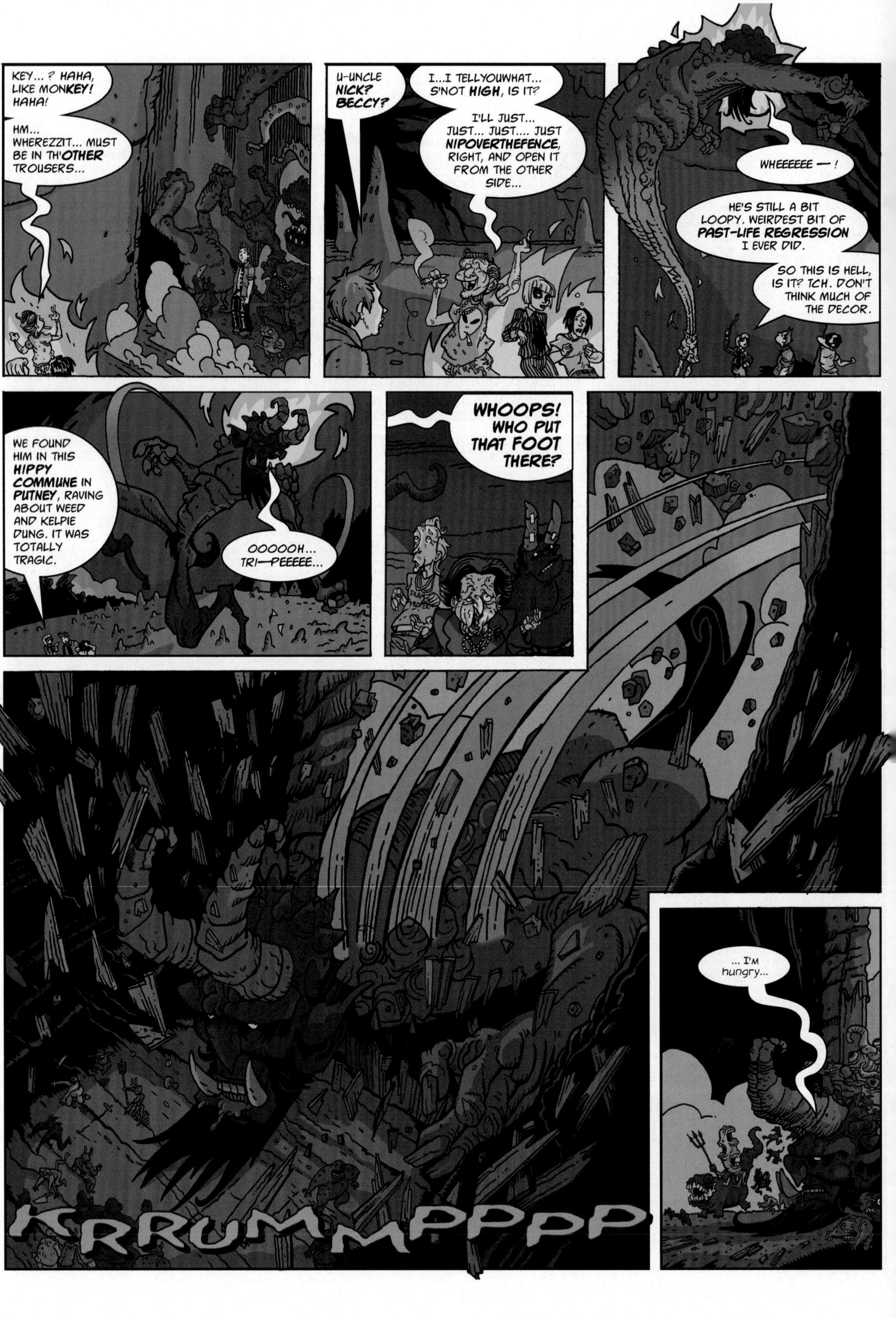
KEY... ? HAHA, LIKE MONKEY! HAHA!
HM... WHEREZZIT... MUST BE IN TH'OTHER TROUSERS...
U-UNCLE NICK? BECCY?
I...I TELLYOUWHAT... S'NOT HIGH, IS IT?
I'LL JUST... JUST... JUST.... JUST NIPOVERTHEFENCE, RIGHT, AND OPEN IT FROM THE OTHER SIDE...
WHEEEEEE — !
HE'S STILL A BIT LOOPY. WEIRDEST BIT OF PAST-LIFE REGRESSION I EVER DID.
SO THIS IS HELL, IS IT? TCH. DON'T THINK MUCH OF THE DECOR.
WE FOUND HIM IN THIS HIPPY COMMUNE IN PUTNEY, RAVING ABOUT WEED AND KELPIE DUNG. IT WAS TOTALLY TRAGIC.
OOOOOH... TRI—PEEEEE...
WHOOPS! WHO PUT THAT FOOT THERE?
KRRUMMPPPPP
... I'M hungry...

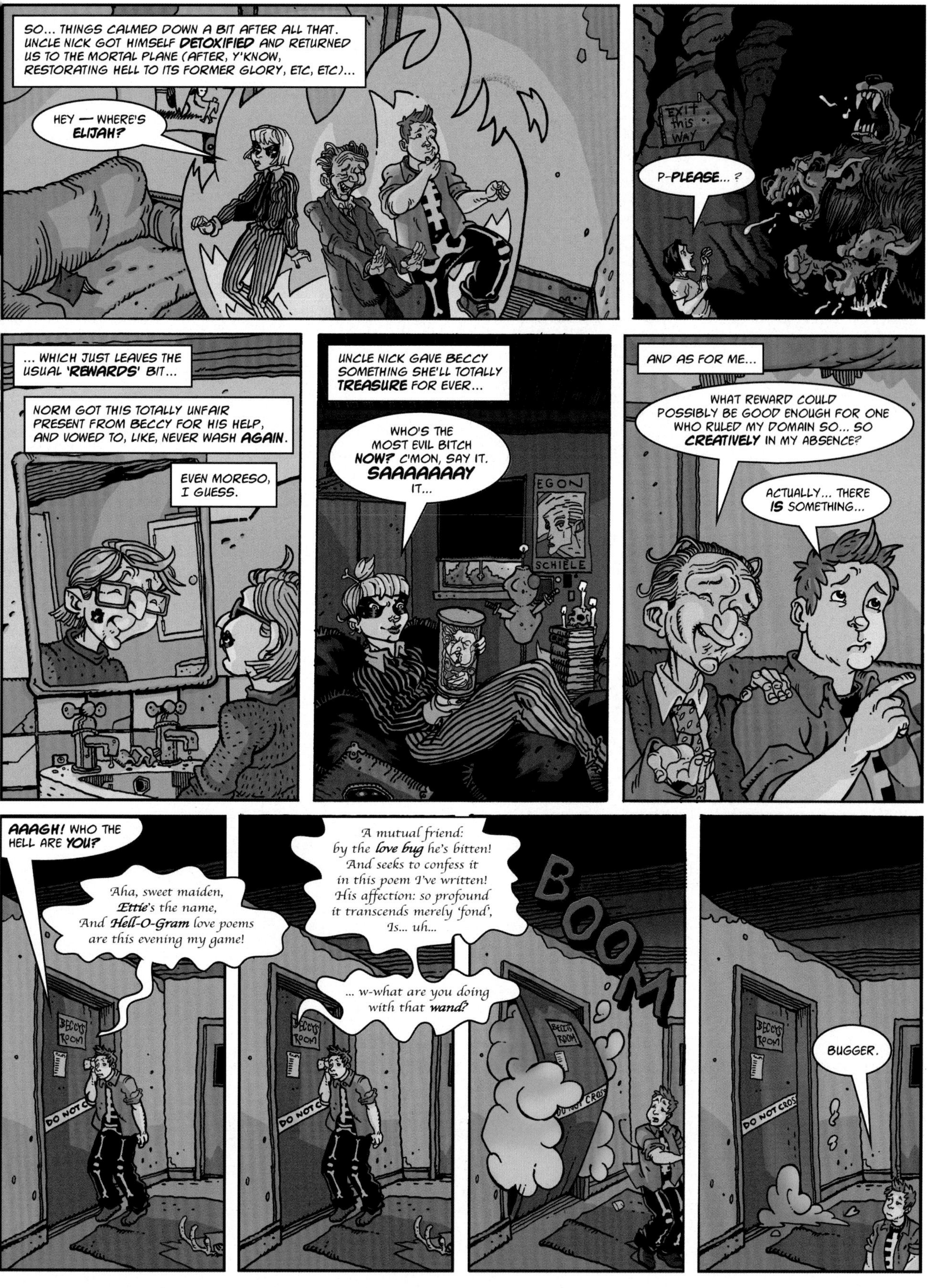

SO... THINGS CALMED DOWN A BIT AFTER ALL THAT. UNCLE NICK GOT HIMSELF DETOXIFIED AND RETURNED US TO THE MORTAL PLANE (AFTER, Y'KNOW, RESTORATING HELL TO ITS FORMER GLORY, ETC, ETC)...
HEY — WHERE'S ELIJAH?
EXIT this WAY
P-PLEASE... ?
... WHICH JUST LEAVES THE USUAL 'REWARDS' BIT...
NORM GOT THIS TOTALLY UNFAIR PRESENT FROM BECCY FOR HIS HELP, AND VOWED TO, LIKE, NEVER WASH AGAIN.
EVEN MORESO, I GUESS.
UNCLE NICK GAVE BECCY SOMETHING SHE'LL TOTALLY TREASURE FOR EVER...
WHO'S THE MOST EVIL BITCH NOW? C'MON, SAY IT. SAAAAAAAY IT...
EGON
SCHIELE
AND AS FOR ME...
WHAT REWARD COULD POSSIBLY BE GOOD ENOUGH FOR ONE WHO RULED MY DOMAIN SO... SO CREATIVELY IN MY ABSENCE?
ACTUALLY... THERE IS SOMETHING...
AAAGH! WHO THE HELL ARE YOU?
Aha, sweet maiden, Ettie's the name, And Hell-O-Gram love poems are this evening my game!
A mutual friend: by the love bug he's bitten! And seeks to confess it in this poem I've written! His affection: so profound it transcends merely 'fond', Is... uh...
... w-what are you doing with that wand?
BOOM
BUGGER.

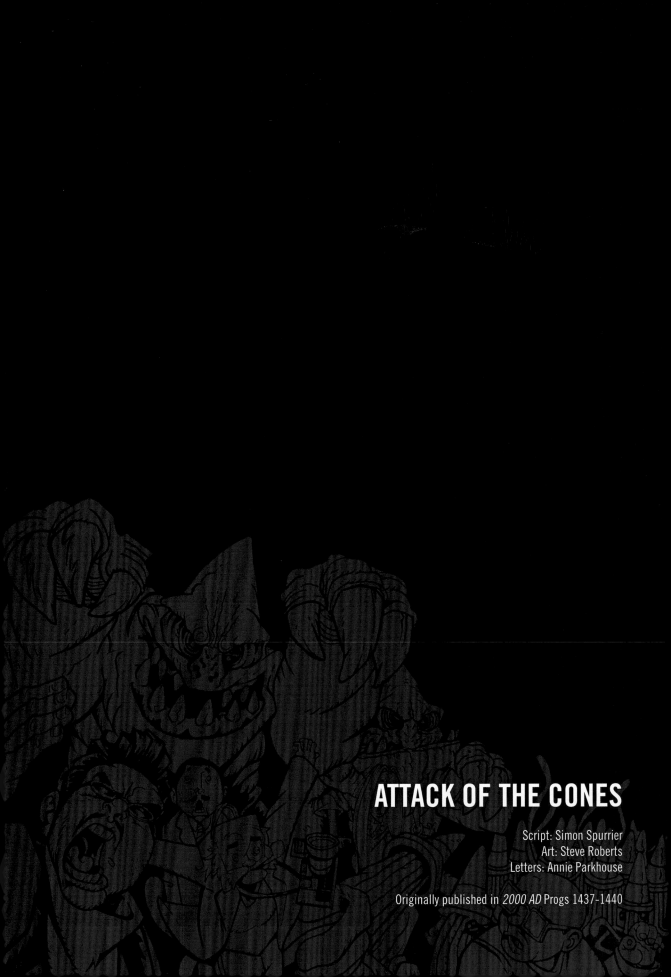

ATTACK OF THE CONES

Script: Simon Spurrier
Art: Steve Roberts
Letters: Annie Parkhouse

Originally published in *2000 AD* Progs 1437-1440

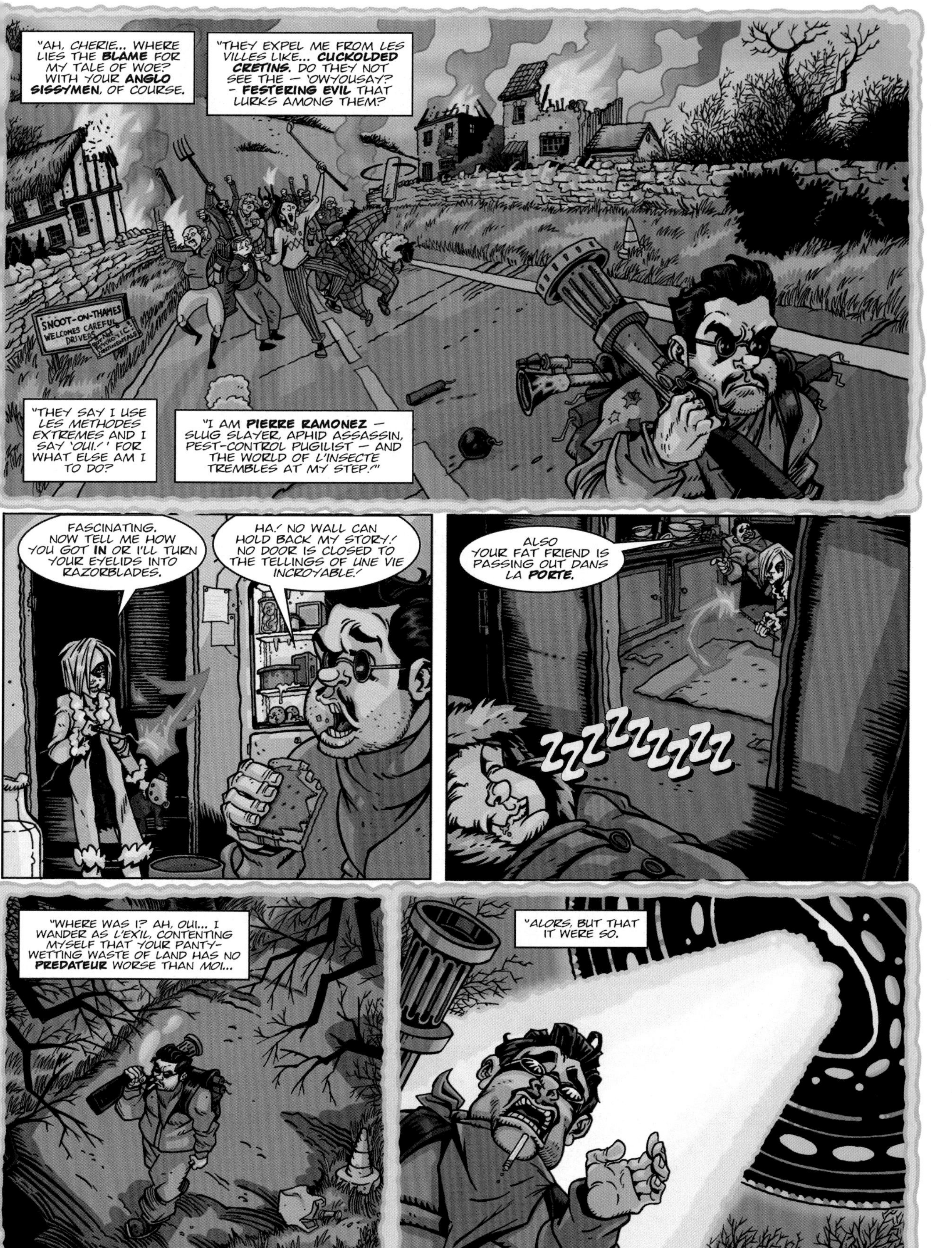

"AH, CHERIE... WHERE LIES THE BLAME FOR MY TALE OF WOE? WITH YOUR ANGLO SISSYMEN, OF COURSE.
"THEY EXPEL ME FROM LES VILLES LIKE... CUCKOLDED CRETINS. DO THEY NOT SEE THE — 'OWYOUSAY? — FESTERING EVIL THAT LURKS AMONG THEM?
SNOOT-ON-THAMES WELCOMES CAREFUL DRIVERS
"THEY SAY I USE LES METHODES EXTREMES AND I SAY 'OUI!' FOR WHAT ELSE AM I TO DO?
"I AM PIERRE RAMONEZ — SLUG SLAYER, APHID ASSASSIN, PEST-CONTROL PUGILIST — AND THE WORLD OF L'INSECTE TREMBLES AT MY STEP!"
FASCINATING. NOW TELL ME HOW YOU GOT IN OR I'LL TURN YOUR EYELIDS INTO RAZORBLADES.
HA! NO WALL CAN HOLD BACK MY STORY! NO DOOR IS CLOSED TO THE TELLINGS OF UNE VIE INCROYABLE!
ALSO YOUR FAT FRIEND IS PASSING OUT DANS LA PORTE.
ZZZZZZZZZZ
"WHERE WAS I? AH, OUI... I WANDER AS L'EXIL, CONTENTING MYSELF THAT YOUR PANTY-WETTING WASTE OF LAND HAS NO PREDATEUR WORSE THAN MOI...
"ALORS, BUT THAT IT WERE SO.

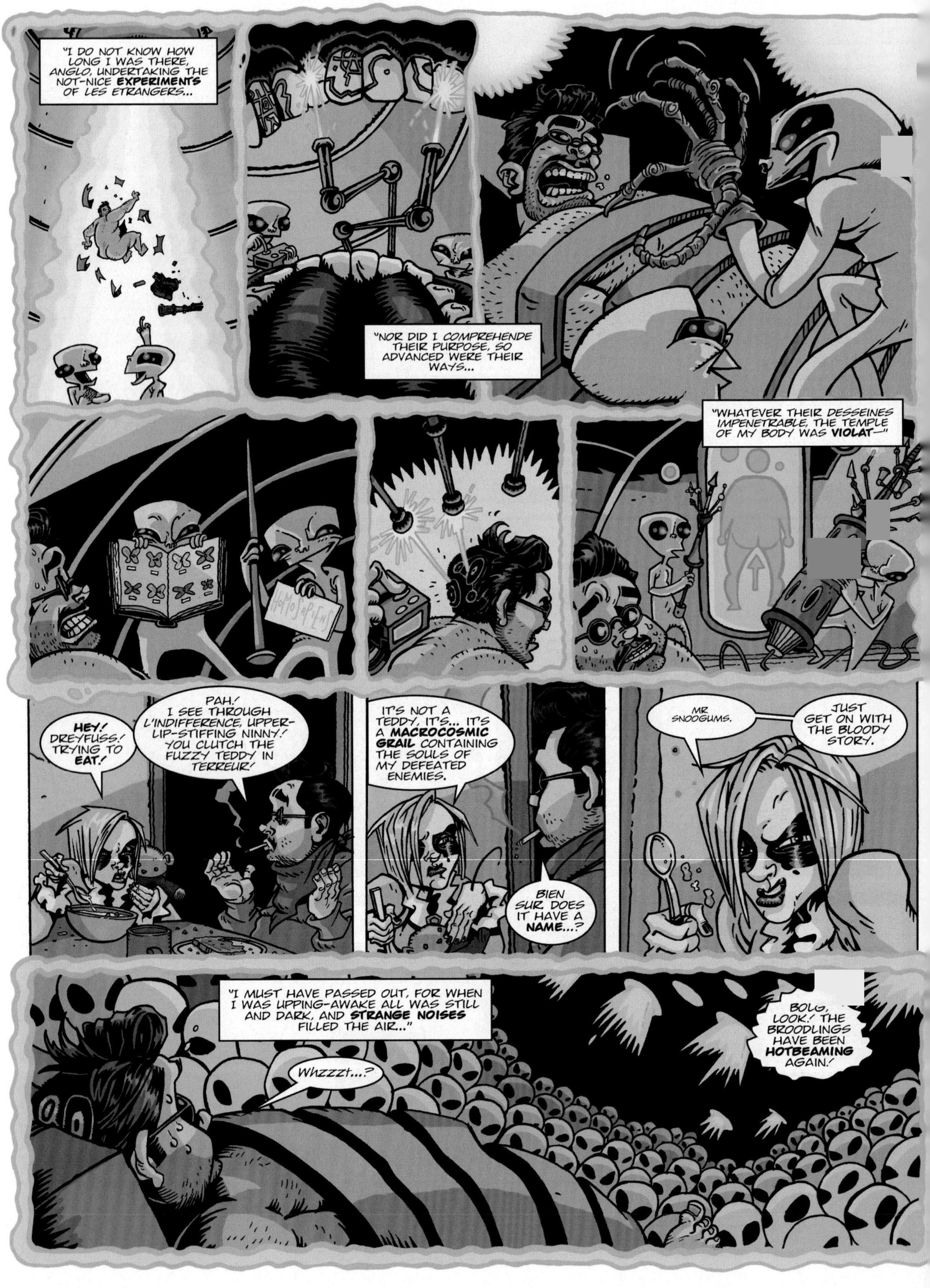

"I DO NOT KNOW HOW LONG I WAS THERE, ANGLO, UNDERTAKING THE NOT-NICE **EXPERIMENTS** OF LES ETRANGERS...
"NOR DID I COMPREHENDE THEIR PURPOSE, SO ADVANCED WERE THEIR WAYS...
HOMO SAPIENS
"WHATEVER THEIR DESSEINES IMPENETRABLE, THE TEMPLE OF MY BODY WAS **VIOLAT**—"
HEY! DREYFUSS! TRYING TO **EAT!**
PAH! I SEE **THROUGH** L'INDIFFERENCE, UPPER-LIP-STIFFING NINNY! YOU CLUTCH THE FUZZY TEDDY IN TERREUR!
IT'S NOT A TEDDY, IT'S... IT'S A **MACROCOSMIC GRAIL** CONTAINING THE SOULS OF MY DEFEATED ENEMIES.
BIEN SUR. DOES IT HAVE A **NAME...?**
MR SNOOGUMS.
JUST GET ON WITH THE BLOODY STORY.
"I MUST HAVE PASSED OUT, FOR WHEN I WAS UPPING-AWAKE ALL WAS STILL AND DARK, AND **STRANGE NOISES** FILLED THE AIR..."
Whzzzt...?
BOLG, LOOK! THE BROODLINGS HAVE BEEN **HOTBEAMING** AGAIN!

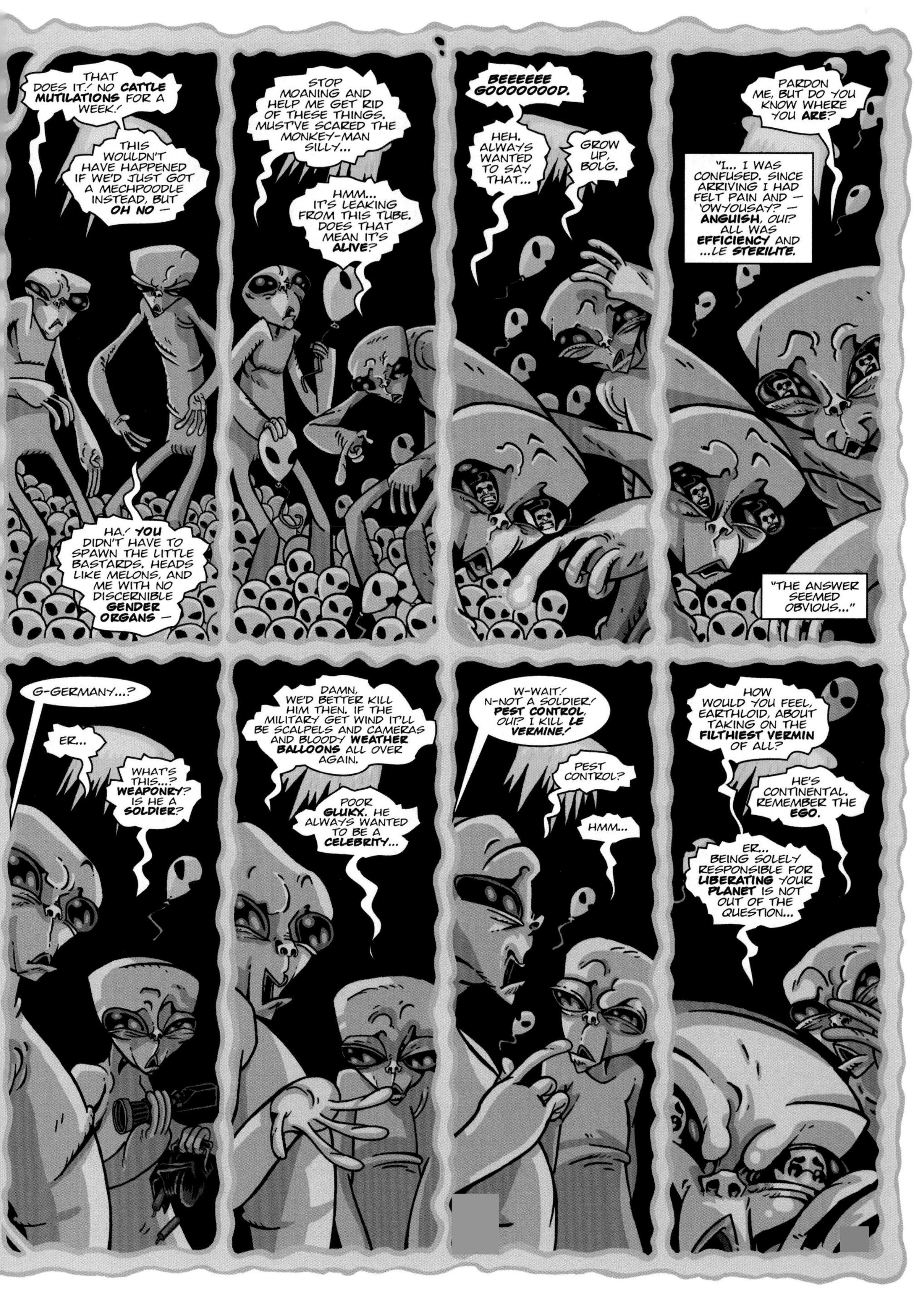

THAT DOES IT! NO CATTLE MUTILATIONS FOR A WEEK!
THIS WOULDN'T HAVE HAPPENED IF WE'D JUST GOT A MECHPOODLE INSTEAD, BUT OH NO —
HA! YOU DIDN'T HAVE TO SPAWN THE LITTLE BASTARDS. HEADS LIKE MELONS, AND ME WITH NO DISCERNIBLE GENDER ORGANS —
STOP MOANING AND HELP ME GET RID OF THESE THINGS. MUST'VE SCARED THE MONKEY-MAN SILLY...
HMM... IT'S LEAKING FROM THIS TUBE. DOES THAT MEAN IT'S ALIVE?
BEEEEEE GOOOOOOOD.
HEH. ALWAYS WANTED TO SAY THAT...
GROW UP, BOLG.
PARDON ME, BUT DO YOU KNOW WHERE YOU ARE?
"I... I WAS CONFUSED. SINCE ARRIVING I HAD FELT PAIN AND — 'OWYOUSAY? — ANGUISH, OUI? ALL WAS EFFICIENCY AND ...LE STERILITE.
"THE ANSWER SEEMED OBVIOUS..."
G-GERMANY...?
ER...
WHAT'S THIS...? WEAPONRY? IS HE A SOLDIER?
DAMN, WE'D BETTER KILL HIM THEN. IF THE MILITARY GET WIND IT'LL BE SCALPELS AND CAMERAS AND BLOODY WEATHER BALLOONS ALL OVER AGAIN.
POOR GLUKX. HE ALWAYS WANTED TO BE A CELEBRITY...
W-WAIT! N-NOT A SOLDIER! PEST CONTROL, OUI? I KILL LE VERMINE!
PEST CONTROL?
HMM...
HOW WOULD YOU FEEL, EARTHLOID, ABOUT TAKING ON THE FILTHIEST VERMIN OF ALL?
HE'S CONTINENTAL. REMEMBER THE EGO.
ER... BEING SOLELY RESPONSIBLE FOR LIBERATING YOUR PLANET IS NOT OUT OF THE QUESTION...

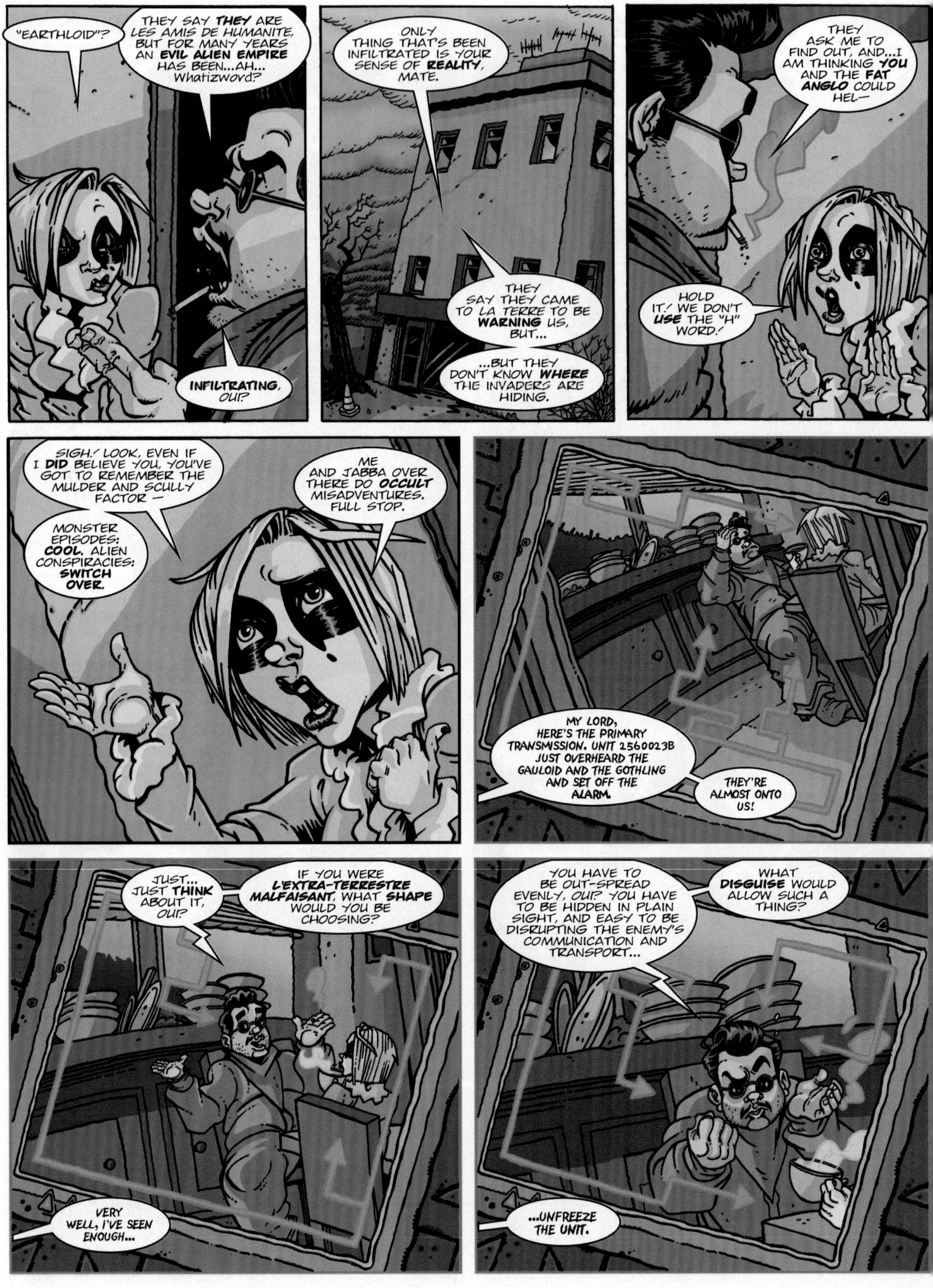
"EARTHLOID"?
THEY SAY THEY ARE LES AMIS DE HUMANITE, BUT FOR MANY YEARS AN EVIL ALIEN EMPIRE HAS BEEN...AH... Whatizword?
INFILTRATING, OUI?
ONLY THING THAT'S BEEN INFILTRATED IS YOUR SENSE OF REALITY, MATE.
THEY SAY THEY CAME TO LA TERRE TO BE WARNING US, BUT...
...BUT THEY DON'T KNOW WHERE THE INVADERS ARE HIDING.
THEY ASK ME TO FIND OUT, AND...I AM THINKING YOU AND THE FAT ANGLO COULD HEL—
HOLD IT! WE DON'T USE THE "H" WORD!
SIGH! LOOK, EVEN IF I DID BELIEVE YOU, YOU'VE GOT TO REMEMBER THE MULDER AND SCULLY FACTOR —
MONSTER EPISODES: COOL. ALIEN CONSPIRACIES: SWITCH OVER.
ME AND JABBA OVER THERE DO OCCULT MISADVENTURES. FULL STOP.
MY LORD, HERE'S THE PRIMARY TRANSMISSION. UNIT 2560023B JUST OVERHEARD THE GAULOID AND THE GOTHLING AND SET OFF THE ALARM.
THEY'RE ALMOST ONTO US!
JUST... JUST THINK ABOUT IT, OUI?
IF YOU WERE L'EXTRA-TERRESTRE MALFAISANT, WHAT SHAPE WOULD YOU BE CHOOSING?
VERY WELL, I'VE SEEN ENOUGH...
YOU HAVE TO BE OUT-SPREAD EVENLY, OUI? YOU HAVE TO BE HIDDEN IN PLAIN SIGHT, AND EASY TO BE DISRUPTING THE ENEMY'S COMMUNICATION AND TRANSPORT...
WHAT DISGUISE WOULD ALLOW SUCH A THING?
...UNFREEZE THE UNIT.

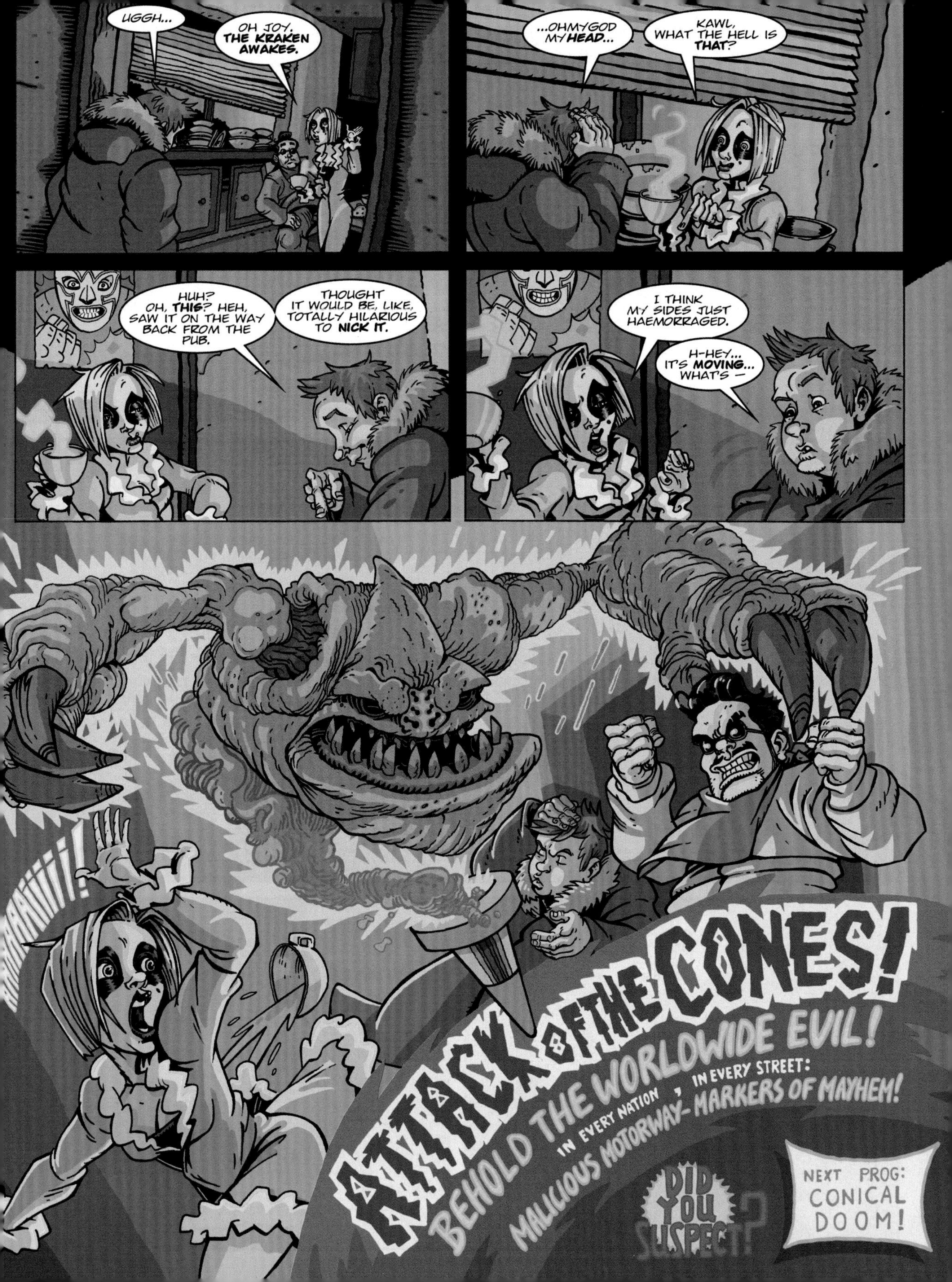
UGGH...
OH JOY. THE KRAKEN AWAKES.
...OHMYGOD MY HEAD...
KAWL, WHAT THE HELL IS THAT?
HUH? OH, THIS? HEH, SAW IT ON THE WAY BACK FROM THE PUB.
THOUGHT IT WOULD BE, LIKE, TOTALLY HILARIOUS TO NICK IT.
I THINK MY SIDES JUST HAEMORRAGED.
H-HEY... IT'S MOVING... WHAT'S —
ATTACK OF THE CONES!
BEHOLD THE WORLDWIDE EVIL!
IN EVERY NATION, IN EVERY STREET:
MALICIOUS MOTORWAY-MARKERS OF MAYHEM!
DID YOU SUSPECT?
NEXT PROG: CONICAL DOOM!

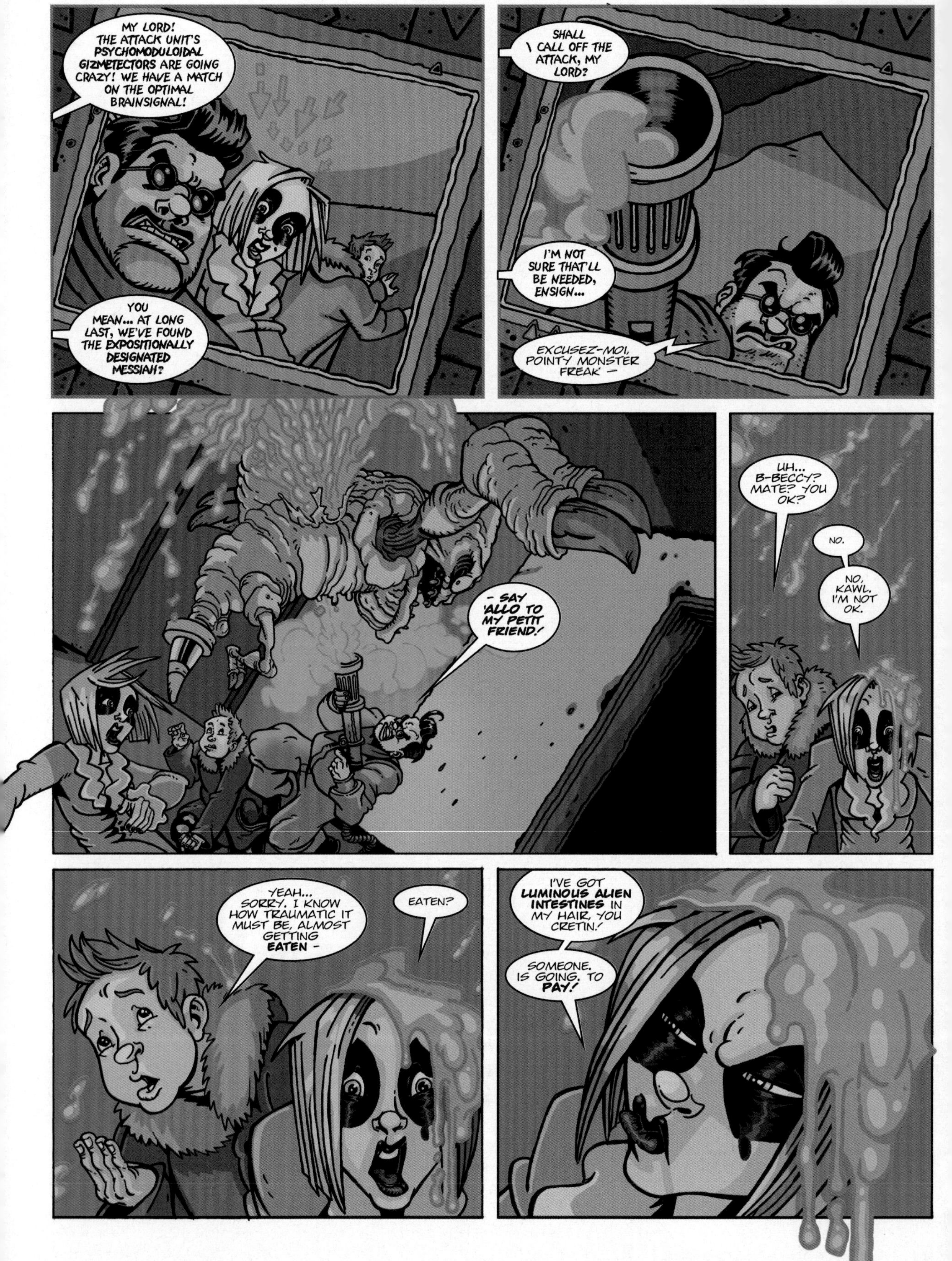

MY LORD! THE ATTACK UNIT'S PSYCHOMODULOIDAL GIZMETECTORS ARE GOING CRAZY! WE HAVE A MATCH ON THE OPTIMAL BRAINSIGNAL!
YOU MEAN... AT LONG LAST, WE'VE FOUND THE EXPOSITIONALLY DESIGNATED MESSIAH?
SHALL I CALL OFF THE ATTACK, MY LORD?
I'M NOT SURE THAT'LL BE NEEDED, ENSIGN...
EXCUSEZ-MOI, POINTY MONSTER FREAK –
– SAY 'ALLO TO MY PETIT FRIEND!
UH... B-BECCY? MATE? YOU OK?
NO.
NO, KAWL. I'M NOT OK.
YEAH... SORRY. I KNOW HOW TRAUMATIC IT MUST BE, ALMOST GETTING EATEN –
EATEN?
I'VE GOT LUMINOUS ALIEN INTESTINES IN MY HAIR, YOU CRETIN!
SOMEONE. IS GOING. TO PAY!

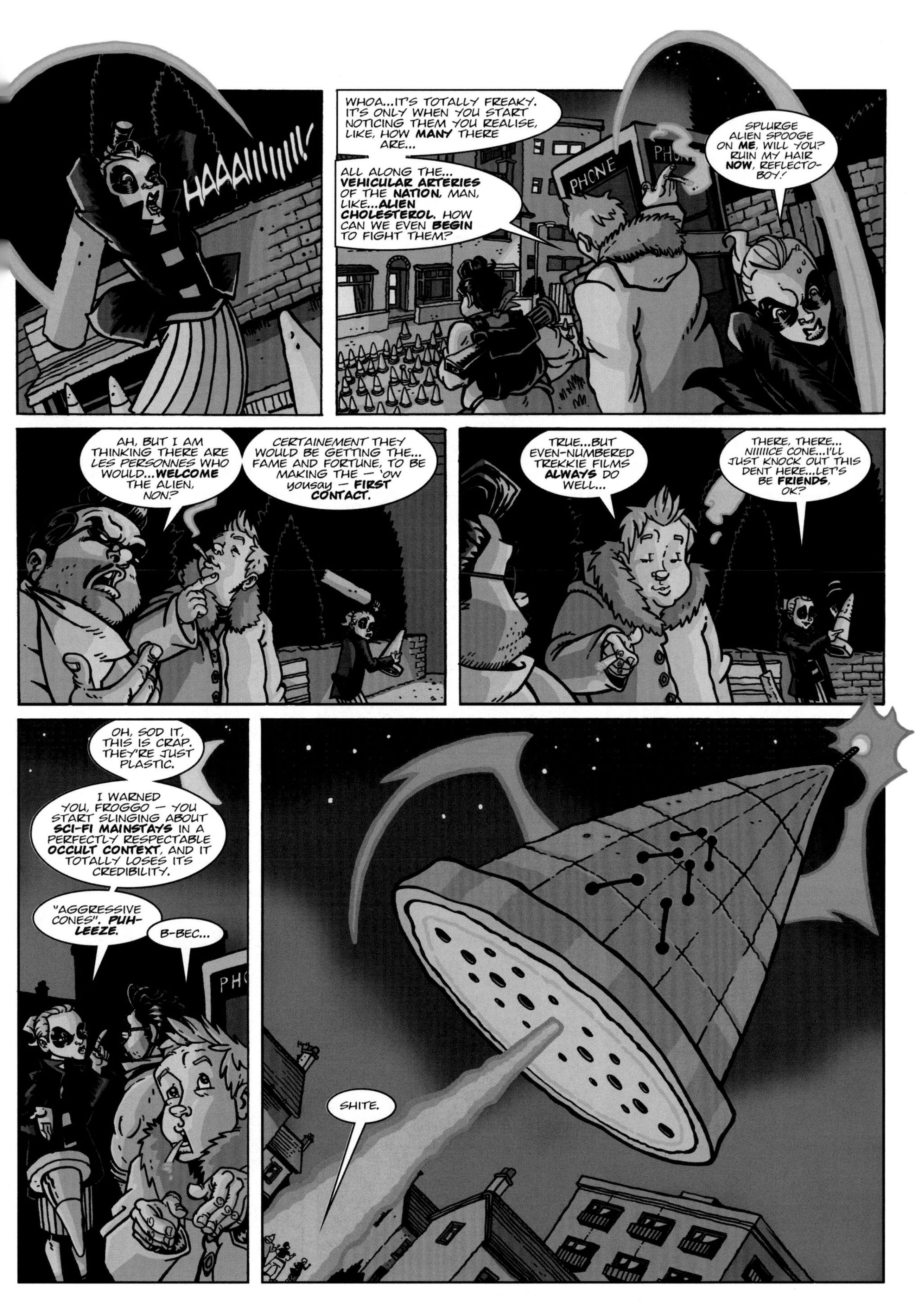
HAAAIIIIIIII!
WHOA...IT'S TOTALLY FREAKY. IT'S ONLY WHEN YOU START NOTICING THEM YOU REALISE, LIKE, HOW MANY THERE ARE...
ALL ALONG THE... VEHICULAR ARTERIES OF THE NATION, MAN, LIKE...ALIEN CHOLESTEROL. HOW CAN WE EVEN BEGIN TO FIGHT THEM?
PHONE
PHONE
SPLURGE ALIEN SPOOGE ON ME, WILL YOU? RUIN MY HAIR NOW, REFLECTO-BOY!
AH, BUT I AM THINKING THERE ARE LES PERSONNES WHO WOULD...WELCOME THE ALIEN, NON?
CERTAINEMENT THEY WOULD BE GETTING THE... FAME AND FORTUNE, TO BE MAKING THE — 'OW YOU SAY — FIRST CONTACT.
TRUE...BUT EVEN-NUMBERED TREKKIE FILMS ALWAYS DO WELL...
THERE, THERE... NIIIIICE CONE...I'LL JUST KNOCK OUT THIS DENT HERE...LET'S BE FRIENDS, OK?
OH, SOD IT, THIS IS CRAP. THEY'RE JUST PLASTIC.
I WARNED YOU, FROGGO — YOU START SLINGING ABOUT SCI-FI MAINSTAYS IN A PERFECTLY RESPECTABLE OCCULT CONTEXT, AND IT TOTALLY LOSES ITS CREDIBILITY.
"AGGRESSIVE CONES". PUH-LEEZE.
B-BEC...
PHO
SHITE.

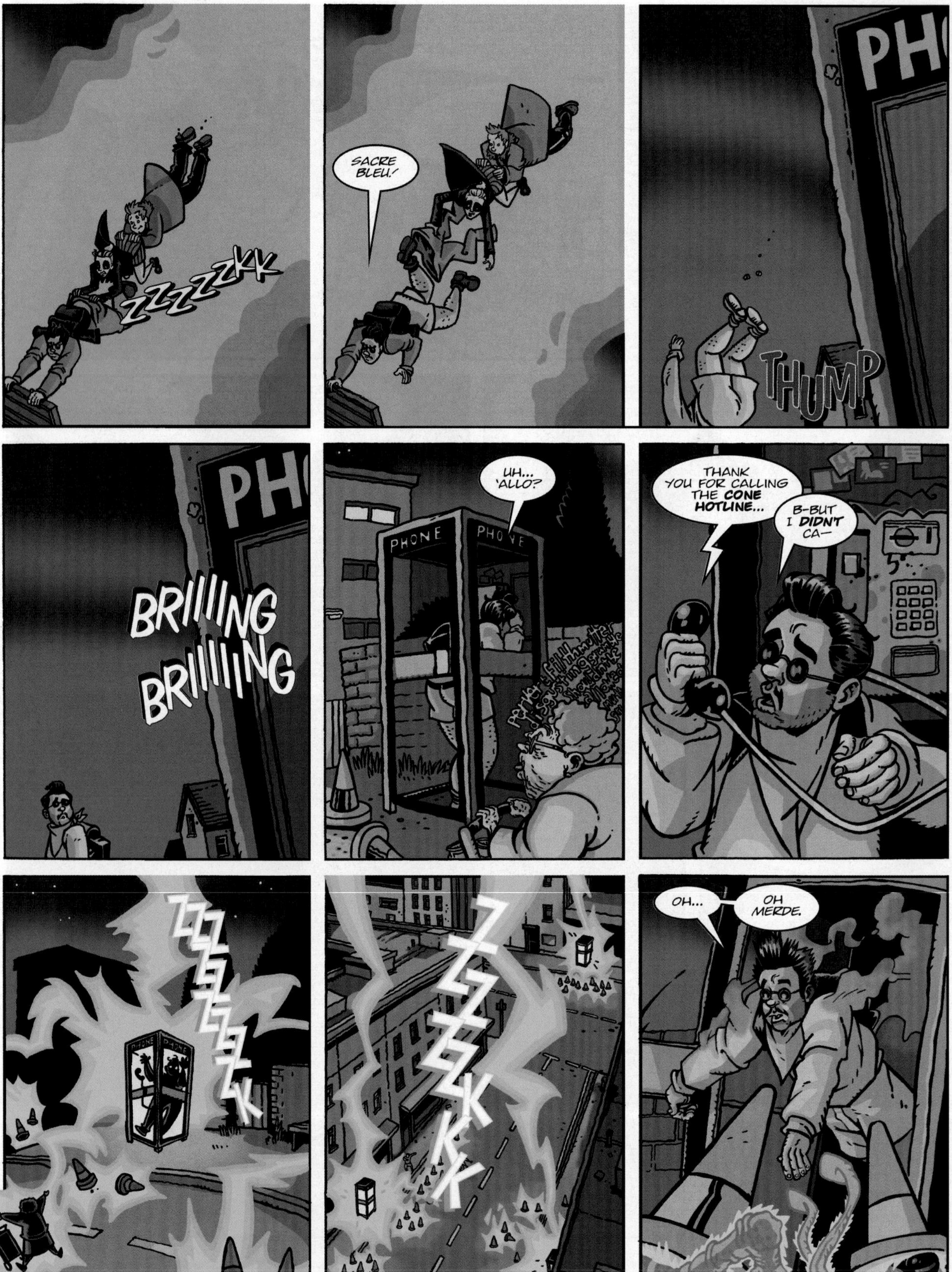
ZZZZZZKK
SACRE BLEU!
THUMP
BRIIIING
BRIIIIING
UH... 'ALLO?
PHONE
PHONE
THANK YOU FOR CALLING THE **CONE HOTLINE**...
B-BUT I **DIDN'T** CA—
OH...
OH MERDE.

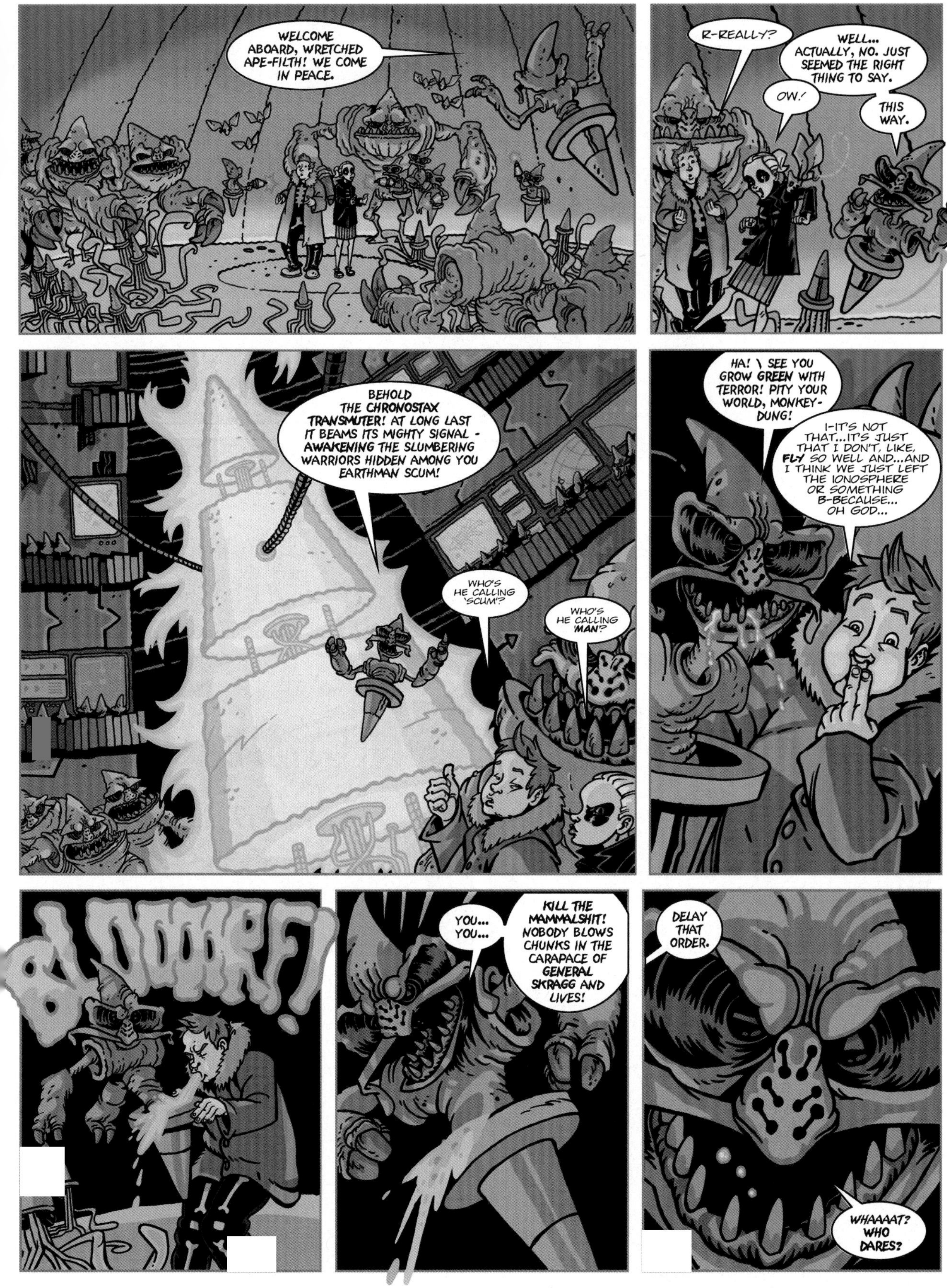
WELCOME ABOARD, WRETCHED APE-FILTH! WE COME IN PEACE.
R-REALLY?
WELL... ACTUALLY, NO. JUST SEEMED THE RIGHT THING TO SAY.
OW!
THIS WAY.
BEHOLD THE CHRONOSTAX TRANSMUTER! AT LONG LAST IT BEAMS ITS MIGHTY SIGNAL - AWAKENING THE SLUMBERING WARRIORS HIDDEN AMONG YOU EARTHMAN SCUM!
WHO'S HE CALLING 'SCUM'?
WHO'S HE CALLING 'MAN'?
HA! I SEE YOU GROW GREEN WITH TERROR! PITY YOUR WORLD, MONKEY-DUNG!
I-IT'S NOT THAT...IT'S JUST THAT I DON'T, LIKE, FLY SO WELL AND...AND I THINK WE JUST LEFT THE IONOSPHERE OR SOMETHING B-BECAUSE... OH GOD...
BLOOOARF!
YOU... YOU...
KILL THE MAMMALSHIT! NOBODY BLOWS CHUNKS IN THE CARAPACE OF GENERAL SKRAGG AND LIVES!
DELAY THAT ORDER.
WHAAAAT? WHO DARES?

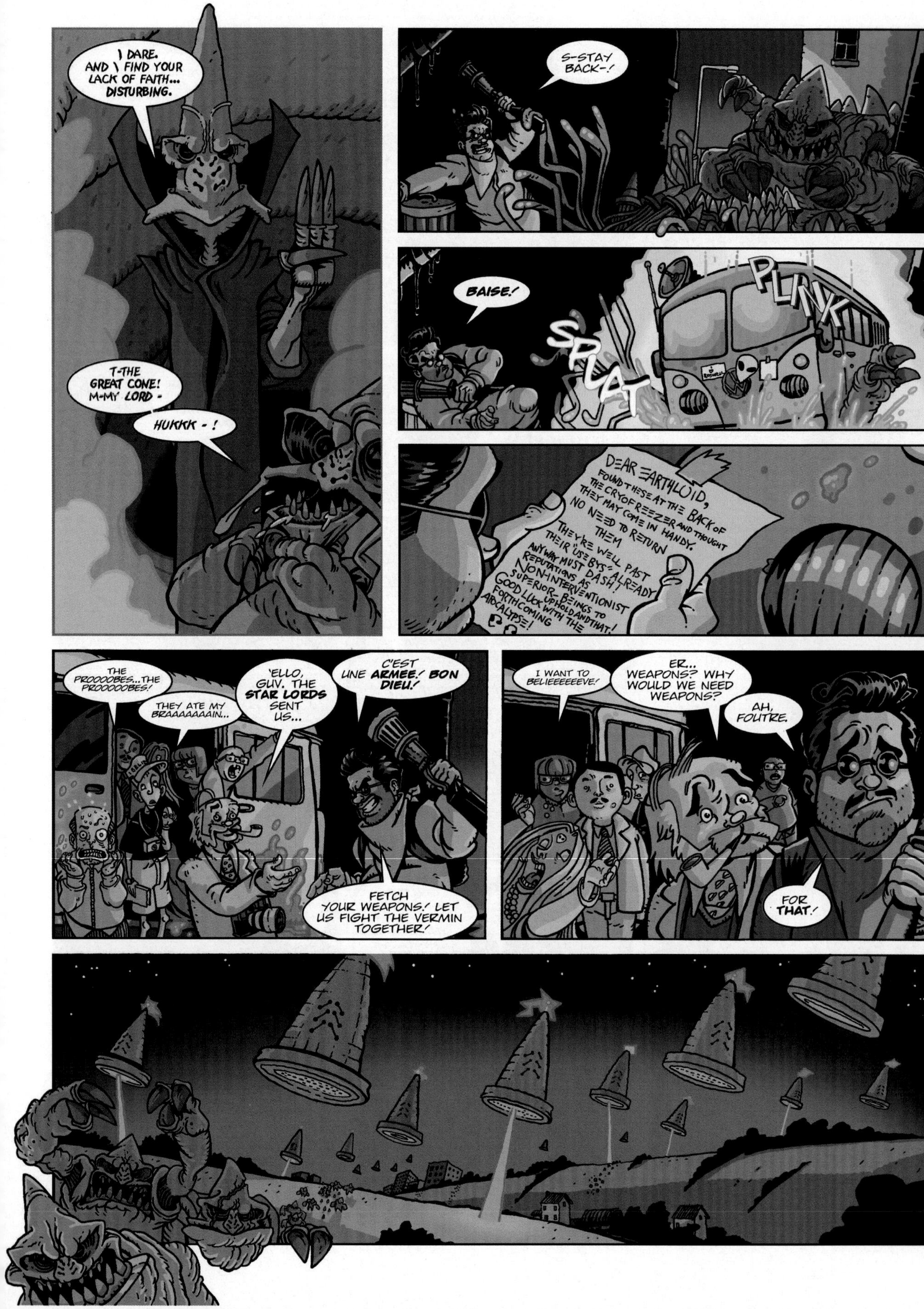
I DARE. AND I FIND YOUR LACK OF FAITH... DISTURBING.
T-THE GREAT CONE! M-MY LORD -
HUKKK - !
S-STAY BACK-!
BAISE!
SPLAT
PLINK
DEAR EARTHLOID,
FOUND THESE AT THE BACK OF THE CRYOFREEZER AND THOUGHT THEY MAY COME IN HANDY.
NO NEED TO RETURN THEM
THEY'RE WELL PAST THEIR "USE BYS" ALREADY
ANYWAY MUST DASH! REPUTATIONS AS NON-INTERVENTIONIST SUPERIOR-BEINGS TO UPHOLD AND THAT!
GOOD LUCK WITH THE FORTHCOMING APOCALYPSE!
THE PROOOOBES...THE PROOOOOBES!
THEY ATE MY BRAAAAAAAIN...
'ELLO, GUV. THE STAR LORDS SENT US...
C'EST UNE ARMEE! BON DIEU!
FETCH YOUR WEAPONS! LET US FIGHT THE VERMIN TOGETHER!
I WANT TO BELIEEEEEEEVE!
ER... WEAPONS? WHY WOULD WE NEED WEAPONS?
AH, FOUTRE.
FOR THAT!

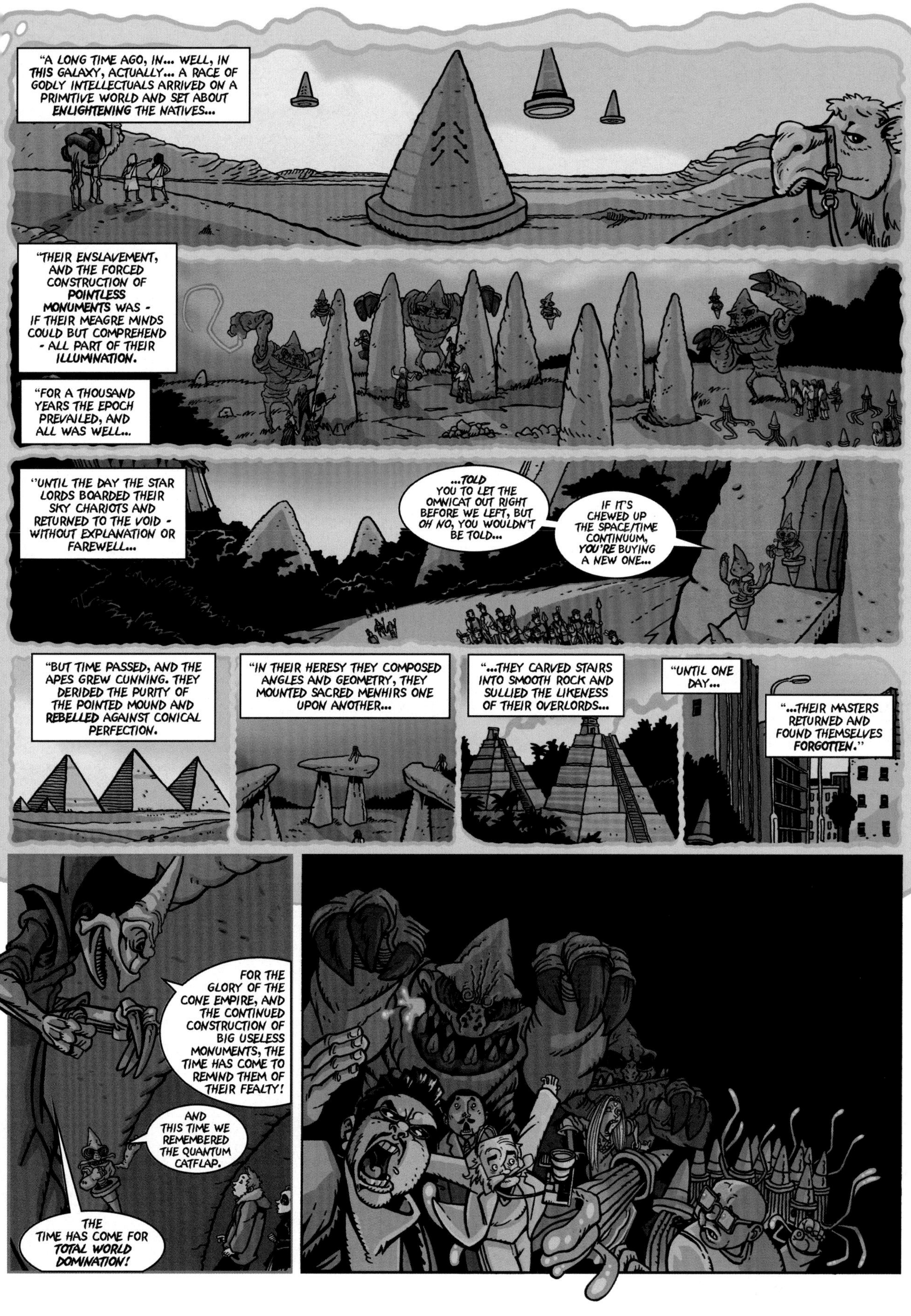
"A LONG TIME AGO, IN... WELL, IN THIS GALAXY, ACTUALLY... A RACE OF GODLY INTELLECTUALS ARRIVED ON A PRIMITIVE WORLD AND SET ABOUT ENLIGHTENING THE NATIVES...
"THEIR ENSLAVEMENT, AND THE FORCED CONSTRUCTION OF POINTLESS MONUMENTS WAS - IF THEIR MEAGRE MINDS COULD BUT COMPREHEND - ALL PART OF THEIR ILLUMINATION.
"FOR A THOUSAND YEARS THE EPOCH PREVAILED, AND ALL WAS WELL...
"UNTIL THE DAY THE STAR LORDS BOARDED THEIR SKY CHARIOTS AND RETURNED TO THE VOID - WITHOUT EXPLANATION OR FAREWELL...
...TOLD YOU TO LET THE OMNICAT OUT RIGHT BEFORE WE LEFT, BUT OH NO, YOU WOULDN'T BE TOLD...
IF IT'S CHEWED UP THE SPACE/TIME CONTINUUM, YOU'RE BUYING A NEW ONE...
"BUT TIME PASSED, AND THE APES GREW CUNNING. THEY DERIDED THE PURITY OF THE POINTED MOUND AND REBELLED AGAINST CONICAL PERFECTION.
"IN THEIR HERESY THEY COMPOSED ANGLES AND GEOMETRY, THEY MOUNTED SACRED MENHIRS ONE UPON ANOTHER...
"...THEY CARVED STAIRS INTO SMOOTH ROCK AND SULLIED THE LIKENESS OF THEIR OVERLORDS...
"UNTIL ONE DAY...
"...THEIR MASTERS RETURNED AND FOUND THEMSELVES FORGOTTEN."
FOR THE GLORY OF THE CONE EMPIRE, AND THE CONTINUED CONSTRUCTION OF BIG USELESS MONUMENTS, THE TIME HAS COME TO REMIND THEM OF THEIR FEALTY!
AND THIS TIME WE REMEMBERED THE QUANTUM CATFLAP.
THE TIME HAS COME FOR TOTAL WORLD DOMINATION!

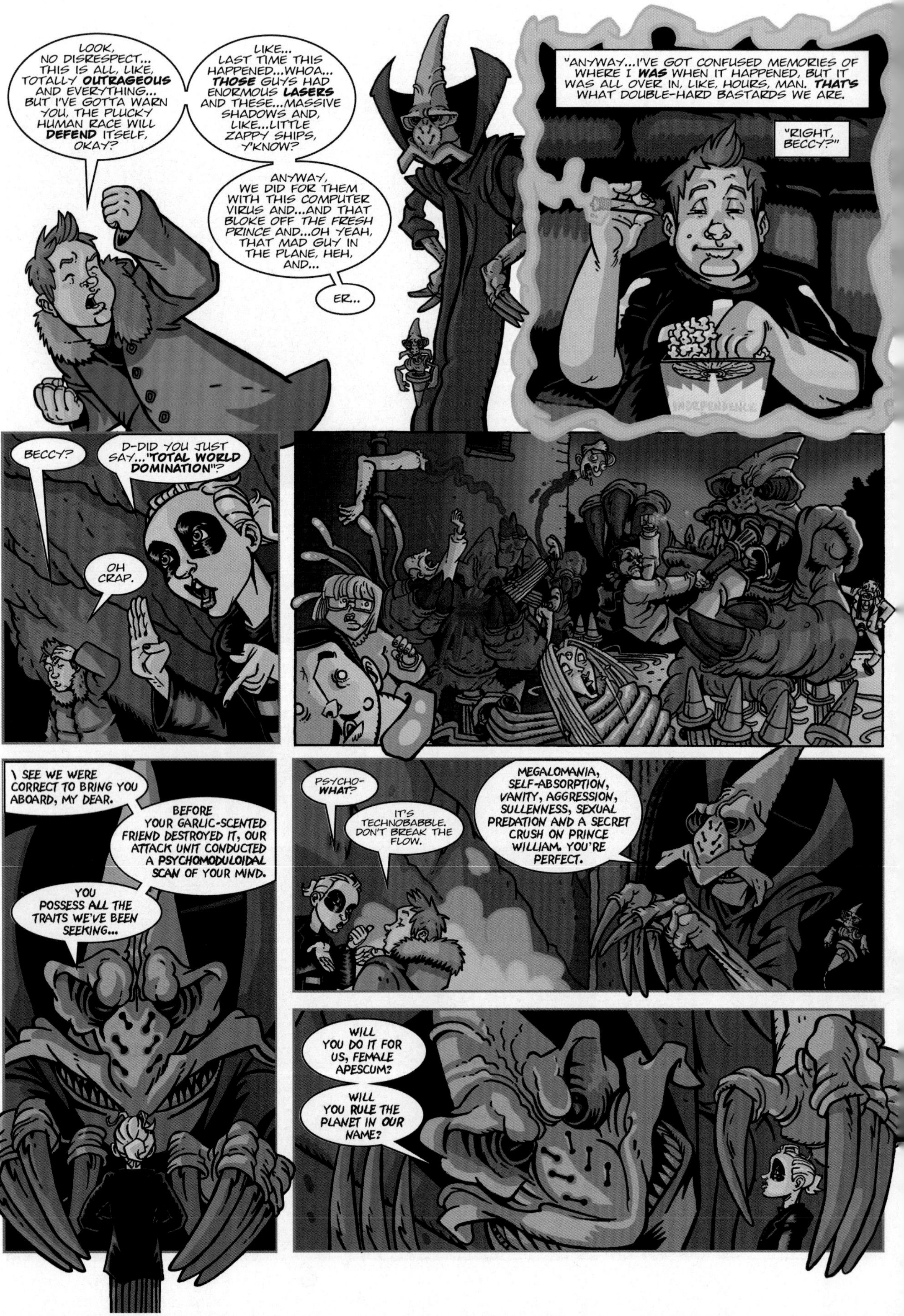

LOOK, NO DISRESPECT... THIS IS ALL, LIKE, TOTALLY OUTRAGEOUS AND EVERYTHING... BUT I'VE GOTTA WARN YOU, THE PLUCKY HUMAN RACE WILL DEFEND ITSELF, OKAY?
LIKE... LAST TIME THIS HAPPENED...WHOA... THOSE GUYS HAD ENORMOUS LASERS AND THESE...MASSIVE SHADOWS AND, LIKE...LITTLE ZAPPY SHIPS, Y'KNOW?
ANYWAY, WE DID FOR THEM WITH THIS COMPUTER VIRUS AND...AND THAT BLOKE OFF THE FRESH PRINCE AND...OH YEAH, THAT MAD GUY IN THE PLANE, HEH, AND...
ER...
"ANYWAY...I'VE GOT CONFUSED MEMORIES OF WHERE I WAS WHEN IT HAPPENED, BUT IT WAS ALL OVER IN, LIKE, HOURS, MAN. THAT'S WHAT DOUBLE-HARD BASTARDS WE ARE.
"RIGHT, BECCY?"
INDEPENDENCE
BECCY?
D-DID YOU JUST SAY..."TOTAL WORLD DOMINATION"?
OH CRAP.
I SEE WE WERE CORRECT TO BRING YOU ABOARD, MY DEAR.
BEFORE YOUR GARLIC-SCENTED FRIEND DESTROYED IT, OUR ATTACK UNIT CONDUCTED A PSYCHOMODULOIDAL SCAN OF YOUR MIND.
YOU POSSESS ALL THE TRAITS WE'VE BEEN SEEKING...
PSYCHO-WHAT?
IT'S TECHNOBABBLE. DON'T BREAK THE FLOW.
MEGALOMANIA, SELF-ABSORPTION, VANITY, AGGRESSION, SULLENNESS, SEXUAL PREDATION AND A SECRET CRUSH ON PRINCE WILLIAM. YOU'RE PERFECT.
WILL YOU DO IT FOR US, FEMALE APESCUM?
WILL YOU RULE THE PLANET IN OUR NAME?

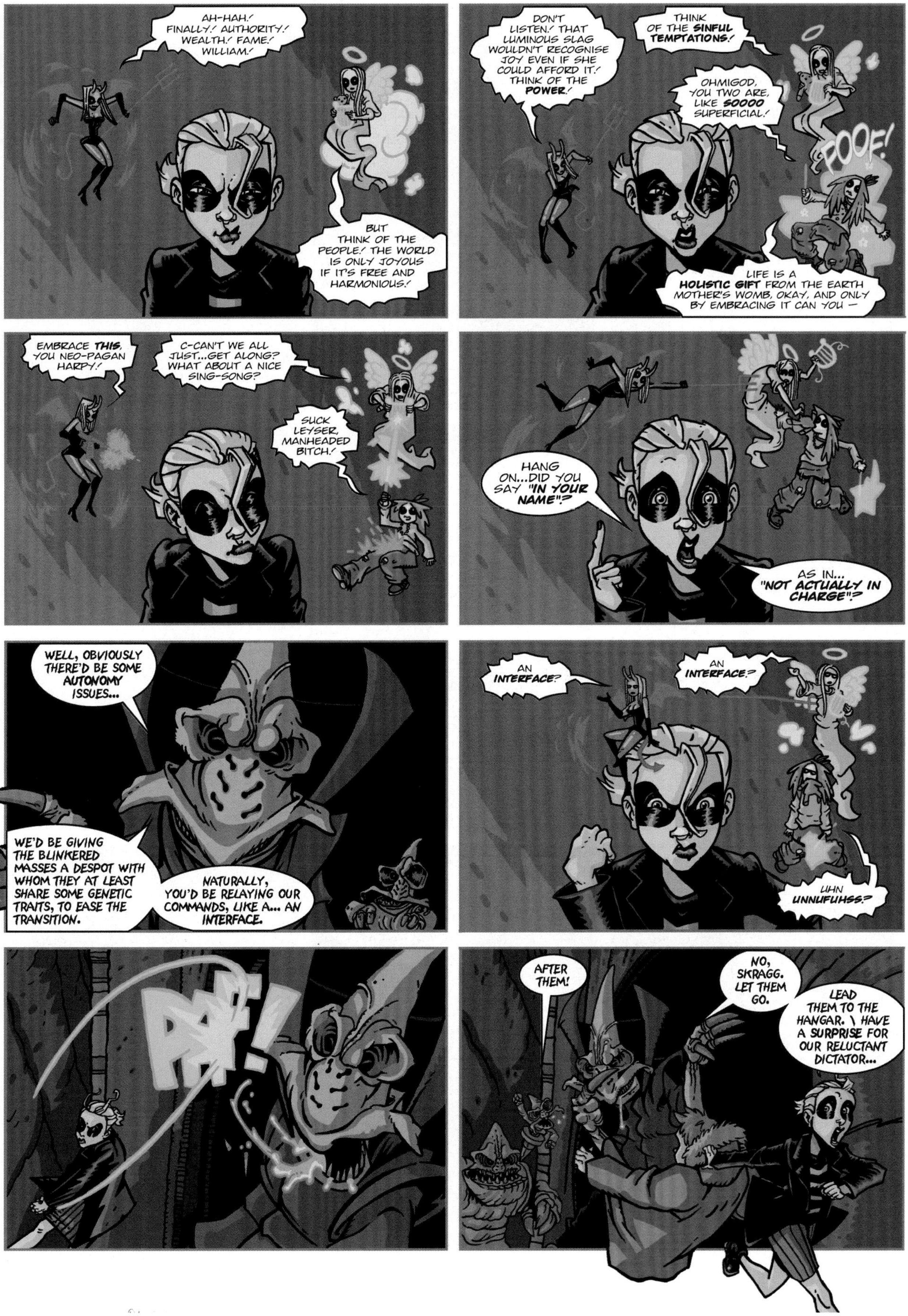

AH-HAH! FINALLY! AUTHORITY! WEALTH! FAME! WILLIAM!
BUT THINK OF THE PEOPLE! THE WORLD IS ONLY JOYOUS IF IT'S FREE AND HARMONIOUS!
DON'T LISTEN! THAT LUMINOUS SLAG WOULDN'T RECOGNISE JOY EVEN IF SHE COULD AFFORD IT! THINK OF THE **POWER**!
THINK OF THE **SINFUL TEMPTATIONS**!
OHMIGOD, YOU TWO ARE, LIKE **SOOOO** SUPERFICIAL!
POOF!
LIFE IS A **HOLISTIC GIFT** FROM THE EARTH MOTHER'S WOMB, OKAY, AND ONLY BY EMBRACING IT CAN YOU —
EMBRACE **THIS**, YOU NEO-PAGAN HARPY!
C-CAN'T WE ALL JUST...GET ALONG? WHAT ABOUT A NICE SING-SONG?
SUCK LEYSER, MANHEADED BITCH!
HANG ON...DID YOU SAY ***"IN YOUR NAME"***?
AS IN... ***"NOT ACTUALLY IN CHARGE"***?
WELL, OBVIOUSLY THERE'D BE SOME **AUTONOMY** ISSUES...
WE'D BE GIVING THE BLINKERED MASSES A DESPOT WITH WHOM THEY AT LEAST SHARE SOME GENETIC TRAITS, TO EASE THE TRANSITION.
NATURALLY, YOU'D BE RELAYING OUR COMMANDS, LIKE A... AN **INTERFACE**.
AN ***INTERFACE***?
AN ***INTERFACE***?
UHN ***UNNUFUHSS***?
PAF!
AFTER THEM!
NO, SKRAGG. LET THEM GO.
LEAD THEM TO THE HANGAR. I HAVE A **SURPRISE** FOR OUR RELUCTANT DICTATOR...

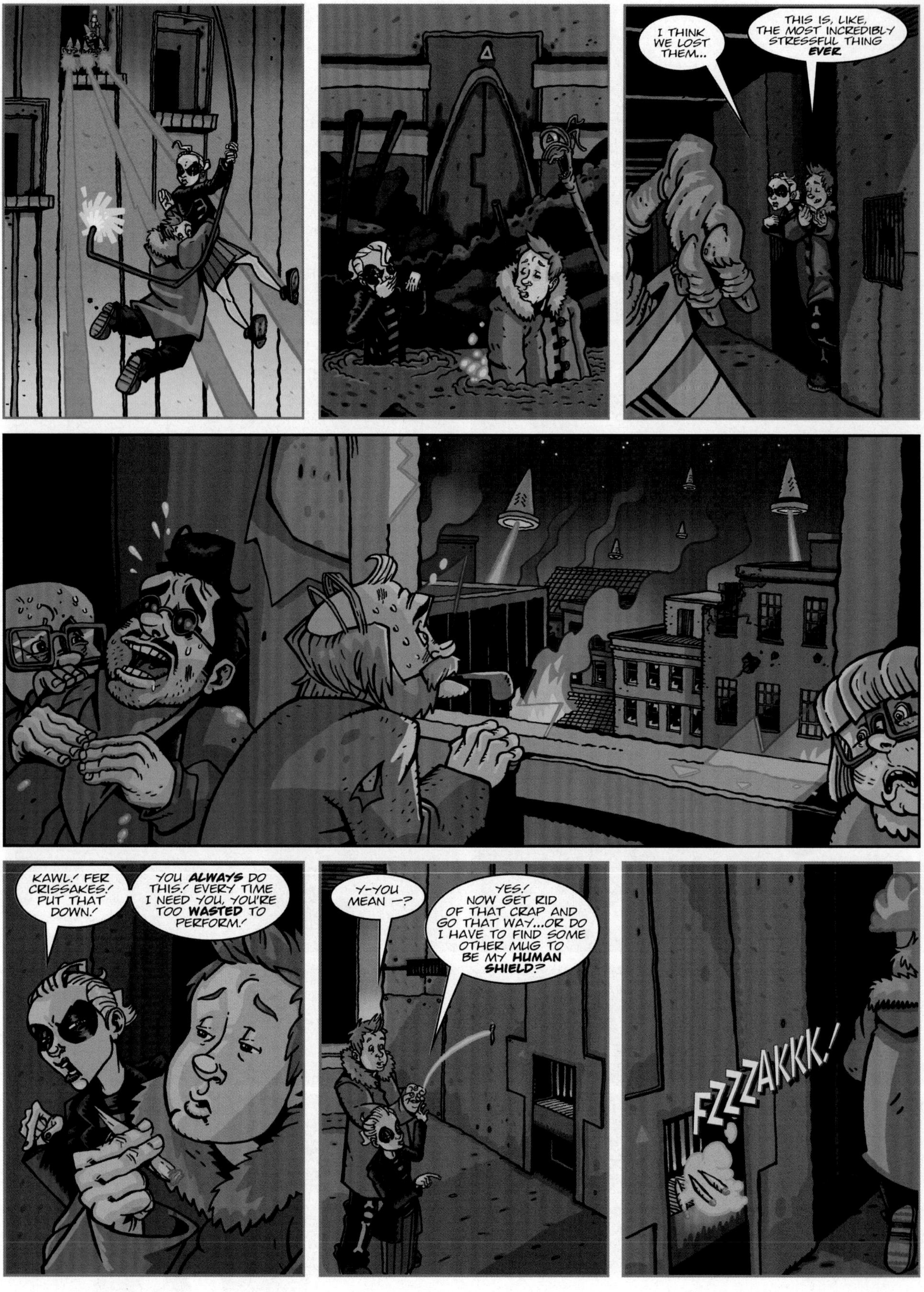
I THINK WE LOST THEM...
THIS IS, LIKE, THE MOST INCREDIBLY STRESSFUL THING EVER.
KAWL! FER CRISSAKES! PUT THAT DOWN!
YOU ALWAYS DO THIS! EVERY TIME I NEED YOU, YOU'RE TOO WASTED TO PERFORM!
Y-YOU MEAN —?
YES! NOW GET RID OF THAT CRAP AND GO THAT WAY...OR DO I HAVE TO FIND SOME OTHER MUG TO BE MY HUMAN SHIELD?
FZZZZAKKK!

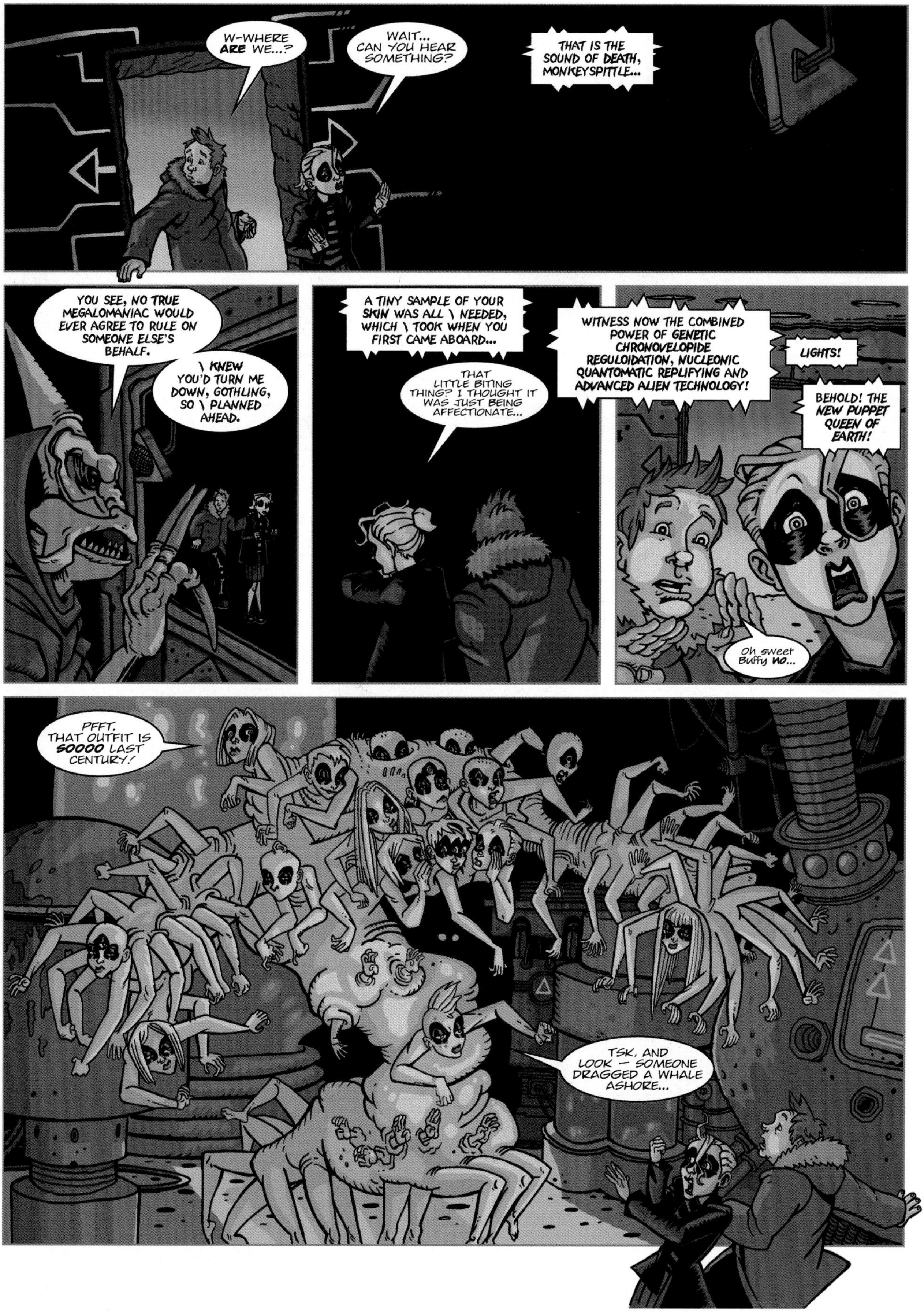
W-WHERE ARE WE...?
WAIT... CAN YOU HEAR SOMETHING?
THAT IS THE SOUND OF DEATH, MONKEYSPITTLE...
YOU SEE, NO TRUE MEGALOMANIAC WOULD EVER AGREE TO RULE ON SOMEONE ELSE'S BEHALF.
I KNEW YOU'D TURN ME DOWN, GOTHLING, SO I PLANNED AHEAD.
A TINY SAMPLE OF YOUR SKIN WAS ALL I NEEDED, WHICH I TOOK WHEN YOU FIRST CAME ABOARD...
THAT LITTLE BITING THING? I THOUGHT IT WAS JUST BEING AFFECTIONATE...
WITNESS NOW THE COMBINED POWER OF GENETIC CHRONOVELOPIDE REGULOIDATION, NUCLEONIC QUANTOMATIC REPLIFYING AND ADVANCED ALIEN TECHNOLOGY!
LIGHTS!
BEHOLD! THE NEW PUPPET QUEEN OF EARTH!
Oh sweet Buffy no...
PFFT. THAT OUTFIT IS SOOOO LAST CENTURY!
TSK, AND LOOK — SOMEONE DRAGGED A WHALE ASHORE...

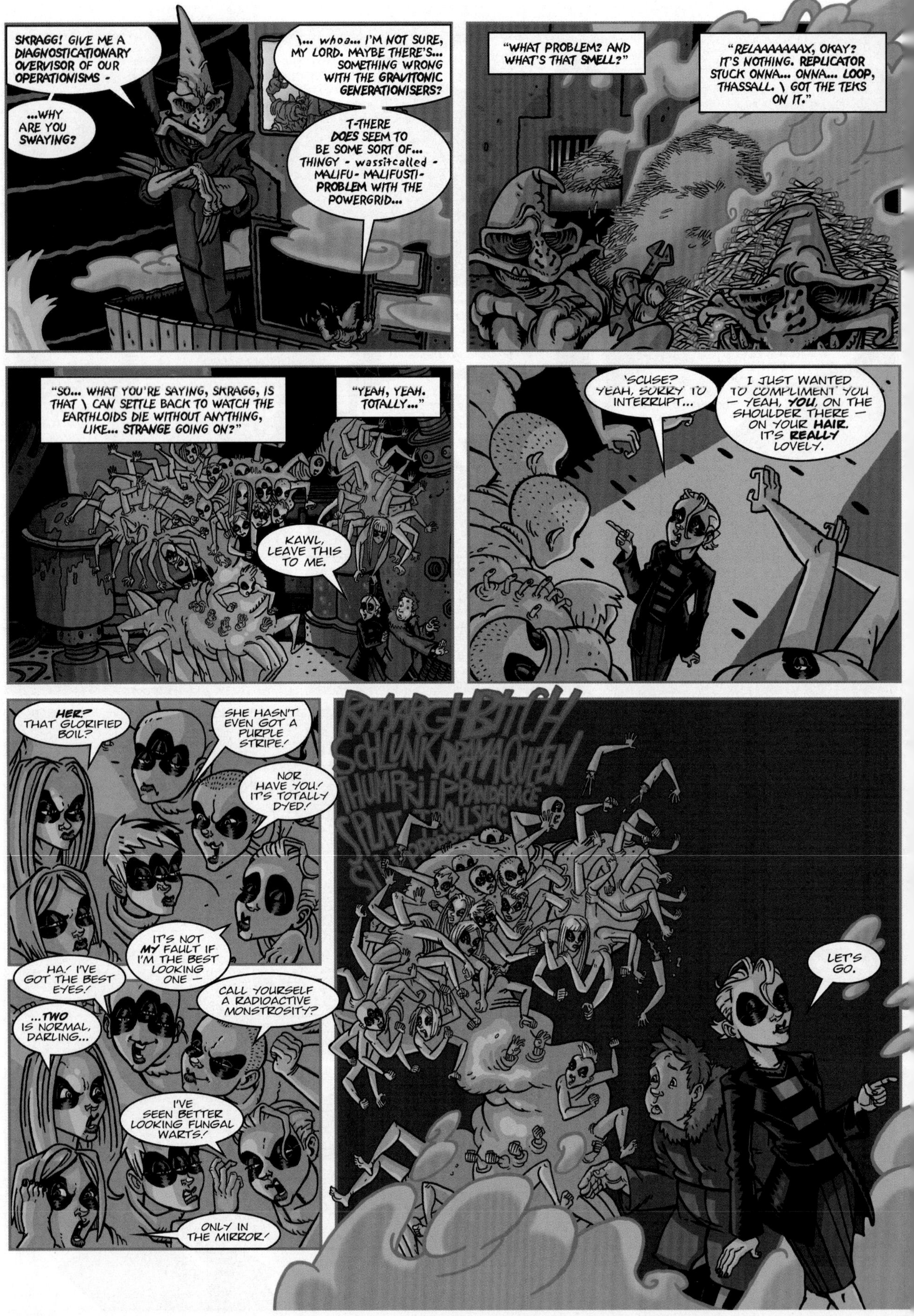
SKRAGG! GIVE ME A DIAGNOSTICATIONARY OVERVISOR OF OUR OPERATIONISMS -
...WHY ARE YOU SWAYING?
I... whoa... I'M NOT SURE, MY LORD. MAYBE THERE'S... SOMETHING WRONG WITH THE GRAVITONIC GENERATIONISERS?
T-THERE DOES SEEM TO BE SOME SORT OF... THINGY - wassitcalled - MALIFU- MALIFUSTI- PROBLEM WITH THE POWERGRID...
"WHAT PROBLEM? AND WHAT'S THAT SMELL?"
"RELAAAAAAAX, OKAY? IT'S NOTHING. REPLICATOR STUCK ONNA... ONNA... LOOP, THASSALL. I GOT THE TEKS ON IT."
"SO... WHAT YOU'RE SAYING, SKRAGG, IS THAT I CAN SETTLE BACK TO WATCH THE EARTHLOIDS DIE WITHOUT ANYTHING, LIKE... STRANGE GOING ON?"
"YEAH, YEAH. TOTALLY..."
KAWL, LEAVE THIS TO ME.
'SCUSE? YEAH, SORRY TO INTERRUPT...
I JUST WANTED TO COMPLIMENT YOU — YEAH, YOU, ON THE SHOULDER THERE — ON YOUR HAIR. IT'S REALLY LOVELY.
HER? THAT GLORIFIED BOIL?
SHE HASN'T EVEN GOT A PURPLE STRIPE!
NOR HAVE YOU! IT'S TOTALLY DYED!
IT'S NOT MY FAULT IF I'M THE BEST LOOKING ONE —
HA! I'VE GOT THE BEST EYES!
...TWO IS NORMAL, DARLING...
CALL YOURSELF A RADIOACTIVE MONSTROSITY?
I'VE SEEN BETTER LOOKING FUNGAL WARTS!
ONLY IN THE MIRROR!
RAAARGHBITCH
SCHLUNK
LET'S GO.

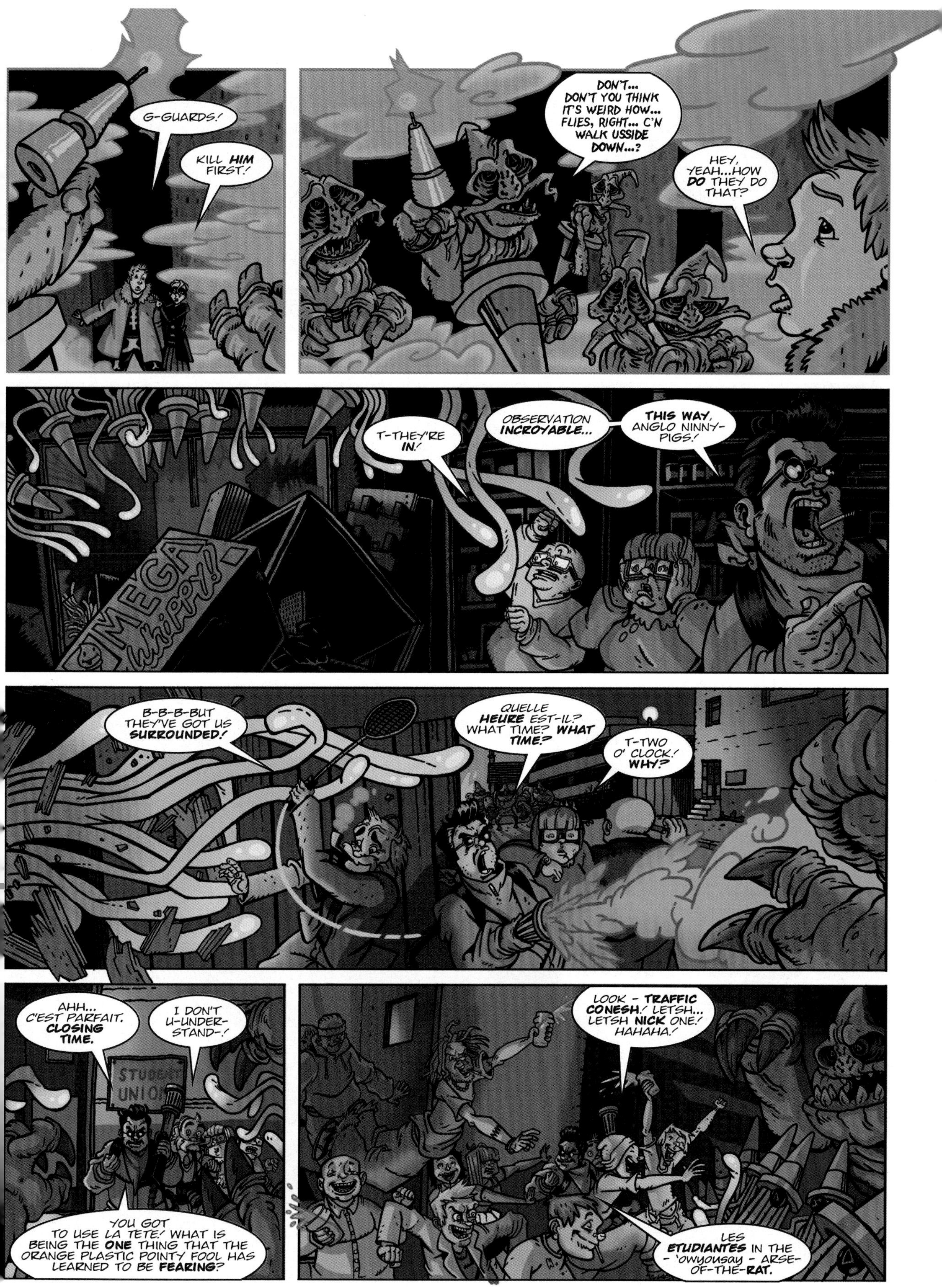
G-GUARDS!
KILL HIM FIRST!
DON'T... DON'T YOU THINK IT'S WEIRD HOW... FLIES, RIGHT... C'N WALK USSIDE DOWN...?
HEY, YEAH...HOW DO THEY DO THAT?
T-THEY'RE IN!
OBSERVATION INCROYABLE...
THIS WAY, ANGLO NINNY-PIGS!
MEGA Whippy!
B-B-B-BUT THEY'VE GOT US SURROUNDED!
QUELLE HEURE EST-IL? WHAT TIME? WHAT TIME?
T-TWO O' CLOCK! WHY?
AHH... C'EST PARFAIT. CLOSING TIME.
I DON'T U-UNDER-STAND-!
STUDENT UNION
YOU GOT TO USE LA TETE! WHAT IS BEING THE ONE THING THAT THE ORANGE PLASTIC POINTY FOOL HAS LEARNED TO BE FEARING?
LOOK - TRAFFIC CONESH! LETSH... LETSH NICK ONE! HAHAHA!
LES ETUDIANTES IN THE - 'OWYOUSAY - ARSE-OF-THE-RAT.

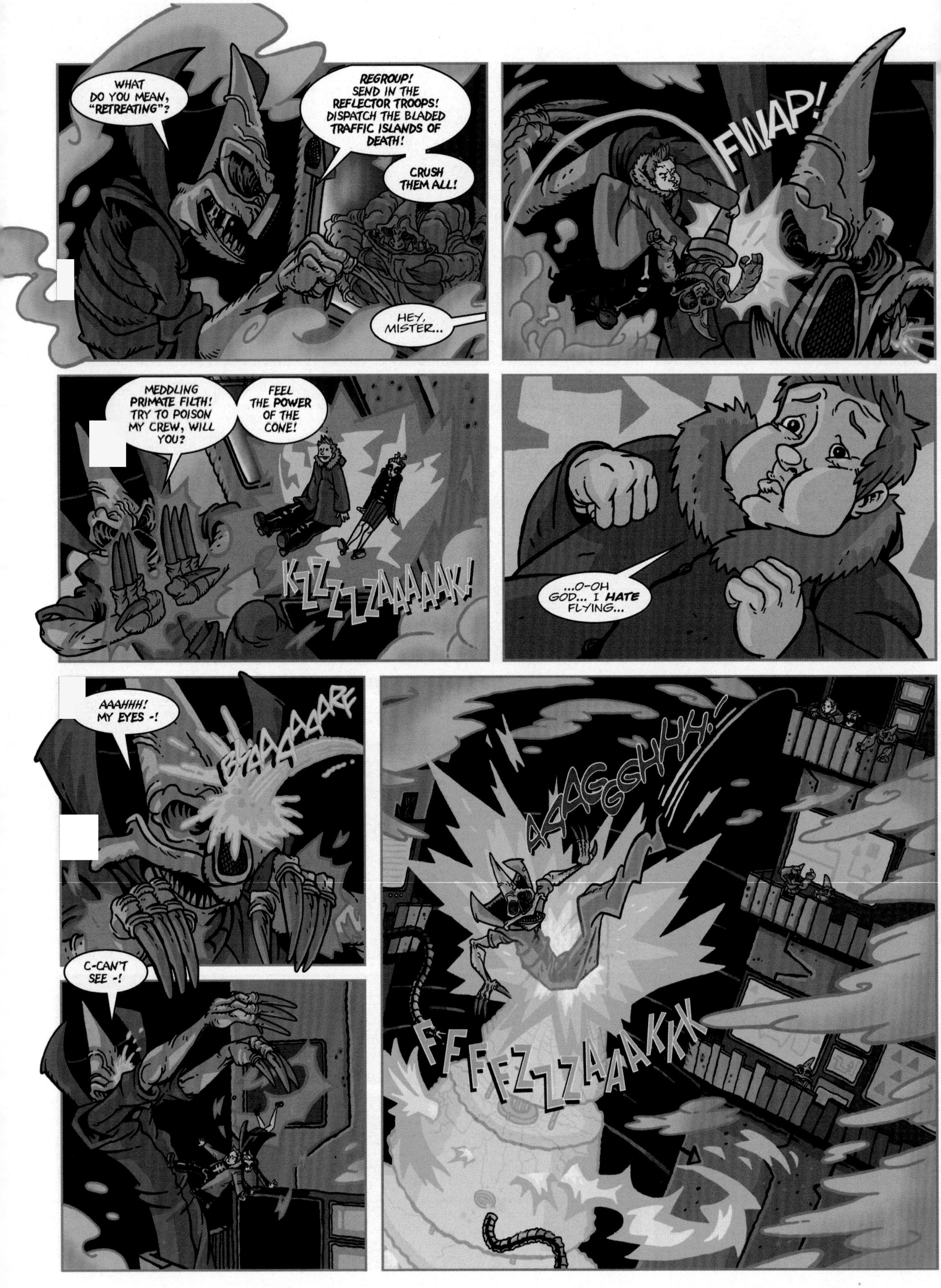

WHAT DO YOU MEAN, "RETREATING"?
REGROUP! SEND IN THE REFLECTOR TROOPS! DISPATCH THE BLADED TRAFFIC ISLANDS OF DEATH!
CRUSH THEM ALL!
HEY, MISTER...
FWAP!
MEDDLING PRIMATE FILTH! TRY TO POISON MY CREW, WILL YOU?
FEEL THE POWER OF THE CONE!
KZZZZZZAAAAAAK!
...O-OH GOD... I HATE FLYING...
AAAHHH! MY EYES -!
BLAAAAARE
C-CAN'T SEE -!
AAAAGGGHHH!
FFFFZZZZAAAAKKK

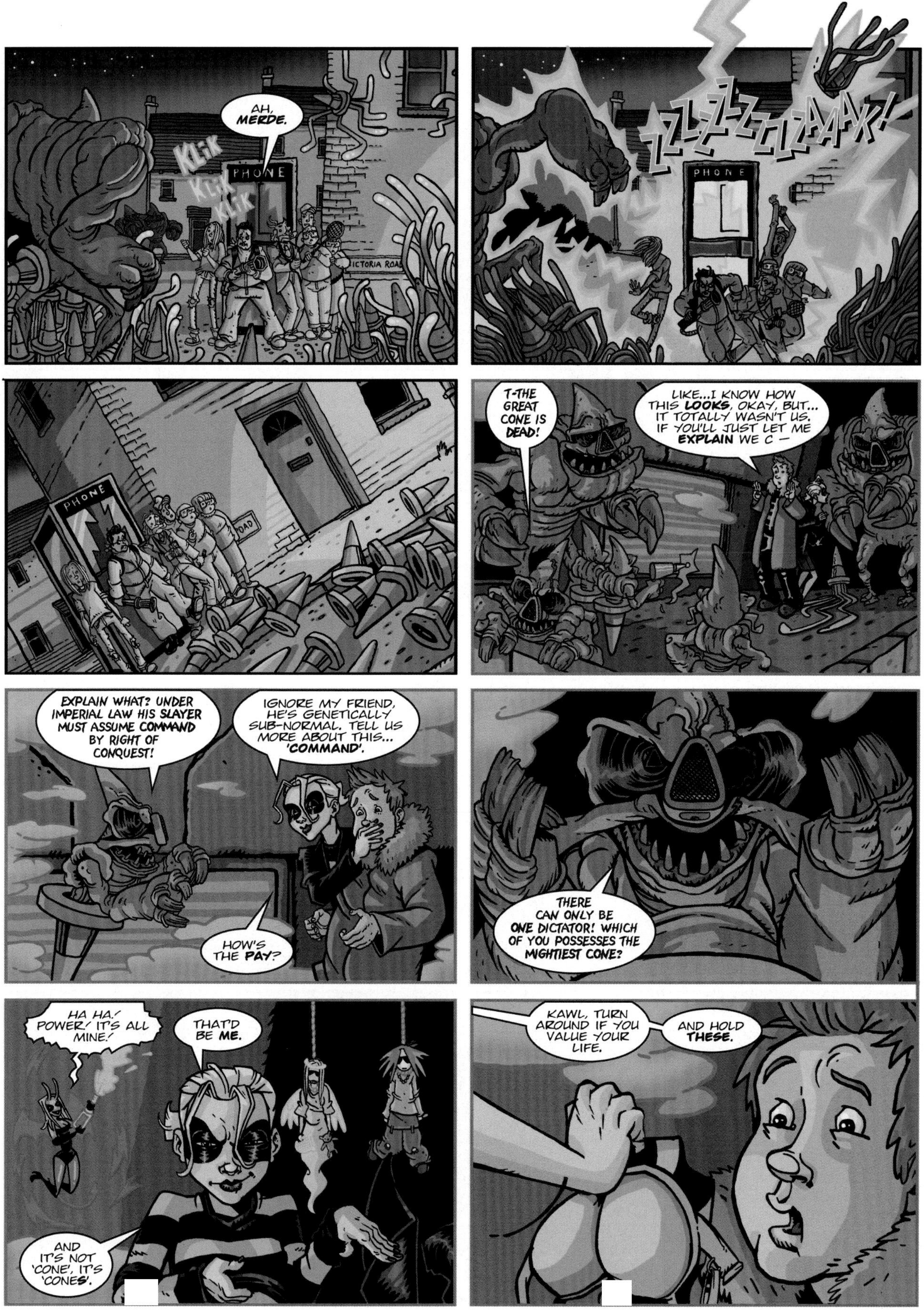
AH, MERDE.
KLIK
KLIK
KLIK
PHONE
VICTORIA ROAD
ZZZZZZZZZZZZZAAAK!
PHONE
PHONE
T-THE GREAT CONE IS DEAD!
LIKE... I KNOW HOW THIS LOOKS, OKAY, BUT... IT TOTALLY WASN'T US. IF YOU'LL JUST LET ME EXPLAIN WE C —
EXPLAIN WHAT? UNDER IMPERIAL LAW HIS SLAYER MUST ASSUME COMMAND BY RIGHT OF CONQUEST!
IGNORE MY FRIEND, HE'S GENETICALLY SUB-NORMAL. TELL US MORE ABOUT THIS... 'COMMAND'.
HOW'S THE PAY?
THERE CAN ONLY BE ONE DICTATOR! WHICH OF YOU POSSESSES THE MIGHTIEST CONE?
HA HA! POWER! IT'S ALL MINE!
THAT'D BE ME.
AND IT'S NOT 'CONE', IT'S 'CONES'.
KAWL, TURN AROUND IF YOU VALUE YOUR LIFE.
AND HOLD THESE.

ALORS... OF ALL THE GIRLY, PANTY-WETTING ANGLOS, **THEY** WERE THE LEAST REPUGNANT.

WE SHALL NEVER SEE THEIR LIKE AGAIN...

...ER...

CRASSSH!

UGGGHH... SOMEBODY STOP THE RIIIIDE...

T-THEY LET YOU **GO**? BUT **WHY**?

SOMETHING ABOUT... BEING REVOLTED BY THE **WOBBLY PINK FLESHINESS** OF OUR **CONES.** AND NEVER BEING ABLE TO TAKE US, LIKE, SERIOUSLY AS LEADERS.

OH... AND THEY SAID WE **ARGUE** WAY TOO MUCH.

ARGUE? ABOUT WHAT?

I DON'T WANT TO TALK ABOUT IT.

LOOK, BEC... I DON'T WANT ANOTHER FIGHT, BUT...

IT'S NOT **MY** FAULT MY CONES ARE BIGGER THAN **YOURS** —

THERE'S ONE THING I DON'T UNDERSTAND...

THOSE BIG-HEADED ALIEN MEN... WHY DO THEY **HELP** US? WHAT DO THEY **GAIN** FROM SCARING AWAY **LES BATARDES CONIQUE?**

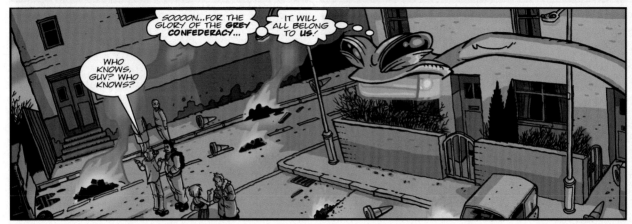

SOOOON...FOR THE GLORY OF THE **GREY CONFEDERACY**...

IT WILL ALL BELONG TO US!

WHO KNOWS, GUV? WHO KNOWS?

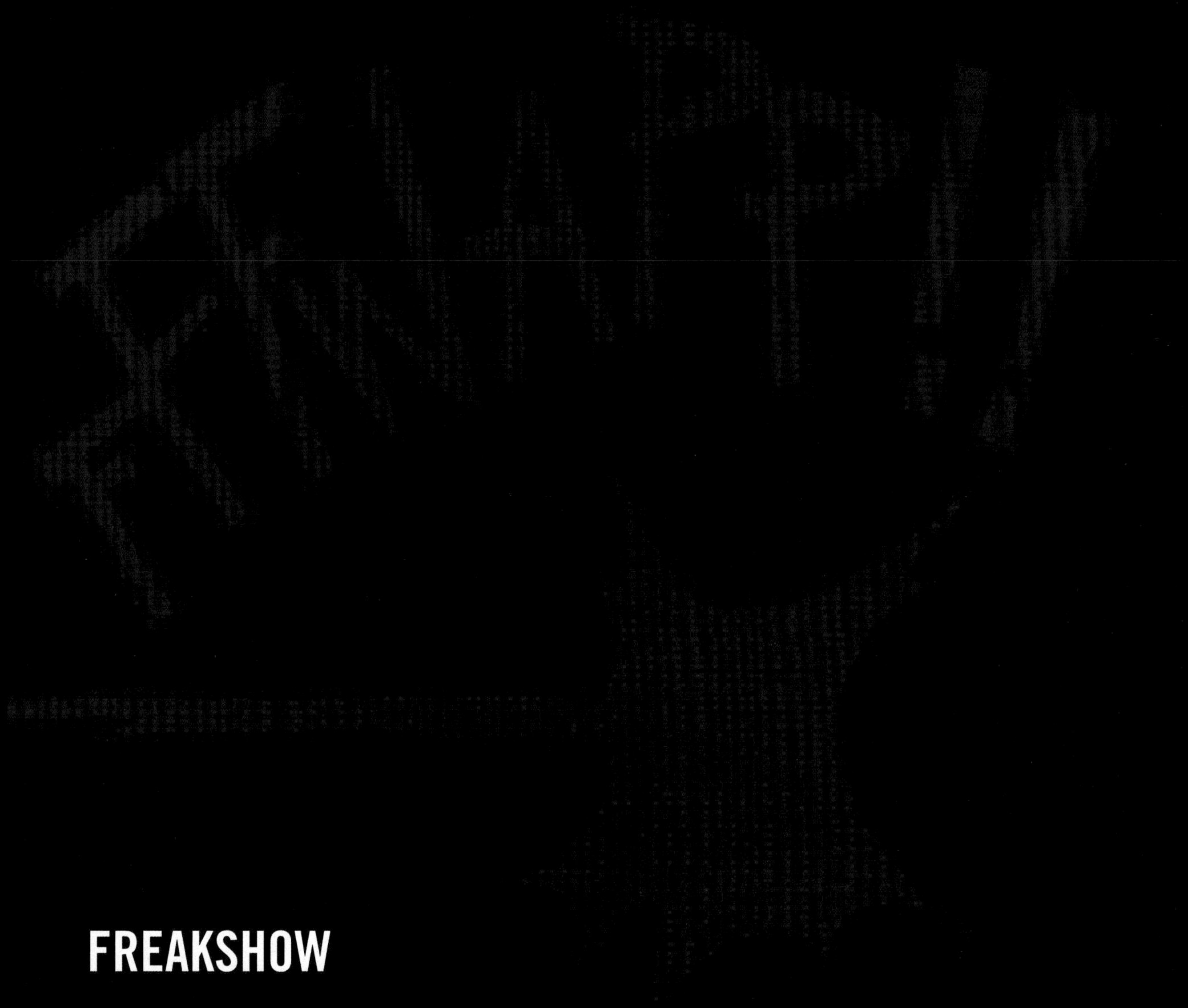

FREAKSHOW

Script: Simon Spurrier
Art: Steve Roberts
Letters: Ellie De Ville

Originally published in *2000 AD* Progs 1477-1481

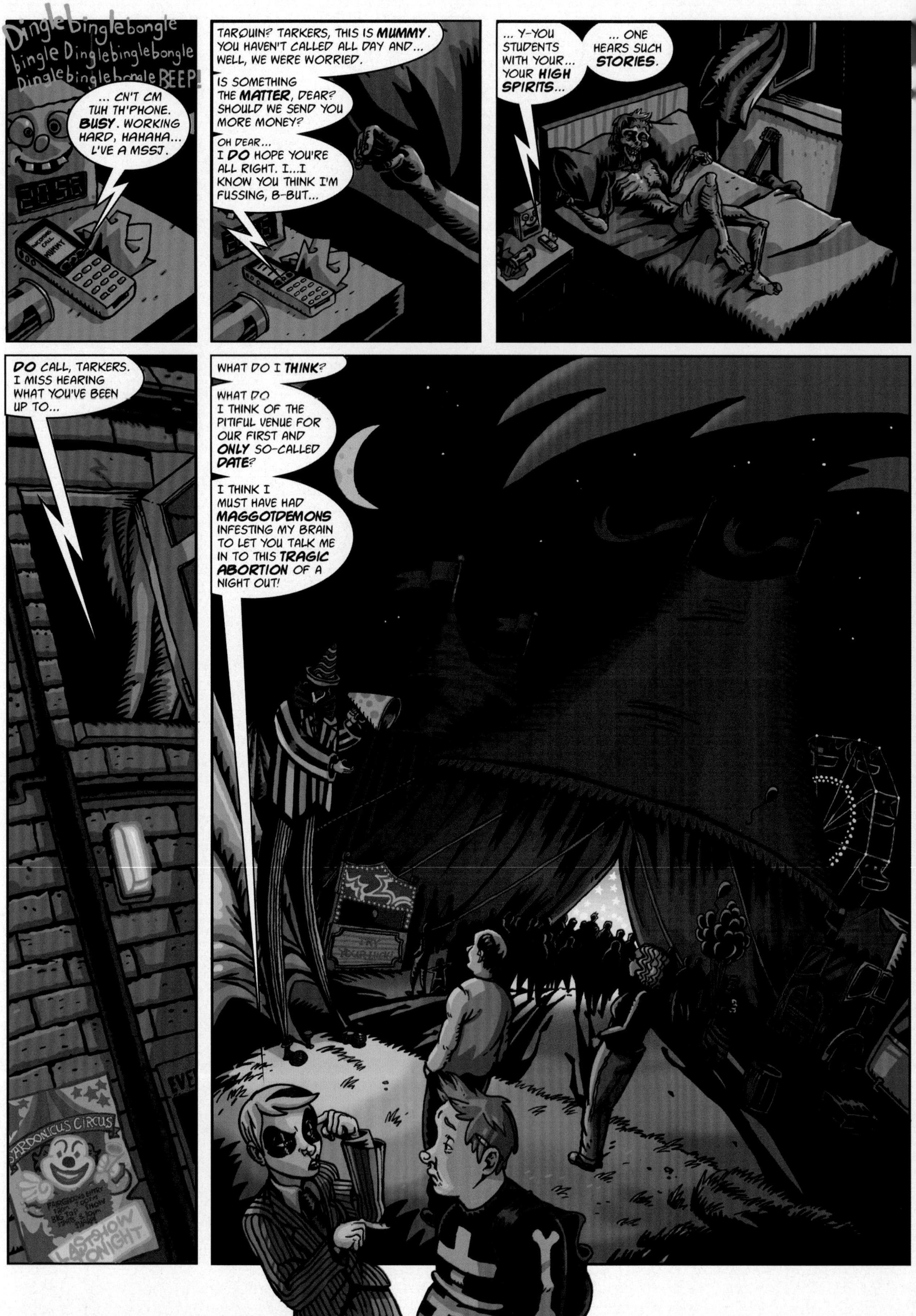

Dinglebinglebongle bingle Dinglebinglebongle Dinglebinglebongle BEEP!
... CN'T CM TUH TH'PHONE. BUSY. WORKING HARD, HAHAHA... L'VE A MSSJ.
TARQUIN? TARKERS, THIS IS MUMMY. YOU HAVEN'T CALLED ALL DAY AND... WELL, WE WERE WORRIED.
IS SOMETHING THE MATTER, DEAR? SHOULD WE SEND YOU MORE MONEY?
OH DEAR... I DO HOPE YOU'RE ALL RIGHT. I...I KNOW YOU THINK I'M FUSSING, B-BUT...
... Y-YOU STUDENTS WITH YOUR... YOUR HIGH SPIRITS...
... ONE HEARS SUCH STORIES.
DO CALL, TARKERS. I MISS HEARING WHAT YOU'VE BEEN UP TO...
SARDONICUS CIRCUS
LAST SHOW TONIGHT
WHAT DO I THINK?
WHAT DO I THINK OF THE PITIFUL VENUE FOR OUR FIRST AND ONLY SO-CALLED DATE?
I THINK I MUST HAVE HAD MAGGOTDEMONS INFESTING MY BRAIN TO LET YOU TALK ME IN TO THIS TRAGIC ABORTION OF A NIGHT OUT!

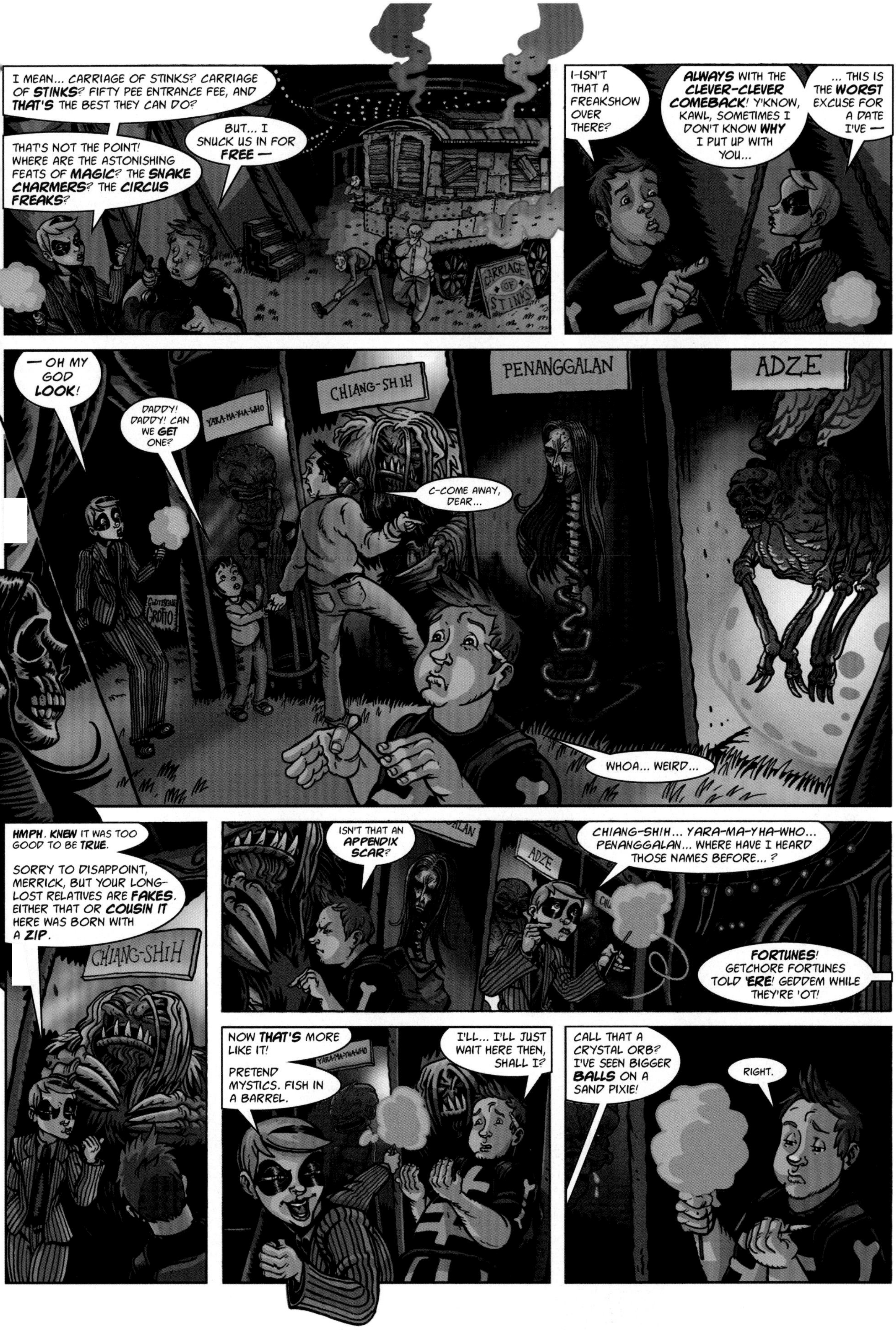
I MEAN... CARRIAGE OF STINKS? CARRIAGE OF STINKS? FIFTY PEE ENTRANCE FEE, AND THAT'S THE BEST THEY CAN DO?
THAT'S NOT THE POINT! WHERE ARE THE ASTONISHING FEATS OF MAGIC? THE SNAKE CHARMERS? THE CIRCUS FREAKS?
BUT... I SNUCK US IN FOR FREE —
CARRIAGE OF STINKS
I-ISN'T THAT A FREAKSHOW OVER THERE?
ALWAYS WITH THE CLEVER-CLEVER COMEBACK! Y'KNOW, KAWL, SOMETIMES I DON'T KNOW WHY I PUT UP WITH YOU...
... THIS IS THE WORST EXCUSE FOR A DATE I'VE —
— OH MY GOD LOOK!
DADDY! DADDY! CAN WE GET ONE?
YARA-MA-YHA-WHO
CHIANG-SHIH
PENANGGALAN
ADZE
C-COME AWAY, DEAR...
WHOA... WEIRD...
HMPH. KNEW IT WAS TOO GOOD TO BE TRUE.
SORRY TO DISAPPOINT, MERRICK, BUT YOUR LONG-LOST RELATIVES ARE FAKES. EITHER THAT OR COUSIN IT HERE WAS BORN WITH A ZIP.
CHIANG-SHIH
ISN'T THAT AN APPENDIX SCAR?
CHIANG-SHIH... YARA-MA-YHA-WHO... PENANGGALAN... WHERE HAVE I HEARD THOSE NAMES BEFORE... ?
ADZE
FORTUNES! GETCHORE FORTUNES TOLD 'ERE! GEDDEM WHILE THEY'RE 'OT!
NOW THAT'S MORE LIKE IT!
PRETEND MYSTICS. FISH IN A BARREL.
I'LL... I'LL JUST WAIT HERE THEN, SHALL I?
CALL THAT A CRYSTAL ORB? I'VE SEEN BIGGER BALLS ON A SAND PIXIE!
RIGHT.

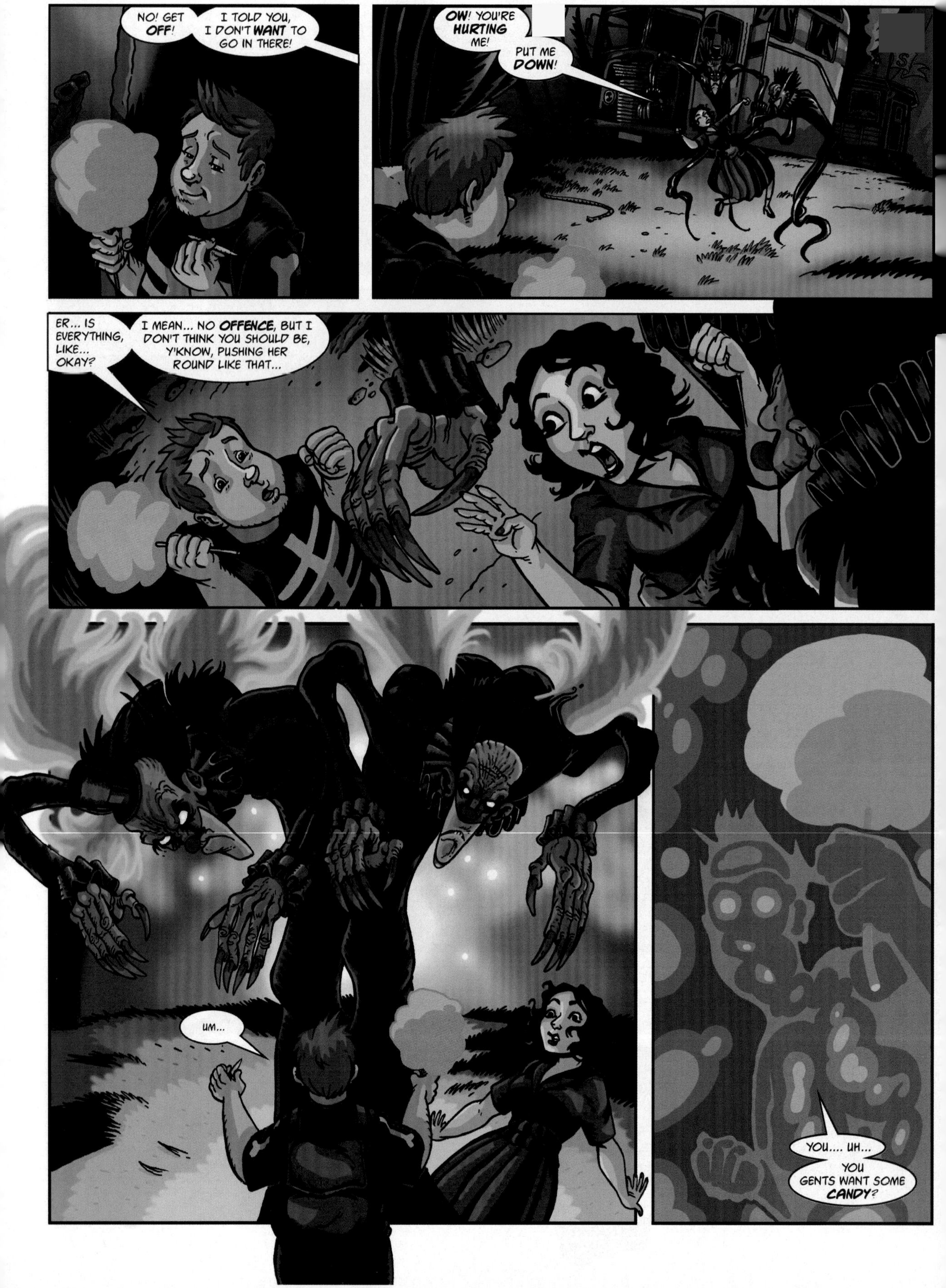
NO! GET **OFF**!
I TOLD YOU, I DON'T **WANT** TO GO IN THERE!
OW! YOU'RE **HURTING** ME!
PUT ME **DOWN**!
ER... IS EVERYTHING, LIKE... OKAY?
I MEAN... NO **OFFENCE**, BUT I DON'T THINK YOU SHOULD BE, Y'KNOW, PUSHING HER ROUND LIKE THAT...
UM...
YOU.... UH...
YOU GENTS WANT SOME **CANDY**?

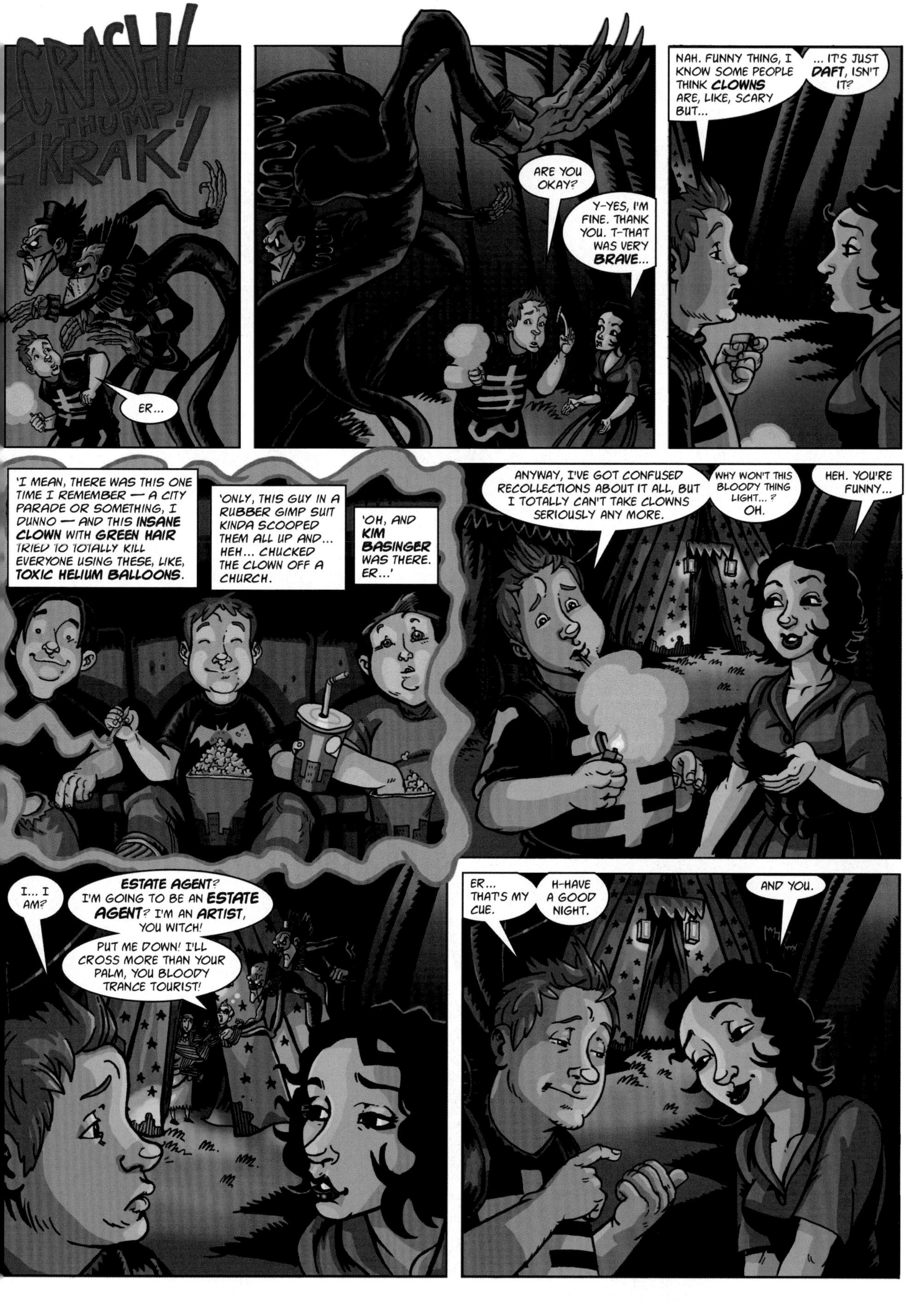
CRASH!
THUMP!
KRAK!
ER...
ARE YOU OKAY?
Y-YES, I'M FINE. THANK YOU. T-THAT WAS VERY BRAVE...
NAH. FUNNY THING, I KNOW SOME PEOPLE THINK CLOWNS ARE, LIKE, SCARY BUT...
... IT'S JUST DAFT, ISN'T IT?
'I MEAN, THERE WAS THIS ONE TIME I REMEMBER — A CITY PARADE OR SOMETHING, I DUNNO — AND THIS INSANE CLOWN WITH GREEN HAIR TRIED TO TOTALLY KILL EVERYONE USING THESE, LIKE, TOXIC HELIUM BALLOONS.
'ONLY, THIS GUY IN A RUBBER GIMP SUIT KINDA SCOOPED THEM ALL UP AND... HEH... CHUCKED THE CLOWN OFF A CHURCH.
'OH, AND KIM BASINGER WAS THERE. ER...'
ANYWAY, I'VE GOT CONFUSED RECOLLECTIONS ABOUT IT ALL, BUT I TOTALLY CAN'T TAKE CLOWNS SERIOUSLY ANY MORE.
WHY WON'T THIS BLOODY THING LIGHT... ? OH.
HEH. YOU'RE FUNNY...
I... I AM?
ESTATE AGENT? I'M GOING TO BE AN ESTATE AGENT? I'M AN ARTIST, YOU WITCH!
PUT ME DOWN! I'LL CROSS MORE THAN YOUR PALM, YOU BLOODY TRANCE TOURIST!
ER... THAT'S MY CUE.
H-HAVE A GOOD NIGHT.
AND YOU.

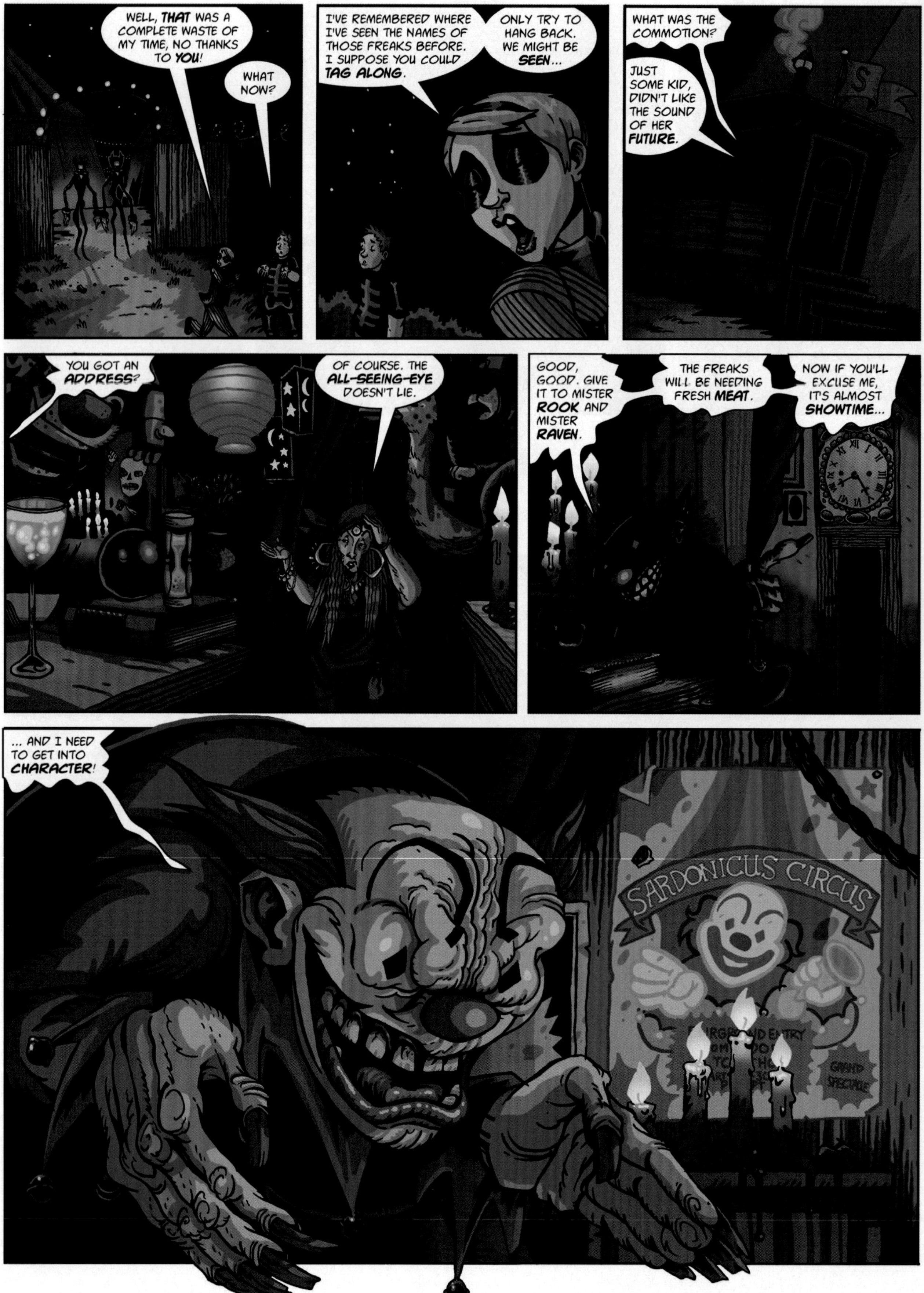
WELL, **THAT** WAS A COMPLETE WASTE OF MY TIME, NO THANKS TO **YOU**!
WHAT NOW?
I'VE REMEMBERED WHERE I'VE SEEN THE NAMES OF THOSE FREAKS BEFORE. I SUPPOSE YOU COULD **TAG ALONG**.
ONLY TRY TO HANG BACK. WE MIGHT BE **SEEN**...
WHAT WAS THE COMMOTION?
JUST SOME KID, DIDN'T LIKE THE SOUND OF HER **FUTURE**.
YOU GOT AN **ADDRESS**?
OF COURSE. THE **ALL-SEEING-EYE** DOESN'T LIE.
GOOD, GOOD. GIVE IT TO MISTER **ROOK** AND MISTER **RAVEN**.
THE FREAKS WILL BE NEEDING FRESH **MEAT**.
NOW IF YOU'LL EXCUSE ME, IT'S ALMOST **SHOWTIME**...
... AND I NEED TO GET INTO **CHARACTER**!
SARDONICUS CIRCUS
GRAND SPECTACLE

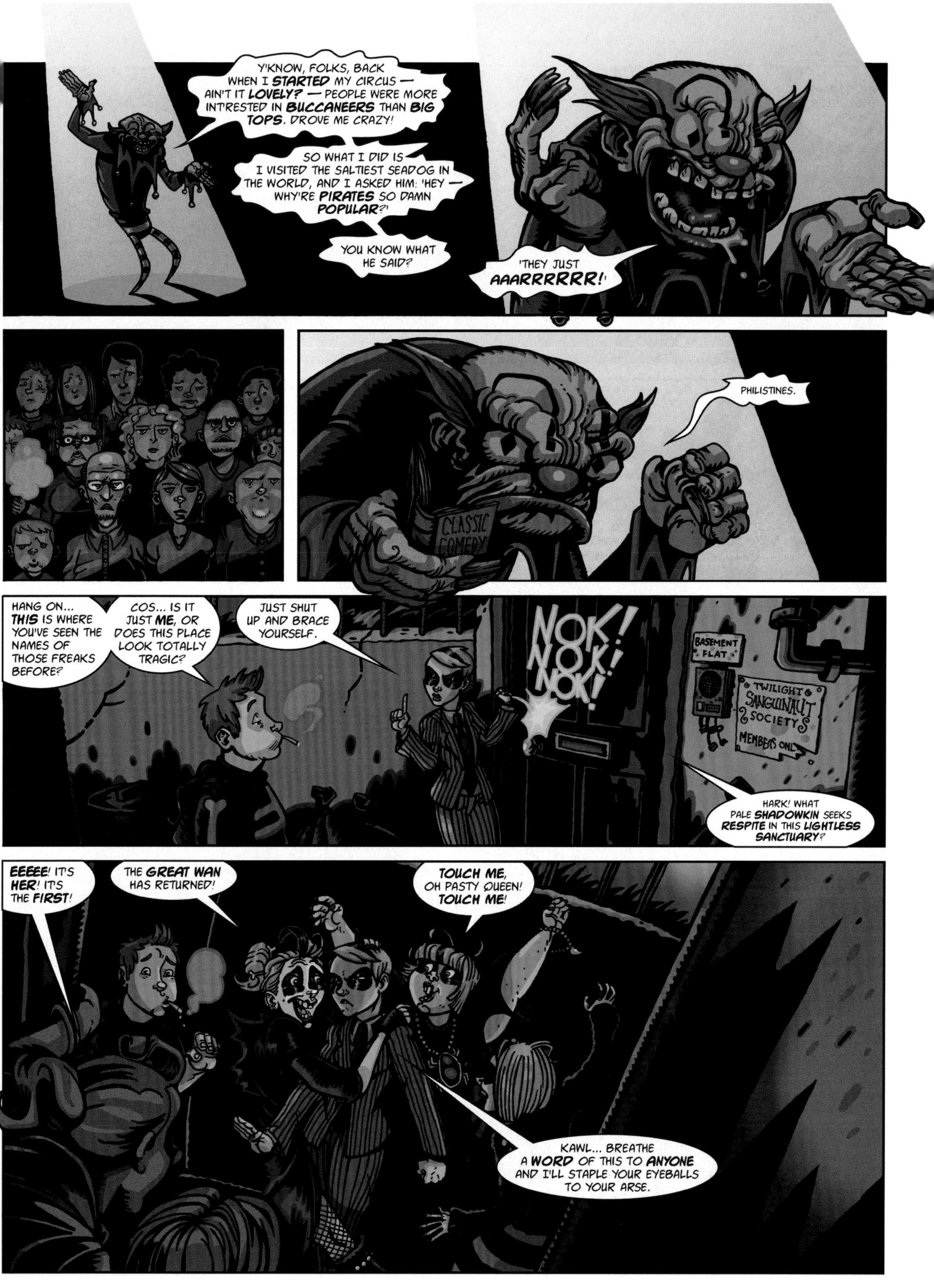

Y'KNOW, FOLKS, BACK WHEN I STARTED MY CIRCUS — AIN'T IT LOVELY? — PEOPLE WERE MORE INTRESTED IN BUCCANEERS THAN BIG TOPS. DROVE ME CRAZY!
SO WHAT I DID IS I VISITED THE SALTIEST SEADOG IN THE WORLD, AND I ASKED HIM: 'HEY — WHY'RE PIRATES SO DAMN POPULAR?'
YOU KNOW WHAT HE SAID?
'THEY JUST AAARRRRRR!'
PHILISTINES.
CLASSIC COMEDY
HANG ON... THIS IS WHERE YOU'VE SEEN THE NAMES OF THOSE FREAKS BEFORE?
COS... IS IT JUST ME, OR DOES THIS PLACE LOOK TOTALLY TRAGIC?
JUST SHUT UP AND BRACE YOURSELF.
NOK! NOK! NOK!
BASEMENT FLAT
TWILIGHT SANGUINAUT SOCIETY
MEMBERS ONLY
HARK! WHAT PALE SHADOWKIN SEEKS RESPITE IN THIS LIGHTLESS SANCTUARY?
EEEEE! IT'S HER! IT'S THE FIRST!
THE GREAT WAN HAS RETURNED!
TOUCH ME, OH PASTY QUEEN! TOUCH ME!
KAWL... BREATHE A WORD OF THIS TO ANYONE AND I'LL STAPLE YOUR EYEBALLS TO YOUR ARSE.

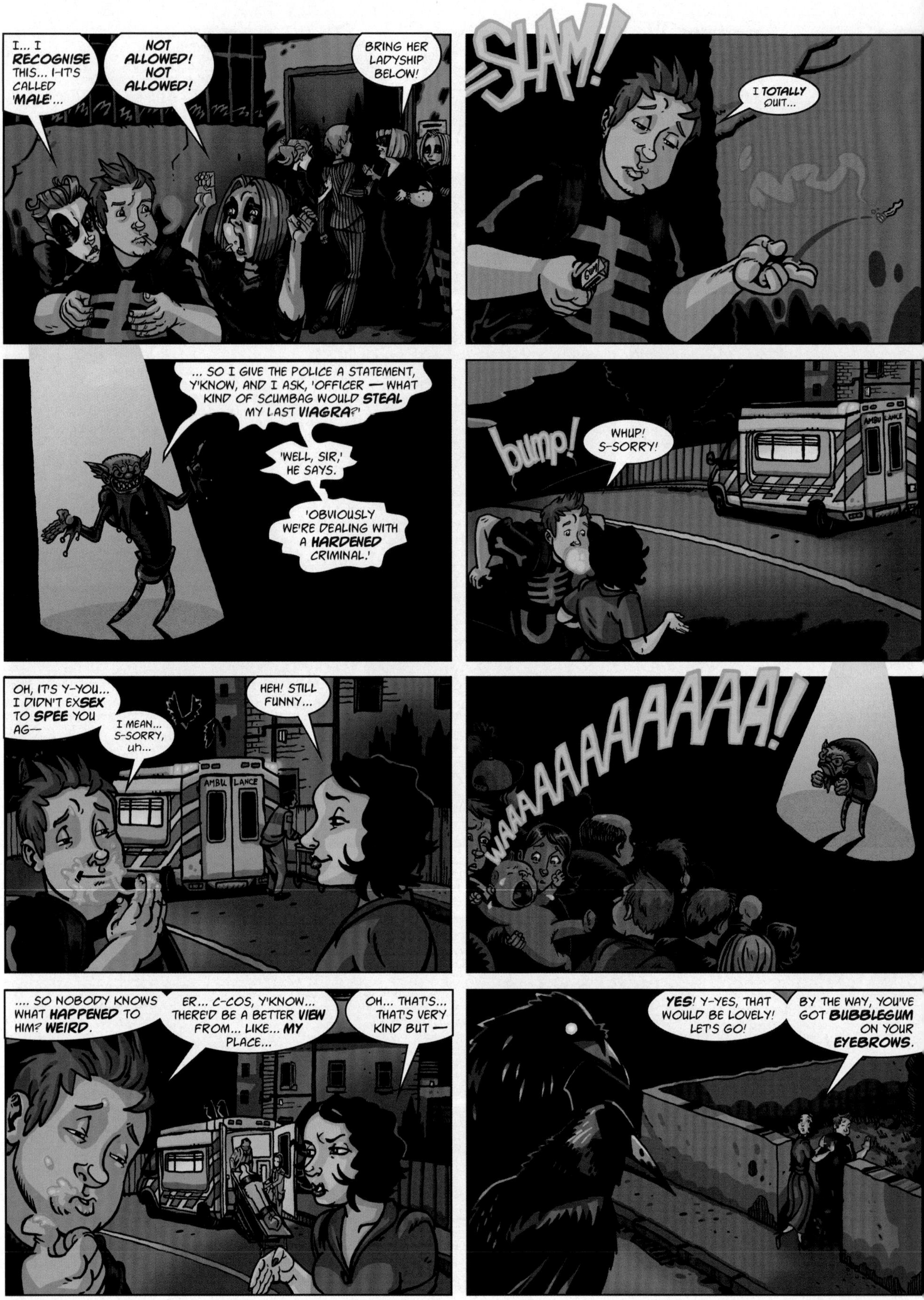
I... I RECOGNISE THIS... I-IT'S CALLED 'MALE'...
NOT ALLOWED! NOT ALLOWED!
BRING HER LADYSHIP BELOW!
SLAM!
I TOTALLY QUIT...
... SO I GIVE THE POLICE A STATEMENT, Y'KNOW, AND I ASK, 'OFFICER — WHAT KIND OF SCUMBAG WOULD STEAL MY LAST VIAGRA?'
'WELL, SIR,' HE SAYS.
'OBVIOUSLY WE'RE DEALING WITH A HARDENED CRIMINAL.'
bump!
WHUP! S-SORRY!
OH, IT'S Y-YOU... I DIDN'T EXSEX TO SPEE YOU AG—
I MEAN... S-SORRY, uh...
HEH! STILL FUNNY...
WAAAAAAAAAAAAA!
.... SO NOBODY KNOWS WHAT HAPPENED TO HIM? WEIRD.
ER... C-COS, Y'KNOW... THERE'D BE A BETTER VIEW FROM... LIKE... MY PLACE...
OH... THAT'S... THAT'S VERY KIND BUT —
YES! Y-YES, THAT WOULD BE LOVELY! LET'S GO!
BY THE WAY, YOU'VE GOT BUBBLEGUM ON YOUR EYEBROWS.

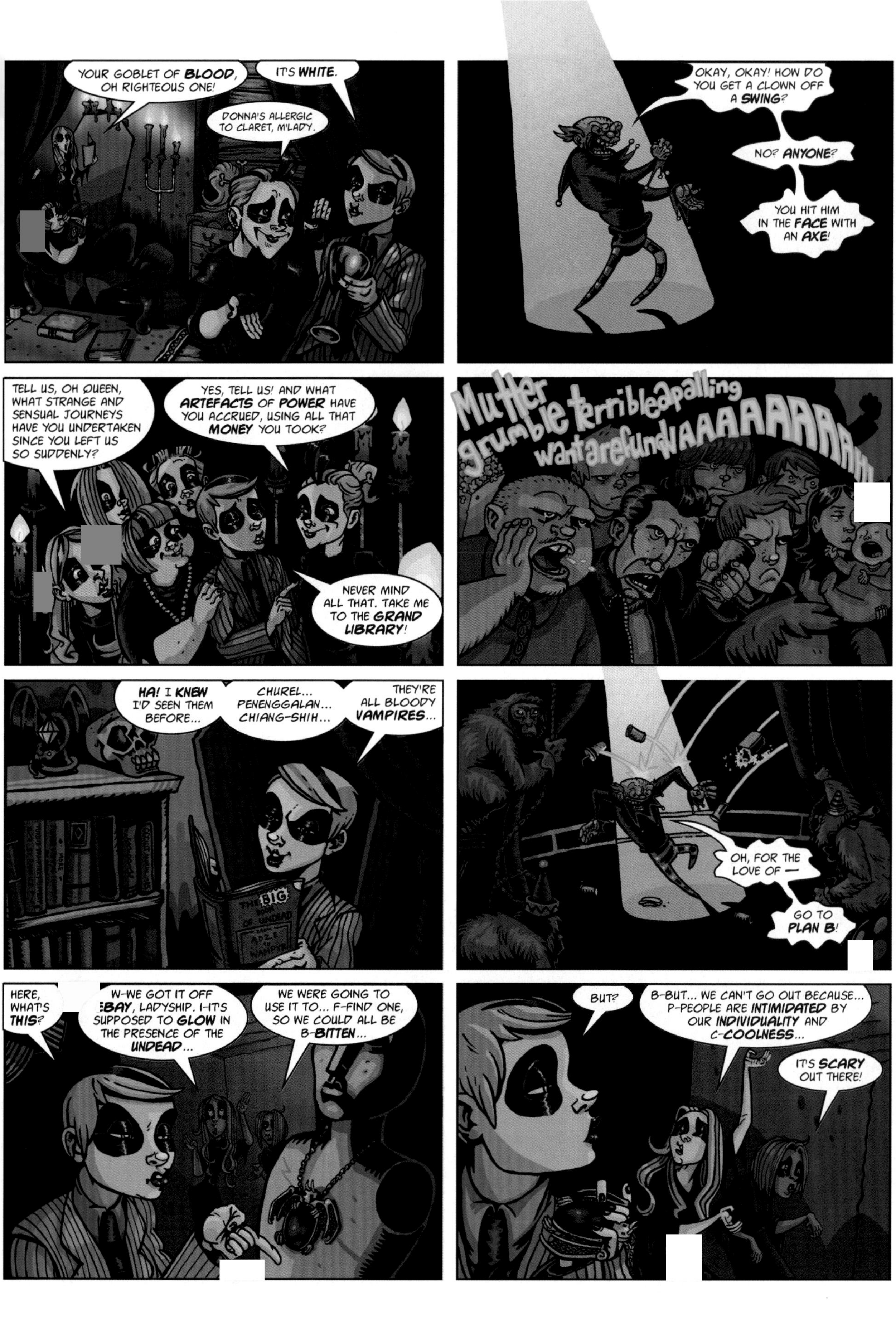
YOUR GOBLET OF BLOOD, OH RIGHTEOUS ONE!
IT'S WHITE.
DONNA'S ALLERGIC TO CLARET, M'LADY.
OKAY, OKAY! HOW DO YOU GET A CLOWN OFF A SWING?
NO? ANYONE?
YOU HIT HIM IN THE FACE WITH AN AXE!
TELL US, OH QUEEN, WHAT STRANGE AND SENSUAL JOURNEYS HAVE YOU UNDERTAKEN SINCE YOU LEFT US SO SUDDENLY?
YES, TELL US! AND WHAT ARTEFACTS OF POWER HAVE YOU ACCRUED, USING ALL THAT MONEY YOU TOOK?
NEVER MIND ALL THAT. TAKE ME TO THE GRAND LIBRARY!
Mutter grumble terribleapalling wantarefundWAAAAAAAAAH!
HA! I KNEW I'D SEEN THEM BEFORE...
CHUREL... PENENGGALAN... CHIANG-SHIH...
THEY'RE ALL BLOODY VAMPIRES...
THE BIG BOOK OF UNDEAD FROM ADZE TO WAMPYR
OH, FOR THE LOVE OF —
GO TO PLAN B!
HERE, WHAT'S THIS?
W-WE GOT IT OFF EBAY, LADYSHIP. I-IT'S SUPPOSED TO GLOW IN THE PRESENCE OF THE UNDEAD...
WE WERE GOING TO USE IT TO... F-FIND ONE, SO WE COULD ALL BE B-BITTEN...
BUT?
B-BUT... WE CAN'T GO OUT BECAUSE... P-PEOPLE ARE INTIMIDATED BY OUR INDIVIDUALITY AND C-COOLNESS...
IT'S SCARY OUT THERE!

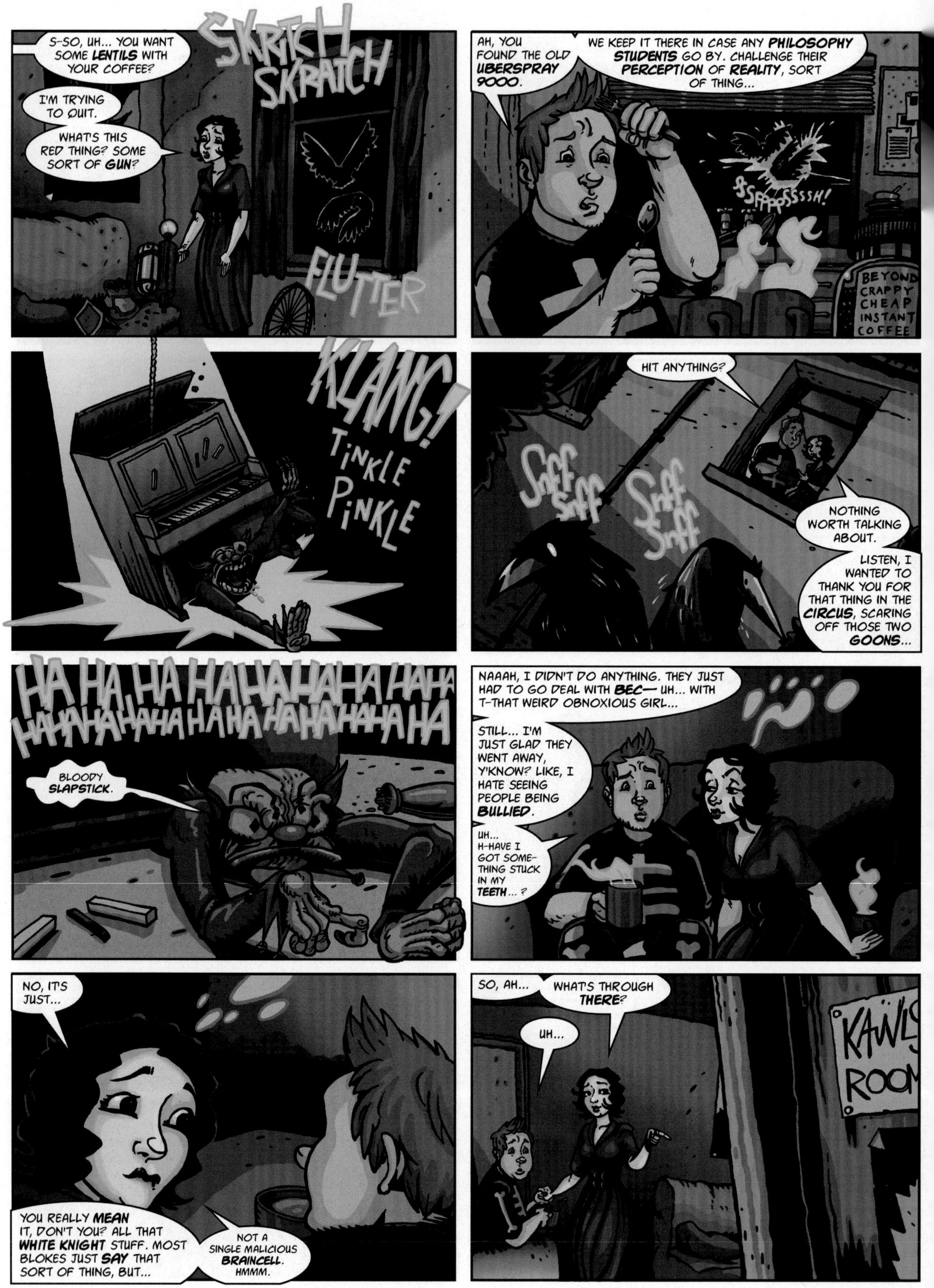

S-SO, UH... YOU WANT SOME LENTILS WITH YOUR COFFEE?
SKRITCH SKRATCH
I'M TRYING TO QUIT.
WHAT'S THIS RED THING? SOME SORT OF GUN?
FLUTTER
AH, YOU FOUND THE OLD UBERSPRAY 9000.
WE KEEP IT THERE IN CASE ANY PHILOSOPHY STUDENTS GO BY. CHALLENGE THEIR PERCEPTION OF REALITY, SORT OF THING...
SSFPPPSSSSH!
BEYOND CRAPPY CHEAP INSTANT COFFEE
KLANG!
TINKLE PINKLE
HIT ANYTHING?
SNIFF SNIFF
SNIFF SNIFF
NOTHING WORTH TALKING ABOUT.
LISTEN, I WANTED TO THANK YOU FOR THAT THING IN THE CIRCUS, SCARING OFF THOSE TWO GOONS...
HA HA, HA HAHAHAHA HAHA HAHAHAHAHA HAHA HA HA HAHAHAHAHA HA
BLOODY SLAPSTICK.
NAAAH, I DIDN'T DO ANYTHING. THEY JUST HAD TO GO DEAL WITH BEC— UH... WITH T-THAT WEIRD OBNOXIOUS GIRL...
STILL... I'M JUST GLAD THEY WENT AWAY, Y'KNOW? LIKE, I HATE SEEING PEOPLE BEING BULLIED.
UH... H-HAVE I GOT SOME-THING STUCK IN MY TEETH...?
NO, IT'S JUST...
YOU REALLY MEAN IT, DON'T YOU? ALL THAT WHITE KNIGHT STUFF. MOST BLOKES JUST SAY THAT SORT OF THING, BUT...
NOT A SINGLE MALICIOUS BRAINCELL. HMMM.
SO, AH...
WHAT'S THROUGH THERE?
UH...
KAWL'S ROOM

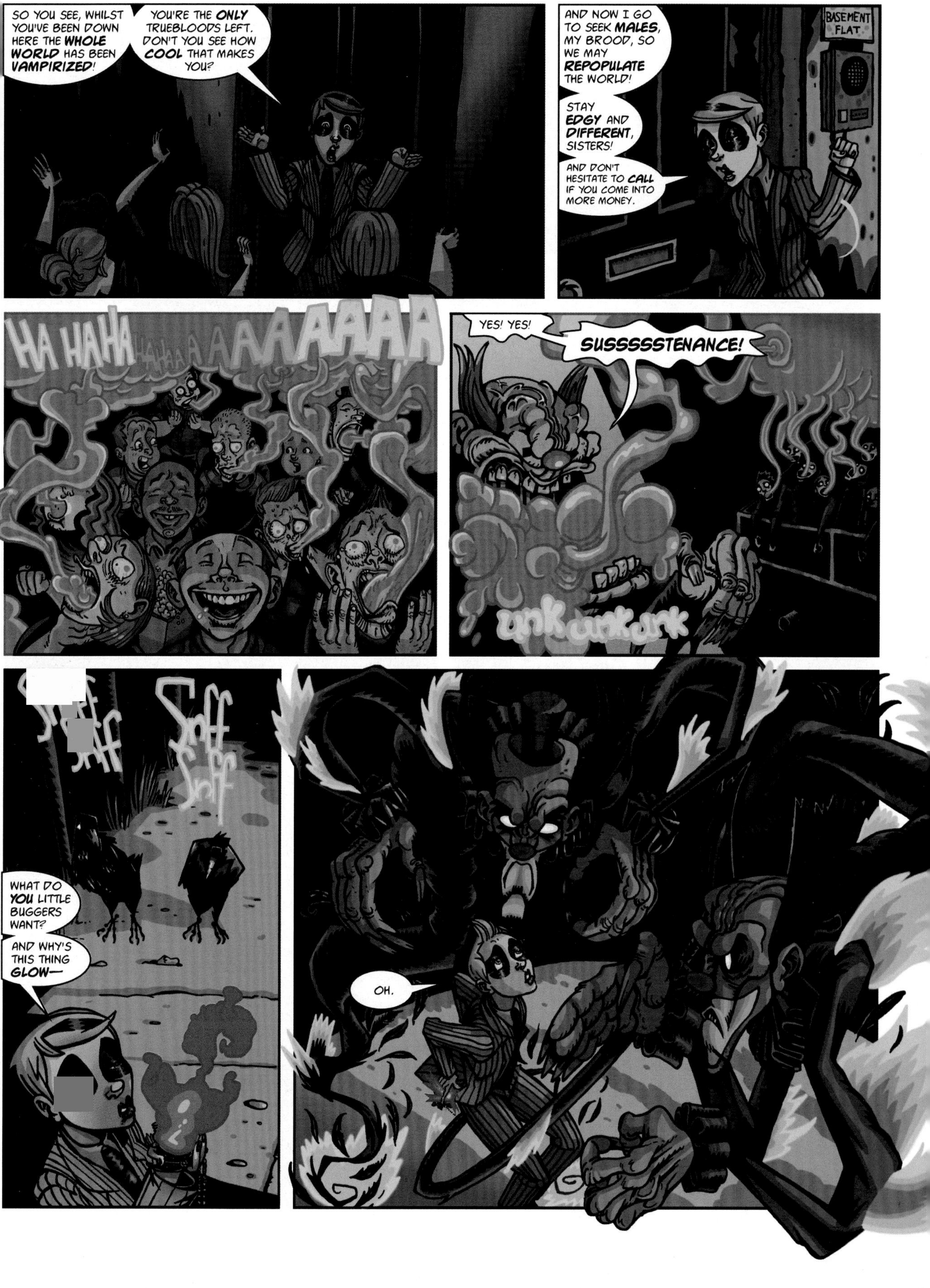
SO YOU SEE, WHILST YOU'VE BEEN DOWN HERE THE **WHOLE WORLD** HAS BEEN **VAMPIRIZED**!
YOU'RE THE **ONLY** TRUEBLOODS LEFT. DON'T YOU SEE HOW **COOL** THAT MAKES YOU?
AND NOW I GO TO SEEK **MALES**, MY BROOD, SO WE MAY **REPOPULATE** THE WORLD!
STAY **EDGY** AND **DIFFERENT**, SISTERS!
AND DON'T HESITATE TO **CALL** IF YOU COME INTO MORE MONEY.
BASEMENT FLAT
HA HAHA
AAAAAA
YES! YES!
SUSSSSSTENANCE!
unkunkunk
Sniff
Sniff
Sniff
WHAT DO **YOU** LITTLE BUGGERS WANT?
AND WHY'S THIS THING **GLOW—**
OH.

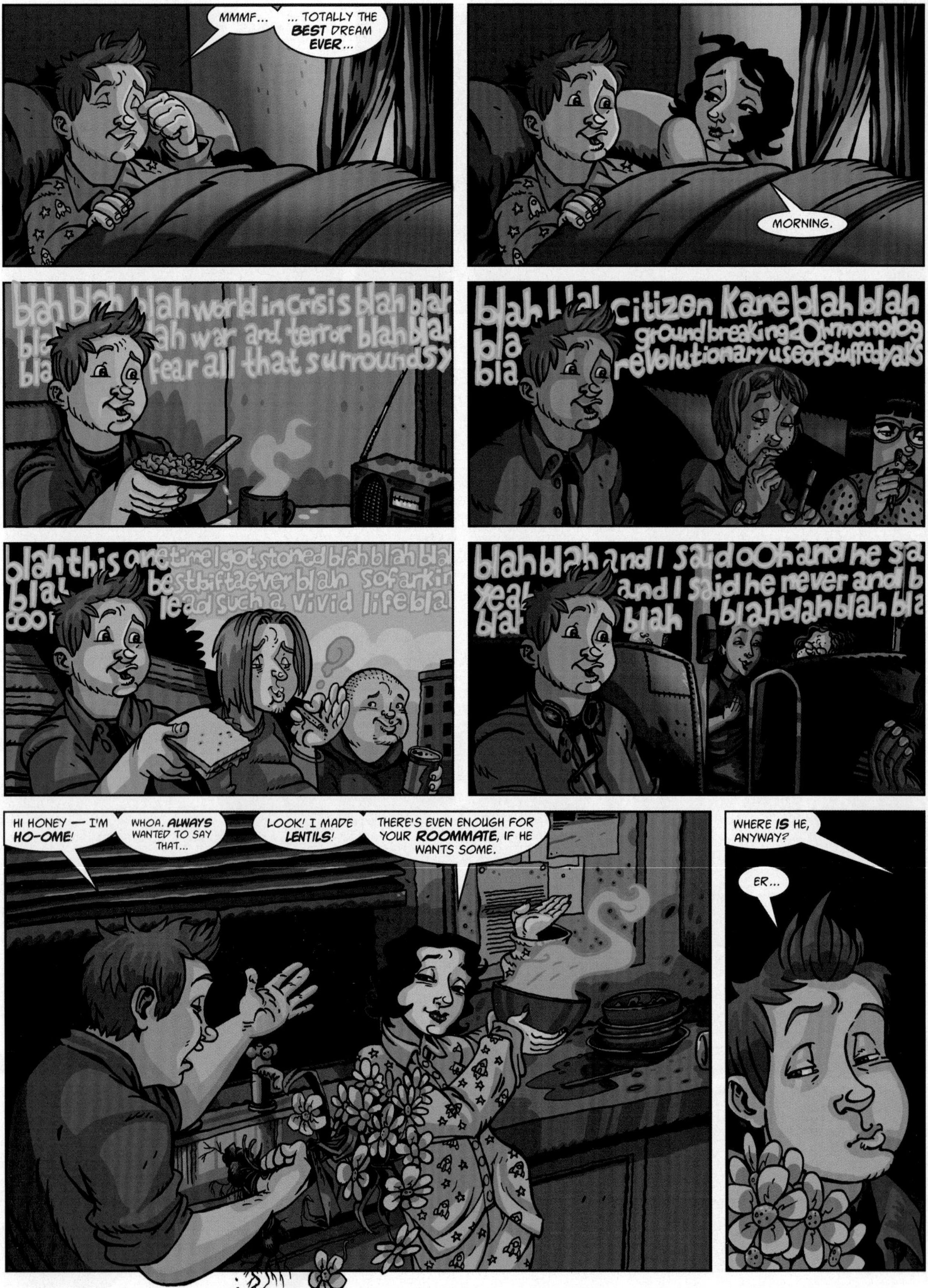
MMMF...
... TOTALLY THE **BEST** DREAM **EVER**...
MORNING.
blah blah blah world in crisis blah blah
bla blah war and terror blah blah
bla fear all that surrounds
blah blal citizen Kane blah blah
bla ground breaking 20 min monolog
bla revolutionary use of stuffed yaks
blah this one time I got stoned blah blah bla
bla best shift ever blah so far kin
cool lead such a vivid life bla
blah blah and I said ooh and he sa
yeah and I said he never and b
blah blah blah blah blah bla
HI HONEY — I'M **HO-OME**!
WHOA. **ALWAYS** WANTED TO SAY THAT...
LOOK! I MADE **LENTILS**!
THERE'S EVEN ENOUGH FOR YOUR **ROOMMATE**, IF HE WANTS SOME.
WHERE **IS** HE, ANYWAY?
ER...

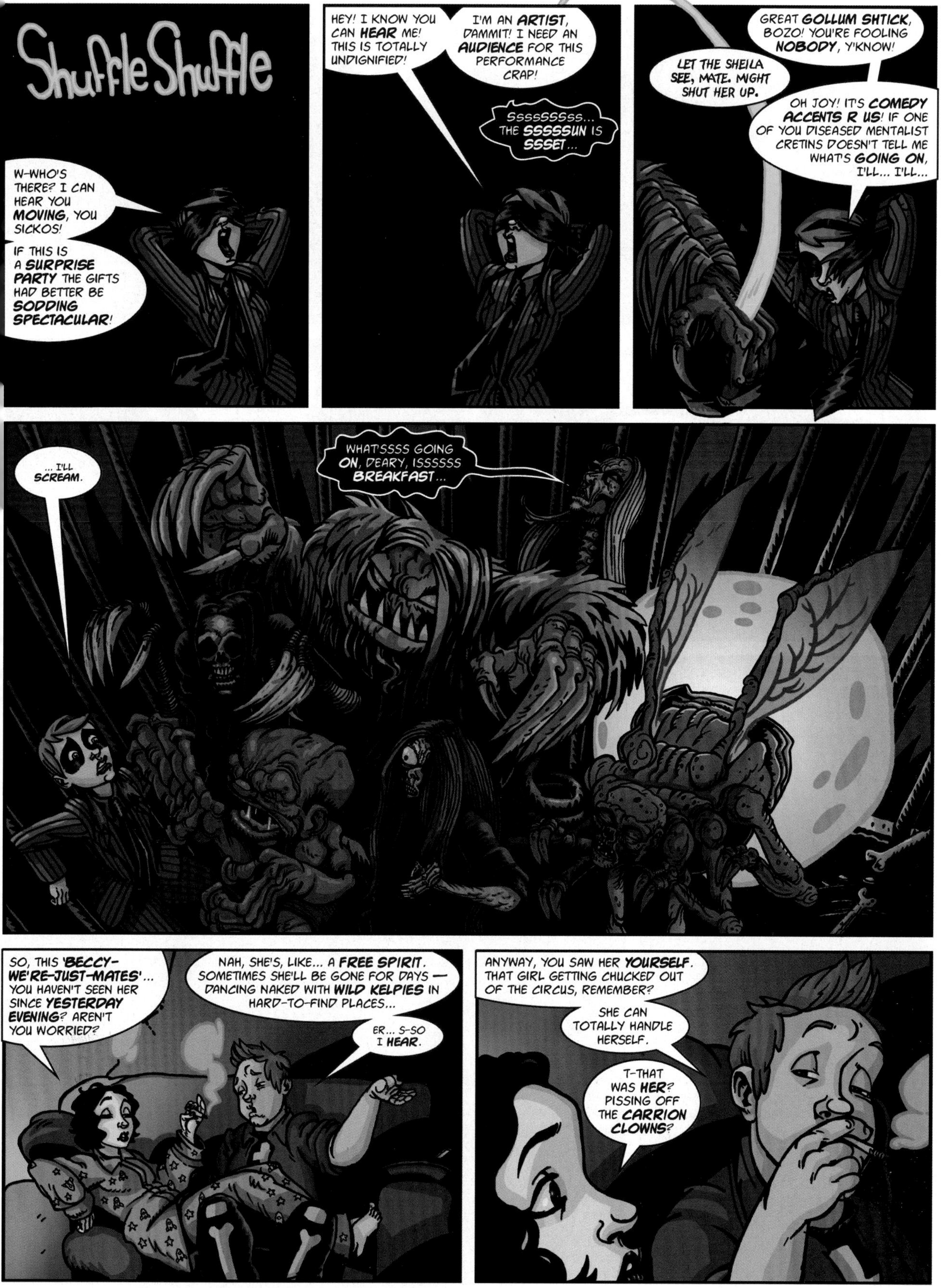
Shuffle Shuffle
W-WHO'S THERE? I CAN HEAR YOU MOVING, YOU SICKOS!
IF THIS IS A SURPRISE PARTY THE GIFTS HAD BETTER BE SODDING SPECTACULAR!
HEY! I KNOW YOU CAN HEAR ME! THIS IS TOTALLY UNDIGNIFIED!
I'M AN ARTIST, DAMMIT! I NEED AN AUDIENCE FOR THIS PERFORMANCE CRAP!
SsssSSSss... THE SSSSSUN IS SSSET...
LET THE SHEILA SEE, MATE. MIGHT SHUT HER UP.
GREAT GOLLUM SHTICK, BOZO! YOU'RE FOOLING NOBODY, Y'KNOW!
OH JOY! IT'S COMEDY ACCENTS R US! IF ONE OF YOU DISEASED MENTALIST CRETINS DOESN'T TELL ME WHAT'S GOING ON, I'LL... I'LL...
... I'LL SCREAM.
WHAT'SSSS GOING ON, DEARY, ISSSSSS BREAKFAST...
SO, THIS 'BECCY-WE'RE-JUST-MATES'... YOU HAVEN'T SEEN HER SINCE YESTERDAY EVENING? AREN'T YOU WORRIED?
NAH, SHE'S, LIKE... A FREE SPIRIT. SOMETIMES SHE'LL BE GONE FOR DAYS — DANCING NAKED WITH WILD KELPIES IN HARD-TO-FIND PLACES...
ER... S-SO I HEAR.
ANYWAY, YOU SAW HER YOURSELF. THAT GIRL GETTING CHUCKED OUT OF THE CIRCUS, REMEMBER?
SHE CAN TOTALLY HANDLE HERSELF.
T-THAT WAS HER? PISSING OFF THE CARRION CLOWNS?

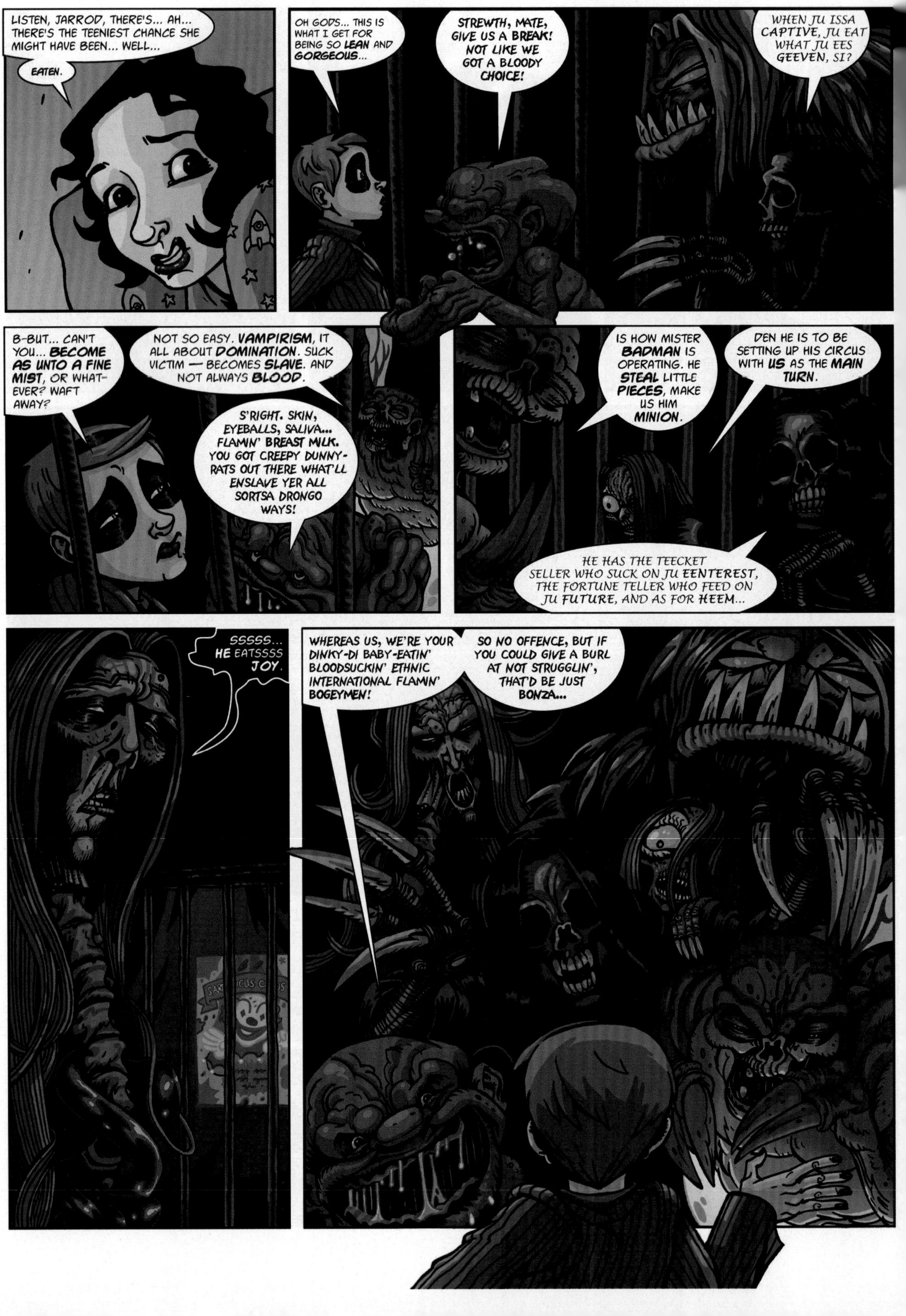
LISTEN, JARROD, THERE'S... AH... THERE'S THE TEENIEST CHANCE SHE MIGHT HAVE BEEN... WELL...
EATEN.
OH GODS... THIS IS WHAT I GET FOR BEING SO LEAN AND GORGEOUS...
STREWTH, MATE, GIVE US A BREAK! NOT LIKE WE GOT A BLOODY CHOICE!
WHEN JU ISSA CAPTIVE, JU EAT WHAT JU EES GEEVEN, SI?
B-BUT... CAN'T YOU... BECOME AS UNTO A FINE MIST, OR WHATEVER? WAFT AWAY?
NOT SO EASY. VAMPIRISM, IT ALL ABOUT DOMINATION. SUCK VICTIM — BECOMES SLAVE. AND NOT ALWAYS BLOOD.
S'RIGHT. SKIN, EYEBALLS, SALIVA... FLAMIN' BREAST MILK. YOU GOT CREEPY DUNNY-RATS OUT THERE WHAT'LL ENSLAVE YER ALL SORTSA DRONGO WAYS!
IS HOW MISTER BADMAN IS OPERATING. HE STEAL LITTLE PIECES, MAKE US HIM MINION.
DEN HE IS TO BE SETTING UP HIS CIRCUS WITH US AS THE MAIN TURN.
HE HAS THE TEECKET SELLER WHO SUCK ON JU EENTEREST, THE FORTUNE TELLER WHO FEED ON JU FUTURE, AND AS FOR HEEM...
SSSSS... HE EATSSSS JOY.
WHEREAS US, WE'RE YOUR DINKY-DI BABY-EATIN' BLOODSUCKIN' ETHNIC INTERNATIONAL FLAMIN' BOGEYMEN!
SO NO OFFENCE, BUT IF YOU COULD GIVE A BURL AT NOT STRUGGLIN', THAT'D BE JUST BONZA...

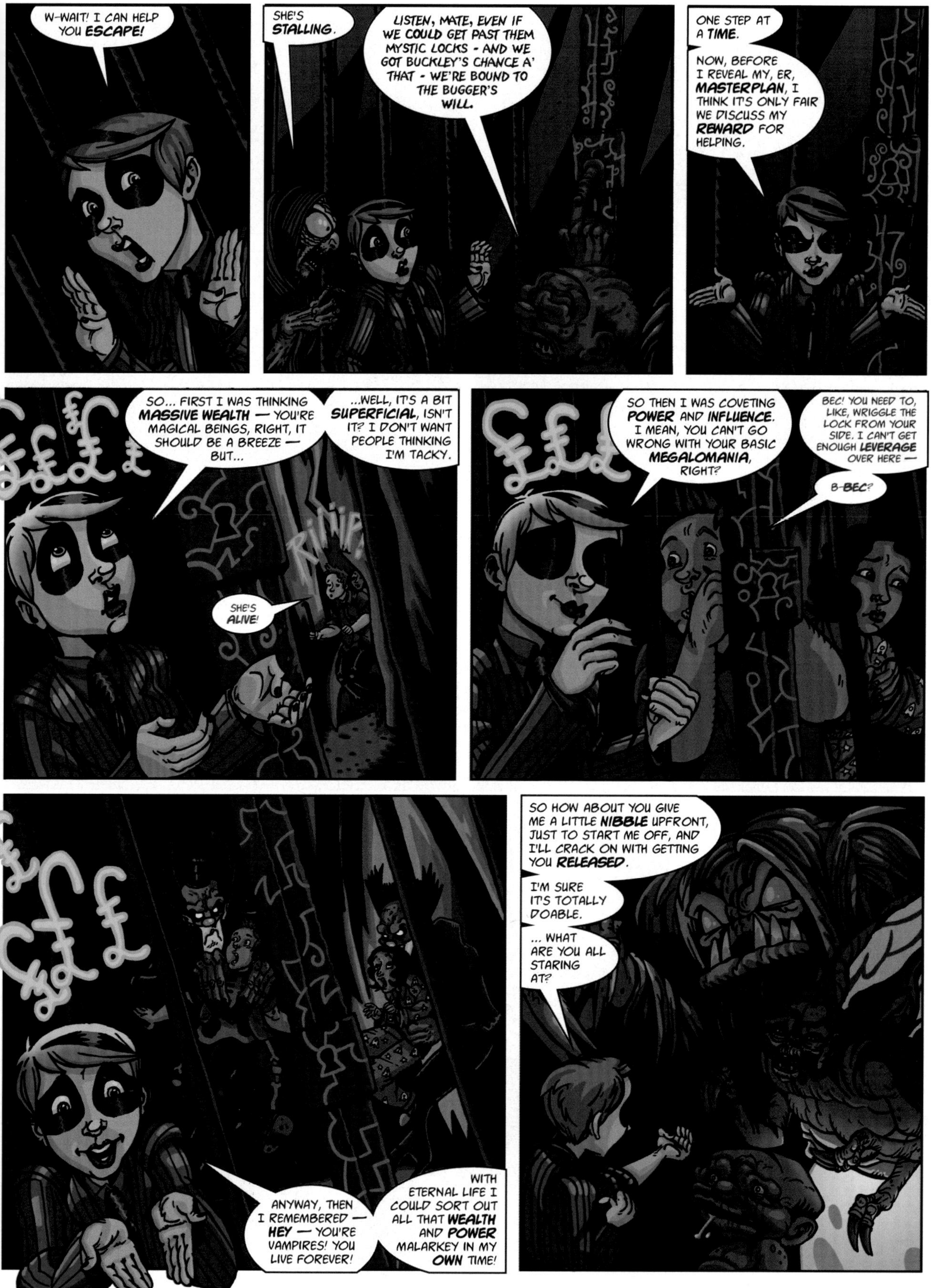
W-WAIT! I CAN HELP YOU ESCAPE!
SHE'S STALLING.
LISTEN, MATE, EVEN IF WE COULD GET PAST THEM MYSTIC LOCKS - AND WE GOT BUCKLEY'S CHANCE A' THAT - WE'RE BOUND TO THE BUGGER'S WILL.
ONE STEP AT A TIME.
NOW, BEFORE I REVEAL MY, ER, MASTERPLAN, I THINK IT'S ONLY FAIR WE DISCUSS MY REWARD FOR HELPING.
SO... FIRST I WAS THINKING MASSIVE WEALTH — YOU'RE MAGICAL BEINGS, RIGHT, IT SHOULD BE A BREEZE — BUT...
...WELL, IT'S A BIT SUPERFICIAL, ISN'T IT? I DON'T WANT PEOPLE THINKING I'M TACKY.
RIIIIP!
SHE'S ALIVE!
SO THEN I WAS COVETING POWER AND INFLUENCE. I MEAN, YOU CAN'T GO WRONG WITH YOUR BASIC MEGALOMANIA, RIGHT?
BEC! YOU NEED TO, LIKE, WRIGGLE THE LOCK FROM YOUR SIDE. I CAN'T GET ENOUGH LEVERAGE OVER HERE —
B-BEC?
ANYWAY, THEN I REMEMBERED — HEY — YOU'RE VAMPIRES! YOU LIVE FOREVER!
WITH ETERNAL LIFE I COULD SORT OUT ALL THAT WEALTH AND POWER MALARKEY IN MY OWN TIME!
SO HOW ABOUT YOU GIVE ME A LITTLE NIBBLE UPFRONT, JUST TO START ME OFF, AND I'LL CRACK ON WITH GETTING YOU RELEASED.
I'M SURE IT'S TOTALLY DOABLE.
... WHAT ARE YOU ALL STARING AT?

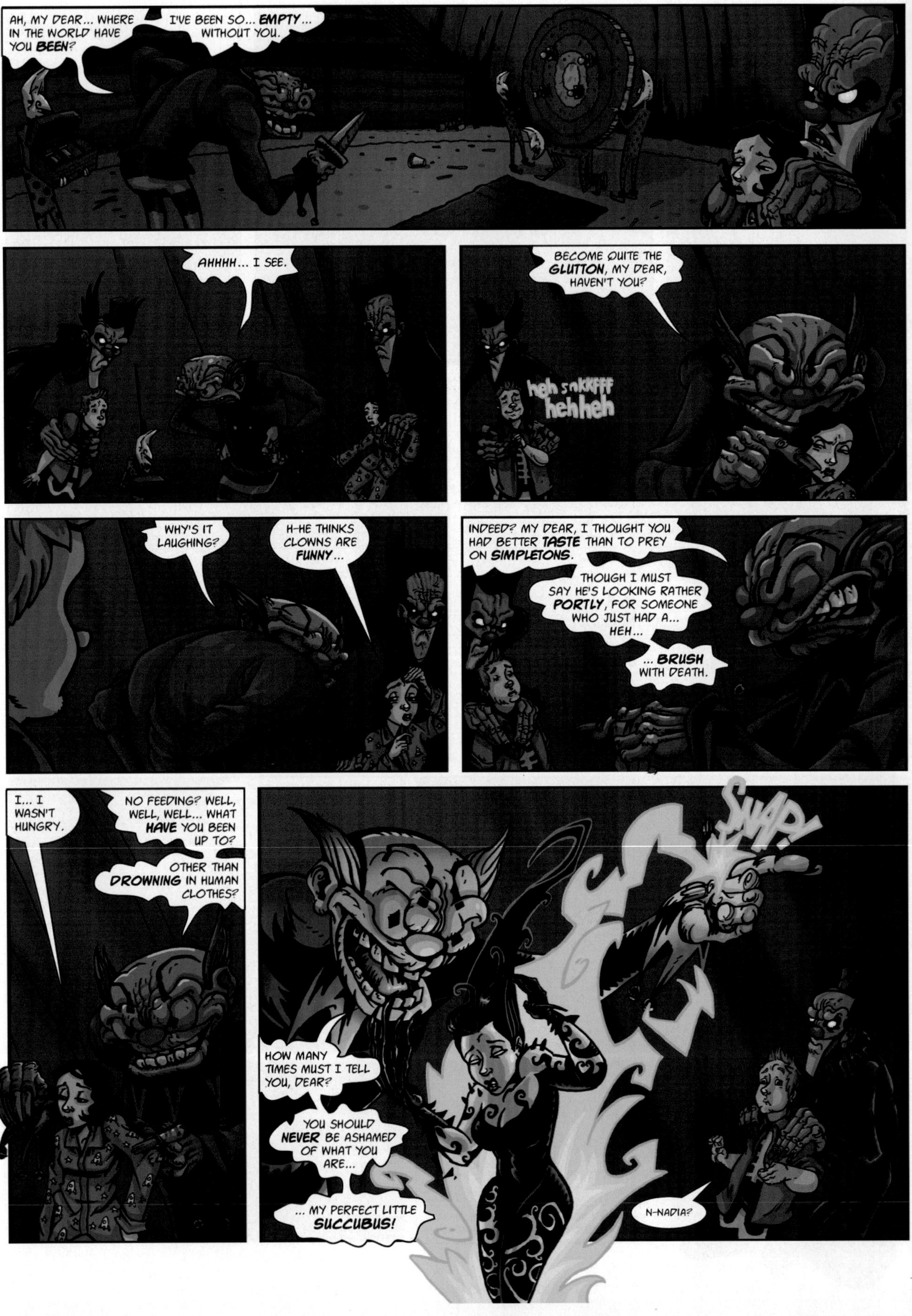
AH, MY DEAR... WHERE IN THE WORLD HAVE YOU BEEN?
I'VE BEEN SO... EMPTY... WITHOUT YOU.
AHHHH... I SEE.
BECOME QUITE THE GLUTTON, MY DEAR, HAVEN'T YOU?
heh snKKFFF hehheh
WHY'S IT LAUGHING?
H-HE THINKS CLOWNS ARE FUNNY...
INDEED? MY DEAR, I THOUGHT YOU HAD BETTER TASTE THAN TO PREY ON SIMPLETONS.
THOUGH I MUST SAY HE'S LOOKING RATHER PORTLY, FOR SOMEONE WHO JUST HAD A... HEH...
... BRUSH WITH DEATH.
I... I WASN'T HUNGRY.
NO FEEDING? WELL, WELL, WELL... WHAT HAVE YOU BEEN UP TO?
OTHER THAN DROWNING IN HUMAN CLOTHES?
SNAP!
HOW MANY TIMES MUST I TELL YOU, DEAR?
YOU SHOULD NEVER BE ASHAMED OF WHAT YOU ARE...
... MY PERFECT LITTLE SUCCUBUS!
N-NADIA?

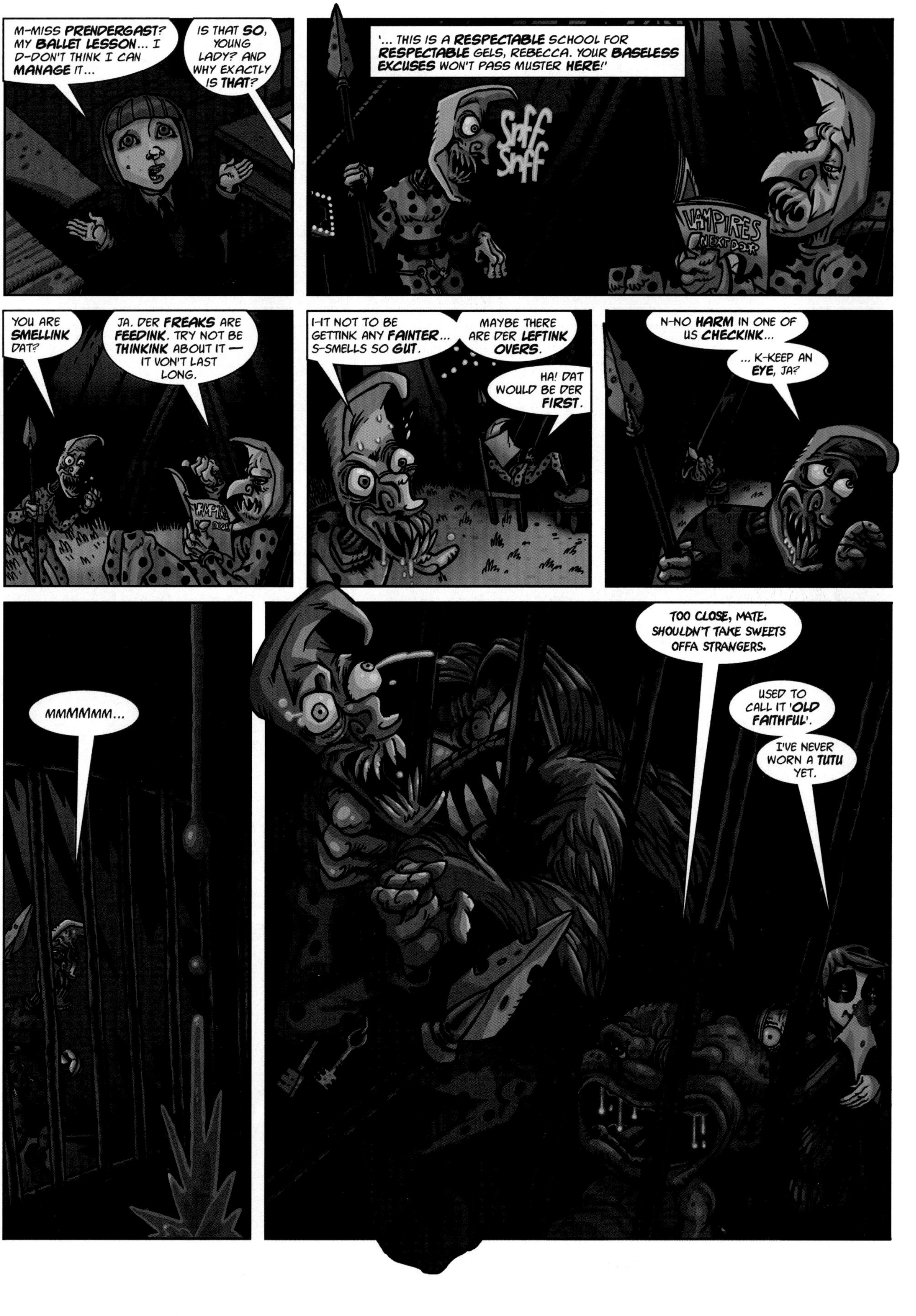
M-MISS PRENDERGAST? MY BALLET LESSON... I D-DON'T THINK I CAN MANAGE IT...
IS THAT SO, YOUNG LADY? AND WHY EXACTLY IS THAT?
'... THIS IS A RESPECTABLE SCHOOL FOR RESPECTABLE GELS, REBECCA. YOUR BASELESS EXCUSES WON'T PASS MUSTER HERE!'
SNFF SNFF
VAMPIRES NEXT DOOR
YOU ARE SMELLINK DAT?
JA. DER FREAKS ARE FEEDINK. TRY NOT BE THINKINK ABOUT IT — IT VON'T LAST LONG.
I-IT NOT TO BE GETTINK ANY FAINTER... S-SMELLS SO GUT.
MAYBE THERE ARE DER LEFTINK OVERS.
HA! DAT WOULD BE DER FIRST.
N-NO HARM IN ONE OF US CHECKINK...
... K-KEEP AN EYE, JA?
MMMMMM...
TOO CLOSE, MATE. SHOULDN'T TAKE SWEETS OFFA STRANGERS.
USED TO CALL IT 'OLD FAITHFUL'.
I'VE NEVER WORN A TUTU YET.

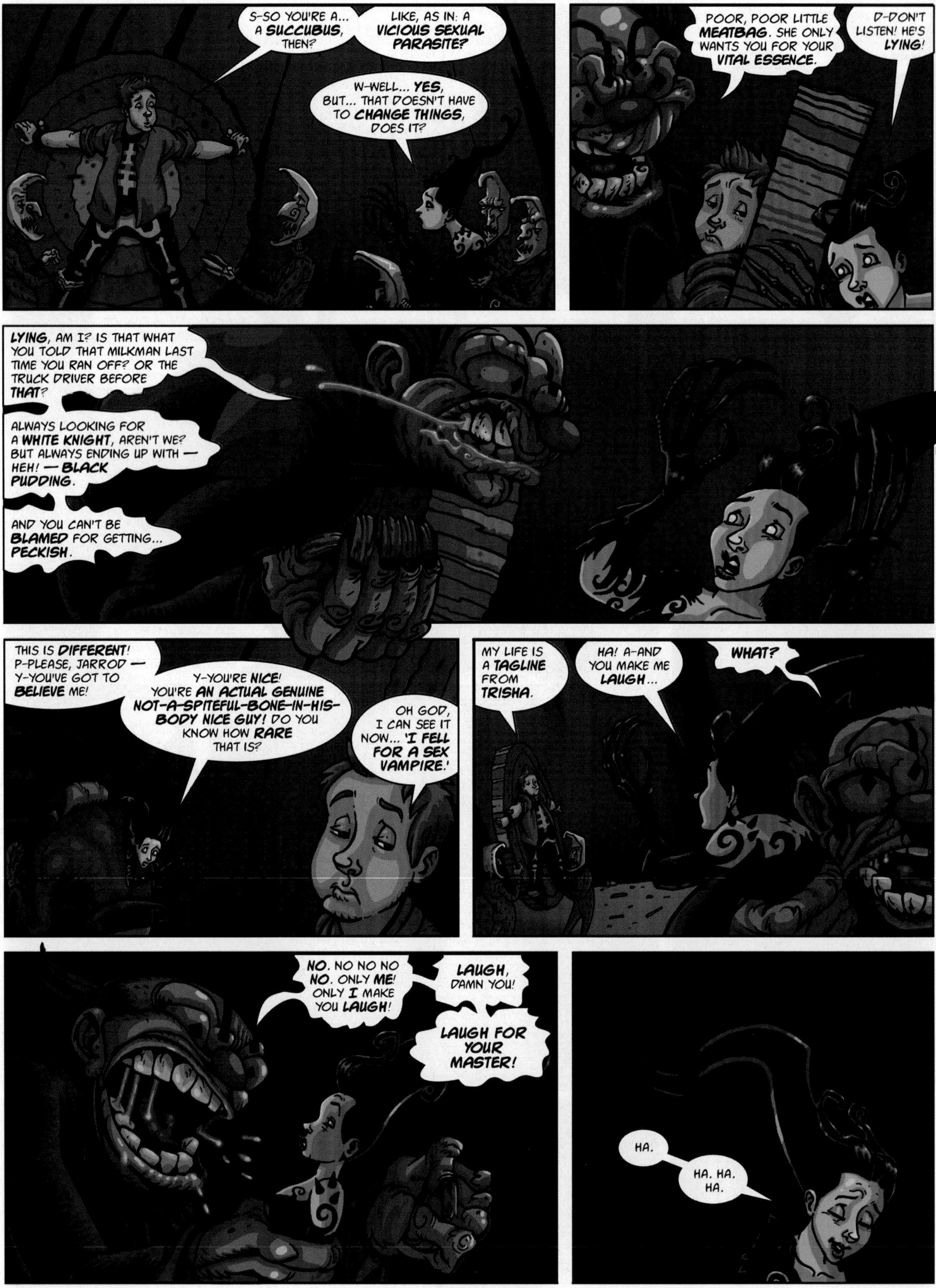
S-SO YOU'RE A... A SUCCUBUS, THEN?
LIKE, AS IN: A VICIOUS SEXUAL PARASITE?
W-WELL... YES, BUT... THAT DOESN'T HAVE TO CHANGE THINGS, DOES IT?
POOR, POOR LITTLE MEATBAG. SHE ONLY WANTS YOU FOR YOUR VITAL ESSENCE.
D-DON'T LISTEN! HE'S LYING!
LYING, AM I? IS THAT WHAT YOU TOLD THAT MILKMAN LAST TIME YOU RAN OFF? OR THE TRUCK DRIVER BEFORE THAT?
ALWAYS LOOKING FOR A WHITE KNIGHT, AREN'T WE? BUT ALWAYS ENDING UP WITH — HEH! — BLACK PUDDING.
AND YOU CAN'T BE BLAMED FOR GETTING... PECKISH.
THIS IS DIFFERENT! P-PLEASE, JARROD — Y-YOU'VE GOT TO BELIEVE ME!
Y-YOU'RE NICE! YOU'RE AN ACTUAL GENUINE NOT-A-SPITEFUL-BONE-IN-HIS-BODY NICE GUY! DO YOU KNOW HOW RARE THAT IS?
OH GOD, I CAN SEE IT NOW... 'I FELL FOR A SEX VAMPIRE.'
MY LIFE IS A TAGLINE FROM TRISHA.
HA! A-AND YOU MAKE ME LAUGH...
WHAT?
NO. NO NO NO NO. ONLY ME! ONLY I MAKE YOU LAUGH!
LAUGH, DAMN YOU!
LAUGH FOR YOUR MASTER!
HA.
HA. HA. HA.

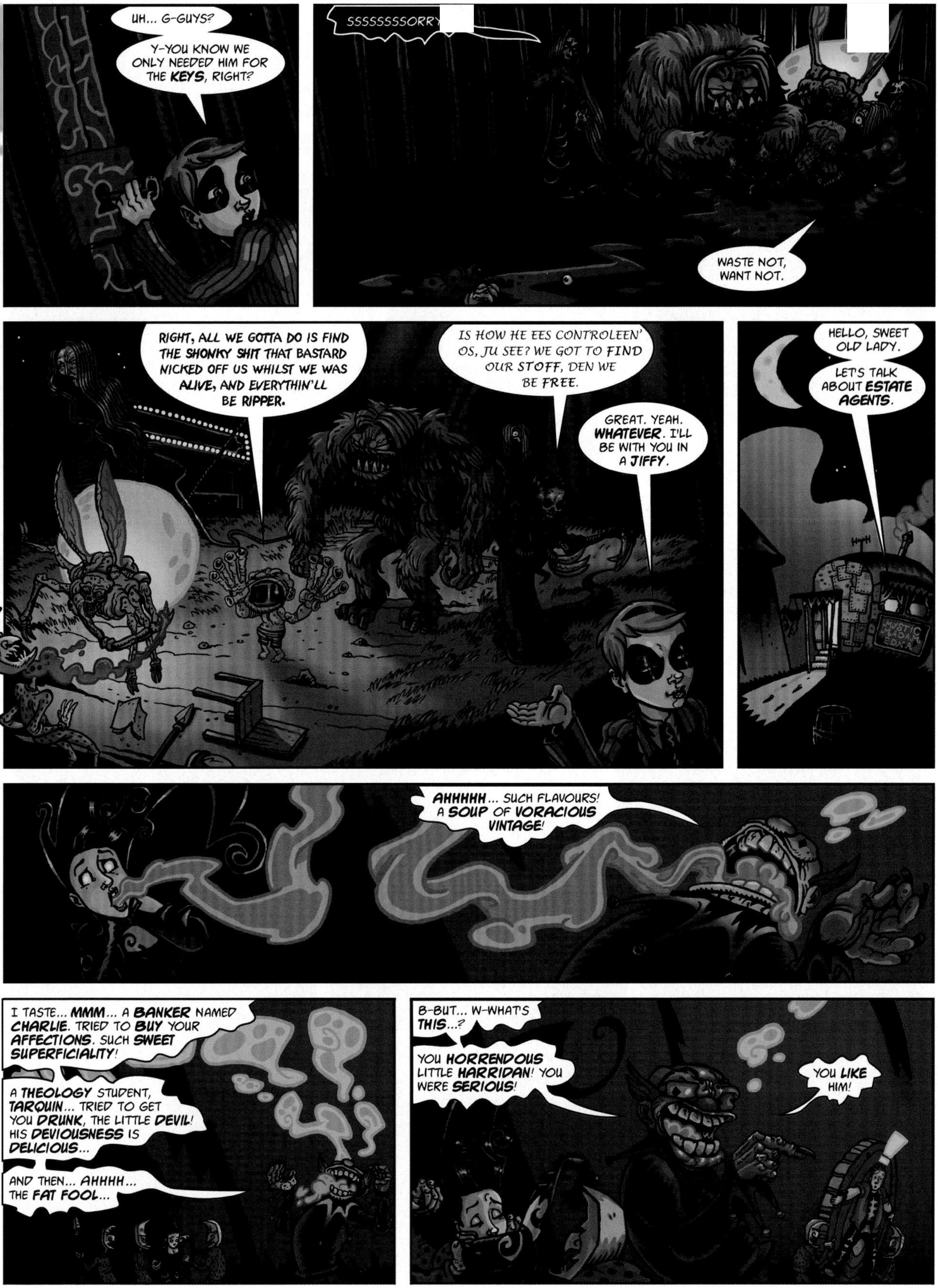
UH... G-GUYS?
Y-YOU KNOW WE ONLY NEEDED HIM FOR THE KEYS, RIGHT?
SSSSSSSSSORRY
WASTE NOT, WANT NOT.
RIGHT, ALL WE GOTTA DO IS FIND THE SHONKY SHIT THAT BASTARD NICKED OFF US WHILST WE WAS ALIVE, AND EVERYTHIN'LL BE RIPPER.
IS HOW HE EES CONTROLEEN' OS, JU SEE? WE GOT TO FIND OUR STOFF, DEN WE BE FREE.
GREAT. YEAH. WHATEVER. I'LL BE WITH YOU IN A JIFFY.
HELLO, SWEET OLD LADY.
LET'S TALK ABOUT ESTATE AGENTS.
MYSTIC MADAM EDNA
AHHHHH... SUCH FLAVOURS! A SOUP OF VORACIOUS VINTAGE!
I TASTE... MMM... A BANKER NAMED CHARLIE. TRIED TO BUY YOUR AFFECTIONS. SUCH SWEET SUPERFICIALITY!
A THEOLOGY STUDENT, TARQUIN... TRIED TO GET YOU DRUNK, THE LITTLE DEVIL! HIS DEVIOUSNESS IS DELICIOUS...
AND THEN... AHHHH... THE FAT FOOL...
B-BUT... W-WHAT'S THIS...?
YOU HORRENDOUS LITTLE HARRIDAN! YOU WERE SERIOUS!
YOU LIKE HIM!

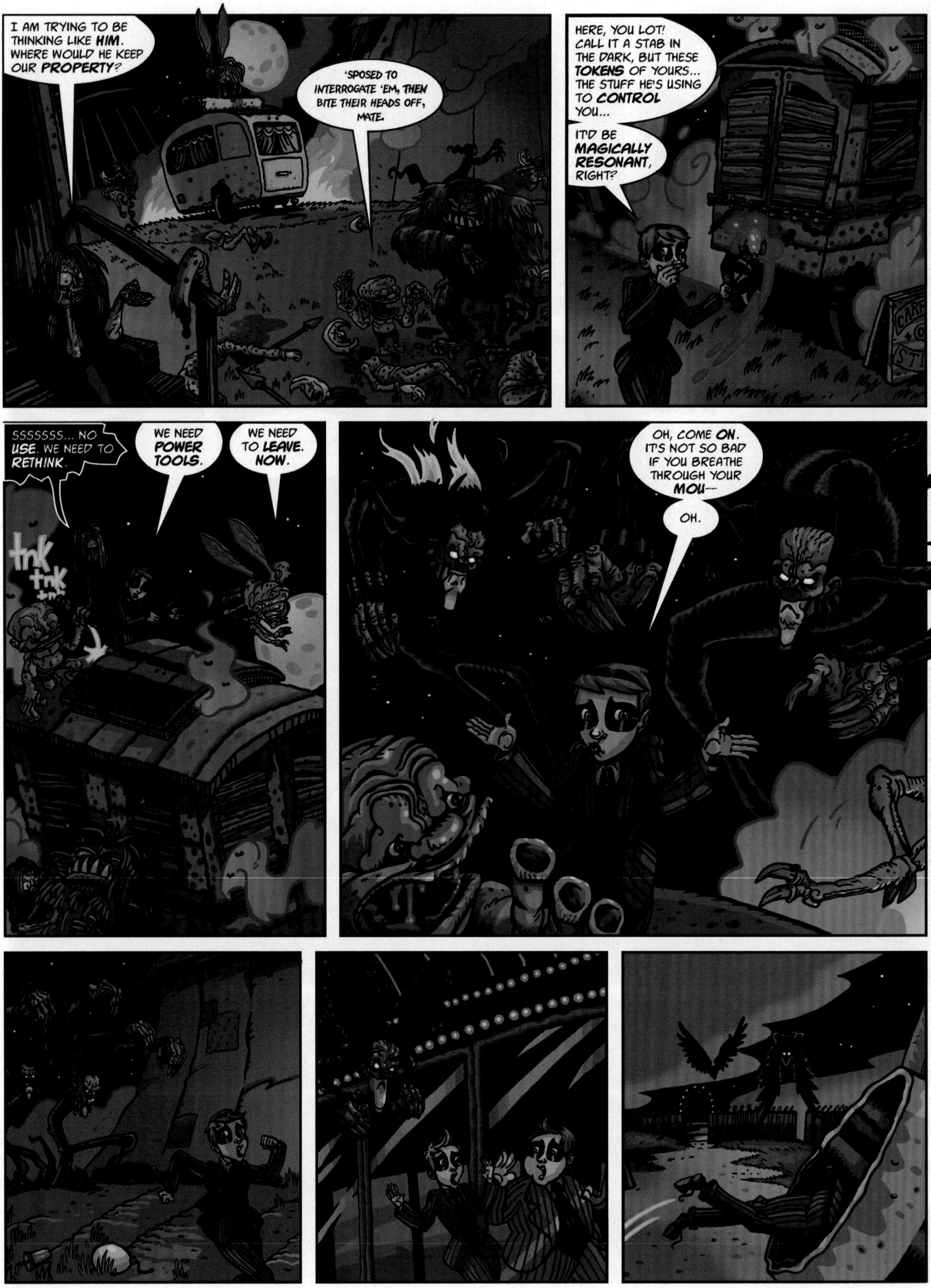

I AM TRYING TO BE THINKING LIKE HIM. WHERE WOULD HE KEEP OUR PROPERTY?
'SPOSED TO INTERROGATE 'EM, THEN BITE THEIR HEADS OFF, MATE.
HERE, YOU LOT! CALL IT A STAB IN THE DARK, BUT THESE TOKENS OF YOURS... THE STUFF HE'S USING TO CONTROL YOU...
IT'D BE MAGICALLY RESONANT, RIGHT?
SSSSSSS... NO USE. WE NEED TO RETHINK.
WE NEED POWER TOOLS.
WE NEED TO LEAVE. NOW.
tnk tnk
OH, COME ON. IT'S NOT SO BAD IF YOU BREATHE THROUGH YOUR MOU--
OH.

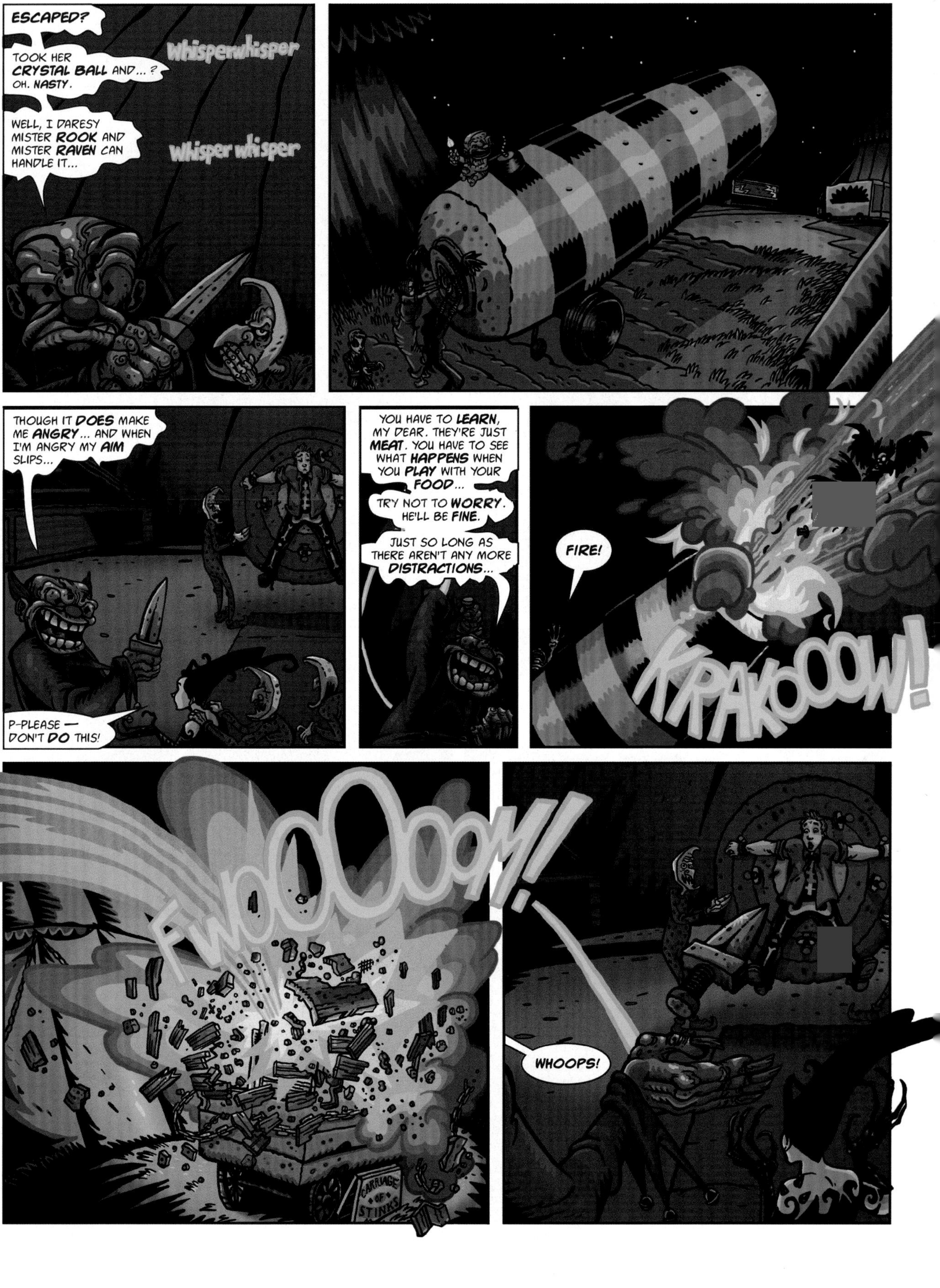
ESCAPED?
TOOK HER CRYSTAL BALL AND... ? OH. NASTY.
whisperwhisper
WELL, I DARESY MISTER ROOK AND MISTER RAVEN CAN HANDLE IT...
whisper whisper
THOUGH IT DOES MAKE ME ANGRY... AND WHEN I'M ANGRY MY AIM SLIPS...
P-PLEASE — DON'T DO THIS!
YOU HAVE TO LEARN, MY DEAR. THEY'RE JUST MEAT. YOU HAVE TO SEE WHAT HAPPENS WHEN YOU PLAY WITH YOUR FOOD...
TRY NOT TO WORRY. HE'LL BE FINE.
JUST SO LONG AS THERE AREN'T ANY MORE DISTRACTIONS...
FIRE!
KRAKOOOW!
FWOOOOOM!!
CARRIAGE OF STINKS
WHOOPS!

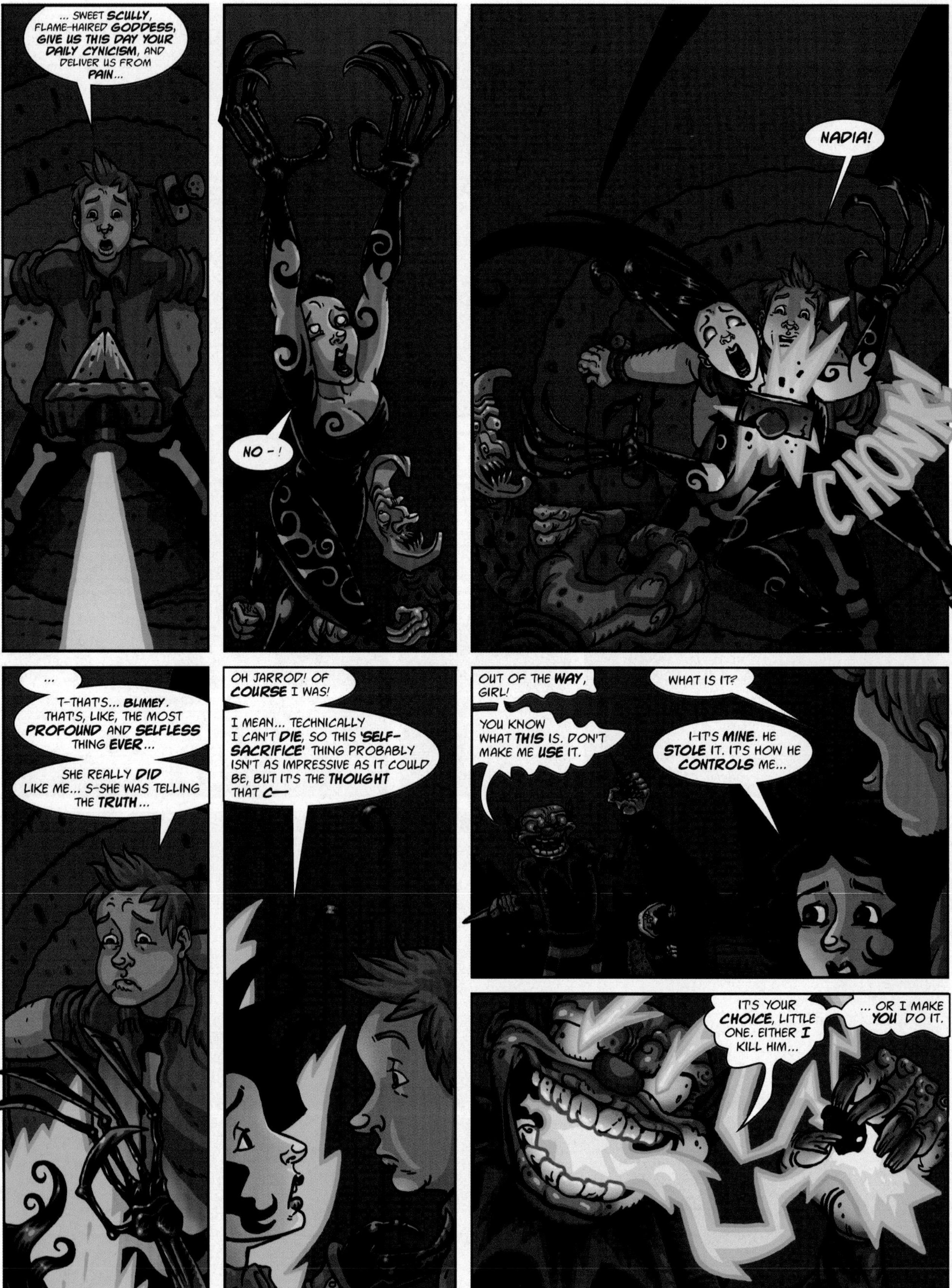
... SWEET SCULLY, FLAME-HAIRED GODDESS, GIVE US THIS DAY YOUR DAILY CYNICISM, AND DELIVER US FROM PAIN...
NO -!
NADIA!
CHONK!
...
T-THAT'S... BLIMEY. THAT'S, LIKE, THE MOST PROFOUND AND SELFLESS THING EVER...
SHE REALLY DID LIKE ME... S-SHE WAS TELLING THE TRUTH...
OH JARROD! OF COURSE I WAS!
I MEAN... TECHNICALLY I CAN'T DIE, SO THIS 'SELF-SACRIFICE' THING PROBABLY ISN'T AS IMPRESSIVE AS IT COULD BE, BUT IT'S THE THOUGHT THAT C—
OUT OF THE WAY, GIRL!
YOU KNOW WHAT THIS IS. DON'T MAKE ME USE IT.
WHAT IS IT?
I-IT'S MINE. HE STOLE IT. IT'S HOW HE CONTROLS ME...
IT'S YOUR CHOICE, LITTLE ONE. EITHER I KILL HIM...
... OR I MAKE YOU DO IT.

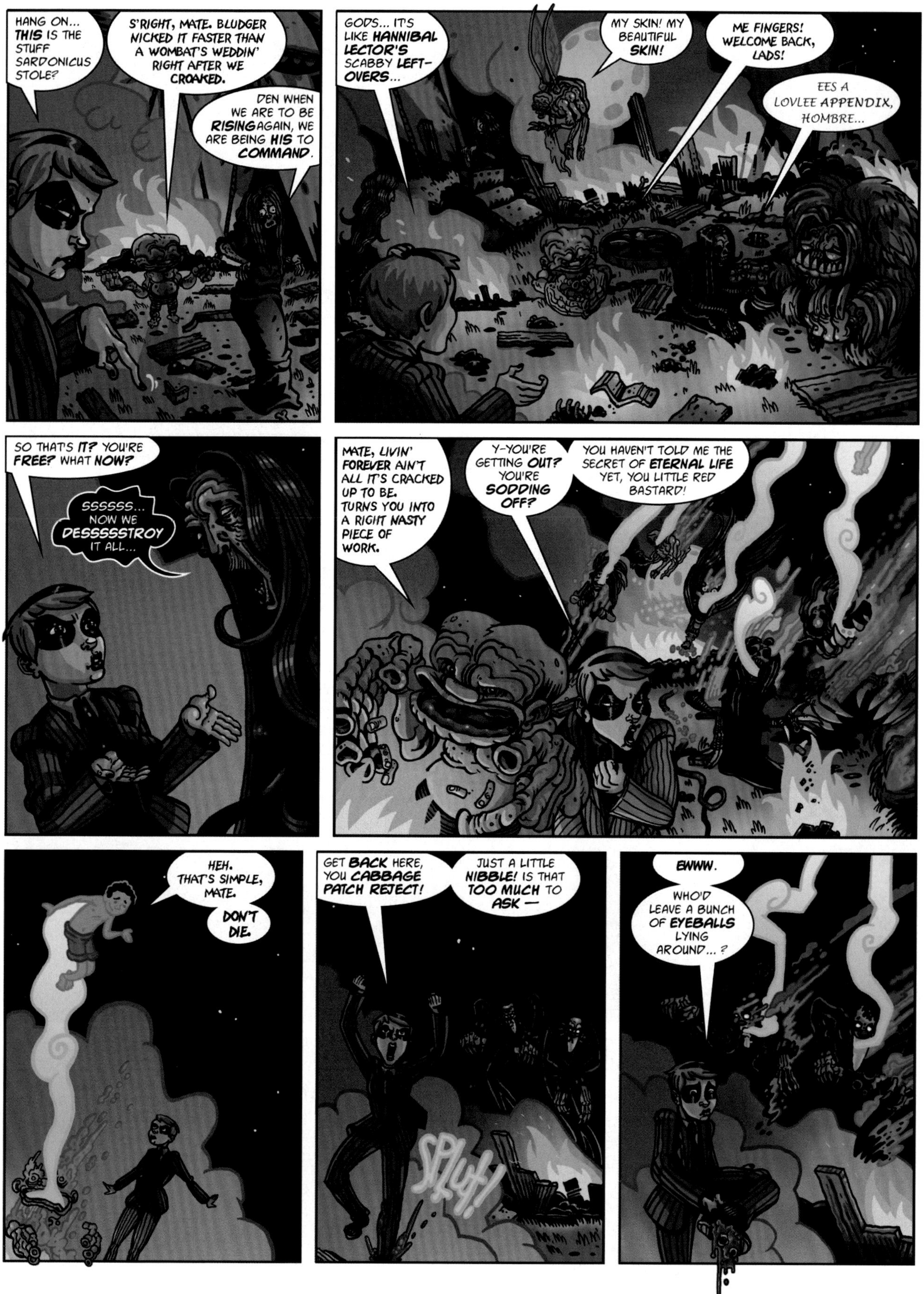
HANG ON... THIS IS THE STUFF SARDONICUS STOLE?
S'RIGHT, MATE. BLUDGER NICKED IT FASTER THAN A WOMBAT'S WEDDIN' RIGHT AFTER WE CROAKED.
DEN WHEN WE ARE TO BE RISING AGAIN, WE ARE BEING HIS TO COMMAND.
GODS... IT'S LIKE HANNIBAL LECTOR'S SCABBY LEFT-OVERS...
MY SKIN! MY BEAUTIFUL SKIN!
ME FINGERS! WELCOME BACK, LADS!
EES A LOVLEE APPENDIX, HOMBRE...
SO THAT'S IT? YOU'RE FREE? WHAT NOW?
SSSSSS... NOW WE DESSSSSTROY IT ALL...
MATE, LIVIN' FOREVER AIN'T ALL IT'S CRACKED UP TO BE. TURNS YOU INTO A RIGHT NASTY PIECE OF WORK.
Y-YOU'RE GETTING OUT? YOU'RE SODDING OFF?
YOU HAVEN'T TOLD ME THE SECRET OF ETERNAL LIFE YET, YOU LITTLE RED BASTARD!
HEH. THAT'S SIMPLE, MATE.
DON'T DIE.
GET BACK HERE, YOU CABBAGE PATCH REJECT!
JUST A LITTLE NIBBLE! IS THAT TOO MUCH TO ASK —
SPLUT!
EWWW.
WHO'D LEAVE A BUNCH OF EYEBALLS LYING AROUND...?

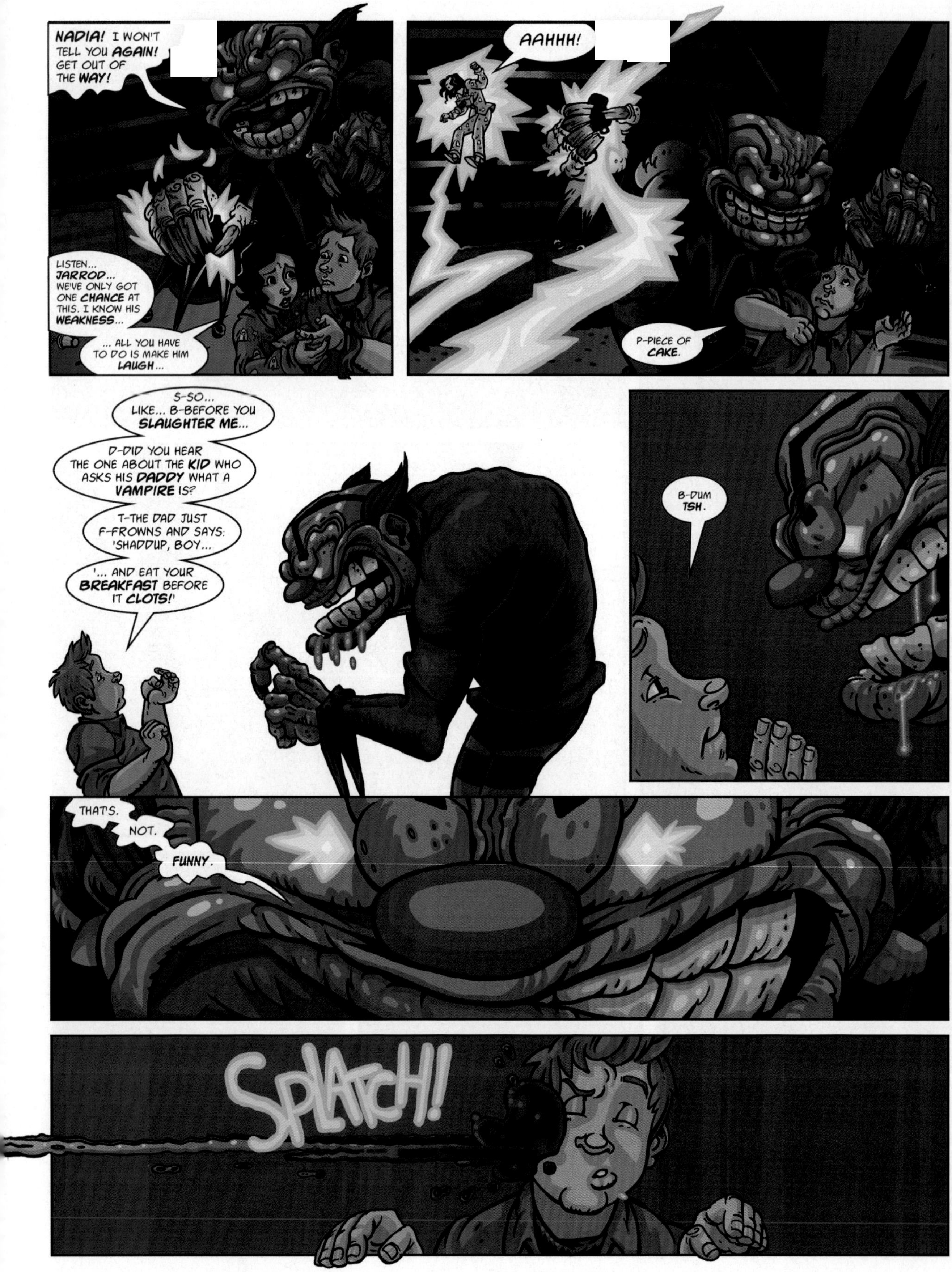
NADIA! I WON'T TELL YOU AGAIN! GET OUT OF THE WAY!
LISTEN... JARROD... WE'VE ONLY GOT ONE CHANCE AT THIS. I KNOW HIS WEAKNESS...
... ALL YOU HAVE TO DO IS MAKE HIM LAUGH...
AAHHH!
P-PIECE OF CAKE.
S-SO... LIKE... B-BEFORE YOU SLAUGHTER ME...
D-DID YOU HEAR THE ONE ABOUT THE KID WHO ASKS HIS DADDY WHAT A VAMPIRE IS?
T-THE DAD JUST F-FROWNS AND SAYS: 'SHADDUP, BOY...
'... AND EAT YOUR BREAKFAST BEFORE IT CLOTS!'
B-DUM TSH.
THAT'S.
NOT.
FUNNY.
SPLATCH!

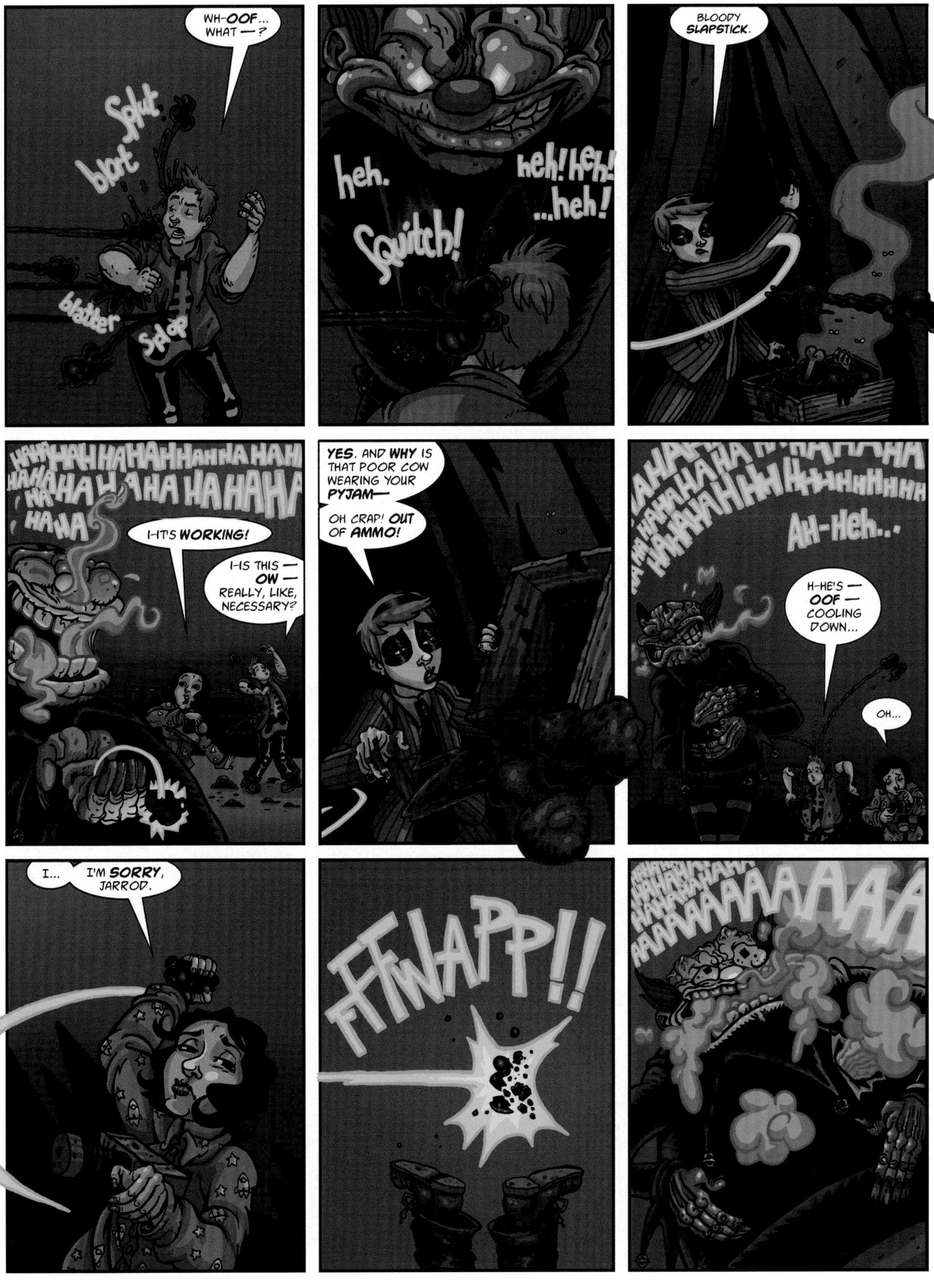
WH-OOF... WHAT—?
Splut
blort
blatter
Splop
heh.
heh! heh! ...heh!
Squitch!
BLOODY SLAPSTICK.
HAHAHAHAHA HAHA HAHA
I-IT'S WORKING!
I-IS THIS — OW — REALLY, LIKE, NECESSARY?
YES. AND WHY IS THAT POOR COW WEARING YOUR PYJAM—
OH CRAP! OUT OF AMMO!
HAHAHAHAHAHA
AH-Heh...
H-HE'S — OOF — COOLING DOWN...
OH...
I...
I'M SORRY, JARROD.
FFFWAPP!!
HAHAHAHAAAAAAA

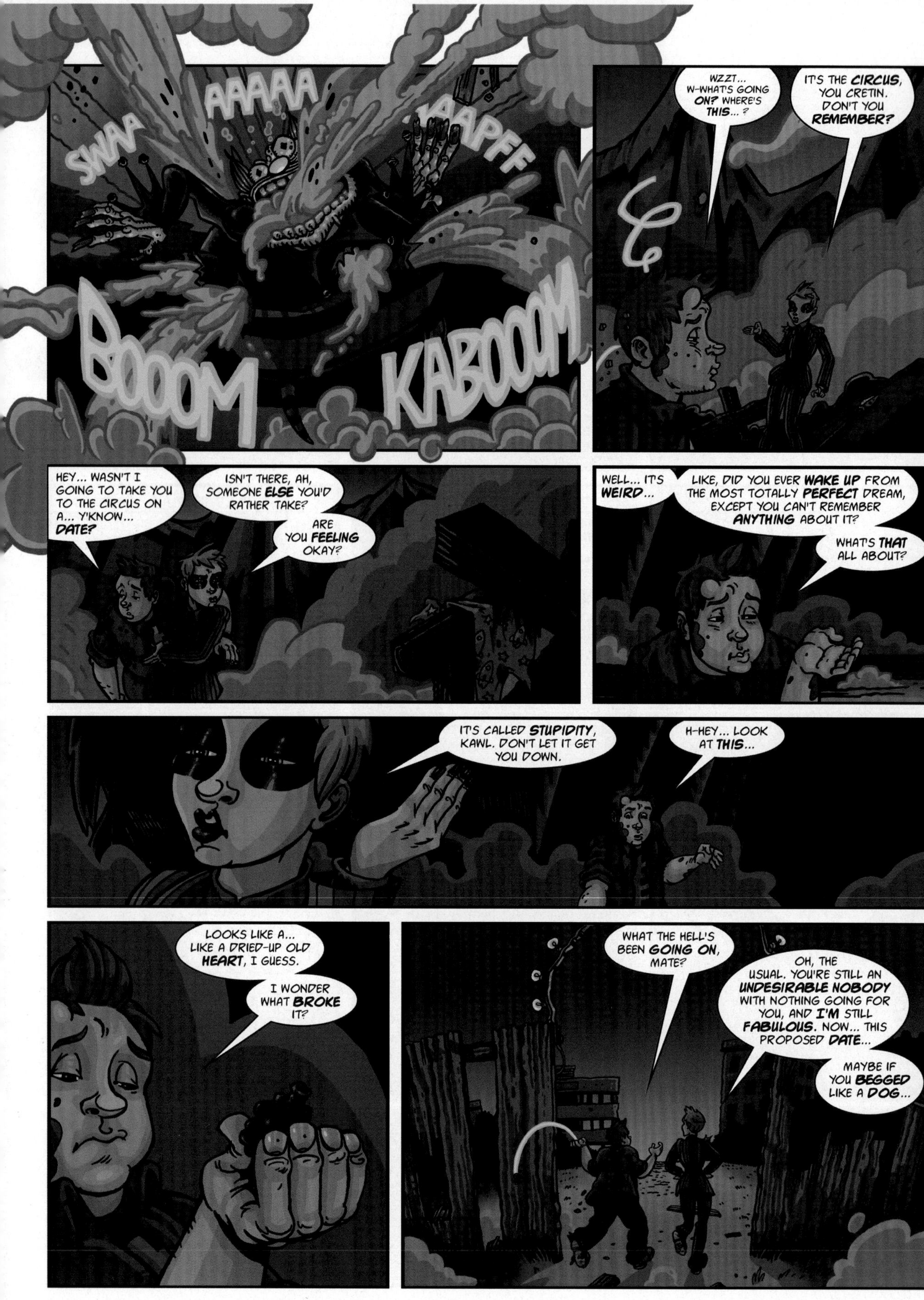
SWAA
AAAAA
AAPFF
BOOOM
KABOOOM
WZZT... W-WHAT'S GOING ON? WHERE'S THIS...?
IT'S THE CIRCUS, YOU CRETIN. DON'T YOU REMEMBER?
HEY... WASN'T I GOING TO TAKE YOU TO THE CIRCUS ON A... Y'KNOW... DATE?
ISN'T THERE, AH, SOMEONE ELSE YOU'D RATHER TAKE?
ARE YOU FEELING OKAY?
WELL... IT'S WEIRD...
LIKE, DID YOU EVER WAKE UP FROM THE MOST TOTALLY PERFECT DREAM, EXCEPT YOU CAN'T REMEMBER ANYTHING ABOUT IT?
WHAT'S THAT ALL ABOUT?
IT'S CALLED STUPIDITY, KAWL. DON'T LET IT GET YOU DOWN.
H-HEY... LOOK AT THIS...
LOOKS LIKE A... LIKE A DRIED-UP OLD HEART, I GUESS.
I WONDER WHAT BROKE IT?
WHAT THE HELL'S BEEN GOING ON, MATE?
OH, THE USUAL. YOU'RE STILL AN UNDESIRABLE NOBODY WITH NOTHING GOING FOR YOU, AND I'M STILL FABULOUS. NOW... THIS PROPOSED DATE...
MAYBE IF YOU BEGGED LIKE A DOG...

COVERS GALLERY

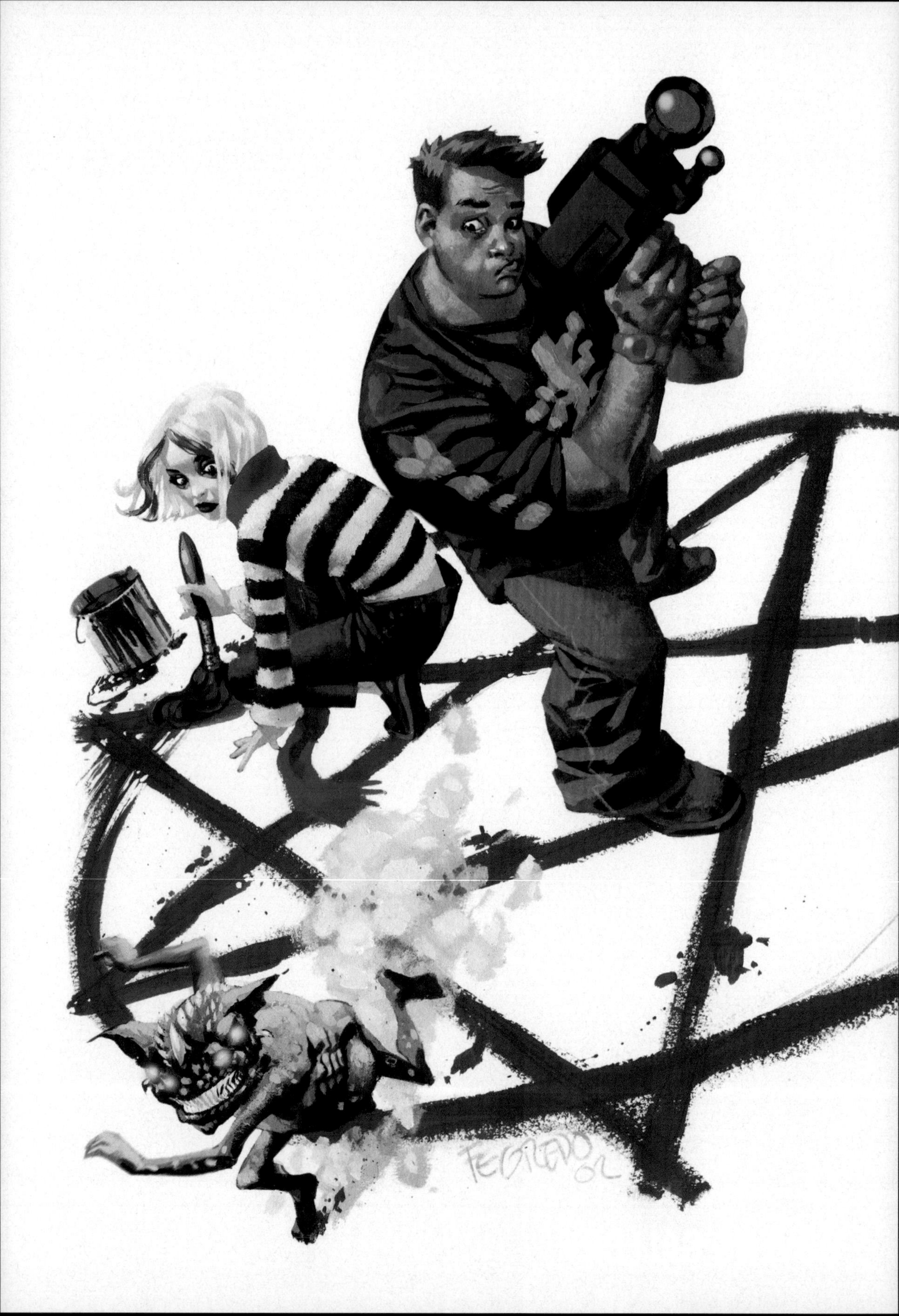
FEGREDO
02

2000 AD Prog 1290: Cover by **Duncan Fegredo**

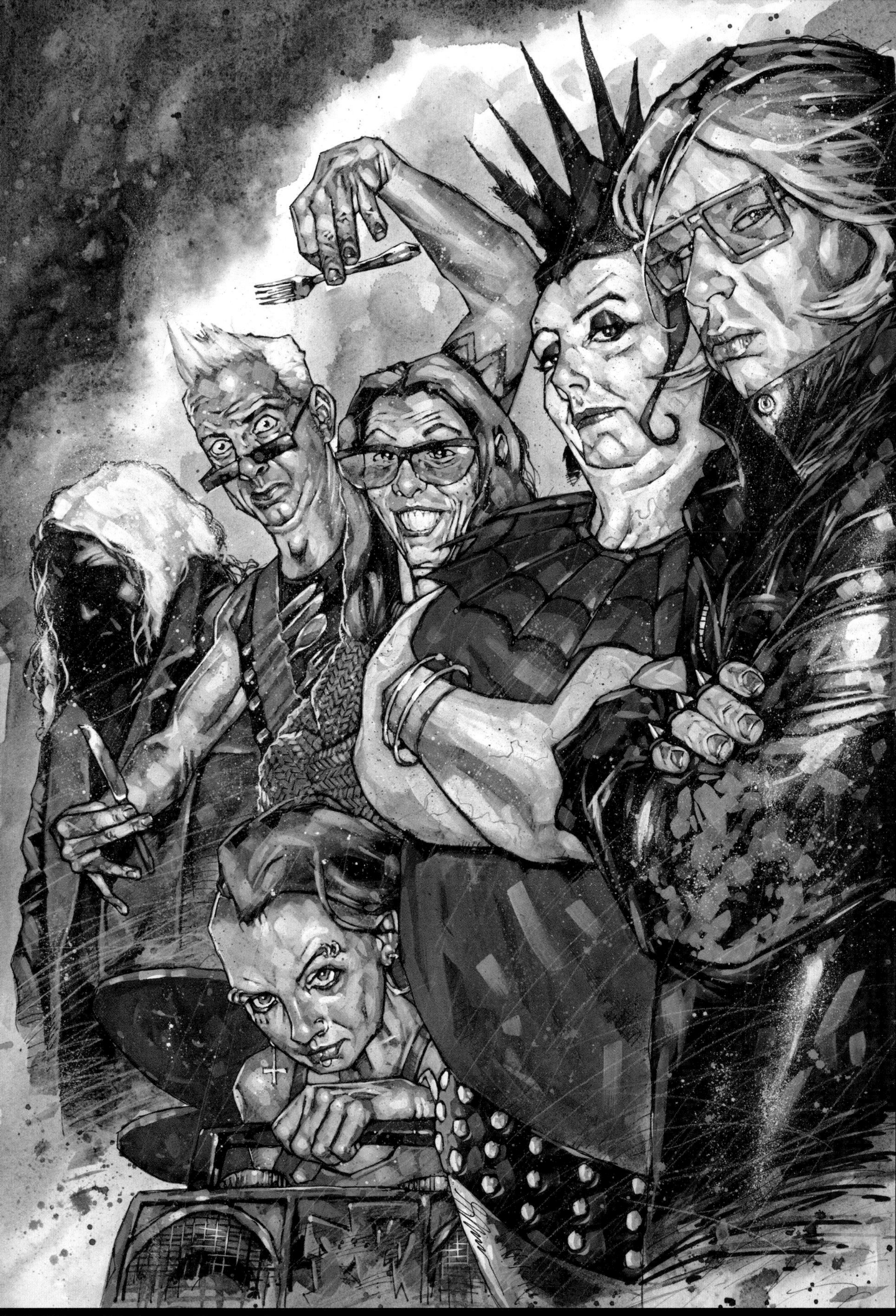

2000 AD Prog 1329: Cover by **Simon Davis**

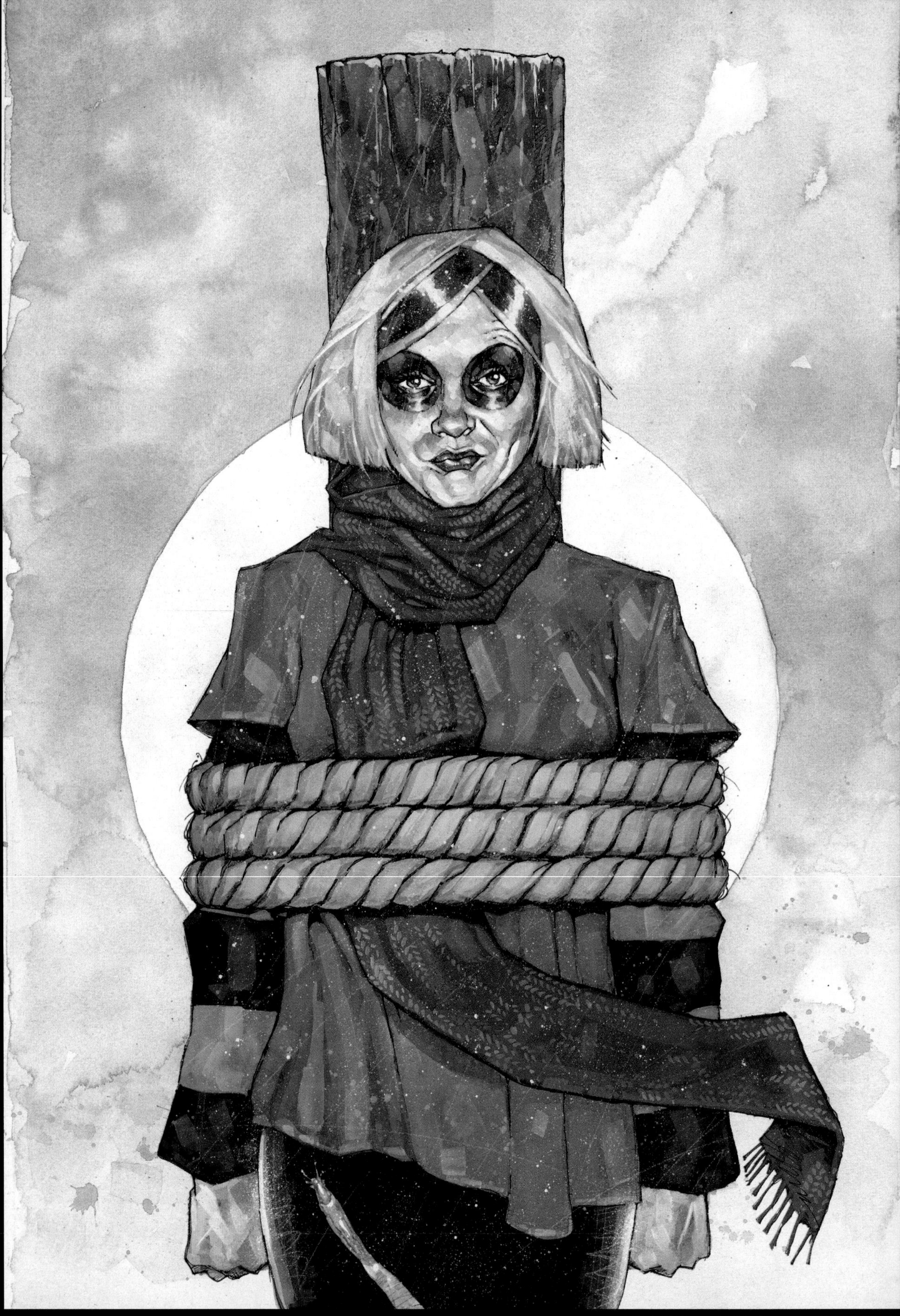

2000 AD Prog 1354: Cover by **Simon Davis**

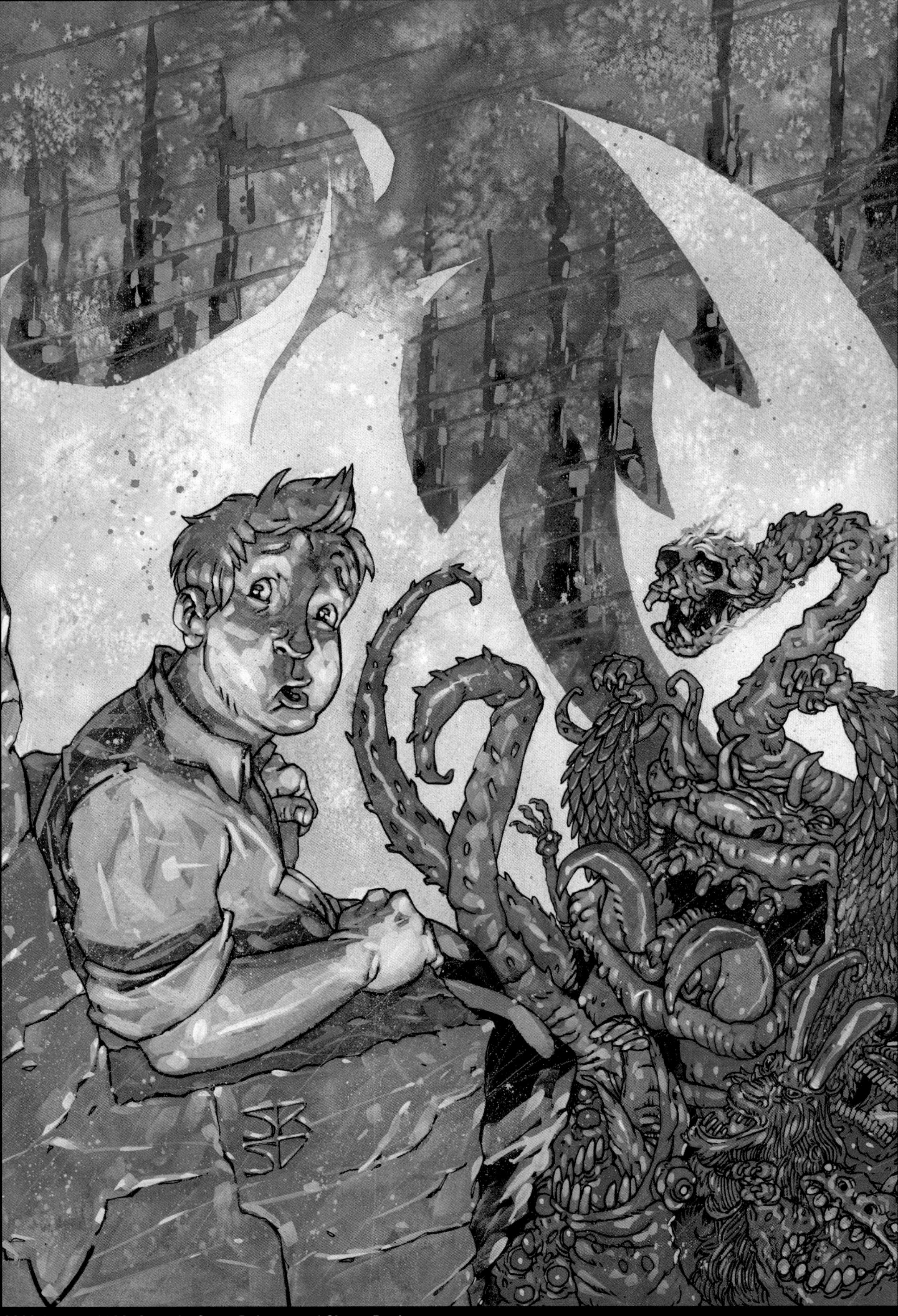

2000 AD Prog 1402: Cover by **Steve Roberts** and **Simon Davis**

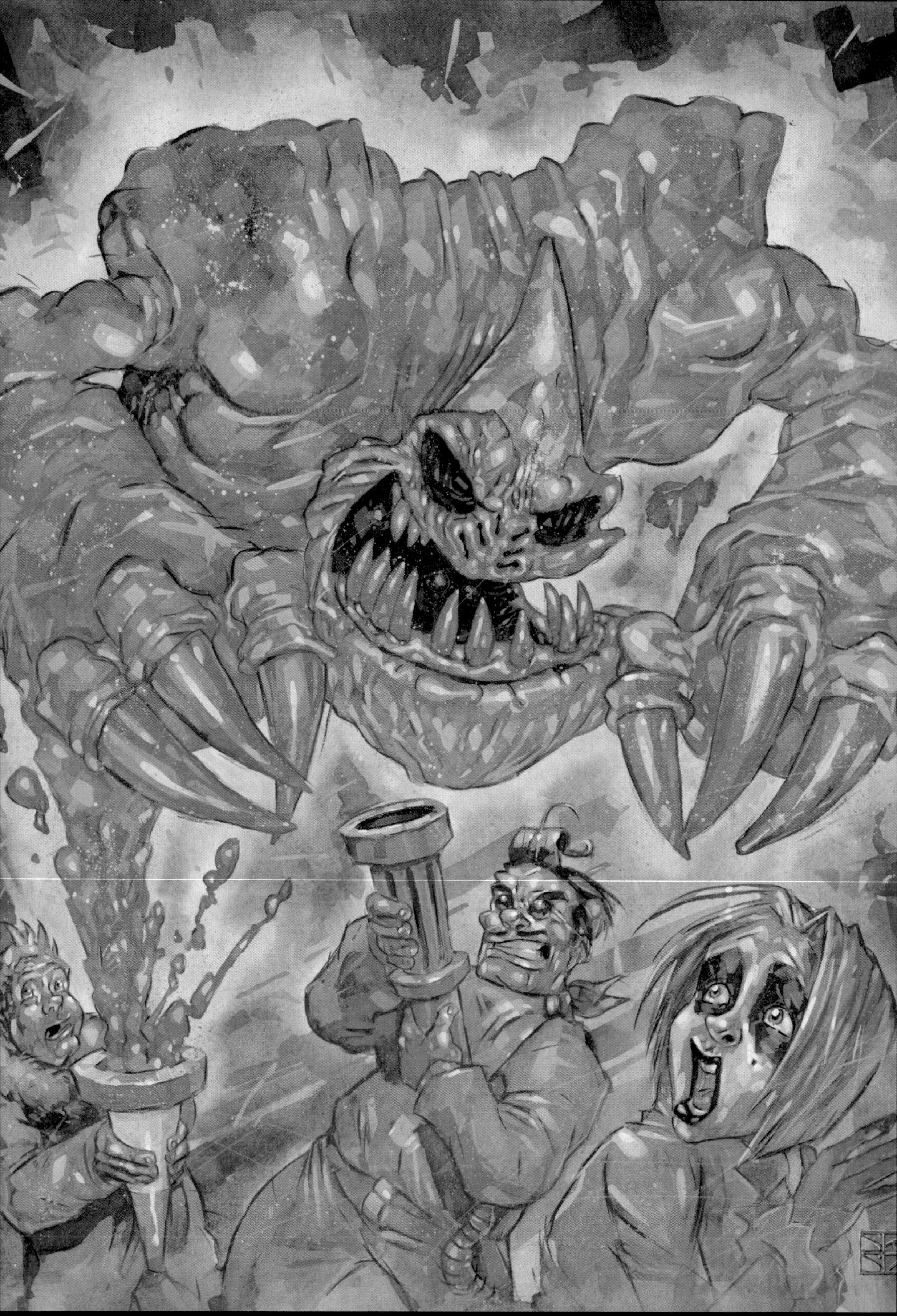

2000 AD Prog 1438: Cover by **Steve Roberts** and **Simon Davis**

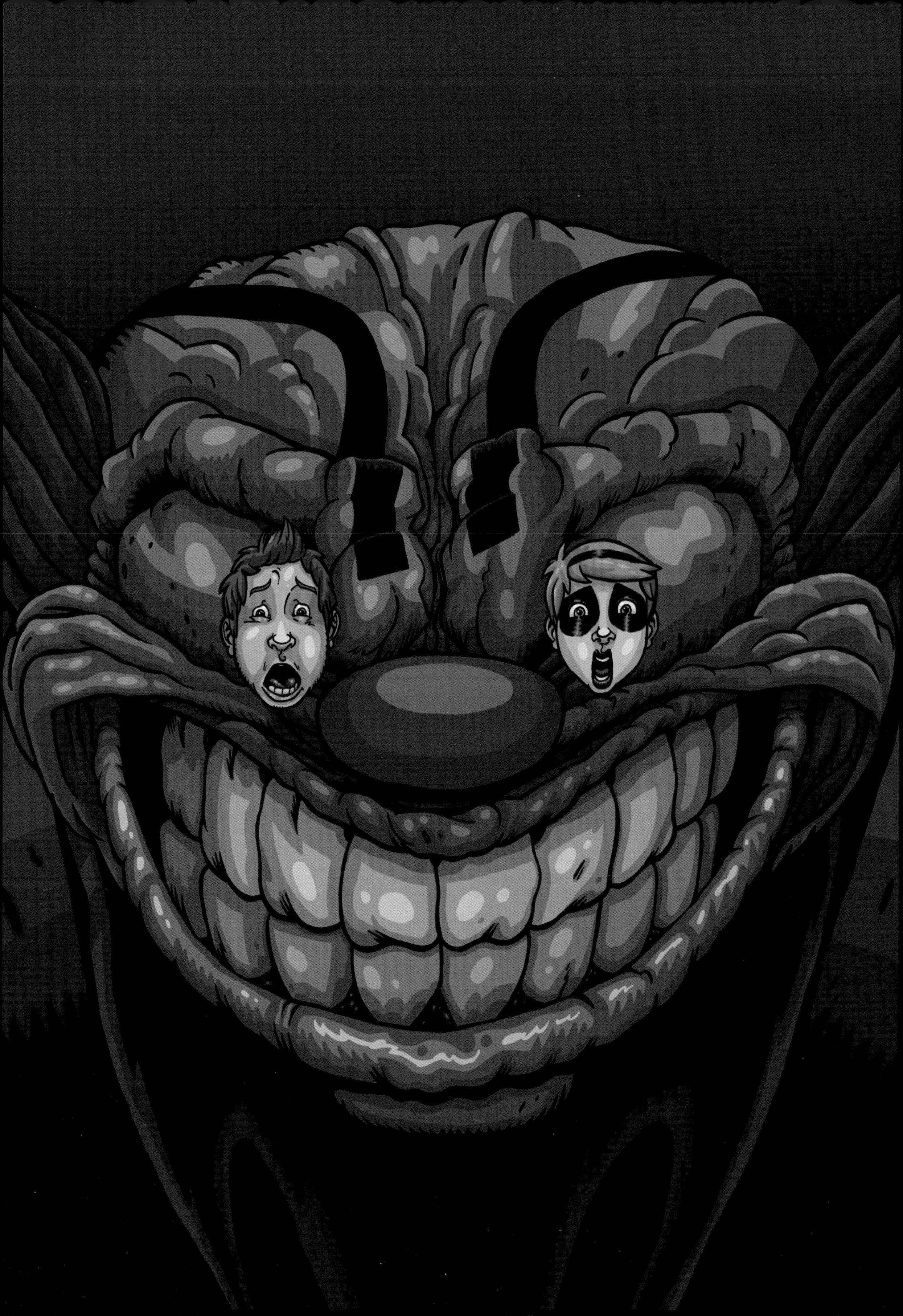

2000 AD Prog 1481: Cover by **Steve Roberts**

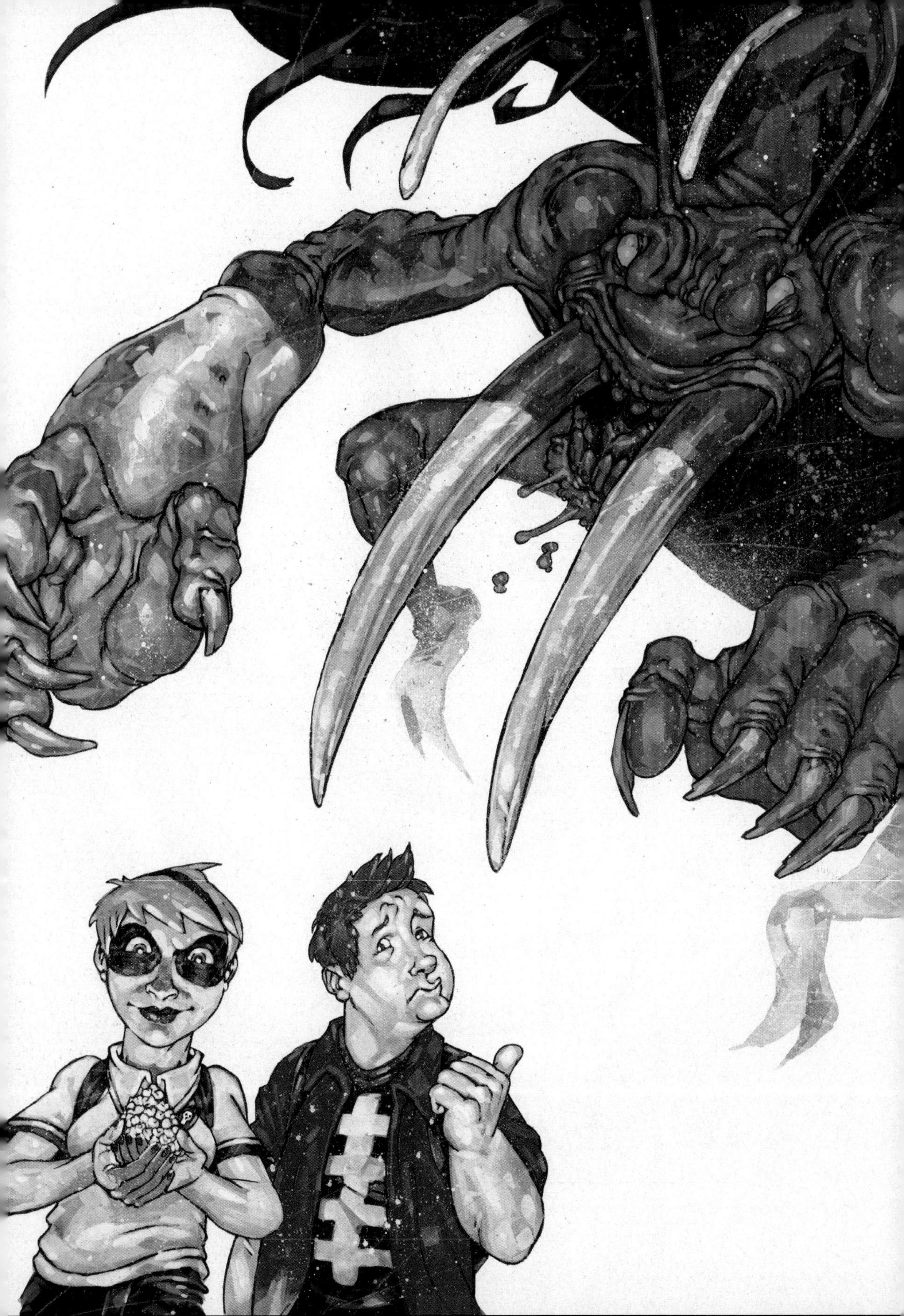

Star Sean originally published in *2000 AD* Prog 1368. Art by **Steve Roberts** and **Simon Davi**

STEVE ROBERTS
SKETCH BOOK

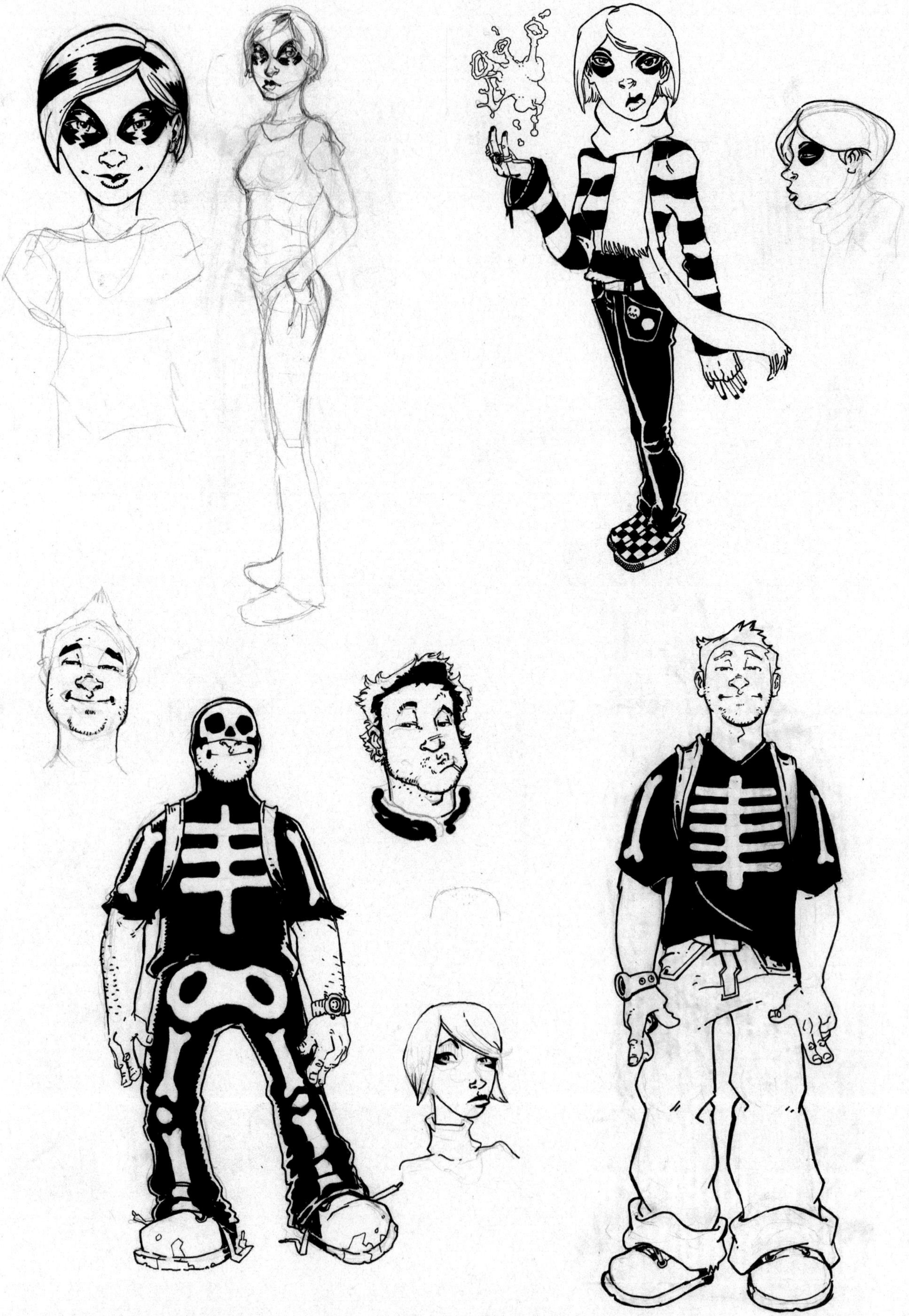

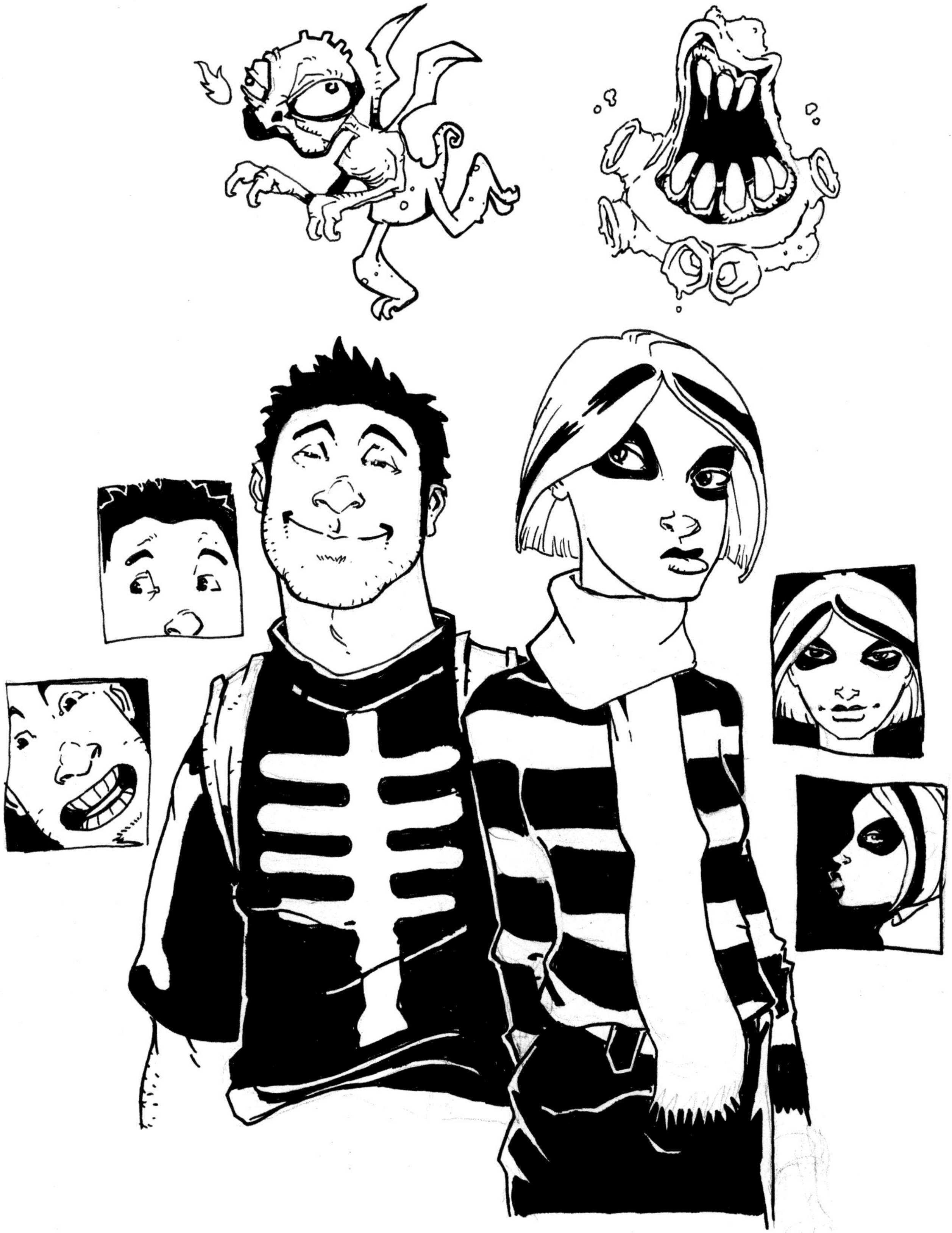

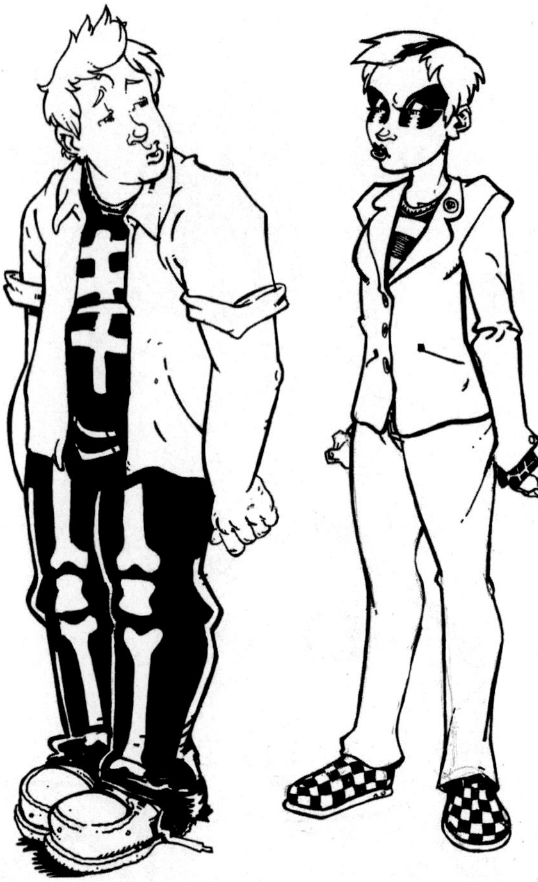

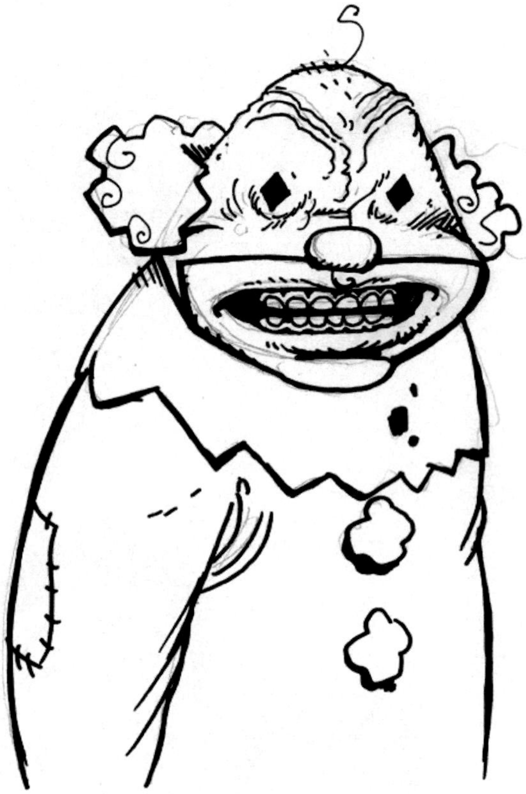

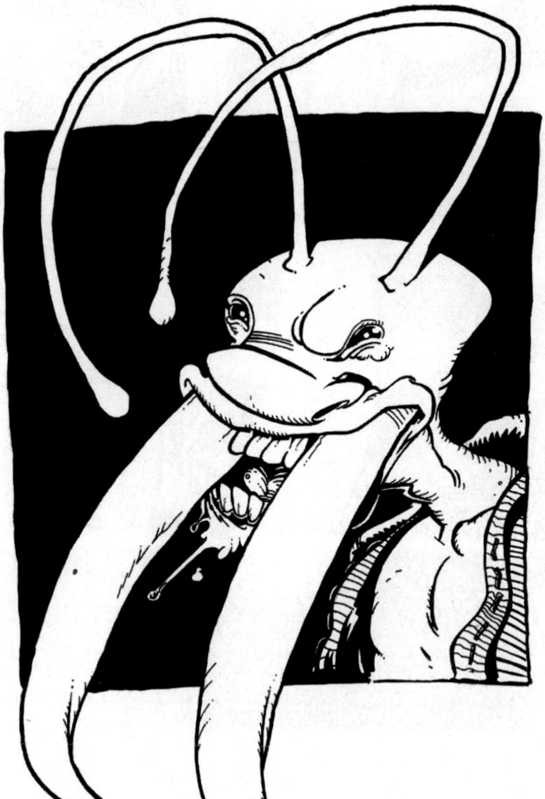

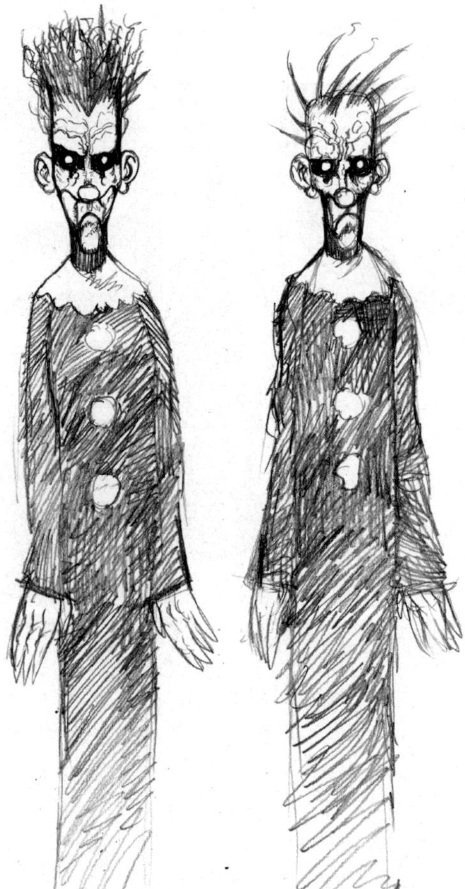

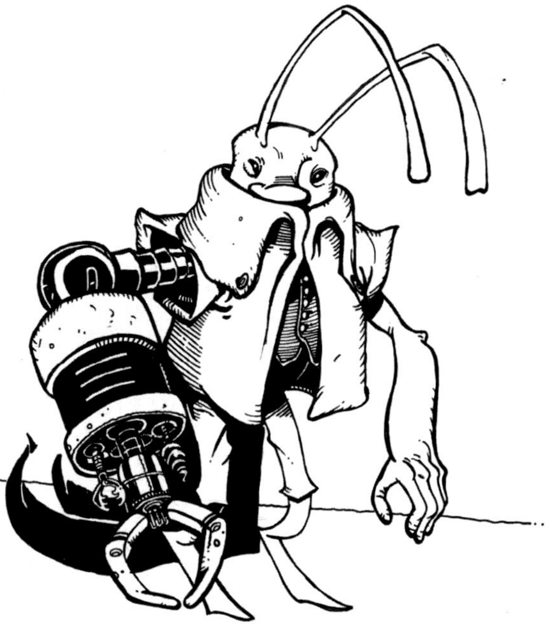

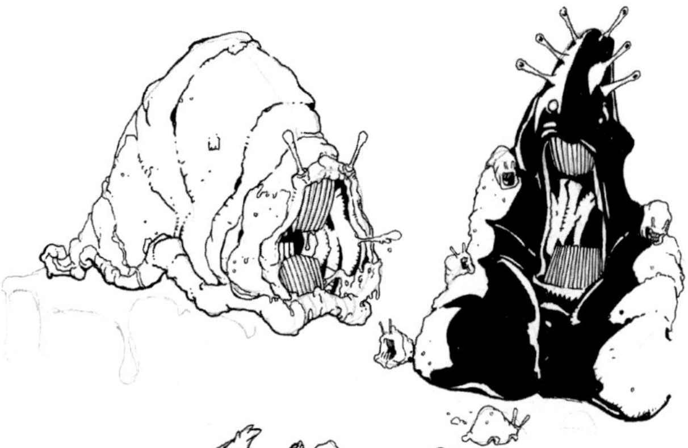

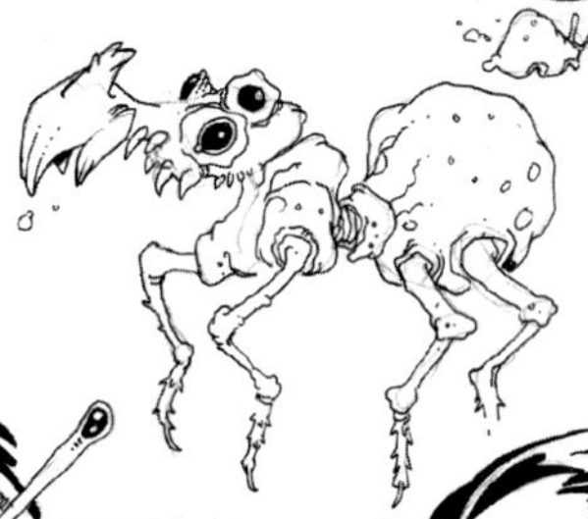

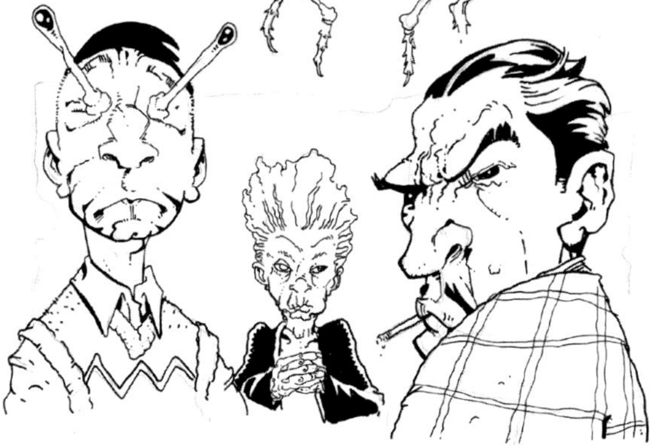

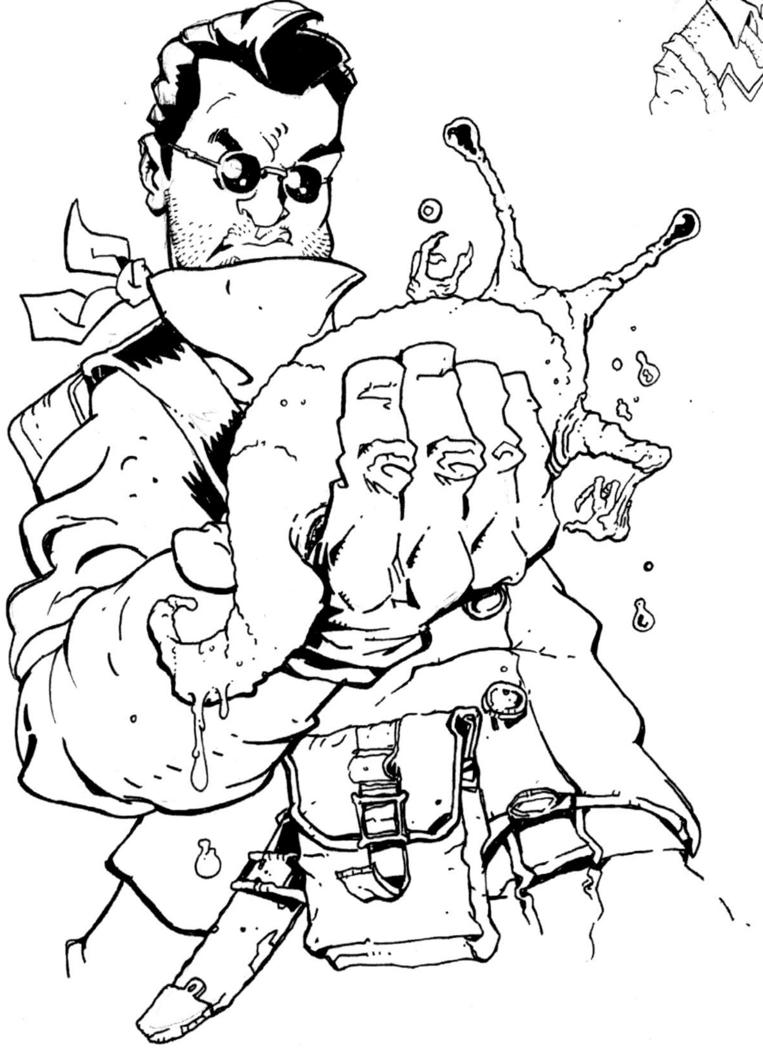

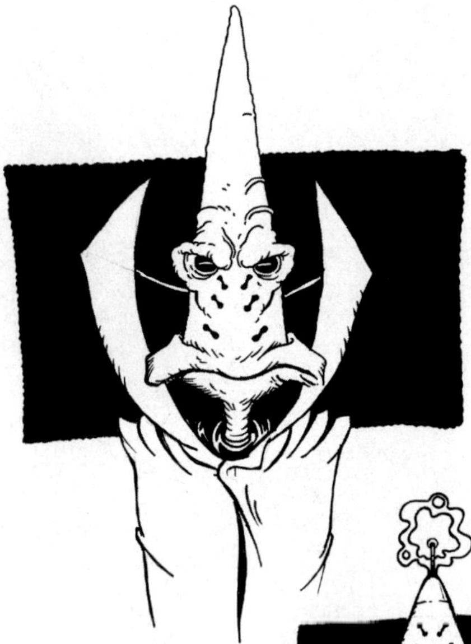

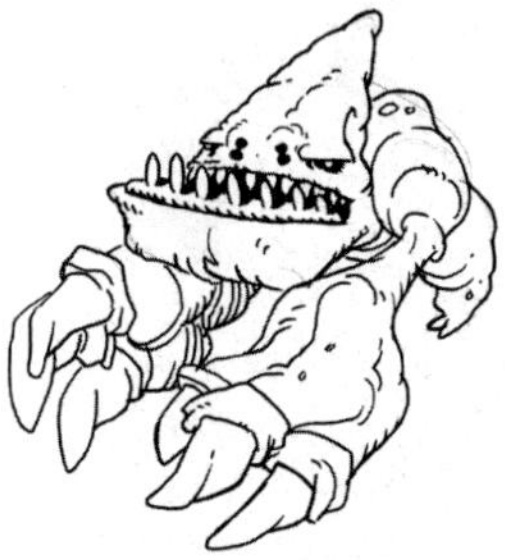

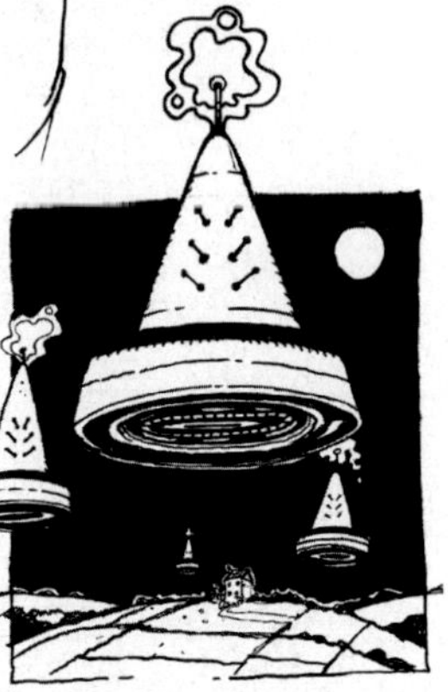

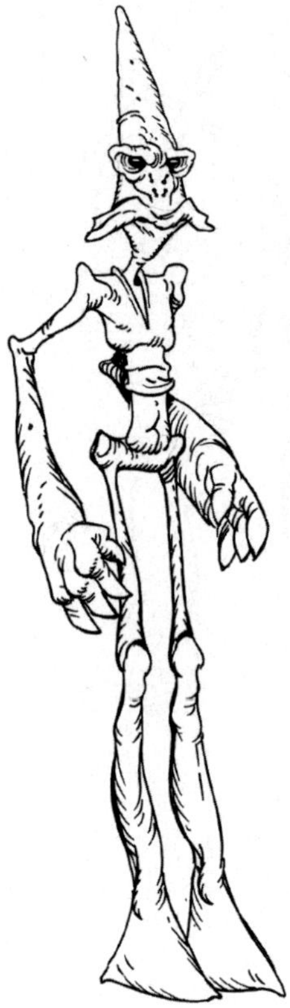

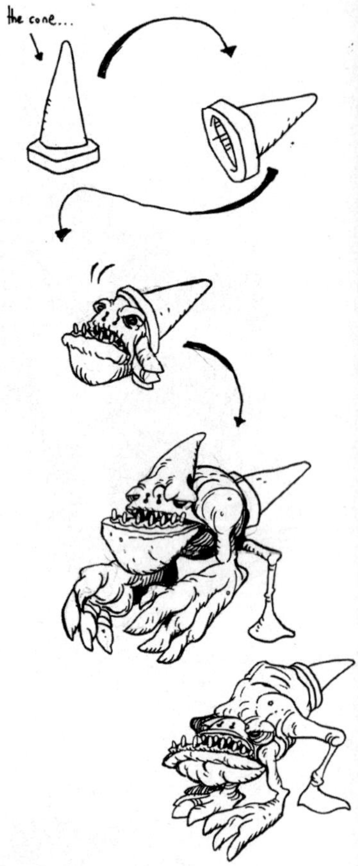
the cone...

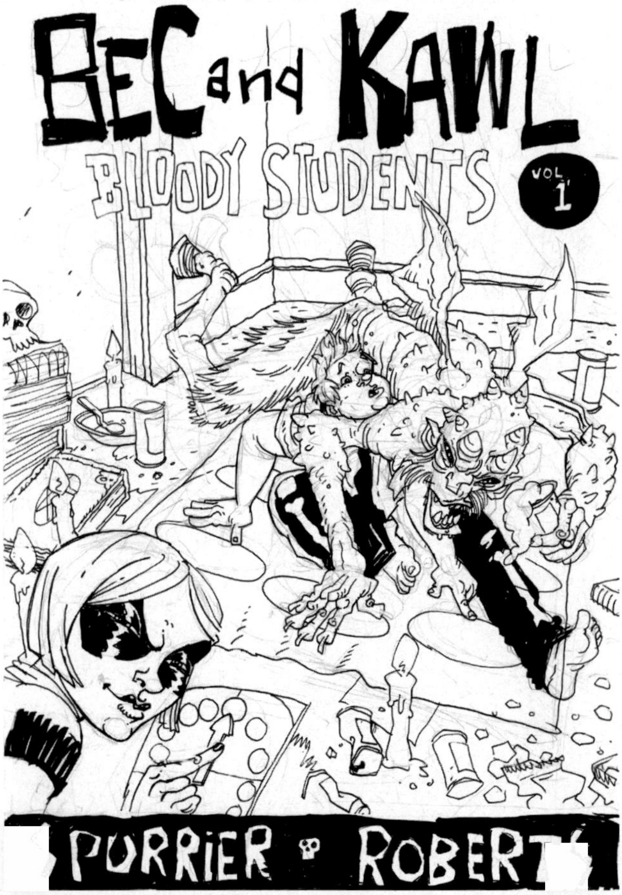
BEC and KAWL
BLOODY STUDENTS
VOL. 1
PURRIER ROBERT

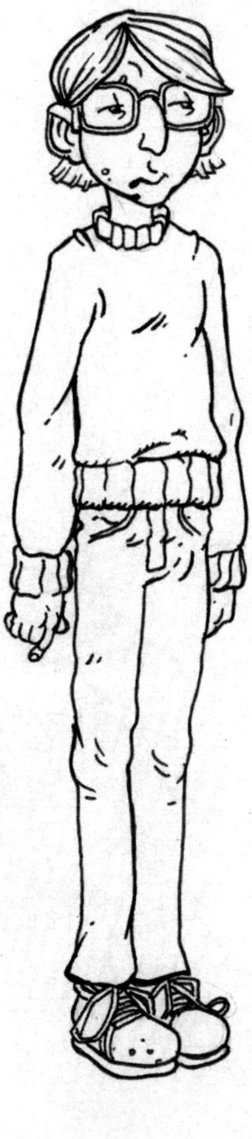

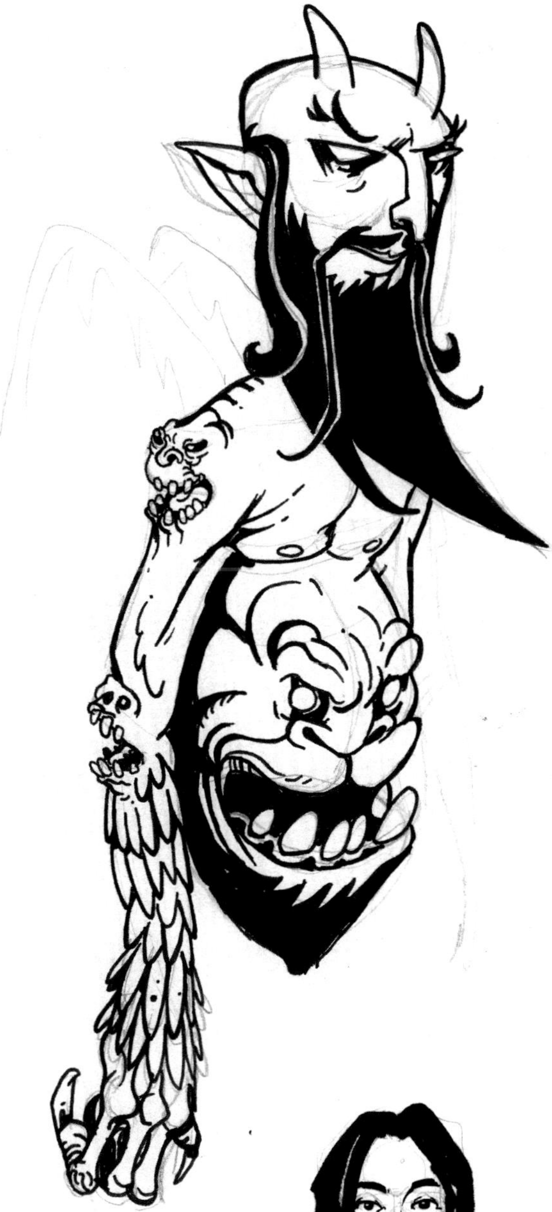

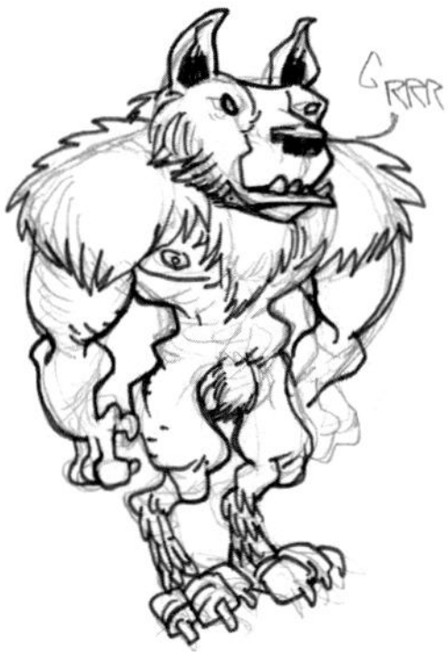
GRRR

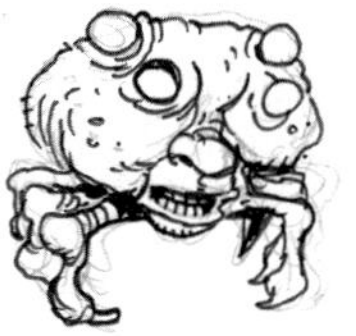

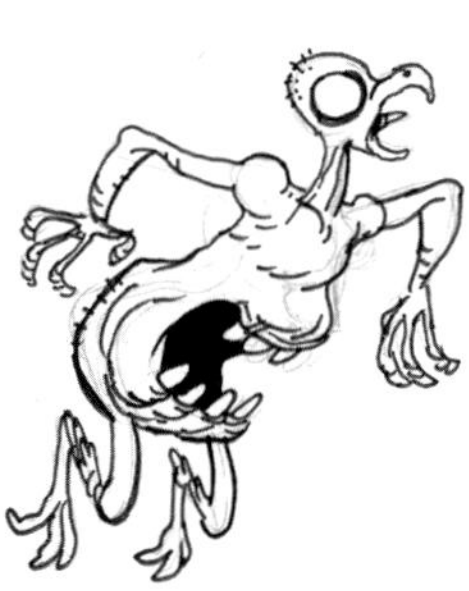

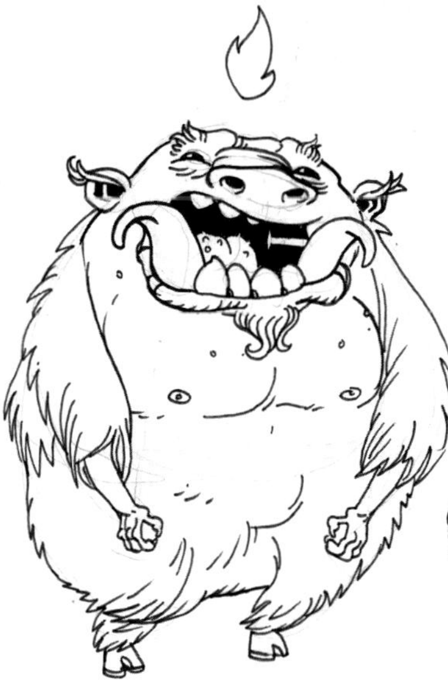

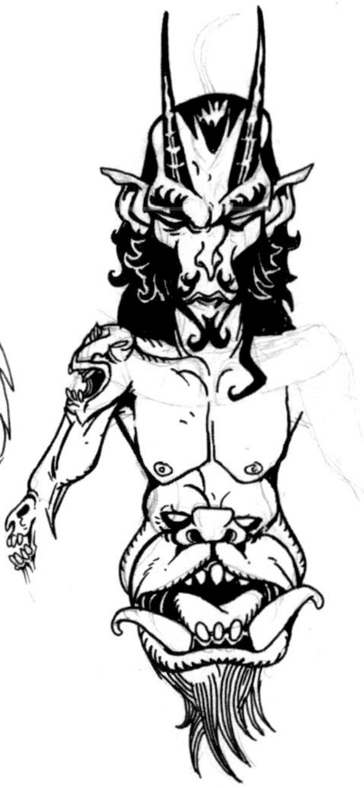

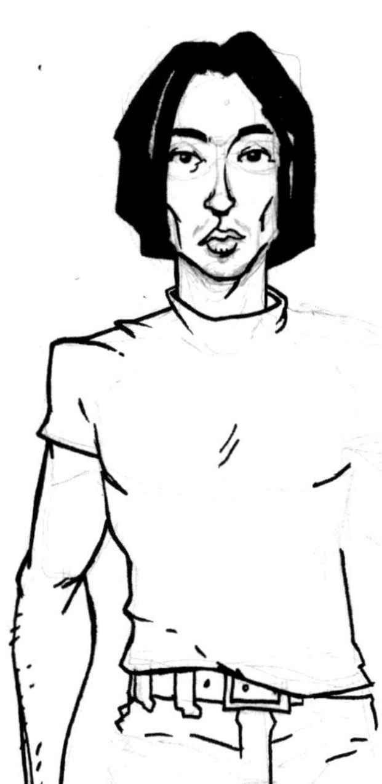

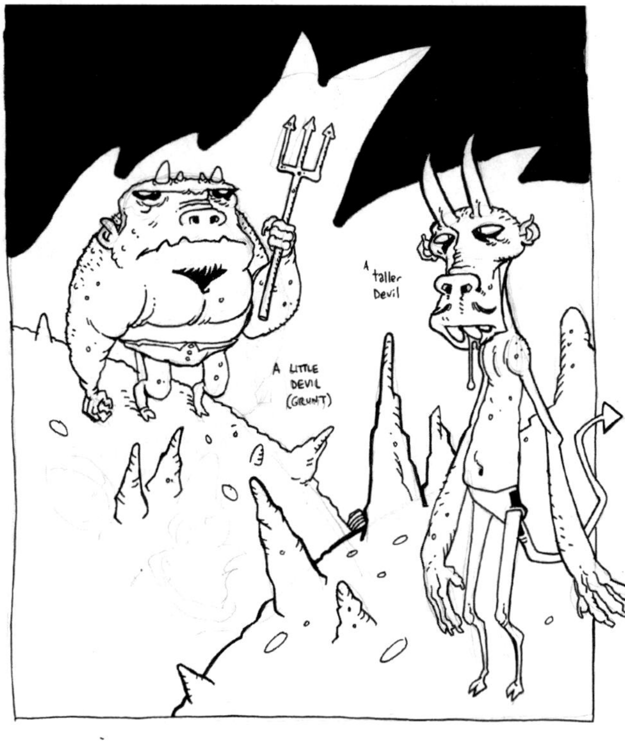
A taller Devil
A LITTLE DEVIL (GRUNT)

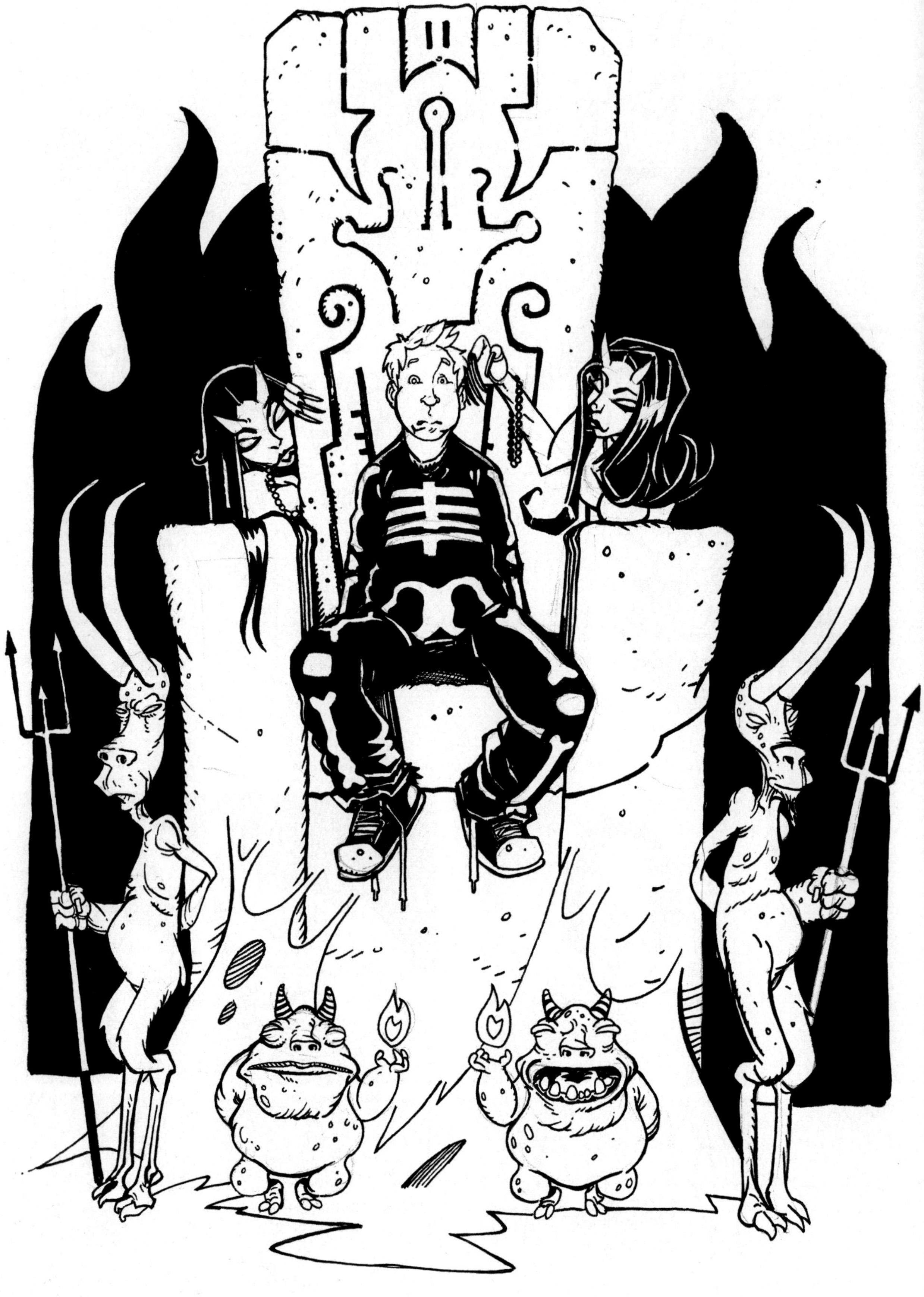

GRAPHIC NOVEL EDITOR, JONATHAN OLIVER, TAKES A MOMENT OR TWO TO CATCH UP WITH SIMON SPURRIER AND FIND OUT WHAT'S GOING ON IN HIS STRANGE AND TWISTED WORLD. .

JO: Tell me a bit how you landed your first job for *2000 AD*.

SS: By being a precocious, overly ambitious, self-deluded teenager. Seriously.

Basically it was a major shock when I found out it's possible to write comics *as a real-world grown-up job*. Sure, all the professionals bitched and whined about how there was no money in it and blah blah blah, but as a world-weary sixteen year old smartarse I *knew* that I was absolutely the best thing since sliced bread, and frankly earning any money was a lot better than earning none. Soon (I decided) the whole world would tremble before my literary might! I would grip the comics world in an iron fist of scripting brilliance!

Clearly my younger self needed a good hard slap, which is more or less what happened to the horrible little troll when he started sending Future Shock pitches to *2000 AD*. It dawned on him very quickly that a) he wasn't anywhere near as good as he thought, and b) there were a thousand other precocious smartarses out there doing exactly the same thing. I sent-in maybe fifteen or twenty diabolical pitches over a couple of years before it even occurred to me to *read* the editor's advice, though by that stage Tharg really was despairing. I have a rejection letter somewhere that simply reads: "*No no, no, no, no.*"

The Big Break came when I was eighteen – still faintly precocious, overly ambitious and self-deluded, but now coming to terms with the fact I had a *lot* to learn. I'd started getting much more promising feedback from Tharg – asking for second drafts and scripts to accompany my rambling, overly-purple breakdowns – and decided to take part in a live pitching event at a *2000 AD* convention. Nervous as hell, I stood up and told a story about a giant space whale shagging a crusty old Space-Captain to death, which just goes to show that you can get away with a lot as long as you sound confident. Booze helps, kids – tell your folks. Anyway, that's how it started: with horny Cosmic Cetaceans, and Tharg's editorial minion Andy Diggle agreeing to print the story.

JO: How did you come up with the characters of Jarrod Kawl and Beccy Miller?

SS: Beccy's basically an exaggerated version of all my less-than-pleasant qualities. Except with, y'know, strange and unfamiliar gender issues and panda eyes attached. Basically I loved the idea of taking that same precocious, overly ambitious, self-deluded cliché that *I* became at college, then ramping it up a notch with dreams of world domination, hellish alliances and occult dabblings… then setting it all in a completely mundane environment. It's very hard to be a megalomaniacal-tyrant-in-waiting when your only stooge is a slob with all the ambition of a twig, and your every attempt to achieve wealth and power is scuppered by your own pretentiousness. Hubris! It's the stuff of Greek Tragedy. Sometimes I think Beccy also has an element of every woman who ever broke my heart, with a dribble of Young Hitler and a dash of Tracey Emin. Except, y'know… likeable.

Kawl is just… *Kawl*. I've come to really love writing this guy. He's just so harmless, so bumbling, so wonderfully cheerful. He hasn't got a bad bone in his body, and it's not his fault that he just happens to've fallen for a psychotic dictatrix. As a writer, there's something wonderfully appealing about characters who are essentially losers: we're so used to having to give our creations defined goals and character arcs that a cloth-headed stoner who doesn't give a fig about anything other than being cheery and making cheap B-movies is a real breath of fresh air.

JO: Did you choose Steve Roberts as the artist for the series, or was he chosen for you by the editor of 2000 AD?

SS: I'm pretty sure the decision was taken by Tharg. Certainly I'd never worked with Steve before then, and didn't really know his stuff. Besides, when you're a 19 year old wannabe and Tharg asks you to come up with a pop-culture-referencing, light entertainment wacky-a-thon, you don't stop to argue about the artist.

Thank crikey I *didn't*, frankly, because it didn't take long for me and Steve to start riffing off each other's foibles, and really start going for it. I think the beauty of this collected edition is that you can really see how two complete rookies went from – let's be honest – *winging it*, to slowly beginning to learn the ropes. I say 'beginning to' because there's really no end to how far an artist or writer can improve themselves, but it's really good to be able to flick back through this stuff

O: What other comic writers and genre writers would you say have influenced your work?

SS: To start with, back when I was writing *The Mystical Mentalist Menace* et al., very few. I'd had as much of a grounding in comics-craft as any reader *could* have, but it's only with hindsight you realise that no matter how much a youngster blazing with ideas and ambitions might deny it, there really is nothing like experience.

As the various series arcs progressed, and I started writing other stuff as well, I started consciously paying a lot more attention to the ways that comics work: watching the masters like John Wagner, Alan Grant, Pete Milligan. It's a curious medium, after all: one that seems so self-intuitive and simple to a reader (and, usually, to a writer), but in fact concerns a *lot* of very complicated mental acrobatics. I began to get a feel for the importance of gullies, bleeds, panel sizes, dialogue progressions, links, pauses, blah blah blah. Go and pick up Scott McCloud's *The Invisible Art* and you'll begin to understand the secret complexities lying behind every simple looking page. Working with an artist to whom all of these rarely-considered gimmicks came totally naturally was an absolute boon: I could experiment to my heart's desire and be safe in the knowledge that Steve would save me from my most ridiculous excesses and improve upon that which was already working well.

Ultimately, if you're going to play with story-telling techniques in a (hopefully) innovative way, then any influence at all is probably a bad thing. But to understand how such tools can be used you simply can't get any better than Will Eisner and his spiritual successor Alan Moore. I also spent a long time going through deliberately 'Out There' masterpieces like Roger Langridge's *Fred the Clown*, Kyle Baker's *Plastic Man* and absolutely anything by Mark Stafford (particularly *Botulism Banquet*), to get a feel for the limits of outrageousness. Being a part of *2000 AD*, B&K can never quite explode into impenetrable oddity, but it's good to be familiar with what lies just beyond your own territory.

O: Were you anything like Jarrod Kawl as a student?

SS: No, not at all. I was driven and fidgety and utterly motivated. I was trying so desperately to be edgy and 'fringe' and 'cool' that I completely neglected to notice what a pillock I was. I went a bit goth for a while (though I couldn't afford leather togs, so it was black jeans, faded band t-shirts and hair-dye), so I guess there's more of me in Beccy (hur hur hur) than in Kawl. Goths who take umbrage at all the mickey taking in this collection honestly shouldn't take it personally: it's all completely self-derisory.

Having said that, I *was* a film student and I *am* passionate about movies, and I *did* get terribly depressed by the pretentiousness of the Beccy Miller fine arts crowd, so it's swings and roundabouts. Certainly I knew a lot of people just like Kawl – or worse… great groups of photosensitive stoners unable to hold conversations about anything except being stoned, or the quality of their gear, or where they were scoring next – and at the time I got massively pissed off with anyone unable to motivate themselves, so I probably would've hated Kawl if I'd known him back then.

Five years of freelancing later, I'm far more inclined towards someone harmless and happy, than someone ruthless and full of shit.

O: If you had to choose a favourite Bec & Kawl moment what would it be?

SS: I think it'd have to be the page from *Freakshow* when Kawl wakes up in the morning and realises what happened the night before. A whole page of him just sitting there, in all sorts of different situations, expression fixed… It's the sort of fun, gimmicky thing you can't do in any other medium.

I also have a soft spot for Steve's depiction of Fairyland-meets-Milton-Keynes, and the splash page of Kawl tumbling into the Mouth of Hell whilst being pestered by a rhyming reporter.

O: Were you always of a fan of *2000 AD* growing up?

SS: Afraid not. In fact, as embarrassing an admission as this is, I don't think I ever really became aware of it until I picked up *Batman Vs. Judge Dredd* in the immediate wake of the Dredd movie. I picked up a couple of progs and for the first time considered the fact that there were people whose job it was to create this stuff. I think up until that point I'd always looked at comics with a sort of youthful acceptance: they just appeared on the shelves by magic.

Anyway, I read the prog for a few weeks and started to wonder whether I could have a crack at the same thing. Back then I fancied myself as a bit of an artist as well, so I made a few DIY efforts – apocalyptic hand-wringing and 'beyond-the-veil' toss, mostly – which went down okay at school. Then the film degree came along and I was s███g so much time writing scripts I slowly re-prioritised in my ████; it was either art or writing, not both, and I stuck to what I enjoyed the most. Looking back I like to think I made the right decision: with a *lot* of practice I could have been a vaguely mediocre comics artist, but even now every time I write something I feel like it's stronger than the last thing I did.

2000 AD slowly took up a place of residence in my heart, and I started to see what all these scary fans around me had been telling me all along. It's not just a comic which varies its quality according to the stories it's running; it's an institution that defines a reader just as much as the music they listen to, the clothes they wear, and their personal politics. Also, it has a green alien as an editor. This, I believe, is the Best Thing Ever.

JO: Will Jarrod and Becky ever finally get it together do you think?

SS: When Hell Freezes Over. Which, given that this is *Bec & Kawl* we're talking about, ain't all that far beyond the realms of possibility...

JO: Which direction would you like to take Bec & Kawl in next?

SS: It's not a conscious thing, really. We haven't got some 10-year plan, working towards Beccy's eventual career-highlight as a shelf stacker and Kawl's bewildered acceptance of the World Presidency. What we *have* got is a lot of ideas, which sort of impinge upon the character arcs as they go.

Again, it's great to see how much the characters and story styles have changed since *B&K* first started, and that's a process of evolution which will hopefully keep on going. Originally they were a pair of vaguely irritating ciphers for pop-culture references, movie parroting and arty pretentiousness. Over the episodes since they've become far more fleshed-out, far darker, far less prone to random quotation and far more able to actually have an impact. We never dreamed, back at the start, we'd be telling grisly tales about laughter-gobbling vampires and slug cults. We never thought we'd be sniffling-along to Kawl's broken-hearted shenanigans, or meeting Beccy's long-lost Clone Sister.

So the future's a big, bright, utterly random and oh-so-unexpected series of oddities. Just the way we like it!

JO: Are there any *2000 AD* characters that you'd like to take a crack at writing, for which you haven't yet had the opportunity?

SS: I've always had a soft spot for Big Dumb Monster stories, so *Shako* the giant forcefield-carrying Polar Bear or *Hookjaw* the insane eco-warrior shark are right up there on the list. Probably in this day and age you'd have to introduce some so-called clever twist ('It's a killer shark... but in SPACE!'... 'It's a Psychotic Polar Bear, but it exists ONLY IN YOUR DREAMS!'), but there's something wonderfully uncomplicated about the whole concept which really appeals: Big Beast Kills Nasty Man. It never gets tired!

Beyond that, I've always been fond of Dredd's old nemeses, the Angel Gang. I know they've all been killed off and resurrected 800 times (this being comics, after all), but I'd love to do some stories about those frothing wackos back when they were the Baddest Thing In The Texas Badlands; staking out varmints in the sun and a-drinkin' Pa's moonshine. Crazy survivialist Mountain-Men of the future. How can it fail? Squeeeeal, radpiggy!

JO: Finally, what advice would you give to budding comic writers?

SS: Be patient. Be aware that no matter how good you think you are, you've got a LOT to learn. Be humble enough to accept criticism, and when your work is being dissected – bleeding and squirting and shrieking on an operating table in front of you – pay attention to the things the surgeons *say* rather than the sharp-sharp slices of their steely evil blades.

Have the tenacity to keep trying, the confidence to believe you'll get there one day, and the strength to pick yourself up when it doesn't work out the first time. Which of course it won't. Above all make sure you are your own worst critic: work and work and work on an idea until it's the best thing you've *ever* seen in your life, then chuck it out and come up with something better.

And maybe, just maybe, be a *smidgeon* precocious, a *fraction* overly-ambitious, and just the teensiest bit self-deluded. Being a teenager, on the other hand, is not recommended.

SIMON SPURRIER

Simon Spurrier is one of the newest additions to the *2000 AD* creative roster, but he has already made his mark with co-created strips *Bec & Kawl*, *From Grace*, *Lobster Random*, *The Scrap* and *The Simping Detective*. He has also written several *Future Shocks*, *Past Imperfects* and *Terror Tales*.

STEVE ROBERTS

Steve Roberts is, relatively speaking, a *2000 AD* newcomer, but his bright cartooning has illuminated both gun-loving criminals *Sinister Dexter* and no-good students *Bec and Kawl*, which he co-created with Simon Spurrier.